# Christian Paths to Health and Wellness

## SECOND EDITION

**Peter Walters, PhD**

**Wheaton College**

**John Byl, PhD**

**Redeemer University College**

**EDITORS**

Human Kinetics

**Library of Congress Cataloging-in-Publication Data**

Christian paths to health and wellness / Peter Walters, John Byl, editors. -- 2nd ed.
  p. cm.
 Includes bibliographical references and index.
 1.  College students--Health and hygiene. 2.  Health--Religious aspects--Christianity.  I. Walters, Peter, 1959- II. Byl, John.
 RA777.3.C47 2013
 613--dc23

2012031881

ISBN-10: 1-4504-2454-6
ISBN-13: 978-1-4504-2454-7

The web addresses cited in this text were current as of October 24, 2012, unless otherwise noted.

**Acquisitions Editor:** Cheri Scott; **Managing Editor:** Amy Stahl; **Assistant Editor:** Rachel Brito; **Copyeditor:** Mark Bast; **Indexer:** Andrea J. Hepner; **Permissions Manager:** Dalene Reeder; **Graphic Designer:** Nancy Rasmus; **Graphic Artist:** Kathleen Boudreau-Fuoss; **Cover Designer:** Keith Blomberg; **Photograph (cover):** © Human Kinetics; **Photo Asset Manager:** Laura Fitch; **Visual Production Assistant:** Joyce Brumfield; **Photo Production Manager:** Jason Allen; **Art Manager:** Kelly Hendren; **Associate Art Manager:** Alan L. Wilborn; **Illustrations:** © Human Kinetics; **Printer:** Versa Press

Printed in the United States of America  10  9  8  7  6  5  4

The paper in this book is certified under a sustainable forestry program.

**Human Kinetics**
Website: www.HumanKinetics.com

*United States:* Human Kinetics
P.O. Box 5076
Champaign, IL 61825-5076
800-747-4457
e-mail: humank@hkusa.com

*Canada:* Human Kinetics
475 Devonshire Road Unit 100
Windsor, ON N8Y 2L5
800-465-7301 (in Canada only)
e-mail: info@hkcanada.com

*Europe:* Human Kinetics
107 Bradford Road
Stanningley
Leeds LS28 6AT, United Kingdom
+44 (0) 113 255 5665
e-mail: hk@hkeurope.com

*Australia:* Human Kinetics
57A Price Avenue
Lower Mitcham, South Australia 5062
08 8372 0999
e-mail: info@hkaustralia.com

*New Zealand:* Human Kinetics
P.O. Box 80
Torrens Park, South Australia 5062
0800 222 062
e-mail: info@hknewzealand.com

E5674

# Contents

## 7  Flexibility Assessment and Training                    **137**

Peter Walters

## Part IV   Understanding Your Behaviors

## 8  Nutritional Health and Wellness                    **161**

Peter Walters

## 9  Emotional Health and Wellness                    **193**

Peter Walters • Doug Needham • Bud Williams

## 10  Sleep Habits and Wellness                    **225**

Peter Walters

## 11 Personal Relationships and Wellness                251
Peter Walters

## Part V   Conclusion

## 12 Offering Your Life as a Living Sacrifice              277
John Byl

# Preface

So God created man in his own image . . .
male and female he created them . . .
God saw all that he had made, and it was very
good.

(Genesis 1:27, 31)

**This textbook** on personal physical wellness is about the woman who delights in mountain biking and the man who loves to run. It is about the people who struggle with body image. It is about the man who hesitates to join an aerobics class and the woman who resists starting a strength-training program but who both overcome their fears and experience lifelong wellness. This book is about helping you "die young," as old as possible—much like Moses who "was a hundred and twenty years old when he died, yet his eyes were not weak nor his strength gone" (Deuteronomy 34:7). It is about developing realistic and helpful resolutions about personal physical wellness and having the tools to accomplish the resolutions. This book is about knowing God and yourself and about how you can enjoy and care for the world God has placed you in; it's about knowing "that you yourselves are God's temple and that God's Spirit lives in you" (1 Corinthians 3:16). This text is about the pursuit of love, health, and happiness—and actually getting closer to them.

## Purpose of This Book

This textbook is contextualized in narrative, supported and illustrated with current research findings, and filtered through the eyes of the Christian faith. It is a multiauthored resource, building on the strengths of a number of Christian academics who teach health and wellness. All the authors focus on assisting you to be positively engaged in personal physical wellness choices, exclaiming with God, after he created Adam and Eve, "It is very good!"

This book is geared toward first-year university or college students enrolled in an introductory course on health and wellness, specifically courses in Christian postsecondary institutions, but it will also benefit others interested in improving their health and wellness for the first time. A general understanding of health and wellness issues will benefit the general audience, and the comprehensive nature and unique perspective of this book will also make the material applicable and interesting to both novices and the experts in the field of health and wellness.

Empowering you to take responsibility and initiative for your health and well-being is a main goal of this book. The book's content helps you, regardless of your interest in physical activity, learn about physical wellness and its importance to the whole person and apply the principles and concepts to daily living. The authors' intent is not to spoon-feed you but to provide well-researched information in the context of narrative, challenging you to make discerning applications to your own lives. The writing of this second edition was in part motivated by including content based on the latest research. In essence this is a book of empowerment and healing. You will develop your awareness of physical wellness issues and develop a passion for proactive and permanent lifestyle changes.

The idea for this book was born out of a commitment to helping you embrace the concepts and lifestyle choices of health and well-being as part of the Christian life. Quick-fix solutions to negative lifestyle choices are not offered in this book. The aim is to help you enter into constructive, positive, and realistic habit formation and transformation. The book provides hope, practical tools, and methods for change with a comprehensiveness that enables you to make gradual and significant permanent change through the wisdom of education and the power of the Holy Spirit.

Physical wellness is a unique topic covering many facets of life. This textbook is specifically focused around four major themes: how God made people, how he made them to move, how he made them to be nourished, and how he made them to rest. Many professors at Christian universities were teaching from books that were not God centered, and they needed a text with a foundation that was God centered. That's the reason behind this book.

# Structure of This Book

Part I, Understanding Your Wellness and Mission, looks at how scripture speaks about the body. Chapter 1, Valuing Wellness, explores a biblical view of a person. Chapter 2, God's Purpose and Your Life's Mission, encourages you to live a focused life fixed on godly physical goals.

Part II, Accepting and Caring for Your Body, explores body image and composition. Chapter 3, Examining Body Image and Eating Disorders in Women and Men, deals with body image and the influence of cultural forces on attitudes toward it. The chapter also includes two powerful personal stories about how a woman and a man came to a positive body image. Chapter 4, Weight Control, examines how excess fat is often so easy to put on and so difficult to permanently remove. These two chapters concern the challenges of being too thin or too fat or being too focused on displaying muscle.

Part III, Moving Your Body, addresses three common areas about how to help the body get and stay active. This part contains three chapters that help you understand how you can develop your cardiorespiratory endurance (chapter 5), muscular strength (chapter 6), and flexibility (chapter 7).

Part IV, Understanding Your Behaviors, focuses on behaviors. People need rhythmic patterns of activity and nutrition, of rest and leisure, and of time with friends and others. Chapter 8, Nutritional Health and Wellness, explores the key components of good nutrition, helping you develop positive and informed choices about your eating habits while fueling the physical body. Rhythmic patterns of rest and leisure greatly improve ability to function normally and to lower unhealthy stress levels. Chapter 9, Emotional Health and Wellness, clarifies the importance of allowing stress to motivate but not debilitate, and it gives guidance about how to work through depression. Chapter 10, Sleep Habits and Wellness, discusses the healing effect of regular, sound sleep. Chapter 11, Personal Relationships and Wellness, talks about how to nurture all relationships to be positive, bringing wellness to all.

Chapter 12 encourages you to pull the content of the whole book together and prepare or construct a comprehensive strategy to maintain and develop personal wellness in a relationship with God. It provides a reflective meditation about the course and how it is up to you to choose to live well.

# Features of This Book

Information in this book is organized into sections, allowing for an easy-to-follow format:

- The objectives of each chapter are clearly identified at the beginning and followed up with review questions at the end of each chapter.
- Specific information is often presented in concise, easy-to-read charts.
- New terms are highlighted in bold, defined, and listed in a glossary at the end of the book, with a list of key terms appearing at the end of each chapter.
- One of the unique features of this book is that the text builds on personal stories pertaining to the topic being covered. The main points of the chapter are explained through a logical narrative style, including some of the authors' personal stories, to foster the learning and practice of lifelong positive health and wellness choices. You will be drawn in by the stories and may find a personal connection to your own experience and that of others. Having been drawn into the stories, you will want to continue reading from one chapter to the next, discovering, understanding, questioning, laughing, wondering, and so on. Many of these stories are found in the Real Life sidebars, noted with the following icon:
- There are often two sides to a story, and the text includes point–counterpoint discussions with brief contrary positions on a topic, which demonstrate the impact ideas have on the way we live. These discussions are noted with the following icon:
- Personal wellness is often achieved through mental and physical discipline. However, it is also important to open yourself to the power of God through the Holy Spirit. The Bible writes, "The fruit of the Spirit is love, joy, peace, patience, kindness, goodness, faithfulness, gentleness and self-control" (Galatians 5:22–23). Ideas from the fruit of the Spirit have been woven through the text, and a couple of chapters offer a brief vignette on a part of the fruit of the Spirit, which demonstrates how the Spirit heals and makes one well.
- The application activities at the end of each chapter help you reflect and make necessary applications to your own life, often by writing your own positive and healing stories.
- A list of print materials (Suggested Readings) and Internet resources (Suggested Websites and Twitter) supports each chapter.

Personal physical wellness is important. Because it is meant for Christians, it is important that the questions posed, the solutions suggested, the actions considered, and the course followed fix "our eyes on Jesus, the author and perfecter of our faith, who for the joy set before him endured the cross, scorning its shame, and sat down at the right hand of the throne of God" (Hebrews 12:2). This same Jesus is preparing a place where "He will wipe away every tear from their eyes. There will be no more death or mourning or crying or pain . . ." (Revelation 21:4). Faculty and students can be a part of "making everything new" (Revelation 21:5).

This textbook, the second edition of a book with a Christian view of health and wellness, has a life of its own and can undoubtedly be strengthened. The authors want to continue to update this book so that it helps more people and brings a bigger smile to God's face. Your input about any concerns or suggestions you have is deeply valued and has shaped this second edition. Please send your suggestions to johnbyl50@gmail.com or peter.walters@wheaton.edu.

# Acknowledgments

**Writing this** book required a community of people. The need for and structure of this text were developed by Christian academics who met at an annual conference hosted by the Christian Society for Kinesiology and Leisure Studies (CSKLS). To each person who helped us formulate this book, and for the prayers of many more, thanks.

CSKLS was founded and nurtured by Glen Van Andel. Without his formative work on CSKLS, the need for this book would not have been so readily apparent, nor its development so speedy. Thanks, Glen, for your formative work with CSKLS and, consequently, the publication of this book.

Several writers shared their work with us. Thanks to Dianne E. Moroz, Doug Needham, Heather Strong, Bob Weathers, and Bud Williams for your valuable contributions. Two particular students, Erin Mulholland and Sarah Jamieson, were immensely helpful at providing a student's perspective of what specific topics were least and most helpful, identifying student concerns in the various chapters, and finally helping with textual revisions that clearly communicated to a student audience. In addition to providing a more "student-sensitive" textbook, they were an absolute joy to work with on this project.

We tested versions of this book during its various stages of development with students at Messiah College, Redeemer University College, Seattle Pacific University, and Wheaton College. Thank you, Jim Gustafson, Dianne E. Moroz, and Bob Weathers, for facilitating that work, and thanks to the students who contributed valuable advice and critiques.

Thanks to the wonderful folks at Human Kinetics for publishing this important text. Thanks especially to Bonnie Pettifor Vreeman and Cheri Scott for your confidence and for nudging the book through to acceptance for both editions. Amy Stahl was awesome in the way she kept us on our time lines, extended grace to us when we were late, and applied her precise and thoughtful editorial skills to sharpening the entire book. Amy, a huge thank-you!

Writing requires time, and those who sacrificed most because of the time we spent writing are Margery and Catherine and our children. Your love and support for us are amazing, and we are blessed by our families.

Thanks to God, who adopted us as his children. We are thankful to be part of his family. We trust this book is a blessing to all.

*Peter Walters and John Byl*

# Credits

Photos are © Peter Walters unless otherwise noted in the following lists.

## Chapter 1

Photo on p. 3, © Mscottparkin | Dreamstime.com.

Photo on p. 5, © Big Cheese Photos.

Photo on p. 6, © Art Explosion.

Photos on pp. 9 and 10, © Human Kinetics.

## Chapter 2

Photo on p. 13, © Charis Verkaik.

Photo on p. 16, © Catherine Byl.

Photo on p. 17, © Human Kinetics/Les Woodrum.

Photo on p. 19, © Human Kinetics.

Table 2.1 on p. 20, adapted from Prochaska, Norcross, and DiClement 1994.

Photo on p. 23, © John Byl.

Photo on p. 24, © Charis Verkaik.

## Chapter 3

Photo on p. 31, Eyewire/Photodisc/Getty Images.

Photos on p. 35, 44, and 46, ©Human Kinetics.

Table 3.1 on p. 48, adapted from ANRED. Available: www.anred.com/causes.html.

Table 3.2 on p. 49, Information from ANRED. Available: www.anred.com/tx.html.

Form 3.1 on pp. 52-53, adapted, by permission, from Bruce Bugbee and Don Cousins. *The Network Curriculum Participant Guide,* © 1994, 2005 by The Willow Creek Community Church and Bruce Bugbee and Don Cousins. (2005) The Zondervan Corporation. For additional resources, go to www.brucebugbee.com.

## Chapter 4

Photo on p. 59, © Bananastock.

Photo on p. 61, © Human Kinetics.

Figure 4.1 on p. 63, reprinted, by permission, from W.L. Kenney, J.H. Wilmore and D.L. Costill, 2012, *Physiology of sport and exercise,* 5th ed. (Champaign, IL: Human Kinetics), 556.

Photo on p. 69, © Hannah Braam.

## Chapter 5

Photo on p. 77, © Eyewire/Photodisc/Getty Images.

Table 5.1 on p. 84, based on National Strength and Conditioning Association, 2008.

Table 5.2, on p. 85, adapted from W.D. McArdle, F.I. Katch, and V. Katch, 2001, *Exercise physiology,* 5th ed. (Baltimore: Lippincott, Williams & Wilkins).

Table 5.6 on p. 101, based on YMCA, 1989, *Y'S way to physical fitness,* 3rd ed. (Champaign, Illinois: Human Kinetics).

Table 5.7 on p. 102, data from ACSM 2000; Cooper 1994; Franklin et al. 2000.

## Chapter 6

Photo on p. 107, © Human Kinetics.

Photo on p. 108, courtesy of Glenda Anderson.

Figure 6.1 on p. 109, © Bev Francis.

Figure 6.2 on p. 110, data from McGlynn and Moran 1997.

Figure 6.3 on p. 110, figure 6.4 on p. 110, figure 6.5 on p. 111, and figure 6.6 on p. 111, courtesy of Zachary Wenger.

Figure 6.7 on p. 112, reprinted, by permission, from W.L. Kenney, J.H. Wilmore and D.L. Costill, 2012, *Physiology of sport and exercise,* 5th ed. (Champaign, IL: Human Kinetics), 428.

Figure 6.10 on p. 115, reprinted from R. Behnke, 2012, *Kinetic anatomy,* 3rd ed. (Champaign, IL: Human Kinetics), 15.

Table 6.2 on p. 116, adapted from McArdle, Katch, and Katch 2001.

Table 6.4 on p. 119, adapted from Dwyer and Davis 2005.

Table 6.5 on p. 120 and table 6.6 on p. 121, data from Cooper-Institute for Aerobics Research 1994.

Table 6.7 on p. 123 and table 6.8 on p. 124, adapted from Dwyer and Davis 2005; Data from Institute for Aerobics Research 1994; Data from Franklin 2006.

Photo on p. 124, Copyright Bettmann/Corbis/AP Images.

## Chapter 7

Photo on p. 137, © Human Kinetics.

Figure 7.2 on p. 139, reprinted from R. Behnke, 2012, *Kinetic anatomy,* 3rd ed. (Champaign, IL: Human Kinetics), 10.

Table 7.1 on p. 143, data from Verran 2007.

Table 7.2 on p. 145, from *ACSM's guidelines for exercise testing and prescription,* 6th ed.; Data: Canada Fitness Survey. All scores are measured in centimeters.

Table 7.3 on p. 146, adapted from W. Hoeger and S. Hoeger, 1991, *Lifetime physical fitness and wellness: A personalized program,* 2nd ed. (Belmont, CA: Cengage Learning-Wadsworth).

## Chapter 8

Photo on p. 161, © Monkey Business/fotolia.com.

Figure 8.1 on p. 162, data from Food Institute 2002.

Figure 8.2 on p. 163, reprinted, by permission, from M. Flegel, 2008, *Sports first aid,* 4th ed. (Champaign, IL: Human Kinetics), 35.

Figure 8.3 on p. 165, adapted from G. Wardlaw and J. Hampl, 2007, *Perspectives in nutrition,* 9th ed. (New York: McGraw-Hill Companies), 42. © McGraw-Hill Companies.

Figure 8.4 on p. 166, adapted from Casey 2012.

Table 8.3 on p. 167, adapted from Powell, Holt, and Brand-Miller 2002.

Figure 8.5 on p. 176, figure 8.6 on p. 177, and figure 8.7 on p. 177, From USDA. Available: www.mypyramid.gov/professionals/index.html.

Figure 8.8 on p. 178, reprinted from USDA and USDHHS. Available: www.choosemyplate.gov/images/MyPlateImages/JPG/myplate_green.jpg.

Table 8.9 on p. 179, adapted from National Heart, Lung, and Blood Institute, 2010, *Portion distortion quiz.* Available:http://hp2010.nhlbihin.net/portion/portion.cgi?action = question&number = 1.

Figure 8.9 on p. 180, reprinted from USDA. Available: www.choosemyplate.gov.

Figure 8.10 on p. 181, reprinted from USDA. Available: https://www.choosemyplate.gov/super-tracker/CreateProfile.aspx\.

Figure 8.11 on p. 181, reprinted from USDA. Available: https://www.choosemyplate.gov/Super-Tracker/mytop5goals.aspx\.

Figure 8.12 on p. 182, reprinted from USDA. Available: https://www.choosemyplate.gov/Super-Tracker/myplan.aspx\.

Figure 8.13 on p. 183, Eating Well with Canada's Food Guide. Health Canada, 2012. Reproduced with permission from the Minister of Health.

Figure 8.14 on p. 185, adapted from Pimentel 1980.

Table 8.12 on p. 186, adapted, by permission, from G. Wadlaw and J. Hampl, 2007, *Perspectives in nutrition,* 9th ed. (New York: The McGraw-Hill Companies), 261. © The McGraw-Hill Companies.

Figure 8.15 on p. 189, reprinted from U.S. Food and Drug Administration, 2012. Available: www.cfsan.fda.gov/ ~ dms/foodlab.html.

## Chapter 9

Photo on p. 193, © Tomasz Niewgowski – Fotolia.

Figure 9.1 on p. 195, adapted from Sax 1999.

Figure 9.2 on p. 196, adapted from Ellis et al. 1997.

Table 9.1 on p. 197, adapted from *Journal of Psychosomatic Research, 11,* T. Holmes and R. Rahe, The social readjustment rating scale, pp. 213-218. Copyright 1967 with permission from Elsevier.

Table 9.2 on p. 198, reprinted from G.E. Anderson, 1972, *College schedule of recent experience* (Fargo, ND: North Dakota State University).

Figure 9.5 on p. 202, based on Gould and Tuffey 1996.

Figure 9.7 on p. 208, results from American College Health Association—National College Health Assessment (ACHA-NCHA) Executive Summary. Updated fall 2011. Available: www.acha-ncha.org/data_highlights.html.

Figure 9.8 on p. 210, reprinted, by permission, from W.L. Kenney, J.H. Wilmore, and D.L. Costill, 2012, *Physiology of sport and exercise,* 5th ed. (Champaign, IL: Human Kinetics), xxii.

Photo on p. 213, © John Byl.

Figure 9.9 on p. 215 and figure 9.10 on p. 216, adapted from Diener et al. 1995.

Figure 9.11 on p. 217, table 9.3 on p. 217, and figure 9.12 on p. 218, adapted from Wallis 2005.

Form 9.1 on p. 220, adapted, by permission, from A.D. Hart, 1998, *Adrenaline and stress* (Waco, TX: Word).

## Chapter 10

Photo on p. 225, © diego cervo/fotolia.com.

Quiz on p. 227, adapted from POWER OF SLEEP by James B. Maas, copyright © 1999 by James Maas (New York: Harper Collins), 19.

Figure 10.1 on p. 228, adapted from National Sleep Foundation 2001.

Figure 10.2 on p. 229 and figure 10.4 on p. 230, based on National Sleep Foundation 2005.

Figure 10.3 on p. 230, adapted from Walters 2005.

Figure 10.5 on p. 230, adapted from J. Schor, 1993, *The overworked American: The unexpected decline of leisure* (New York: Basic Books).

Form 10.1 on p. 231, adapted from National Sleep Foundation, 1999, *The sleep quiz* (Washington, DC: National Sleep Foundation).

Figure 10.6 on p. 234, data from Kribbs and Dinges 1994.

Figure 10.7 on p. 237, adapted from Encarta 2004.

List on p. 238, adapted from Wells 2012; Becker 2005.

Table 10.1 on p. 238, adapted from Condor 2001.

Photo on p. 239, © John Byl.

## Chapter 11

Photo on p. 251, © Andres Rodriguez/fotolia.com.

Photo on p. 252, © NASA/NOAA/GSFC/Suomi NPP/VIIRS/Norman Kuring.

Table 11.1 on p. 254, based on Buss 1985.

Table 11.2 on p. 255, based on Walters et al. 2006.

Table 11.3 on p. 261, scripture quotations are taken, with exceptions noted, from the *Holy Bible,* New International Version. 1973, 1978, 1984 by International Bible Society. (Colorado Springs, CO: Zondervan).

Form 11.1 on pp. 266-267, adapted, by permission, from Bruce Bugbee and Dan Cousins. Copyright © 1994, 2005. *The Network Curriculum Participant Guide*, by The Willow Creek Community Church and Bruce Bugbee and Don Cousins. © (2005) The Zondervan Corporation. For additional resources go to www.brucebugbee.com.

Form 11.2 on pp. 268-269, based on Kise, Stark, and Hirsh 2005.

## Chapter 12

Three photos on right side of p. 277, © Human Kinetics.

Left photo on p. 277, © Brand X Pictures.

## Appendix A

Appendix A on p. 283, reprinted with permission from the National Eating Disorder Information Centre, Toronto, Canada, www.nedic.ca.

## Appendix B

Table B.1 on p. 286, adapted from Thompson and Comeau 2000.

Table B.2 on pp. 287-288 and table B.3 on p. 289, ©Copyright 1989. K. Kim Lampson, PhD, 206-232-8404, www.eatingdisordersupport.com.

## About the Editor photos

Peter Walters photo, © Peter Walters.

John Byl photo, © Daniel Banko.

## Text Credit Lines

Chapter 2 text on pp. 17-19, adapted, by permission, from J. Byl, 2002. *Intramural recreation* (Champaign, IL: Human Kinetics), 13-19.

Chapter 3 text #2 on p. 35, adapted, by permission, from M. Bear, 2000, *Dieting and weight loss facts and fiction* (Toronto, Canada: National Eating Disorder). www.nedic.ca

Chapter 3 text #1 on p. 36, adapted from Bear 2000.

Chapter 3 text #3 on p. 40, from NEDIC 1997.

Chapter 3 text #4 on pp. 41-42, adapted, by permission, from J.J. Robert-McComb, 2000, *Eating disorders in women and children: Prevention, stress management, and treatment.* (New York: Taylor and Francis).

Chapter 3 text #5 on p. 49, Information from ANRED: Anorexia Nervosa and Related Eating Disorders, Inc. www.anred.com.

Chapter 3 text #6 on p. 43, adapted from Moriarty and Moriarty 1993.

Chapter 3 text #7 on p. 50, adapted, by permission, from ANRED, 1999, *Treatment and recovery.* Available: www.anred.com/tx.html.

Chapter 11 text #1 on p. 264, from *The Peacemaker: A Biblical Guide to Resolving Personal Conflict* ©Kenneth Sande (Baker Books, 3rd edition, 2004). Used by permission. Visit www.Peacemaker.net and www.RW360.org for additional information about biblical peacemaking.

# Part I

# Understanding Your Wellness and Mission

# Valuing Wellness

John Byl

After reading this chapter, you should be able to do the following:

1. Describe a biblical view of the human body.
2. Explain your view of the human body.
3. Begin to examine how you should view and treat your body.

**You've probably** had days when you felt great and were happy to be alive and active. This book encourages each person to bring honor to God by the way he or she lives. It advocates enjoying, improving, and serving through physical wellness in relation to others.

I prepared to write this chapter by exploring the question "Does God really care about our physical being?" I found that people have very different perceptions of a person's value, particularly when they consider the value of their own bodies. Think about how you view your body and how you believe God views your body. As you serve God, it is helpful to have a sense of his perspective and to remember how God created "male and female . . . [and] God saw all that he had made, and it was very good" (Genesis 1:27, 31).

This chapter explores a view of the body by looking at the implications of the Bible's teachings on creation, the fall, redemption, and fulfillment. If you view the body like the fasting student and Plato do (see the What Value Is Your Body? sidebar), then concern for physical wellness matters only insofar as you are able to let the good spirit control the evil body. On the other hand, if your view is more like the second student's (also mentioned in the What Value Is Your Body? sidebar), who viewed her body as "the me that God made," then concern for physical wellness matters.

## What Value Is Your Body?

Let's take a look at several personal views. Which best reflects your own? One student writes honestly about this topic:

> When I first fell in love with Jesus, I stopped loving my body. I thought that to be spiritual was to abstain from foods; fasting was a great door to a living relationship with God. However, my physical state became poor. Many of my friends alerted me to this, but I ignored them, seeing it as my way of becoming poor. (Byl, 1999, p. 73)

Socrates, coming from a similar perspective, constructs his argument as follows:

> When soul and body are both in the same place, nature teaches the one to serve and be subject, the other to rule and govern. In this relation which do you think most resembles the divine and which the mortal part? Don't you think it is the nature of the divine to rule and direct, and that of the mortal to be subject and serve?

> I do.

> Then which does the soul resemble?

Obviously, Socrates, soul resembles the divine, and the body the mortal (Socrates, 1954, p. 131).

Plato, also viewing a person's body negatively, argues that the soul is "marred by association with the body and other evils, but when she has regained that pure condition which the eye of reason can discern, you will then find her to be a far lovelier thing" (Plato, 1945, p. 345). The fasting student, Socrates, and Plato conclude that a person's body is something that "mars" the true person. Is that your view?

Another student writes about her body in a positive manner:

> I believe that I do love myself, but explaining that love is the hard part. You know, God has blessed me with so many things. I think that it would be like an insult to say that I did not love the me that God made. I love my sense of humor, my nose; yes, I love me. (Byl, 1999, p. 73)

Gabriel Marcel, a Christian existentialist, also appreciates people's physical selves, and argues, "I am my body. . . . I cannot validly say 'I and my body'" (Marcel, 1965, p. 18). The second student and Marcel view the body positively. Marcel goes even further by stating that he cannot talk about his body apart from who he is.

Think of the various statements you just read about the body. Did they make sense to you? Why or why not? Which student or philosopher seems to best reflect the Christian tenets regarding the view of who people are, particularly in the physical being?

# Creation

As you know, the scriptures begin with God creating everything, including man and woman. God looked at all of **creation** and declared not that it was good, but that it was *very* good. God saw all of Adam and all of Eve—their emotions, their thoughts, their noses, their toes—and "it was very good" (Genesis 1:27–31):

This first chapter of the Bible teaches at least two important preliminary lessons. The first lesson is that God made all things. Other writers in the scriptures reemphasize this point (Psalm 33:9; 11:3; 147:15–20; and 2 Peter 3:5–7). The second lesson is that God created all things "very good." The first chapter in Genesis makes no distinction that some things of creation are very good, others are okay, and others are undesirable. God looked at all of creation at the very end and declared that all of it was "very good." In the New Testament, Paul reiterates this point: "For everything God created is good, and nothing is to be rejected" (1 Timothy 4:4). From the beginning to the end of the Bible a good creation, including good physical people, is a consistent theme.

Creation is about a personal God who walked in the garden with Adam and Eve and among everything he made. It is about a personal God who talks with his people. Creation is not about man and woman finding their origins in the impersonal process of time and chance that characterizes an **evolutionist** position on the origin of people.

God recognized and provided for the needs of this first man and woman. He knew of their need for food and provided plants to nourish them (Genesis 1:29). He knew of their need for emotional companionship and provided that in each other. Calvin Seerveld, an **aesthetician**, imagines Adam and Eve's first meeting as follows: "When Adam first discovered Eve and Eve saw Adam for the first time, I imagine they were amazed. Their skin rather tingled with anticipation. God was going to surprise them with something exciting, but they didn't know yet what it was. In the beginning, Adam and Eve probably smiled at one another, invitingly, a little bashfully" (Seerveld, 1976, p. 19).

But what does it mean to be created in the image of God? In the chapter titled "The Meaning of the Image" in his book *Man: The Image of God*, G.C. Berkouwer (1962) writes, "The image of God is something which concerns the whole man, his place in this world and his future, his likeness in his being a child of a Father, of his Father in heaven" (p. 117). In other words, the image of God is not limited to a person's soul, body, or relationships; the image of God is potentially expressed through all aspects of a person, and in the garden the imaging was very good. Think about what kind of pictures Adam and Eve would put on their blogs and how they would finish the following sentence: "This past week we . . ."

When you read Genesis 5, notice how the word *image* comes up: "When Adam had lived 130 years, he had a son in his own likeness, in his own image; and he named him Seth" (Genesis 5:3). Like parent, like child. People often comment on how much a newborn child looks like the father or mother. The comparison isn't surprising because indeed that is the child's origin.

The announcement that Seth was like Adam begins a list of many boys and girls born to Adam's descendants. Notice these words that precede the explanation of Seth in verse 3: "When God created man, he made him in the likeness of God. He created them male and female and blessed them" (Genesis 5:1–2). The equation is simple: Inasmuch as I am in the image of my father and mother, I am also in the image of God. In Genesis 1:26, God said, "Let us make man in our [my] image, in our [my] likeness." God made people in his image and "crowned" humans "with glory and honor" (Psalm 8:5). People represent God wherever they go because they are in his image.

One aspect of being created in God's image is that God and people are "creators." All of Genesis 1 is about a God who creates, as opposed to Greek gods who came from creation. The Christian God is a creator God—a God who gets involved in the creative tasks. Jesus came into this world as a son of a carpenter and a homemaker. Genesis 2:15 says

Children are made in the image of their parents and of God.

the Lord God took a man and woman and put them into the Garden of Eden, "to work it and take care of it" and to extend that same care to animals (Genesis 1:26). One of God's commandments calls for rest on the Sabbath, but that follows six days of doing work (Exodus 20:8–11). Adam and Eve, their children, and all people are created in the image of God, to be busy working in and caring for creation. People, created in God's image, are cultivators. Caring for your physical body is one of those creative tasks.

Not only did God create Adam and Eve, but he also provided for them so they could survive and fully enjoy his creative goodness. Like Adam and Eve, you are created to be like God. The creation of you was also "very good," and you are called to care for and develop his creation, which includes your body.

# Fall

Man and woman turned their backs on God in the center of the Garden of Eden (not unlike temptations that challenge people and are often also in the center of their lives) and ate the fruit God had declared off-limits. Consequently, they broke their perfect relationship with God, with each other, and with all of creation. The painful reality of broken relationships soon became evident when Adam and Eve's son Cain killed his brother Abel (Genesis 4:8). The implications of Adam and Eve's **fall** are not limited to them. As the scripture points out, "We all, like sheep, have gone astray, each of us has turned to his own way" (Isaiah 53:6). Romans 3:23 adds, "All have sinned and fall short of the glory of God." The *fall* refers to a universal and pervasive disposition of people to turn their backs on God. A result of the fall was that people would find gathering food and caring for themselves more difficult. In addition, people's decisions would be influenced by "conflicting spirits," or conflicting internal voices that influence toward what is good and toward what is bad.

## Damaged Intimacy

The most intimate relationship in the world—the one between husband and wife—was also damaged as a result of the fall. Before the fall, Adam and Eve walked openly and unashamedly with each other and with God, and their relationship was great. After the fall they were more closed, ashamed, and quick to blame each other for wrongs. From that point on, maintaining good relationships would require hard work. Because of Adam and Eve's sin, even the closest relationships have discord and will require effort for growth.

## Desolate Creation

Creation itself experienced the fall. As Paul writes, "We know that the whole creation has been groaning as in the pains of childbirth right up to the present time" (Romans 8:22). This groaning, or response to pain and discomfort, is made worse by people's disobedience to God (Jeremiah 12:11). In other words, all of creation is hurting because of the fall and personal sin.

People still are inclined to reject God (to sin) even though sinning brings negative consequences. Consider the "seven deadly sins" (Proverbs 6:16–19). Think about their everyday meaning in your life and in the lives of those around you. Each of these sins adds brokenness to the world and to individuals' lives.

### Pride

Pride goes before a fall. Pride is thinking you are the center of the world. You exhibit pride when you get upset and become impatient when stoplights turn red as you approach, when you're stuck in a traffic jam, or when your line for the bank teller is long.

### Envy

To envy is to resent someone else's good fortune so much that you are tempted to destroy it or steal it from them. If your friend is doing well in a fitness program, you would exemplify envy if you sabotage the program so that you can gloat about his or her failure and your own success. The scripture teaches that "envy rots the bones" (Proverbs 14:30).

The whole of creation groans because of the fall and personal sin.

## Anger

Experiencing anger means that you allow contempt for another to rule over you. A girl who is not loved by her father and turns to controlling food to vent her anger may find food controlling her life. A girl who is overweight and is heavily criticized by her father may overeat as a response to her anger and hurt over her father's remarks. The scripture teaches that uncontrolled "anger is cruel and fury overwhelming" (Proverbs 27:4).

## Laziness and Apathy (Sloth)

The laziness in people may be part of why they dream of fitness but don't get off the couch to do anything about it. Scripture teaches that the lazy person wants to go but doesn't do anything to get anywhere (Proverbs 13:4). In other words, although the "couch potato" says he wants to be fit, his lack of action indicates he doesn't really want anything—and that's what he gets!

## Greed and Materialism (Avarice)

Greed makes people want the best fitness equipment and finest fitness clubs to produce the finest body around, and they'll do anything to get it. The scriptures remind us, "Whoever trusts in his riches will fall" (Proverbs 11:28). If you count on money and material things, you will fail.

## Overindulgence (Gluttony)

The glutton is captive to food because her thoughts are consumed by wanting more food or, in cases of anorexia nervosa, less food. The Scripture says that "their god is their stomach" (Philippians 3:19).

## Misguided or Sinful Desire (Lust)

People who let their bodies direct them into a lustful obsession to continually satisfy cravings for pleasure become captives of a vicious cycle, wanting more and more. Scripture describes the situation this way: "Having lost all sensitivity, they have given themselves over to sensuality so as to indulge in every kind of impurity, with a continual lust for more" (Ephesians 4:19). Addictions come from those kinds of cravings. One more drink or one more look at a sexy picture seems so innocent, but the taste or the look calls for one more, and another, and another. Those desires are like sponges that never become saturated.

Let's face it: Because Adam and Eve blew it, you are susceptible to doing your own thing, no matter the consequences. But that behavior ultimately

- damages your body,
- holds you in a prison of the things you crave, and
- leaves you dissatisfied and searching for what you're missing.

Falling into sin increases the suffering of this world and of your body.

# Redemption

Rebellion against God causes people to be miserable, unhealthy, and unwell—but there is hope. Christ says, "I have come that they may have life, and have it to the full" (John 10:10). Christ died and rose again to bring life. God wants to change all things through Christ (Colossians 1:19–20). Through Christ's redemptive work, people are reconciled to God and are challenged to make all things as they were created and meant to be—very good. **Redemption** means that all things are made new in Christ.

At the beginning of this chapter, you read about a new Christian abstaining from food and not caring for his body as a way of worshipping the Lord. This new Christian may also have quoted from Proverbs 31:30: "Charm is deceptive, and beauty is fleeting but a woman who fears the Lord is to be praised." Or he could have quoted from Psalm 147:10–11: The Lord does not delight "in the legs of a man; the Lord delights in those who fear him." Is part of becoming reconciled to God doing what this new Christian did? I think the answer is no! The key part of each of these verses is the last one—the need to fear the Lord. Then, out of reverence for God, people need to glorify God in everything they do (1 Corinthians 10:31) because "everything God created is good" (1 Timothy 4:4) and needs to be redeemed, including the body.

## Opposite of Sinning Causes Healing

The seven deadly sins cause much brokenness, but the opposite of each sin brings healing. Instead of feeling the pain caused by self-centered pride, give and receive love to feel healing. Instead of the rot caused by envy, experience the peace that gives life to the body (Proverbs 14:30). Instead of injury through furious, irrational anger, experience healing through gentle, irrational forgiveness, as God forgave you (Matthew 6:12; Ephesians 4:32). Instead of experiencing obesity caused by laziness, experience the promise of fullness in Proverbs 13:4: "The desires of the diligent are fully satisfied." Instead of being greedy for self-serving riches, live simply. Trust the scripture that says, "God will meet all your needs according to his glorious riches in Christ Jesus" (Philippians 4:19).

Instead of being a captive to food, "eagerly await a Savior from [Heaven], the Lord Jesus Christ, who, by the power that enables him to bring everything under his control, will transform our lowly bodies so that they will be like his glorious body" (Philippians 3:20–21). Instead of being a captive to lust, follow the scripture that teaches this: "Do not offer the parts of your body to sin, as instruments of wickedness, but rather offer yourselves to God" (Romans 6:13).

Even in falling into sin, you are still created in God's image. Moses asks this rhetorical question: "Is he [God] not your Father, your Creator, who made you and formed you?" (Deuteronomy 32:6) Elders praise God before his throne, saying, "You are worthy, our Lord and God, to receive glory and honor and power, for you created all things, and by your will they were created and have their being" (Revelation 4:11). Fallen? Yes! But you are created by God, held in his loving embrace, and asked to join God in caring for and developing creation. Amazing!

Even though you are created in God's image and you rebel against God, he still wants you to renew all things, including your physical wellness and your body (which is created in his image). Paul states, "God was reconciling the world to himself in Christ. . . . And he has committed to us the message of reconciliation. We are therefore Christ's ambassadors, as though God were making his appeal through us" (2 Corinthians 5:19–20). The psalmist states this more forcefully: "You made [people] ruler over the works of your hands; you put everything under his feet" (Psalm 8:6). Through your body you are God's hands and feet in this world, created to do good.

God wants to renew the world—to reconcile it to him—and he wants you to be his ambassador on earth. Jesus said, "Go into all the world and preach the good news to all creation" (Mark 16:15). Notice that Jesus does not say "to all *people*" but "to all *creation*," every bit of it and of you. The good news of salvation found in Jesus Christ is important not only in your relationship to God and to each other but also in your relationship to plants, animals, your body, and all of creation. Paul urges "in view of God's mercy, to offer your bodies as living sacrifices, holy and pleasing to God—this is your spiritual act of worship" (Romans 12:1–2). Spiritual acts of worship are to be physical.

When John the Baptist's disciples asked if Jesus was the Messiah, Jesus did not reply with philosophical or theological or other theoretical arguments; instead he replied, "Go back and report to John what you hear and see: The blind receive sight, the lame walk, those who have leprosy are cured, the deaf hear, the dead are raised, and the good news is preached to the poor" (Matthew 11:4–5), all physical stuff. Elsewhere the scripture says, "Be holy, because I, the Lord your God, am holy" (Leviticus 19:2; also Leviticus 11:44, 20:7). Did God intend for holiness to mean only sitting in temple courts, singing and praying? No! Examples of holiness in the Old Testament included honoring parents, taking a break from work, not turning to idols, not eating old meat, caring for the poor (Leviticus 19), not eating swarming things (Leviticus 11), and not hurting or killing children because other things had a higher value than they did (Leviticus 20:1–5). To be spiritual and holy today remains a physical act and includes patterns of sleeping, eating, and exercising.

Your body is so important to God that he refers to it as his temple. "Do you not know that your body is a temple of the Holy Spirit, who is in you, whom you have received from God? You are not your own; you were bought at a price. Therefore honor God with your body" (1 Corinthians 6:19–20). Take some time to read 1 Kings 6–7 for a description of the beauty of the temple—a place where people met God. God invites you to live in such a way that people see and meet him when they are in your physical presence (2 Corinthians 4:10–12).

## God's Care for Your Body

God describes his **providence** for the body in Matthew 6:31–33: "Do not worry, saying 'What shall we eat?' or 'What shall we drink?' or 'What shall we wear?' . . . your Heavenly Father knows that you need them. But seek first his kingdom and his righteousness, and all these things will be given to you as well." Psalm 104:14–15 adds, "He makes grass grow for the cattle, and plants for man to cultivate—bringing forth food from the earth: wine that gladdens the heart of man, oil to make his face shine, and bread that sustains his heart." God is a providential God. *Providence* is God's loving care and protection, and we can be confident in it.

God's concern for your body is also demonstrated through his many acts of healing (Exodus 15:26; Matthew 4:23, 8:16, 9:35, 10:8, 12:22, 21:14; Luke 22:51): "This healing was the sign of the reconciling and victorious Kingdom which in Him and with Him came to be" (Berkouwer, 1962, p. 230). His concern is also noted in laws to protect life. He commands: "You shall not murder" (Exodus 20:13). Why? "For in the image of God has God made man" (Genesis 9:6). God gives you the knowledge and power generally to keep you well and to make yourself well

physical wellness is a part of abundant living, of glorifying God with all that you are, and of redeeming this world for God.

# Fulfillment

But what happens to people when they die? The scripture teaches, "Whoever believes in the Son has eternal life" (John 3:36). Notice the word *has.* The text does not say "will get" but "*has* eternal life." Today is a part of eternity. Death is only a passing from this life to the next. **Fulfillment** is God's honoring his promise that all things will be made new and that there will be an eternal "new heaven and a new earth" (Revelation 21:1).

So what does the future hold for people after death? Jesus said, "Do not let your hearts be troubled. Trust in God; trust also in me. In my Father's house are many rooms; if it were not so, I would have told you. I am going there to prepare a place for you. And if I go and prepare a place for you, I will come back and take you to be with me that you also may be where I am" (John 14:1–3).

The Apostles' Creed, written soon after the death of Christ, confesses, "I believe in the resurrection of the body, and life everlasting." The scriptures describe in 1 Corinthians 15:51–58 how people will be resurrected (see the passage in the Transition at Death sidebar).

Jesus is living proof of the resurrection. After he rose from the dead he met with his disciples, ate with them, and let them touch him. His resurrection was physical (Luke 24:37–42). Jesus' resurrection is important because it assures Christians of their resurrection (1 Corinthians 15:16–19). Certainly, a living relationship with God gives purpose to life, but there is more to life than the present.

What are Christians being physically resurrected to? The scripture teaches that God "will create new

Jesus came so you can have a full life.

when you are ill; and from time to time he provides special healing.

God typically does not expect you to live an **ascetic** lifestyle that is austere, harshly self-disciplined, and devoid of material comforts. God "richly supplies us with everything for our enjoyment" (1 Timothy 6:17). Jesus came so that you "may have life, and have it to the full" (John 10:10). John prayed, "Dear friend, I pray that you may enjoy good health and that all may go well with you" (3 John 1:2). Preserving your

## Transition at Death

Listen, I tell you a mystery: We will not all sleep, but we will all be changed—in a flash, in the twinkling of an eye, at the last trumpet. For the trumpet will sound, the dead will be raised imperishable, and we will be changed. For the perishable must clothe itself with the imperishable, and the mortal with immortality. When the perishable has been clothed with the imperishable, and the mortal with immortality, then the saying that is written will come true: "Death has been swallowed up in victory." "Where, O death, is your victory? Where, O death, is your sting?" The sting of death is sin, and the power of sin is the law. But thanks be to God! He gives us the victory through our Lord Jesus Christ. Therefore, my dear brothers, stand firm. Let nothing move you. Always give yourselves fully to the work of the Lord, because you know that your labor in the Lord is not in vain. (1 Corinthians 15:51–58)

heavens and a new earth" (Isaiah 65:17; see also 66:22 and 2 Peter 3:13). Biblical scholars do not know exactly what this new heaven and earth will be like, but the Bible shows glimpses. The writer of Revelation states that it will be a place where God "will wipe every tear from their eyes. There will be no more death or mourning or crying or pain, for the old order of things has passed away" (Revelation 21:4). This new earth will be creation as it was meant to be—a place where resurrected Christians will be physically whole. Work on living a healthy life now, to be as you were created to be, and continue to experience wellness in eternity.

The Bible looks forward to a time when, in the New Jerusalem (i.e., heaven), "the city streets will be filled with boys and girls playing there" (Zechariah 8:5). It records how the "infant will play near the hole of the cobra, and the young child put his hand into the viper's nest. They will neither harm nor destroy on all my holy mountain" (Isaiah 11:8–9). The new heaven and new earth will be amazing. If God looks forward to seeing children playing and discovering his universe in heaven, he must certainly enjoy his children doing the same today.

A minister once told me that when he got to the new heaven and new earth he would like to become an astronaut. He was curious what all the planets looked like and wanted to explore them. Because he knew people live forever, he felt he had lots of time. Heaven for this minister was a continuation of what happens on earth. He wanted to glorify God by discovering more of his majesty as displayed in the planets, stars, and galaxies. After hearing the minister's story, I've decided that I want to play a lot more squash when I get to heaven. Can you imagine having forever to understand and develop your running speed or your ability to jump? To kick a ball? To throw? To catch? All this activity will be done simply for enjoyment and to praise the Maker, not to please anyone else. After the resurrection, Christians and God will together find delight in the physical body. Why not experience those delights in your life now, by healing brokenness, enjoying your wellness, and worshipping God actively?

God enjoys active worship.

## Next Steps

Remember the two students who held different views of how to love God with their body? They wrote these words:

> When I first fell in love with Jesus, I stopped loving my body. I thought that to be spiritual was to abstain from foods; fasting was a great door to a living relationship with God. (Byl, 1999, p. 73)

> God has blessed me with so many things. I think that it would be like an insult to say that I did not love the me that God made. I love my sense of humor, my nose; yes, I love me. (Byl, 1999, p. 73)

How do you value your physical self and your relationships with others? How do you offer your life and body as a spiritual act of worship? Thoughtfully consider whether you agree or disagree with the biblical arguments in this chapter. Talk about your thoughts with some other people. Ask yourself if you need to make some changes in the way you live so that what you do is consistent with what you say.

## Key Terms

| | | |
|---|---|---|
| aesthetician | evolutionist | providence |
| ascetic | fall | redemption |
| creation | fulfillment | |

## Review Questions

For each of these questions, choose at least two relevant scripture passages and explain how they support your position.

1. How does this chapter argue that creation affects who you are physically?

2. How does this chapter argue that the fall affects who you are physically?

3. How does this chapter argue that God's redemptive work affects who you are physically?

4. How does this chapter argue that God's ultimate fulfillment affects who you are physically?

## Application Activities

Write your responses to the following questions in your journal.

1. How do you like yourself—all your parts?

2. How do you honor God with all of you, particularly with your physical body?

3. If you're a Christian, how do you hope to please and enjoy God when you pass on to the new heaven and new earth? Are you already doing some of that today?

4. Based on your answers to the previous three questions, do you need to make changes in your views of what it means to be a person and of who you are?

## References

Berkouwer, G.C. (1962). *Man: The image of God.* Grand Rapids: Eerdmans.

Byl, J. (1999). Spirituality and wellness: Student perspectives. In J. Byl & T. Visker (Eds.), *Physical education, sports, and wellness: Looking to God as we look at ourselves.* Sioux Center, IA: Dordt College Press.

Marcel, G. (1965). *Being and having.* London: Fontana Library.

Plato. (1945). *The republic of Plato* (F. M. Dornford, Trans.). London: Oxford University Press.

Seerveld, C. (1976). Gallantry as a recreative moment in life. *Vanguard* (October): 19–21.

Socrates. (1954). Phaedo. In H. Tredennick (Trans.), *The last days of Socrates.* Baltimore: Penguin.

## Suggested Readings

Byl, J., & Visker, T. (Eds.). (1999). *Physical education, sports, and wellness: Looking to God as we look at ourselves.* Sioux Center, IA: Dordt College Press.

For readings on various Christian views of the body, read two chapters in this book:

Chapter 1: The Bible and the Body: A Biblical Perspective on Health and Physical Education, by John Cooper.

Chapter 2: The Incarnation and the Flesh, by Bud B. Williams.

Wolters, A. (2005). *Creation regained* (2nd ed.). Grand Rapids: Eerdmans.

This is a book about using all created things in a way that pleases God.

## Suggested Websites

www.gospelcom.net

This is a great website that helps you explore the Bible.

## Twitter

On Twitter, follow @YouVersion.

# God's Purpose and Your Life's Mission

## John Byl • Dianne E. Moroz

After reading this chapter, you should be able to do the following:

1. Understand how life choices and practices are affected by external pressures.
2. Understand how to live all areas of your life with your own choices.
3. Write a personal mission statement.
4. Understand how to methodically change certain aspects of your lifestyle through goal setting.

## Alice Goes Nowhere in Particular

When people are "on a mission," they know exactly where they're going and are focused on getting there. Alice, in *Alice's Adventures in Wonderland*, exemplifies a lack of focus:

Alice . . . went on. "Would you tell me, please, which way I ought to go from here?"

"That depends a good deal on where you want to get to," said the Cat.

"I don't much care where—" said Alice.

"Then it doesn't matter which way you go," said the Cat.

"—so long as I get somewhere," Alice added.

"Oh, you're sure to do that," said the Cat, "if you only walk long enough." (Carroll, 1960, p. 62)

Alice will get somewhere, but clearly she is not on a well-considered mission. She may make positive choices and end up in good places, or she may make bad choices and end up in bad places. The story of the race between the hare and the tortoise makes the same point. As slowly as the tortoise goes, all its energies were focused on crossing the finish line.

You can also think about it this way: "Run water through a water pipe six feet in diameter and you have great volume with great potential. Force that same water through the nozzle of a fire hose and you have great impact. You were created for a life that makes that kind of impact. You are being shaped and positioned by God Himself to make a unique contribution for the kingdom" (Hoke et al., 2011). The question for you is this: How do you develop a mission for your life and develop goals to accomplish it? That's the question addressed in this chapter.

**The process** of answering important questions helps you discover the direction you want your life to go. For example, are you influenced by the "bigger is better" ideal? To what extent is materialistic gain important? David Myers (2006), a well-known writer on psychology, argues that as affluence has increased, depression has skyrocketed in North America: More than ever people have big houses and broken homes, high incomes and low morale.

Robert Putnam (2000) asks in his penetrating book *Bowling Alone* why people watch the TV show *Friends* instead of having friends. Researchers reporting in the *American Sociological Review* made some important observations. Comparing survey responses in 1985 and 2004, the researchers found that the "number of people saying there is no one with whom they discuss important matters nearly tripled" (McPherson et al., 2006, p. 353); and on average the number of people with whom they discussed important matters decreased from approximately three to two people during those 20 years. To what extent is this true in your life? How does your place of affluence and spiritual hunger affect your wellness choices? Ask yourself, What do I do to contribute to peace or to brokenness for myself, those around me, and the creation I need to care for? Remember that "whoever is kind to the needy honors God" (Proverbs 14:31), and those who pursue kindness will be blessed by finding "life, prosperity and honor" (Proverbs 21:21).

Scripture speaks to Christians who, like Alice, lack focus. Have you ever been tossed around by big waves in the ocean or a lake? The Bible warns its readers against being tossed around like that, moving from one fad to another, but encourages people to lovingly stand firmly with God (Ephesians 4:14–15). This book gives you tools to respond in a biblically rooted, scientifically validated manner to Paul's urging in Romans 12:1–2 to "offer our bodies as living sacrifices, holy and pleasing to God." This chapter helps you to be more intentional in your walk with God and to be encouraged in it because you know you are on a chosen path.

As you go through this text discovering how activity, nutrition, and life's rhythms can be used in ways to offer your body to God, please do two things. First, be committed to deliberately writing and living your own story. Map out your life so that you plan to go to great places more often. In other words, don't travel through life aimlessly as Alice did, and don't let your life be swayed by every wind of teaching. Second, read this text and other literature with **discernment** because you need to "continue to work out your salvation with fear and trembling, for it is God who works in you to will and to act according to his good purpose" (Philippians 2:12–13).

Begin mapping where you wish to travel. Questions are offered to help you look at the pressures that shape your choices. Next, consider God's mission for people. Finally, work through the steps designed to help you articulate your personal life's mission and your physical wellness goals.

## God's Mission

I am certain God has a plan for all people. For example, God creates and preserves his creation. He does not decide to go one way one day and a completely different way another day. Scripture confirms that God has a plan for his people; it is a plan of hope and a plan with a future (Jeremiah 29:11). God has a mission. What images do you see in God's mission described by Isaiah in chapter 9 (see the Part of God's Mission sidebar)? The words I see in God's mission have to do with light, joy, harvest, shattered yokes, wonderful counsel, peace, and eternity. These concepts are part of God's mission, and each leads to wellness.

Jesus' purpose on earth wasn't just to walk aimlessly around for a while and live with humanity. He had a mission. He did walk among people, but he came for a specific purpose. Luke states that purpose by recording Jesus' words: "The Spirit of the Lord is on me, because he has anointed me to preach good news to the poor. He has sent me to proclaim freedom for the prisoners and recovery of sight for the blind, to release the oppressed, to proclaim the year of the Lord's favor" (Luke 4:18–19). Jesus had a healthy and healing mission that directed everything he did. This same Spirit empowers, for "God did not give us a spirit of timidity, but a spirit of power, of love and of self-discipline" (2 Timothy 1:7).

## Making God's Purposes Your Purposes

If God has a mission, then it is helpful for his people to have a mission. If you want to honor God, then it is good when your mission is consistent with God's and empowered by him. A mission needs to be something that resonates deep within you, not something superficial that you devise quickly. Stephen Covey argued that "the power of transcendent vision is greater than the power of the scripting deep inside the human personality and subordinates it, submerges it, until the whole personality is reorganized in the accomplishment of that vision" (Covey et al., 1994, p. 106). A Christian's mission needs to be transcendent and thoroughly connected to God's vision.

Here are some questions to help you discover your mission: What are the biggest areas of suffering that touch my life? What can God's mission bring to that suffering? What role can I play as an agent of God? Or think about your part in the Lord's Prayer: "Your kingdom come, your will be done on earth as it is in heaven" (Matthew 6:10). God's eternal kingdom is a place of no mourning, crying, or pain (Revelation 21:4), because **love** is central and, significantly, listed first in the aspects of the fruit of the Spirit (Galatians 5:22–23). Is deliberately demonstrating love central to your life? What role do you play in helping God's kingdom to come "on earth as it is in heaven"?

Scripture encourages people to "throw off everything that hinders and the sin that so easily entangles, and let us run with perseverance the race marked out for us" (Hebrews 12:1). Do you have that kind of focus in your life?

Do you have the kind of focus that allows you to interpret your daily choices against what is considered cool by culture and what God thinks? Think this

---

### Part of God's Mission

The people walking in darkness have seen a great light; on those living in the land of the shadow of death, a light has dawned. You have enlarged the nation and increased their joy; they rejoice before you as people rejoice at the harvest, as men rejoice when dividing the plunder. For as in the day of Midian's defeat, you have shattered the yoke that burdens them, the bar across their shoulders, the rod of their oppressor. Every warrior's boot used in battle and every garment rolled in blood will be destined for burning, will be fuel for the fire. For to us a child is born, to us a son is given, and the government will be on his shoulders. And he will be called Wonderful Counselor, Mighty God, Everlasting Father, Prince of Peace. Of the increase of his government and peace there will be no end. He will reign on David's throne and over his kingdom, establishing and upholding it with justice and righteousness from that time on and forever. The zeal of the Lord Almighty will accomplish this. (Isaiah 9:2–7)

through very practically: Are your choices about these things—where you shop, the clothes you wear, how or where to vacation, what you drive, the way you spend your time, the way you spend money, where you go out with friends, and the way you care for your body—directly determined by biblical principles? As you read the following verses, think about how they speak to your lifestyle in those areas.

> Do not be afraid, little flock, for your Father has been pleased to give you the kingdom. Sell your possessions and give to the poor. Provide purses for yourselves that will not wear out, a treasure in heaven that will not be exhausted, where no thief comes near and no moth destroys. For where your treasure is, there your heart will be also. (Luke 12:32–34)

> For we are God's workmanship, created in Christ Jesus to do good works, which God prepared in advance for us to do. (Ephesians 2:10)

What do you really treasure? Where is your heart? You are created to do good. Do the things you treasure encourage you to do good? Don't just pay lip service to these questions, because they form the basis of your life and of this textbook. If your heart is focused on acquiring more and more things, you won't take

Take time to think about your life's purposes.

the time to care for your body. If your heart is focused on pleasing God, you will take the appropriate time to care for your physical health because you are in the image of God.

## Pressures That Shape Life's Mission

Many influences shape desires, judgments, and ultimately even goals. Some of these influences contribute to wellness and others take away from wellness. Two major influences are peer pressure and mass media. Think about how those two influences shape your answers to the questions you answered about your daily choices. If you were to create a collage of pictures from magazines or newspapers about what is cool, what would it look like? Do the violence, alcohol, and promiscuity in some corporate advertising, television shows, magazines, movies, and video games affect your sense of what is cool?

### Peer Pressure

Peer pressure can both help and hinder health and wellness. When students were asked what the greatest victories in their lives were, one student responded this way: "The biggest victory in my life was to leave my old life behind. I was dating an alcoholic non-Christian. . . . I did things and have been to the wrong places. I knew my life was going downhill. . . . God took me out of that life and brought me back to him" (Byl & Visker, 1999, p. 74). Another student shared how "through a friend at school, God began the process of freeing me from the bondage in my life" (Byl & Visker, 1999, p. 74). Friends had a huge influence in both of these stories. The influence in the first story was negative; in the second story it was positive. You can look at your own life and see how friends kept you accountable to do good or how they took you down unhealthy paths. Ultimately you make the choices to follow or not, but the pressure to follow is often enormous.

### Mass Media

Mass media have a powerful influence in shaping values and opinions. Some media products deal with significant issues and encourage people to live whole and healthy lives. However, as William D. Romanowski writes in his penetrating look at popular culture in the United States, "We need to be more aware of self-interest and self-reliance, a lust for power, violent resolutions to problems, materialism stereo-

What shapes your view of what's cool?

types . . . and even a humanistic outlook. American values? Perhaps, but definitely not Christian values" (Romanowski, 2007, p. 134). How much do media, particularly television and movies, shape the way you think about yourself and the way you live?

# Your Mission Statement*

*Adapted by permission from Byl 2002.

You've learned so far in this chapter what some of God's purposes are, how difficult it is to change, and how important it is to live with direction. Now it's time to clearly develop your personal **mission statement** that will direct your life and wellness. There are seven steps.

## Step 1: Begin With a Central Theme

Think of a statement that describes the central theme of your mission. The statement should explain who you are, what you stand for, and why you exist. This statement is the focus of your life. Complete the four steps requested in the Making a Godly Difference sidebar.

Here's how I've described how I can redeem things for God.

I know my life passions and gifts include sport, health, fun, and games. In the big picture I know God loves the world and is deeply grieved by its brokenness. I want to love the world as he wants me to and to be a healing influence. In the world of health I see and delight in people who actively walk, run, jump, and skip with smiling faces and healthy bodies. I love the feeling of a long, hard cycle on a warm day. I also see and grieve for people who are inactive, sad, and in poor health, and I'm unhappy with my own increased body fat and stressed lifestyle. I am really bothered when people don't get along and there is conflict. I totally enjoy watching and being a part of a group of people who are having fun with each other. I want all of us to be happy. I want us all to know the joy of the Lord, celebrating God's victories in our lives (Psalm 30:11; Jeremiah 31:13; Luke 24:40-41; Psalm 126:1-2). I want to build myself, my city, my country, and this world in a way that pleases God.

## Step 2: Write the Mission Statement

Begin to write your mission statement. Be realistic, though. The mission statement should push you to new and positive roads, but roads that are within reach. Don't worry if you can't get it just right at first or if you ramble a bit. Getting something down on paper gets you closer to a more specific mission statement. Here's an example of how I might start: "Because I'm in God's image, I want to joyfully and gently walk with God in my whole being and to share that encouraging walk with my wife, children, students, readers, and others, especially the marginalized and oppressed. I want to live more simply so that others may simply live. Stated briefly, I want to walk joyfully and gently with God and to encourage others to do the same."

## Making a Godly Difference

1. Answer this question: How does God want me to make a difference in this world?

   a. Think about the following passage. What does it say about God's leading? "Many are the plans in a man's heart, but it is the Lord's purpose that prevails" (Proverbs 19:21).

   b. Jesus is referred to as a shepherd. It is interesting that shepherds do not stand still but are usually on the move. What does it mean for your mission statement that you follow a dynamic God?

2. Find stillness to discern God's will. Listen to God's voice from your past; through scripture, prayer, the needs of others, your gifts and talents, your dreams, your broken places, and your imagination; and by picturing new possibilities (Sine & Sine, 2002). How does each of these situations help you focus your life?

3. Determine some practical ways to make a difference and list some scripture passages that speak to you about your purpose.

   a. Think about the following two passages. What do they say about God's love for people and the world?

      i. "For God was pleased to have all his fullness dwell in him, and through him to reconcile to himself all things, whether things on earth or things in heaven, by making peace through his blood, shed on the cross" (Colossians 1:19–20).

      ii. "For God so loved the world that he gave his one and only Son" (John 3:16).

   b. Listen to Bruce Cockburn's song "Laughter." He sings about people wanting to make a New Jerusalem and ending up with New York. Look at the full lyrics at http://cockburnproject. net/songs&music/l.html or listen to it at http://www.youtube.com/watch?v=x39HBT7XuDo. To what extent are people's priorities laughable?

4. Find and describe positive ways you can redeem things for God. It's important that the mission statement be about you, not about someone else. Remain true to yourself.

## Step 3: Refine Your Mission Statement

Refine the statement by keeping it short and simple so you can live by it in your daily life, because "faith by itself, if it is not accompanied by action, is dead" (James 2:17). The statement now should be one sentence long—two at the most. Maybe a Bible verse works as the framework for your mission statement. A colleague chose Jesus' words found in Mark 12:30: "Love the Lord your God with all your heart and with all your soul and with all your mind and with all your strength." I simplified my previous statement this way: "I want to joyfully and gently walk with myself, God, and others."

## Step 4: Build Excitement and Inspire Action

Choose words for your mission statement that build excitement and inspire action. Your mission statement should not be a weight that hangs around your neck but rather wings that help you soar. Use inspiring and strong verbs and adverbs to communicate your mission. My own statement began weakly with "I want to." I realized I needed to make a decision to *do* it, so I deleted "I want to." *Running* is a more inspiring word than *walking*, but I don't want to run through life. I did change *walking* to *walk*. Finally, "myself, God, and others" was still a mouthful, so I changed that phrase to *companions* but then decided to assume my walking included us all! My statement at this point: "Walk joyfully and gently."

## Step 5: Get Others' Input on Your Mission Statement

Talk to other people about their mission in life. Live prayerfully and listen to the Lord's leading. Study scripture to give you focus for your mission. Choose friends that love you and will remind you when you're focused too much or too little on yourself and your own well-being. They will also remind you when you are trying to be someone you're not or when your actions are consistent with your abilities and interests. Listen to your heart and what others say as you decide on the best route to take.

## Step 6: Make Your Mission Statement Visible

Post copies of your mission statement in your room, put a copy in your wallet, or write it on your calendar. A bathroom mirror is both a personal and somewhat public space to remind you of your mission statement every day. The screen saver on your computer is another good place to put it.

## Step 7: Revisit and Evaluate Your Mission Statement

Evaluation is key to the success of any plan. You need to evaluate your mission statement from time to time and adjust it as necessary, either to improve the statement or to reflect more closely on your life's purpose. Part of these changes may revolve around changing life stages. A person's focus may change somewhat from being a student to being a worker to being a parent. Everyone is shaped by these different stages. Be open to the leading of the Holy Spirit. Don't go through life as Alice did, blown around by every fad (Ephesians 4:14), but focus on God (Hebrews 12:2) and run his race (Hebrews 12:1; see also 1 Corinthians 9:24 and Galatians 5:7).

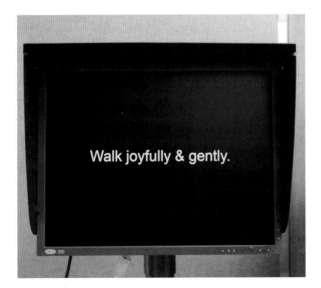

Walk joyfully & gently.

Make your mission statement visible by using it as your screen saver on your computer or mobile device.

## Goals for the Journey

You now have the tools to establish a mission statement. Someone once told me that a mission statement is the place God calls you, the place where your deep gladness and the world's deep sadness meet. You've learned how God created people good, in his image, and that the body is his temple. The rest of this book explores more thoroughly the concept of the body as God's temple, the holy of holies, and how the Holy Spirit provides power to heal. An old gospel song says, "Little by little He is changing me." Your developing a mission statement and setting and achieving health and wellness goals are part of the process of sanctification and of becoming more like God.

## Making Permanent Lifestyle Changes

You will refine your mission statement and develop more specific Christian paths to your health and wellness goals through the rest of this book. It's sometimes necessary to make permanent changes to your lifestyle or attitudes to achieve the goals you put in your mission statement or to improve health and well-being. For example, you may wish to quit smoking, start an exercise program, or become more sociable. Changes that are permanent usually begin slowly. Psychological perceptions change first, sometimes years before actual behavior change is made.

Prochaska et al. (1994) developed the Transtheoretical Model of Stages of Change (shown in table 2.1), which identifies six interactive stages in developing and implementing any permanent behavior. Note that for a lifestyle change to be considered permanent, your behavior must match your goal fairly consistently for about five years! That may seem like a long time, but these are *permanent* changes, so five years devoted to making a change is only a small fraction of a life span over which you will reap the benefits. It is also important to recognize that relapse to a prior stage is possible throughout the stages, more likely in early stages, less likely in the latter years of the maintenance stage, and much less likely in the termination stage.

After you have committed to making a change in your behavior, you need to develop a plan of action. It is most valuable to write this plan down so it's concrete and because it provides a document for future reference.

"I can do all things through Christ who strengthens me" (Philippians 4:13).

## Table 2.1  Transtheoretical Model of Stages of Change

| | |
|---|---|
| **Precontemplation** | You are unaware of any need for behavior change. Others may suggest a change in your behavior, but you are unconvinced. |
| **Contemplation** | You recognize that a behavior change would be beneficial and decide to implement a change sometime in the distant future. No firm commitment is made, but you make a sort of mental note that it would be a good idea sometime. |
| **Preparation** | You prepare to make a change. For example, if your goal is fitness, you may gather information about benefits of exercise, cycle with friends once in a while, and buy running shoes. You prepare yourself mentally and physically before committing to a regular exercise program. |
| **Action** | A plan is established and implemented. This is the most difficult stage, and relapse into the previous stage occurs frequently. This stage is only complete once the plan of action has been maintained for 6 months. |
| **Maintenance** | The behavior is maintained for about 5 years but requires compliance with a specific program. Assessment of the plan and of compliance to it are still necessary, and there is a threat of relapse to previous stages. |
| **Termination** | The termination stage is defined when the behavior has been consistently maintained for 5 years. The behavior is now incorporated into your life and has become part of your identity. For example, you see yourself as a fit individual who runs 4 times per week. You no longer require self-monitoring, and relapse is unlikely (although possible) even when the program faces obstacles. |

Adapted from Prochaska, Norcross, and DiClement 1994.

## Designing an Action Plan for a Permanent Lifestyle Change

The following seven steps will help you design a personal plan for permanent lifestyle change. These steps are all part of the Action stage of the Transtheortical Stages of Change Model. It is important to be realistic and concrete with every step of your plan. Map out each step prior to implementing your behavior change so that the entire plan is clear to you and therefore your expectation of progress is clear and realistic. Although the primary concern is with permanent lifestyle changes like achieving and maintaining fitness, the Action stage of change and the steps within it are equally useful for short-term goals, such as training for a marathon. There are five steps to the Action Plan that, if implemented with the proper attitude, will ensure success in achieving your overall goal. Make sure you complete the plan before implementing it.

### Step 1: State the Overall Goal

Simply but specifically state your **goal**. Some goals may be fairly standard to healthy living and be very similar to the goals of others. For example,

I will eat nutritiously according to our national food guide, Canada's Food Guide for Healthy Eating.

I will be physically active enough to achieve and maintain cardiovascular fitness.

Other goals may be tailored to your specific needs. For example,

I will engage in more social activities and develop more (or deeper) friendships.

I will develop my spiritual life by beginning my day with devotions and reading scripture each night before bed.

Changing your life requires patient work, but the rewards are amazing (Isaiah 40:31; Psalm 40:1-3; Psalm 130). It's tempting to change or abandon goals that are difficult to achieve. Writing your goal down with the reasons that you believe the goal is important will help to motivate you, particularly at times of difficulty. It's also important to develop a positive mind-set about life's challenges, and setting positive goals is one way of doing that. Instead of writing something like, "I will stop eating fast foods," you might write, "I will eat balanced and healthy meals three times a day, seven days a week."

Also, be realistic in establishing goals. Don't set them so high that they are unattainable or so low that they are not useful. Set goals for your own situation; don't try to set goals by other people's standards and programs because goals are unique to each individual, and even similar goals may have different individual emphases.

### Step 2: Assess Your Present Lifestyle

It is very helpful to have a full understanding of the present behaviors and attitudes surrounding your goal before you develop a plan of action. For one week, write down habits and activities or other information that affect your goal. Collect information long enough to note trends. If you record for just a short time, like for a day, you may get a skewed impression of your daily activity or habits. Include specific information about the behavior you are planning to change. For example, if you plan to quit smoking, record specific information about where, when, and why you smoke. You may even include information about who you're with and how you feel when you smoke. A chart is an effective way to record information and assess it at a glance (see table 2.2). Daily logs, journals, diaries, and graphs are also useful tools and can be used as an intervention strategy once you begin to implement your plan.

### Step 3: Design a Specific Plan

Use the assessment information to form a specific plan. The more specific the plan, the more likely you are to achieve your goal. The plan must include measurable, concrete actions that specify what you will do, when, where, and how. For example, a plan like this is too general: "I plan to run two hours per week." It may leave you slapping your forehead on Saturday night when you realize you are out of time and didn't run. In contrast, this is much more specific: "I plan to run around my neighborhood for 30 minutes, from 7:00 to 7:30 p.m., Monday, Wednesday, Friday, and Saturday." When 7:30 p.m. on Monday rolls around, you can immediately judge if you implemented your plan. If so, note your accomplishment. If you didn't, examine the reason and either reschedule or adjust your plan accordingly. For example, you may not have run because you were tired after dinner and then realize that you are unlikely to run at that time of day. Thus, you can adjust your plan to run when it is more convenient and enjoyable such as immediately before or after school or at lunch time. When you write a *specific* plan it's easy to monitor your compliance and moderate it when necessary. This is when many people have great difficulty and often abandon their goal. The critical part of implementing a behavior change plan is recognizing why you are not compliant and then adjusting the plan accordingly rather than giving up.

Sometimes the drive toward immediate gratification forces people to set unrealistic goals. Another critical part of the Action Plan is to break your overall goal down into small, achievable, measurable steps. Each of those adjectives is important on its own: *small, achievable, measurable.* Small enough that you don't feel overwhelmed. Achievable so that you experience success that promotes further success. Measurable so that you get instant, specific feedback about whether or not you are implementing your plan. For example, some people will plan to go from a sedentary lifestyle to running for one hour every day. Few people, if anyone, would be able to accomplish

## Table 2.2  Daily Activity and Barriers to Daily Activity

|  | Monday | Tuesday | Wednesday | Thursday | Friday | Saturday | Sunday |
|---|---|---|---|---|---|---|---|
| Week 1 | Squash at noon | Take a break | Golfed | Need to finish assignments | Tired at the end of the week | Need to do homework and shopping | Walked for 1 hour |
| Week 2 | Meeting at noon | Scheduled break | Golfed | Need to get to work. I got behind because of golfing. | Tired at the end of the week | Need to do homework and shopping | Rained; stayed inside |
| Week 3 | Squash at noon | Rained; stayed inside | Too wet to golf | Went for a walk with a friend | Too cold to go outside | Too cold to go outside | Too cold to go outside |
| Week 4 | Meeting at noon | Too tired to walk | Partners could not golf | Played a game of squash | Tired at the end of the week | Need to do homework and shopping | Walked for 1 hour |

such a goal. One of the greatest reasons for giving up a plan is "biting off more than you can chew." Even active people would have trouble running for an hour straight. How many people can suddenly find seven hours (actually, much more including shower and changing time) in the week? Therefore, break that goal into small, achievable, measurable goals. See the example at the end of the chapter under "Step 3" in the application activities.

For another example, if your plan to quit smoking "cold turkey" doesn't work and you keep sneaking a cigarette during the day, your plan isn't effective for you. Redesign it by breaking your goal into small, easily achievable steps. Use the behavior assessment (step 2) to rank the cigarettes you smoke in a day from favorite to least favorite. Maybe you could start by eliminating the least favorite cigarettes once every three days. If at some point you find that a cigarette you've eliminated leaves you craving to the point where you give in and smoke, then select another cigarette to eliminate. You may even continue without eliminating anymore until you feel you're ready. At

this point, you will already have eliminated some cigarettes, which is progress. Time is on your side when you're trying to change behaviors or attitudes. Because you're working on a *permanent* lifestyle change, the several months it may take to implement a plan is inconsequential if, ultimately, the behavior change improves health and wellness in the long run.

### Step 4: Predict Obstacles

You will inevitably encounter obstacles as you work through your program, including illness, exams, financial problems, stress, and unforeseen demands on your time. Predict some of the most likely obstacles and decide ahead of time how you'll overcome them. This serves two purposes. First, it prepares you for predictable obstacles. Second, it gives you the confidence that your plan can survive other obstacles when they come up. It helps you to realize that the plan is a work in progress, requiring modification as you advance through it. Table 2.3 shows you how six barriers can affect a plan and how you can overcome them.

### Table 2.3    Barriers to Change

| Barrier | Effect | Solution |
|---------|--------|----------|
| Procrastination | Rather than jump into action, you may believe that your life is busy and the timing for a new action will be better later. | Ask yourself why you are waiting. Assess the relative importance of the behavior so you can assign appropriate priority. |
| Success or failure attitude | You believe that if you don't complete the plan as outlined, you have failed and change is impossible. | Recognize that there is no failure. If you cannot comply with your plan, the plan must be revised, not abandoned. |
| Education | People tend to feel invincible unless they understand the significance of lifestyle to disease prevention and wellness. | Devastating diseases such as cancer and heart disease are processes that begin as early as adolescence. The earlier you begin a healthy lifestyle, the greater the quality and quantity of life. |
| Instant gratification | Society has a mind-set toward instant gratification. People would rather purchase quick-fix gimmicks to improve wellness than work hard. | Wellness is a lifelong process that is achieved and maintained only through frequent evaluation and action. Gratification is long-term, not instant. |
| Nonindividualized plan | You may turn to programs for diet or exercise that are not consistent with your lifestyle and enjoyment. A program that emphasizes activities you dislike has little value. | Individualize a plan so that you have selected the kinds of specific activities that are suited to your lifestyle and preferences. |
| Short-term change vs. permanent change | People tend to assume an intense exercise program until goals such as weight loss are met, only to return to unhealthy eating and the sedentary lifestyle that contributed to their desire to change in the first place. | Recognize that you are trying to make a permanent change in order to maintain a level of health and wellness. Slow, progressive change is permanent. Temporary change doesn't even guarantee temporary wellness, as in the case of restrictive diets that are unhealthy. |

## Implementing a Permanent Lifestyle Change

So far, you've developed a mission statement and analyzed and assessed your past. Steps 5 through 7 support gradual but significant life changes. Do not underestimate the difficulty in making changes. I have sometimes asked my students to move from their normal seat to sit on the opposite side of the classroom. They say that they feel strange, weird, or odd. Students don't like staying in their new seats, and they go back to their "normal" seating position the next time they come to class. Or try folding your hands as if praying. Which thumb is on top? Now fold your hands but have the other thumb on top. How weird does that feel? If something as inconsequential as taking a different seat or switching which thumb goes on top is challenging, how much more challenging it is to make a significant and permanent lifestyle change.

### Step 5: Plan Intervention Strategies

Making a permanent lifestyle change requires a great deal of time, motivation, and commitment. A relapse is a real risk, especially in the beginning. Design strategies to keep you compliant and to act as motivators. Here are six strategies that can help:

1. **Write a behavior contract.** This contract is a written promise to another person that you will complete activities according to plan. It usually includes a statement of the goal and the steps you will take to achieve it. Sign it and ask the person to whom you are accountable to sign it as a witness.

2. **Use positive and negative reinforcements.** It is important to reinforce success. Let's say, for example, that you follow your plan of cycling for three weeks. You could reward yourself by buying some cycling shorts or bike tools (positive reinforcement). On the other hand, if you didn't follow your plan, you might stay in on a Friday night instead of going out with friends (negative reinforcement).

3. **Get a support group.** This group may be a formal group, such as those for substance abusers, or just a group of friends you exercise with. The purpose of such a group is to keep you focused on your goals and to provide you with structure in your plan. If several friends are waiting for you at 7:00 a.m. to go for a walk, you are more likely to get out of bed and go for a walk than if you did not have friends waiting for you. It also indicates your commitment publicly and provides accountability to your goal.

4. **Use behavior shaping.** In **behavior shaping,** you modify situations or behavior to be consistent with your plan. If you have planned to study and the

Too big an obstacle to overcome at once: You climb a mountain one step and one stage at a time.

dorm is too noisy, for example, move to the library each night for your study time. Shape your behavior by making certain areas study areas and other areas play areas, rather than confusing the two. Many students now try to combine homework with text or instant messaging. Try to separate the two. Concentrate on homework, and then do messaging at another time. **Behavior substitution** is when you replace an undesirable behavior with a healthy one. For example, instead of having coffee and a cigarette after dinner, take a brisk walk. Remember, though; don't replace a bad habit with another bad habit. A common example of doing this is smoking to avoid overeating.

5. **Keep a journal or diary.** If developing a healthy sleep habit is your goal, for example, write a brief journal entry about how many hours of sleep you got, your bedtime and rising time, and your habits before sleep. With busy school demands, some students find they no longer spend enough time in devotions and prayer. If that's you, you could use a journal to formalize time spent with God by writing about prayers, devotions, or thoughts about scripture.

6. **Graph or chart your results.** Use a chart or graph to record compliance with your plan. For example, you could chart servings of each food group consumed per day, miles run, or hours of sleep. Charts and graphs provide information about progress and compliance with your plan at a glance. Take pride in your accomplishments.

## Step 6: Assess Compliance With the Plan

Use the charts, graphs, or records you developed in step 5 to assess whether you are compliant with your program. These may be the same as those used as intervention strategies. If you find you are not compliant with the plan, then reassess the plan. You may wish to go back to the previous step in your plan until you are ready to progress further. Never give up! If you don't manage to achieve your goal, your plan probably isn't appropriate for you at this time. Adjust your plan so that there are small, *easily achievable* steps that lead to the final goal. The only failure is abandoning the plan. Changes are made one step at a time. If you continue to be noncompliant with plans despite several adjustments, you may not be truly committed to the plan. Go back to your mission statement and make sure that the goal you have set is one that you value in your walk with God. If the goal is set for poor reasons, it simply may not be valuable enough to you to justify the work and dedication it takes to make a permanent change.

## Step 7: Assess Progress of Your Overall Goal

In addition to assessing compliance with your plan, evaluate whether your plan is helping you achieve your overall goal. For example, you may be compliant with your weight-loss program by reducing dairy and

Each step brings you closer to your goal; enjoy each step and the journey.

meat servings, but if you are substituting those foods with high-calorie items, the plan may not be reducing your body mass. Measure body mass (weight) periodically to ensure you are meeting your goals, but do it infrequently to avoid discouragement. For example, if your goal is weight loss, measure body weight weekly, rather than daily, because the common, day-to-day fluctuations can be disheartening and tempt you to abandon your program.

## Next Steps

Paul offers a partial mission statement in his letter to the Romans when he urges Christians to "offer your bodies as living sacrifices, holy and pleasing to God—this is your spiritual act of worship. Do not conform any longer to the pattern of this world, but be transformed by the renewing of your mind. Then you will be able to test and approve what God's will is—his good, pleasing and perfect will" (Romans 12:1–2). You should now have a mission that will help you become very deliberate in running your race, running your life, and running in a deliberate way in conformity with God's will. The rest of this book helps you develop specific goals for your health and wellness based on your mission statement.

## Key Terms

| | | |
|---|---|---|
| behavior shaping | discernment | love |
| behavior substitution | goal | mission statement |

## Review Questions

1. List several external factors that shape the way you think and live.

2. What are some characteristics of God's mission?

3. What are the seven steps in preparing an effective mission statement?

4. What are the seven steps in preparing goals to make permanent lifestyle changes?

## Application Activities

1. Reflect on the song "Today." You can find the lyrics for the song at www.lyricstime.com/brian-doerksen-today-lyrics.html or follow on YouTube at http://www.youtube.com/watch?v = XFs1d32K_ro. Do you agree with the lyrics of the song? Does your life agree with the lyrics of the song? Is your whole life, including your physical health and wellness, focused on serving and living for God?

2. Imagine that you are 70 years old and are reflecting on the most important things that happened in your life as you write a letter to someone you love. What are those things?

3. Write your personal mission statement (subsequent chapters revisit the mission statement and ask you to set specific goals for the different areas of your life, such as muscular strength, nutrition, and sleep):

   a. Write your central theme.

      i. How does God want you to make a difference in this world?

      ii. Take quiet time to discern your answer.

      iii. List three scripture passages and explain how they help you, in practical ways, to understand your place in this world.

      iv. What are some positive steps you can take in redeeming some things for God?

   b. Write a realistic mission statement that is simple to remember and inspires you to action.

   c. What are some steps you can take or are taking to remind yourself of your mission statement?

4. Use the following examples (and the text provided in this chapter) to help you develop your goals and make a plan to achieve them. Pick one area of your life that you're concerned about and develop a goal and a plan for achieving it.

   a. **Step 1:** State the goal. Write your overall goal in a sentence or two. You might write something like this: I would like to improve cardiorespiratory fitness by training for 45 minutes three times per week.

b. **Step 2:** Assess your present lifestyle. This is an example: I hate cycling, but I've tried running and liked that, so I will plan to run. I know that I get breathless quickly when I run, so I will start by walking and will work up to running. I work long days on Tuesdays and Thursdays and am too tired to work out on those days. Friday nights I play volleyball with my church group. I've checked my heart rate during the games, and I found that it doesn't fall within my target training heart rate zone of 142 to 175 beats per minute, so I can't really use that to improve fitness. I don't enjoy exercising in the morning and would prefer to work out in the evening. I think I would prefer to do my exercise alone, at least at first. Maybe later, when I'm more comfortable with my fitness, I'd enjoy exercising with others.

c. **Step 3:** Design a specific plan. Develop realistic, specific, measurable, and concrete steps. Goals should start out small to ensure some degree of success and then proceed in easily achievable increments until you are exercising for 45 minutes three times a week. Take a look at this example:

- *Week 1.* I will walk around the streets in my neighborhood on Monday, Wednesday, and Friday, from 7:00 p.m. to 7:30 p.m.

- *Week 2.* I will run for 5 minutes, walk 10, run 5, and walk for 10 minutes.

- *Week 3.* I will run for 10 minutes, walk 5, run 10, and walk 5. I'll try to run fast enough to keep my heart rate within my target heart rate zone.

- *Week 4.* I will run the whole 30 minutes. If this is too hard, I will walk for 1 minute after each 10 minutes of running.

- *Weeks 5, 6, and 7.* I will increase the duration of those runs by 5 minutes a week, to a total of 45 minutes.

- *Weeks 8, 9, and 10.* I will run the same route but increase my speed so that I'm running the same distance but in only 40 minutes by the end of 10 weeks. I'll check my heart rate to be sure I'm working harder.

- *Weeks 10 and 11.* I will run the same route in 37 minutes to increase intensity.

- *Week 12.* I will add more streets (or distance) to my route so that it takes 45 minutes to complete. I'll work at the midrange of my target heart rate zone.

Therefore, within only 12 weeks I will meet my goal of running 45 minutes on three days per week and within my target heart rate zone so that the overall goal of increasing fitness is achieved.

d. **Step 4:** Predict obstacles. Predict at least two obstacles and describe how you would overcome them. These are common obstacles and some ideas for overcoming them:

- *Illness:* If I am well enough to walk, I'll walk for only 20 minutes to 30 minutes so I stay in the routine of exercising. If I'm too sick to walk, I will plan to get back to my program as soon as I start attending classes again. I will reduce my intensity and duration when I resume exercising, and I'll build each day until I'm back to the place I was in my program before I got sick.

- *Exams:* During exam preparation I sleep less, have less time, and am more stressed. That is a time I should exercise to reduce stress and improve energy levels, but I always feel that I don't have enough time. To overcome this, I will exercise during exam weeks, but I will decrease the duration to 30 minutes while I maintain the intensity. I can use the time exercising to review memory work for exams or to plan out an essay.

e. **Step 5:** Plan intervention strategies. Formulate intervention strategies to help you stick with your plan. For example, you might include some of these strategies:

- I will keep a logbook of my running to record the days, times, and how long I run and to record my heart rate.

- I will buy running clothes if I'm compliant for three weeks.

- If I miss a day of running, I'll make it up on Saturday.

- I will write a contract and ask a friend to ask me regularly about my training.

f. **Step 6:** Assess compliance with the plan. Evaluate how well you're sticking to your plan. Here's one way to do that: Weekly, I will examine my running log to see if I've been compliant with my plan. If I find I haven't been following my plan, I'll adjust it accordingly. For example, if I see that I can't seem to get out on Wednesdays, I'll plan to switch my exercise to another day or time.

If the intensity is too hard I'll alter the plan so that I run slower and then slowly build up the intensity to meet my goal. I could also implement the "run 10 minutes, walk 1 minute" rule that even some seasoned marathoners use.

g. **Step 7:** Assess progress of your overall goal. Here's an example of how you can plan to measure your progress: To determine whether I am achieving cardiorespiratory fitness, I'll take my resting heart rate every three weeks to see if it is decreasing. Before training and at the end of six weeks, I will use one of the walking or running tests to estimate aerobic power ($\dot{V}O_2$max) and see if it has improved.

# References

Byl, J. (2002). *Intramural recreation.* Champaign, IL: Human Kinetics.

Byl, J., & Visker, T. (Eds.) (1999). *Spirituality and wellness: Looking to God as we look at ourselves.* Sioux Center, IA: Dordt College Press.

Carroll, L. (1960). *Alice's adventures in Wonderland.* New York: New American Library.

Covey, S., Merrill, R., & Merrill, R. (1994). *First things first.* New York: Simon & Schuster.

Hoke, S., Mayes, G., & Walling, T. (2011). Your personal mission statement exercise. In *Send me! Your journey to the nations* (p. 107). www.worldevangelicals.org/resources/rfiles/res3_196_link_1292601056.pdf.

McPherson, M., Smith-Lovin, L., & Brashears, M.E. (2006). Social isolation in America: Changes in core discussion networks over two decades. *American Sociological Review, 71*(3): 353–75.

Myers, D.G. (2006). *Wealth, well-being, and the new American dream.* www.davidmyers.org/Brix?pageID=49.

Prochaska, J.O., Norcross, J.C., & DiClemente, C.C. (1994). *Changing for good.* New York: Morrow.

Putnam, R.D. (2000). *Bowling alone: The collapse and revival of the American community.* New York: Simon & Schuster.

Romanowski, W.D. (2007). *Eyes wide open: Looking for God in popular culture* (2nd ed.). Grand Rapids: Brazos Press.

Sine, C., & Sine, T. (2002). *Living on purpose.* Grand Rapids: Baker Book House.

# Suggested Readings

Sine, C., & Sine, T. (2002). *Living on purpose.* Grand Rapids: Baker Book House.

This is a helpful book that further promotes the ideas of living with a mission or purpose.

Romanowski, W.D. (2007). *Eyes wide open: Looking for God in popular culture* (2nd ed.). Grand Rapids: Brazos Press.

This is an award-winning and widely read book that discourages mindless acquiescence or blanket condemnation of popular culture but encourages thoughtful engagement and critique of mass media.

# Suggested Websites

**www.franklincovey.com/missionbuilder**

The FranklinCovey organization shares an exercise to help you to create your own personal mission statement. Taking the time to seriously consider your answers to the questions will help you to define your values, principles, and priorities in your life.

**www.mapnp.org/library/plan_dec/str_plan/stmnts.htm**

The Free Management Library: Basics of Developing Mission, Vision and Values Statements site will help you develop your mission statement.

**www.toolkit.cch.com/text/P03_4001.asp**

The Business Owner's Toolkit site will help you develop your mission statement.

**www.lyricsmode.com/lyrics/b/bruce_cockburn**

This website contains the lyrics of a number of Bruce Cockburn's songs.

# Part II

# Accepting and Caring for Your Body

# Examining Body Image and Eating Disorders in Women and Men

Heather Strong • John Byl

After reading this chapter, you should be able to do the following:

1. Describe body image concerns and eating disorders in men and women.
2. Outline what causes eating disorders and how they can affect men and women.
3. Describe how eating disorders are treated and list resources for those struggling with an eating disorder.
4. Describe how people distort a biblical view of themselves.
5. Appreciate God's love for people and their bodies.

**You read** in chapter 1 that you were created in God's image. You explored the biblical idea that God created people "very good"—short and tall, small framed and large framed. Some people agree with God's evaluation of them as "very good"; others skew this evaluation and view themselves as "very bad."

 ## My Struggles With Eating

My name is Heather. During high school I was a straight-A student. I was on the school swim team, was in the concert band, and went to the youth group at our church. I always had a boyfriend and lots of other friends, but I never felt pretty or thin.

By the end of high school, life at home with my parents was tense, so I was looking forward to going away to a university, living on my own, and being able to be more independent. I was confident I would do well because I was a good student. However, my first year was a disaster. I failed most of my courses. I spent way too much time on my social life, and I gained a couple of extra pounds. I didn't realize at the time that I was struggling with low self-esteem and depression. I felt pretty awful about myself, and I thought that I would never go back to school. I decided I needed to take back some control of my life to prove to everyone that I was not stupid, even though I had convinced myself that I was.

I began exercising, and over the course of several months I began slowly taking control of my emotional state. I became very disciplined and structured with what I ate and how much I exercised. I dropped weight like crazy and got so many positive comments about my body that I felt I was finally doing something right. But there was a problem. I felt worse and worse inside every day. I couldn't hold myself together. I was sleeping more during the day and losing a lot of my motivation for life. Something inside me was eating me alive.

Eventually I decided to give the university a second try. I was still convinced I was ugly, stupid, and no good to society, but I thought that maybe it was time for a fresh start. My unhealthy, regimented eating and exercise patterns persisted, but I was adamant that I was merely an advocate for healthy living. I was really very unhealthy, though. I was teaching aerobics five times a week and was also hitting the weight room for cardio and weights every day. It looked to others like I was in control of my life, but for some reason I felt out of control. Something inside me was hurting and I could not figure it out.

When I woke up each morning I would be thinking about the food I would consume that day. Planning my meals and daily activity became a higher priority for me than planning when to study or do my class assignments. Even as I sat in class and shivered because I had very little body fat, all I could think about was what I would have for lunch. At that point my weight was pretty low. I hadn't had a menstrual period for almost eight months, and I wasn't feeding my body for the amount of activity I was doing. I was cold all the time, and I found it hard to concentrate in classes because my body was so tired.

Something inside me wasn't right. I hurt. I would sleep all the time during the day because I had trouble sleeping at night. I'd miss a lot of classes, and I couldn't understand my life. This was supposed to be my second chance, but I couldn't even get out of bed in the mornings. One night I told my resident assistant (RA) that I needed to talk to her. I told her I couldn't stop thinking about food and that I found it difficult to get out of bed each morning. I had lost enthusiasm for life, and I was disappointed in myself for my lack of effort at school. My RA told me she thought I had an eating disorder. I laughed at that, because I was still eating. I was just really health conscious. I thought that to have an eating disorder you couldn't eat at all. Was I wrong! I searched the Internet for information about eating disorders. I could hardly believe my eyes. Every symptom I was experiencing was right there on the screen, under the heading *anorexia nervosa*. I was shocked. I didn't know what to do.

It took me a few days to take in all I had just learned. I thought the next logical step was to talk to my parents and make an appointment with my family doctor. My doctor told me that I had obsessive–compulsive behaviors, depression, and an eating disorder. She described the many physical complications of an eating disorder, which scared me. I didn't know until then that people could die from an eating disorder or ruin their chances of bearing children.

Soon after my visit with the doctor I began therapy with a psychologist. I started taking medicine, and I felt, finally, that I was improving. I learned from uncovering my pain that I was a perfectionist at heart. I had such high expectations for myself that I felt worthless when I failed during my first year at the university. I discovered I had placed my self-worth in things that were not dependable, like appearances, grades, boyfriends, and other friends. I discovered I wanted to go back to a time in life where things seemed "perfect," because I felt very guilty for failing in my first year at the university and for rebelling against my parents when I was a teenager.

Slowly (and let me emphasize the word *slowly* here) I began to learn to accept small things about myself. I struggled to confront the hurt and the pain I felt and to learn to love the person I was, inside and out. The most incredible thing I learned during my struggle was that, as a Christian, I could depend on God for support and unconditional love. I knew he wouldn't change and would love me no matter what. He had already proven to me that he was taking care of me; I just needed to accept it.

I learned to replace the terrible lies in my head—that I was worth nothing and that I was stupid—with the truth: God loves me. That was the spiritual awakening of my life. I had never needed to depend on God so much or to face evil so directly. What it all came down to was acceptance.

I knew that God accepted me no matter what, but I had a hard time accepting me because I was not perfect according to society's standards, and society's standards had become my own. Unfortunately, I could never measure up to them.

I realized that society tells people a lot about how they need to live, what to wear, what to buy, and how to love. It became obvious to me that society's values rest on a superficial foundation. None of those values provided me with happiness. I could have the skinniest body in the world and still be unhappy. I could have a boyfriend, a closet full of clothes, and tons of friends. I could go to parties, I could have sex, but I could still be hurting inside. Thinness becomes a religion, but one that "offers false promises of freedom and fulfillment that leaves followers feeling unsatisfied and incomplete" (Lelwica, 2009a, cover).

A materialistic culture implies that those superficial things are fulfilling and bring happiness. People can rent that kind of happiness for a short period, but it won't fulfill their deepest needs. Those needs can be met in only one way and that is through a relationship with Christ. He is the constant in a world filled with so many lies and inconsistencies.

# Introduction to Dieting, Weight Preoccupation, and Body Image

Western culture has seen a dramatic increase in the number of young women and men suffering from **weight preoccupation** in the last 25 years (Braun et al., 1999; Cash et al., 1986; Polivy & Herman, 2002). The term *weight preoccupation* encompasses a variety of topics in this chapter, including dieting, body image, eating disorders, and other obsession tendencies with weight and food.

Women and men alike are experiencing more dissatisfaction with their bodies than ever before. Americans spend an estimated $60 billion a year on diets or diet-related products (Lelwica, 2009a). Studies show that as many as 80 percent of 10-year-old girls have dieted, and the same percentage of women in their midfifties also report wanting to be thinner. More than three-quarters of healthy-weight adult women in the United States think they are "too fat," and nearly two-thirds of high school girls are dieting, compared to just 16 percent of boys (Lelwica, 2009b, p. 20). Researchers have reported that half of American women are on a diet (Cash & Henry, 1995; Smolak, 1996), 25 percent of men are on a diet (Smolak, 1996), and 91 percent of women on a college campus had dieted (Kurth et al., 1995). Five-year-old girls report an awareness of dieting practices (Abramovitz & Birch, 2000). Between 60 percent and 80 percent of middle school and high school girls report dieting behavior (Lock & LeGrange, 2006). If men and women could only love themselves as the woman did in the opening pages of this book where she wrote, "I believe that I do love myself, but explaining that love is the hard part. You know, God has blessed me with so many things. I think that it

My name is Tom. I was pretty shy as a kid, and I didn't get involved in too many sports. My family always went to church together. My parents split up when I was young, and I always felt really bad about it. I was very angry at God for breaking up my family. I was also teased a lot for being skinny when I was young, which made me feel really bad about myself. I didn't want to join any school sports teams, and I ended up avoiding friends and keeping to myself. By the time I reached high school I had grown taller and had a few friends, but I was still pretty skinny. I still didn't have a girlfriend. I remember like it was yesterday the day I decided I would try working out to get bigger. I thought I would definitely get a girlfriend if I worked out and had bigger muscles.

I started working out at our local gym and spent almost three hours a day, seven days a week, in the gym. I was after that V-shaped upper body that supposedly drives girls crazy. I was pretty tired and sore at the end of most workouts, but I believed the "no pain, no gain" philosophy. When I looked at muscle magazines in stores, I used to envy the guys in them and wish I had a chest as developed as those weightlifters. I remember thinking I would do almost anything to get that kind of shape.

I started working out with a few new friends at the gym, and we became such good friends that we rarely spent time with anyone else. When I wasn't working out, I was thinking about which exercises I was going to focus on at my next workout. The weight training was making significant changes to my body, but I still wanted to get bigger. Some of the guys suggested I take a variety of nutritional supplements to develop my muscles even more. I tried about five kinds of supplements and kept working out. The changes became even more pronounced. By the end of a year I had tried every program out there. I was taking protein supplements and fat burners and trying the latest training programs to get the edge I needed to get bigger. I was getting amazing results.

I was in amazing shape by the time I went to the university. I had put on about 26 pounds (12 kilograms) of pure muscle. It was great, because for the first time in my life I was the cool guy. I felt other guys looked up to me, and lots of girls wanted to hang out with me.

I kept working out like crazy and taking crazy amounts of supplements until they just stopped working. I then decided I needed to look for a new product that would take me to the next level. One day (I remember this day so clearly) I overheard some of the guys in the changing room talking about some steroids they were using. I decided immediately that steroids were the key to getting the best results and helping me get even bigger.

I had heard in my health class about some negative side effects of steroids, but I ignored the information. I thought, *If these guys are taking them and getting huge, and the steroids aren't hurting them, why shouldn't I take them?* So I tried the steroids. After about a month, my upper body was awesome. I had huge arms and pecs, and my abs looked like the abs on the guys in the muscle magazines.

Soon after I started to take the steroids I began to have massive mood swings and got really bad acne. I was freaking out on my girlfriend and family all the time and was completely obsessed with working out. It didn't matter if it was Christmas day or my girlfriend's birthday—my first priority was to hit the gym for three hours to get my workout in.

Everyone close to me started to worry about me. They told me that my obsession with my body was taking over my life. My girlfriend dumped me because she said I wasn't making her a priority. My mom and sister wanted me to see a doctor because they knew I was on some kind of drug. I knew I needed to change some parts of my life, but I didn't want to give up my new body and the rush I felt from working out. I felt trapped.

My mom and sister love me and are always there for me, but my dad has not been a big part of my life. I remember wishing from a really young age that he was closer to me, but I never knew how to make that happen. When I was working out so much I didn't have time or make time for my relationship with God. I don't think God was happy with my taking drugs, but I felt amazing, and I was getting so many great comments about my body.

Since my family confronted me I have seen my family doctor and a couple of therapists. I don't take the steroids anymore, but I am still in the gym two to three hours a day. At this point it is hard for me to accept the changes I need to make, because I might have to change my body. I know I have a long way to go, but I am learning new things every day. I'm much better than I was a year ago. I've started reading my Bible again and discovering new insights into what God wants me to believe about my body and who I am. This has been the hardest experience of my life, but I know it is worth it.

---

would be like an insult to say that I did not love the me that God made. I love my sense of humor, my nose; yes, I love me" (Byl, 1999, p. 73).

According to the National Eating Disorder Information Centre (NEDIC), **dieting** is a futile, often harmful, process of restrictive eating, usually caused by body dissatisfaction, preoccupation with thinness, and the false belief that self-worth is dependent on body size (Bear, 2000). Unlike healthy eating, which involves eating well-balanced snacks and meals from a variety of foods that give you energy to carry out your daily activities, dieting creates a physiologically driven preoccupation with food and can have devastating results, such as eating disorders, weight-loss surgery, and even suicide. Most people who diet do not understand or believe that healthy people come in all shapes and sizes (Bear, 2000).

The effects of dieting include a preoccupation with food, irritability, depression, and social withdrawal, as well as lowered self-esteem when diets fail (Bear, 2000). Depression is often associated with body dissatisfaction, and increases in body image dissatisfac-

tion are associated with increases in depression—it is a vicious negative spiral (Fulkerson et al., 2004; McCarthy, 1990; Stice & Bearman, 2001). In cultures where acceptance and self-esteem are often linked to physical appearance, people seem increasingly to be judged by the way they look. Information everywhere tells people they can shape their lives by shaping their appearance. This reshaping usually starts with dieting and maybe a new exercise program. People who feel unloved, ineffective, out of control, or unlovable may try to take back control by controlling their physical appearance (Bear, 2000).

Adapted, by permission, from M. Bear, 2000, *Dieting and weight loss facts and fiction* (Toronto, Canada: National Eating Disorder). www.nedic.ca.

When people continually diet, they are attempting to alter their body or their physical appearance. They are also trying to alter the image they have of their body. **Body image** is a multidimensional construct and is defined as the picture you hold in your mind of your own body (Thompson et al., 1999). Body image encompasses four dimensions: cognitive,

Body image includes how you think, feel, and act toward your body shape and size.

affective, perceptual, and behavioral. The cognitive component is what you *think* about your body (e.g., I think my hips are too wide). The affective component includes the *feelings* that you have about your body (e.g., I feel ugly or fat). The perceptual component includes how you *visualize* your body in your mind (e.g., I see myself as having wide hips). Finally, the behavioral component includes the things you *do* to try to change your body (e.g., exercising, dieting).

The concept of body image can be measured along a continuum. Some people may like the way their bodies look. Those positive thoughts have been linked to increased self-esteem, self-confidence, success in business, and success with interpersonal relationships (Thompson et al., 1999). On the other hand, a negative body image may induce negative thoughts, which may lead to depression, excessive dieting and exercise, steroid abuse, and substance abuse (Thompson et al., 1999).

Every person has a body image—an idea of what he or she looks like. However, a distorted body image or an unhealthy emphasis on physical appearance may influence how a person thinks and feels about his or her body and what he or she decides to do about it.

# Causes of Body Image Concerns for Men and Women

Many factors, such as puberty, peer pressure, family influences, the media, and gender differences, contribute to the development of body image concerns for both men and women. You'll learn about puberty and peer pressure briefly in this section, and you'll read about family, media, and gender differences when the causes of eating disorders are covered later in the chapter.

## North American Cultural Ideals

For women in North America the currently accepted ideal body shape is a thin and lean physique that is very difficult for most women to attain (Garner, 1997; Wiseman et al., 1992). The cultural pressure to be thin may be transmitted to young women directly through parents or peers encouraging their daughter or friend to diet or, indirectly, through advertisements promoting the beauty and weight-loss industry. Research has found that perceived pressure for girls to be thin (either direct or indirect) was related to increases in their body dissatisfaction (Field et al., 2001; Stice & Whitenton, 2002).

## Facts About Dieting and Weight Loss

- Anyone who goes on a restrictive diet will initially lose weight.
- An initial weight loss often makes people feel better about themselves because they experience a sense of control.
- Over time bodies on a restrictive diet become malnourished and begin to conserve energy, and dieters reach a weight plateau.
- The restrictive behavior makes people feel deprived of a normal existence and robs them of enjoyable meal times. Being malnourished brings mood swings and a desire to binge.
- The diet fails and dieters begin to regain the lost weight.
- The initial problems are still there and are compounded by feelings of failure from not losing enough weight or not keeping it off.
- Dieting can lead to lowered self-esteem, which is bad for health.
- Dieting can lead to increased weight through lowered basal metabolic rate.
- Dieting can lead to bingeing and eating disorders.
- Dieting can cause depression, mood swings, reduced sexual interest, and impaired concentration and judgment. Severe weight loss can bring heart disorders, elevated cholesterol, anemia, higher risk of infertility, hair loss, loss of muscle tissue, changes in liver function, and other complications.
- The risk of dying from heart disease is 70 percent higher in those with fluctuating weights than in those whose weight remains stable, regardless of initial weight, blood pressure, smoking habits, cholesterol level, or level of physical activity.

Adapted from Bear 2000.

Cultural pressures to attain an ideal physique also contribute to body dissatisfaction for men. However, the culturally accepted ideal physique for men is the V-shaped, lean and muscular body type (Olivardia, 2002). As for women, these cultural ideals are transmitted to men both directly and indirectly. One study found that young men who perceived their parents and their friends to be pressuring them to be a certain body size and shape were more likely to engage in strategies to alter their body size and shape (i.e., working out, taking supplements; McCabe & Ricciardelli, 2003). Approximately 4.7 percent of high school boys and 1.6 percent of high school girls reported using supplements weekly to improve physical appearance and strength (Field et al., 2005). In addition, another study (Field et al., 2001) found that parents who were concerned about their personal weight gain influenced the weight concerns that their adolescent boys experienced. Research has also found that young boys who claimed to try to alter their body size and shape to look like same-sex models and actors in the media were more likely to develop weight concerns and engage in negative dieting behaviors (Field et al., 2001). As many as 10 percent of anorexia and bulimia sufferers and 25 percent of binge eating disorder sufferers have been reported to be men (Weltzin et al., 2005).

## Value Placed on Cultural Ideals

The body dissatisfaction and weight concerns that many young men and women experience can come from how much they internalize the culturally accepted ideals for their gender. For example, one study found that adolescent males who scored high on drive for muscularity (high value placed on looking muscular) were more likely to have low self-esteem and to engage in strategies to increase their body size (McCreary & Sasse, 2000; Smolak et al., 2001). Other research has found that male adolescent football players were more dissatisfied with their body shape and size than adolescent cross-country runners. This finding was potentially due to the cross-country runner's body shape more closely resembling the culturally accepted ideal male body type (Parks & Read, 1997).

Similar results have also been found for women. For example, one research study found that women who placed greater value on the culturally accepted ideal body type experienced increases in body dissatisfaction (Stice & Bearman, 2001). Other research has found that adolescent and college-aged women who placed a greater emphasis and commitment on appearance ideals experienced greater body dissatisfaction (Cusumano & Thompson, 2000; Jones et al., 2004; Smolak et al., 2001; Stice et al., 1994).

## Puberty

Puberty is one major contributor to the onset of body image concerns. Young adolescents' bodies start to develop and change during puberty in ways they are unfamiliar with. Many young girls feel threatened by the natural weight gain and the physiological changes that come during this period of development. As they try to control their feelings about their new bodies, young women may develop negative thoughts about their bodies. These young women may end up in a cycle that begins with dieting to control their new images and that leads to further dissatisfaction with the body (DeCastro & Goldstein, 1995).

## Peer Pressure

Peer pressure is another contributing factor to body image and the subsequent need for societal approval. Appearances are intensely important for adolescents, especially adolescent girls. Young girls will often compare themselves to others and talk about their bodies, how much they weigh, and what they do to stay in shape. Research has demonstrated that adolescents who are a part of friendship groups have similar levels of body image concerns, are similarly preoccupied with thinness, and are on the same diet (Levine & Smolak, 2002).

Some of the other factors that play a role in the development of a negative body image are discussed later in this chapter. Some of them are avoidable and some aren't. However, some ideas and attitudes may need to be challenged to prevent or recover from a negative body image and to cultivate a healthy body image.

# How to Deal With a Negative Body Image

There are several ways to overcome the negative thoughts and feelings a person may feel about the body. Martha Homme's (1999) Turning Point workbook, *Seeing Yourself in God's Image*, is an excellent resource with a step-by-step guide to help people overcome a negative body image and eating disorders. The workbook outlines several useful steps, summarized in the paragraphs that follow.

First, as hard as it may be, it is necessary to "accept that bodies come in a variety of shapes and sizes" (Homme, 1999, p. 33). It is also important to not let your physical body or physical appearance define who you are (2 Corinthians 5:1). Society's definition of beauty is very narrow and constantly changing, but God's definition of beauty never changes. For example, 1 Peter 3:3–4 states, "Your beauty should not come from outward adornment, such as braided hair and the wearing of gold jewelry and fine clothes. Instead it should be that of your inner self, the unfading beauty of a gentle and quiet spirit, which is of great worth in God's sight."

People are often their own worst critics and pick apart every aspect of themselves or others to make themselves feel better. Instead of picking yourself apart, try looking for the qualities about your appearance that you do like, and focus on those. After all, all people were created unique by an amazing designer.

Love yourself and the God who personally created you. Because of the emphasis given to love in 1 Corinthians 13, it's no surprise that love is listed as the first fruit of the spirit. There will be no more "mourning or crying or pain" (Revelation 21:4) in the new world (heaven) because it is filled with love. God also gives the opportunity in the present world to experience the healing power of love. People can experience great healing when they know that God loves them and that Jesus died on the cross to pay for their sin; when they can give and receive forgiveness, a caring handshake, and a hug; when their love finds expression in living obediently with God; and when they are committed to lovingly building others up and they get the same in return. Does your mission include letting God's love flow through you?

In a recent randomized, controlled study, patients in an intensive inpatient eating disorders program were assigned to either a weekly emotional support group, a cognitive therapy group, or a spirituality group in which they received spirituality readings and self-help exercises (Richards et al., 2006). "For all patients, these weekly sessions supplemented an already intensive and effective treatment program. All groups experienced large pretreatment to post-treatment improvements; however, women in the spirituality group experienced the most reductions in disordered eating symptoms, negative emotionality, relationship distress, and social role conflict. They also experienced increases in their sense of being loved by God and having a purpose or meaning in life" (Homan & Boyatzis, 2010, pp. 241–42).

Second, recognize that your weight and shape will change at various times in your life. You probably experienced this when you went through puberty and perhaps during your first year at a university. There are other times when bodies commonly change: when women have children; when starting a new, sedentary desk job; and during aging. You can do things now to make those transition periods easier, such as eating a balanced, healthy diet; getting enough sleep; and figuring out what kind of exercise you like to do and doing it. Research has shown that a moderate amount of exercise is one of the most

effective (and enjoyable) ways you can improve your body image (Hausenblas & Fallon, 2006; Martin & Lichtenberger, 2002). A National Survey in the United States in 2000 indicated that 72 percent of women and 64 percent of men were inactive (Barnes & Schoenborn, 2003).

Third, explore who you are and who you were created to be, and take a good look at your "internal self—emotionally, spiritually, and as a growing human being" (Homme, 1999, p. 33). When you do, you will decide where you want to spend your energy. Do you want to focus on pursuing the "perfect image" or on your spiritual growth and personal needs?

Finally, remember that attractiveness comes from within, and thinness or beauty does not always equal happiness. Joy is the ability to respond to God's triumphs: seeing, feeling, and expressing celebration in God's victories. Jesus brought joy to the world before his birth (Luke 1:44) and after he rose from the dead (Matthew 28:8). Jesus's followers lived in "joy and amazement" (Luke 24:40–41) and worshipped him with great joy (Luke 24:52–53). They recognized his victories and allowed joy to overtake them.

Joy is also a response to God's blessing. When the Israelites returned from captivity they were filled with gladness. The psalmist wrote that the Israelites were "like men who dreamed. Our mouths were filled with laughter, our tongues with songs of joy" (Psalm 126:1–2). Those people were so happy they were drunk with laughter! Proverbs reminds readers that "a happy heart makes the face cheerful" (Proverbs 15:13; see also Proverbs 10:28; 12:20; 15:13) and a cheerful heart is "good medicine" (Proverbs 17:22) and "has a continual feast" (Proverbs 15:15). Can you allow gladness and joy to overtake you (Isaiah 35:10; 51:3, 11; 52:8)? Remember how David danced for joy when the ark returned and how his wife, Michal, remained barren because she was a killjoy (2 Samuel 6:17–23)?

For those too crushed by circumstances to experience joy, think of David. In his confession about the sin with Bathsheba, he asked God, "Let me hear joy and gladness; let the bones you have crushed rejoice. . . . Restore to me the joy of your salvation" (Psalm 51:8, 12). David was also able to confess that God's "consolation brought joy to my soul" (Psalm 94:19). Isaiah later asked God, "Strengthen the feeble hands, steady the knees that give way; say to those with fearful hearts, 'Be strong, do not fear. . . .' Then will the lame leap like a deer, and the mute tongue shout for joy" (Isaiah 35:3–4, 6; see also Romans 15:13; Acts 8:8). God will provide victory and joy even in the painful times of life.

Paul says, "Rejoice in the Lord always, I will say it again: Rejoice!" (Philippians 4:4). Sometimes people need to be told to rejoice as a reminder to get off the track of "Go, go, go! Produce, produce, produce!" Then they can openly receive the gift of joy and celebrate God's triumphs.

Count God's blessings to you and give thanks for each of them. Take a moment to relax and enjoy God's goodness to you. Can you feel the healing? Do you remember how good it felt to receive a genuine smile, to give one, and to laugh your head off with friends? The Holy Spirit offers joy to those who open their hearts to him.

Feeling positive about yourself will affect how others view you, and you will always benefit from treating your body with the respect it deserves. Maybe respecting your body means taking up a new exercise program, spending some time in nature learning to relax, and rediscovering your relationship with God. Maybe it means hanging out with a different group of friends who respect you for who you are and not for what you look like. On a final note, make sure you "are aware of your own weight prejudice and what you think about people who don't fit the 'perfect image'" (Homme, 1999, p. 33), and realize that maybe your definition of beauty needs to change.

# What Are Eating Disorders?

A person who feels very dissatisfied or unhappy with his or her body may take extreme measures to try to alter body size and shape. According to the American Psychiatric Association (2000), one of the key defining features of people with eating disorders is extreme dissatisfaction with body image.

Eating disorders are classified into three categories according to the *Diagnostic and Statistical Manual of Mental Disorders* (American Psychiatric Association, 2000): anorexia nervosa (AN), bulimia nervosa (BN), and eating disorders not otherwise specified (EDNOS). Binge eating disorder is classified under the EDNOS category. Other identified disorders that are related to eating disorders include anorexia athletica, female athlete triad syndrome, body dysmorphic disorder, and muscle dysmorphia. For a comprehensive overview on detecting disordered eating, managing athletes with disordered eating, preventing disordered eating, and additional studies, view the National Athletic Trainers' Association Position Statement (Bonci et al., 2008). Each of these disorders is explored further in the following sections.

## Anorexia Nervosa

**Anorexia nervosa** is characterized by a person's refusal to maintain a minimal body weight, an intense

fear of gaining weight, significant disturbance in the perception of the shape or size of his or her body, and, in females, no menstrual period (American Psychological Association, 2011). These are signs of anorexia:

- Dramatic weight loss
- Preoccupation with weight, food, calories, fat content, and dieting
- A refusal to eat certain foods

People with anorexia will frequently comment about feeling "fat" or overweight, despite their weight loss, and experience anxiety about gaining weight or being "fat." Often these people will develop food and exercise rituals, find consistent excuses to avoid mealtimes or situations involving food, and withdraw from spending time with friends or participating in usual activities. Approximately 0.9 percent of women and 0.3 percent of men suffer from anorexia (Hudson et al., 2007).

## Bulimia Nervosa

**Bulimia nervosa** is characterized by repeated episodes of **bingeing** (eating an abnormally large amount of food at one time) followed by behaviors designed to eliminate food from the body (e.g., self-induced vomiting, fasting, or excessive exercise; American Psychological Association, 2011). The warning signs of bulimia include evidence of binge eating, like disappearance of large amounts of food in short periods of time, as well as **purging** behaviors. People with bulimia will frequently make trips to the bathroom after meals, use laxatives or diuretics, or follow excessively rigid exercise regimens. People with bulimia are usually at a normal weight but, like those with anorexia, are obsessed with food and weight. Individuals with bulimia may also have cuts or calluses on the back of the hands and knuckles (caused by teeth scraping the hand during purging), discolored teeth, and damage to the esophagus. Binge eating has increased among adolescent girls in recent years, with 20 percent to 60 percent of girls in community samples reporting episodes of binge eating (Ackard et al., 2003; Hudson et al., 2007; Shisslak et al., 2006; Sierra-Baigrie et al., 2009).

## Eating Disorders Not Otherwise Specified

**Eating disorders not otherwise specified (EDNOS)** is a broad category that encompasses binge eating disorder (BED), compulsive exercising (e.g., anorexia

*(continued)*

## Risk Factors Contributing to Muscle Dysmorphia

- Being overweight as a child
- Early history of dieting practices
- Participation in a sport that demands thinness
- Having a job or profession that demands thinness (e.g., models, actors)

Adapted, by permission, from J.J. Robert-McComb, 2000, *Eating disorders in women and children: Prevention, stress, management, and treatment* (New York: Taylor and Francis).

### Muscle Dysmorphia

**Muscle dysmorphia** is a preoccupation with the idea that one's body is insufficiently lean or muscular (Pope et al., 2005). Muscle dysmorphia is believed to be a subtype of the more general body dysmorphic disorder (Pope et al., 2005); and so, although it shares similar characteristics with eating disorders, it isn't a classified eating disorder. Generally speaking, muscle dysmorphia affects men more than women. Men and women with muscle dysmorphia view themselves as being "too small," when in reality they look normal or even incredibly muscular. As a result, they may neglect important social or occupational activities because of the way they believe they look or because they need to attend to a meticulous diet and regimented workout schedule (Kanayama et al., 2006; Phillips et al., 1997; Pope et al., 2000). A warning sign of muscle dysmorphia is a constant need for affirmation of physical appearance attributes (because the person with muscle dysmorphia sees himself or herself as small). Individuals with muscle dysmorphia may be engaged in compulsive weightlifting or bodybuilding routines and may take steroids or other muscle-building drugs to get bigger. Achieving the societal ideal of the perfect male physique is often the draw for males to be engaged in bodybuilding (Olson et al., 2009; Parish et al., 2010).

## How Prevalent Are Eating Disorders?

In the United States, conservative estimates suggest that as many as 10 million females and 1 million males are struggling with eating disorders such as anorexia or bulimia, and as many as 25 million more people are struggling with binge eating disorder (Hoek & vanHoeken, 2003; Shisslak et al., 1995). One study indicated that more than half of adolescent girls in the United States reported unhealthy weight control behaviors such as fasting and skipping meals (Neumark-Sztainer et al., 2002). Although women are

at higher risk for developing body image concerns and eating disorders, research has demonstrated that men are slowly becoming more and more at risk (Furnham & Calnan, 1998; Neumark-Sztainer et al., 1999).

Eating disorders affect both men and women, but they typically are expressed in very different ways. For example, women (like Heather) often strive to be thinner than they are, whereas men (like Tom) often want to be bigger, or at least more muscular and lean. But the most alarming statistic about eating disorders is that "according to the National Institute of Mental Health, one in ten anorexia cases ends in death from starvation, suicide, or medical complications like heart attack or kidney failure" (American Psychological Association, 2011).

Eating disorders typically develop during adolescence; the typical age of onset is between 13 and 18 years (Robert-McComb, 2001). On average, adolescents begin developing eating disorders at around age 17, which is usually their last year in high school or first year at a college or university.

Each year eating disorders increase on college campuses across North America. Many students are excited about leaving home, gaining independence, and pursuing their goals. However, students who feel that the responsibility placed on them is too great may turn to inappropriate methods to hide or control their feelings of inadequacy or fear. It is often in these situations that college students develop eating disorders to help them cope with their new feelings. An article about college students and eating disorders reported the following:

When the pressures get to be too much, some [college students] may turn to anorexia as a way to block out what is happening. If they spend all of their time focusing on calories and their weight, they don't have time to think about anything else. Others might believe that the only way they will be accepted is if they are thin. If someone is having trouble in their courses and not getting the marks they wanted or expected to, they might also develop anorexia. As the scale goes down they start to believe that losing weight is the one thing they can succeed at and it makes them feel like they are accomplishing something. Others may turn to bulimia or compulsive eating as a way to deal with the pressures and all of the emotions they are experiencing. If they are feeling lonely, sad, tired, overwhelmed, depressed, scared, or confused, food can bring them a false sense of security and can also comfort them. When they binge, all their negative feelings disappear. When the bulimics purge, whether by vomiting or by compulsive exercising, it may help them to feel like they are releasing all of those feelings. Because food can only temporarily help deal with negative feelings, the binge–purge cycle will continue. (Thompson, 2000)

You might think that Christians are not affected by eating disorders. Research has indicated that assumption is false. A study by Cook and Reiley (1991) examined the prevalence of eating concerns among four college campuses for both women and men. Two campuses held an explicitly Christian worldview and two campuses were nonsectarian. The results of the study suggested that eating concerns were more prevalent among women than among men and that there were no significant differences in eating concerns between the campuses with a Christian worldview and the nonsectarian campuses.

Furthermore, the study reported that women on all four college campuses experienced significant eating and dieting concerns consistent with eating disorders, such as an intense fear of fat, persistent dieting, tendencies to overeat, abuse of laxatives, and purging. In the study, 52 percent of the women and 40 percent of the men identified themselves as overweight.

The study concluded that eating concerns are not exclusively a non-Christian or nonsectarian issue. The results from this study imply that eating concerns and eating disorders are prevalent on different kinds of college campuses, even those that espouse a Christian worldview.

# What Causes Eating Disorders?

Eating disorders are complex psychological disorders, and their onset may be influenced by sociocultural factors, psychological factors, biological influences, and conflict within the family (Epling & Pierce, 1988; Garfinkel et al., 1987; Sundgot-Borgen, 1994). Health professionals work to understand where eating disorders come from so they can attempt to explore and eventually change the way people think, feel, and act toward the body and their physical appearance.

## Sociocultural Influences

Society in general has a very narrow definition of beauty and incessantly places more emphasis on the outer appearance of an individual than on inner strengths and qualities. North American cultural pressures glorify thinness and place value on obtaining the "perfect" body. In general, people in these cultures think only men and women who are thin and shapely are beautiful (EDAP, 2000).

Western culture has confused and betrayed women and men by establishing unattainable ideals. Dick Moriarty, a professor at the University of Windsor, identified five sociocultural influences of eating disorders:

1. Cultural overemphasis on thinness
2. Glorification of youth
3. Changing roles of women and men in society
4. A fitness-crazed culture
5. Presence of the media

Adapted from Moriarty and Moriarty 1993.

Three examples of media that flood people with messages about the advantages of being thin are TV, movies, and magazines. Impressionable readers and viewers are told—sometimes directly and sometimes indirectly, by the choice of actors and models—that goodness, success, power, approval, popularity, admiration, intelligence, friends, and romantic relationships all require physical beauty in general and thinness in particular. The corollary is also promoted: People who are not thin and beautiful are failures. Media have recently portrayed the ideal female body image as more unrealistically thin than in the past (Koyuncu et al., 2010). People who are overweight are portrayed as bad, morally lax, weak, out of control, stupid, laughable, lonely, disapproved of, and rejected.

Research has demonstrated that, for women, reading teen or fashion magazines and watching television are related to body dissatisfaction (Jones et al., 2004; Tiggemann, 2003), the perception of being overweight (McCreary & Sadava, 1999), and eating disorder symptoms (Harrison, 1997, 2000a, 2000b; Thomsen et al., 2002). It's not hard to see where the dissatisfaction may come from. An article in *Health* magazine, for example, reviewed the body shapes and sizes of television network females and found

The ideal North American body shapes for women and men.

that 32 percent of the women were underweight and only 3 percent were larger than the average girl. The numbers are actually flipped in the U.S. population at large. Fewer than 5 percent of the female viewers are underweight and about 25 percent are heavier than the average female (ANRED, 1999a).

Mary Pipher, author of *Reviving Ophelia*, states, "Girls compare their own bodies to our cultural ideals. They started developing eating disorders when our culture developed a standard of beauty that they couldn't obtain by being healthy. When unnatural thinness became the object of health, girls did unnatural things to be thin" (1994, p. 184).

A summary article of 25 experimental research studies provided more empirical data. The article reported that women in the United States had greater body dissatisfaction after they were exposed to media images of thin people than when they saw images of people who were average or plus sized. Women who were particularly vulnerable to body dissatisfaction after exposure to these media images included those who were younger than 19 years and who placed a lot of value on being thin (Groesz et al., 2002).

For men, research has shown that men's magazines often show men in advanced fitness activities and muscularity (Berry & Lauzon, 2003). Studies have shown that North American media are using more male models that are bare chested, muscular, and have a marked V shape than they used in previous years (Law & Labre, 2002; Parks & Read, 1997; Pope et al., 2001). Studies have demonstrated that males are affected by visual signals. For that reason, media play a significant role in shaping the views of men (Barthel, 1992).

One media study, for example, created two 30-minute video segments. One contained appearance-loaded advertisements, and the other contained advertisements not related to appearance. The study revealed that "males exposed to appearance-related advertisements had significantly higher reports of muscle dissatisfaction. . . . Males who viewed the body image ideal advertisements became significantly more depressed following exposure" (Agliata & Tantleff-Dunn, 2004, p. 16).

A more recent study concluded that "participants who viewed advertisements with male models showed an increase in body dissatisfaction, while those who viewed only products demonstrated no change in body dissatisfaction. The importance of this finding is that the body dissatisfaction experienced through exposure to idealized images of men in the media is only the beginning of possible outcomes such as anabolic steroid use, eating disorders, and muscle dysmorphia" (Baird & Grieve, 2006, p. 115).

Magazines and other media vehicles focus more on muscularity, beauty, and thinness than on fitness or health. The advertising industry is a major culprit (Labre, 2005; Toro et al., 2005). Altered photographs in magazine advertisements enhance both the female and male physique, setting an unrealistic standard for body shapes most people can't attain.

On a positive note, the Dove skin care company launched the Campaign for Real Beauty in September 2004 to change the way women think about beauty. Dove uses real women in several commercials, posters, and magazine ads that challenge women's perceptions of beauty. One hopes this campaign will serve as an effective, positive media tool to get women and men around the world to reframe their definitions of what real beauty is. One market researcher stated that the campaign was successful on two fronts. The first success was that more women sensed that "Finally! Someone understands!" The second success was an increase in sales in Europe and North America for products featured in the advertisements; in the first two months of the campaign, sales were up 600 percent (Barletta, 2007).

## Psychological Influences

Many psychological and interpersonal factors contribute to the development of an eating disorder:

- Distorted body image (discussed previously)
- Depression
- Perfectionism
- Low self-esteem

Hinrichsen et al., 2004; Lunner et al., 2000; Robert-McComb, 2001.

Thirty to fifty percent of people with anorexia also have mood disorders such as depression or anxiety (Mullen, 1999). Research has demonstrated that eating disorders may cause depression. For example, Stice and colleagues (2000) found that symptoms of eating disorders and dietary restraint predicted subsequent depression in initially nondepressed individuals.

Because eating disorders and mood disorders both involve chemical imbalances in the brain, the mind is altered and becomes flooded with negative thoughts. Antidepressants can correct the imbalance and restore normal mood and thought control. When the obsessive thoughts stop, the person can relax about weight and begin to resume normal eating patterns. People with these disorders need to receive counseling because the disorders come with significant emotional issues (Mullen, 1999).

According to Dr. Mullen, emotions are one of the three fundamental, God-given building blocks of human personality. The others are intelligence and will. People must be healthy in all three areas to function at the level of wholeness God intends. If a person's emotions are damaged, he or she will not function at the level that intelligence or will would permit. Success in life depends on emotional health, whether or not people acknowledge that (Mullen, 1999).

Perfectionism may also contribute to the development of an eating disorder (Hasse & Clopton, 2001). Perfectionists develop exceptionally high and unrealistic standards for themselves on achievement tasks. You can see some characteristics of a perfectionist in Heather's story at the beginning of the chapter. Her world collapsed when she failed in her first year at the university. She didn't reveal, though, that even though she was struggling with depression at the time, she failed only two courses. Even in her depression her standards were so high for herself that she couldn't fathom why she could let herself fail. Failing, to Heather, meant her world was falling apart and she was worthless.

Related to perfectionism is the persistence of obsessive thoughts and tendencies. People with eating disorders commonly spend a substantial amount of their time obsessing about food: what they will eat, how much they weigh, and how they can change their shape (Gleaves et al., 2000; Polivy & Herman, 2002). A research study in the United States demonstrated that approximately 74 percent of individuals with eating disorders spent more than three hours a day thinking obsessively about food and weight. As many as 42 percent spent more than eight hours a day thinking about food, weight, and shape. Sixty-two percent of those with eating disorders in the study had fewer than three hours a day entirely free of such obsessive thoughts, and 37 percent had no free hours at all (Sunday et al., 1995).

These statistics are alarming and demonstrate that eating disorders are all-consuming. Average people quantifying where they spend their energy would say they spend less than 5 percent of their time thinking about food and weight. An individual with an eating disorder, on the other hand, thinks about food and weight all the time. It isn't surprising, then, that people with eating disorders struggle with working productively, going to classes, and maintaining friendships.

Self-esteem also plays a role in the development of eating disorders and body dissatisfaction. Some people argue that body dissatisfaction causes low self-esteem, but the converse may also be true: Low self-esteem may cause body dissatisfaction (Furnham et al., 2002). Most women and men have body types that don't match their ideal. Striving for that unreasonable standard can contribute to lower self-esteem and depression in both women and men (Pope et al., 2000). People's wholeness is compromised as they use unwholesome ways to achieve the ideal they aspire to. Healthy self-esteem should come from a personal relationship with God, not because a person compares favorably with a digitally enhanced image.

## Biological Influences

Eating disorders are typically characterized by and labeled with their most obvious features—a preoccupation with food and unhealthy behaviors surrounding appetite. Researchers have been curious about the biological basis of medical conditions where appetite is a central focus, as is the case with eating disorders (Polivy & Herman, 2002).

According to a review by Polivy and Herman (2002), studies of twins and families have provided evidence that eating disorders are transmitted genetically. Therefore, if a family member has had an eating disorder, you have a high risk of developing one, too. Family studies have also indicated that eating disorders appear to have a genetic line. In other words, certain families are more predisposed to eating disorders than other families (Spelt & Meyer, 1995).

## Family Influences

Scientists have also found that, in addition to passing on genetic traits, families pass along concerns, fears, and preoccupations about weight (Klump et al., 2000). Parents who have eating disorders are more likely to have children with these deadly disorders. This happens through genetic transmission, as you just read, but environmental factors also come into play. For example, family members often praise individuals with eating disorders for their slenderness, and they envy the self-control and discipline required to achieve the thin physique (Branch & Eurman, 1980). Unfortunately, family members may be blind to their relative's eating disorder, and they may continue to praise and reinforce the weight loss even when the person becomes severely ill (Polivy & Herman, 2002).

Family dynamics have also been implicated in a person's developing and maintaining an eating disorder (Haworth-Hoeppner, 2000; Minuchin et al., 1978). An individual with an eating disorder will often describe family members as intrusive, hostile, disrespectful of emotional needs (Minuchin et al., 1978), and overprotective (Shoebridge & Gowers, 2000). People with eating disorders may come from a critical and intimidating family environment (Haworth-Hoeppner, 2000) or one in which parents impose their beliefs and standards on their children (Thøgersen-Ntoumani et al., 2010).

Mothers may also play a significant role in young girls' developing eating disorders. Many mothers who think their daughters should lose more weight say so, and they describe their daughters to others as being less attractive than the ideal (Hill & Franklin, 1998; Pike & Rodin, 1991). Research has found that direct comments from a mother about the weight and shape of her daughter influence the daughter more powerfully than when a mother only models weight and shape concerns through dieting or extreme exercising (Ogden & Steward, 2000; Smolak et al., 1999). That's not to say modeling has an insignificant role. In a study of young elementary school children, Smolak et al. (1999) found that the behaviors and attitudes a mother models to her young child do affect the child's weight- and shape-related attitudes and behaviors. Other research found that mothers' critical comments prospectively predicted eating disorder outcomes for their daughters (Vanfurth et al., 1996).

Mothers who have an eating disorder or an extreme preoccupation with food and weight negatively influence their children's attitudes and behaviors. Polivy and Herman (2002) showed that mothers with eating disorders tend to feed their children irregularly, use food for rewards and punish-

The family plays an important role in what people think and feel about their bodies.

ments, and express concern about their daughters' weight when the girls are as young as two years. Research by Agras et al. (1999) demonstrated that by the time these children reach kindergarten, they exhibit more negative moods and are at serious risk for developing eating disorders. In sum, the family environment—especially the mother's role—has a significant influence on how children think and feel about their bodies and physical appearance. This is especially true for daughters.

## Differences Between Men and Women

Men and women express body image concerns and eating disorders differently (Anderson, 1992, 1998; Cumella, 2003). Typically, women want only to get thinner and leaner. For example, one study indicated that 69 percent of girls wanted to lose weight (Furnham et al., 2002). Men, on the other hand, generally want to get leaner or more muscular (Anderson & Di Domenico, 1992; Furnham et al., 2002).

When using healthy standards of weight, women tend to view themselves as too heavy and men tend to view themselves as too light (Cash et al., 1986; Furnham & Calnan, 1998). One study discovered that men thought they would be more attractive to women if they had about 30 pounds (14 kg) more muscle but that women actually preferred more average-looking men (Pope et al., 2000). Women, on the other hand, thought their most attractive weight was lower than their current weight, but men preferred women heavier than the women's preference (Fallon & Rozin, 1985; Grieve et al., 2005). Another study demonstrated that almost 47 percent of males wanted to become bigger, compared to fewer than 4.5 percent of females (Silberstein et al., 1988).

Although men and women differ in what they want their bodies to look like, the motivation behind why they want to change their bodies is often the same. Both sexes struggle with how they view their bodies and how they accept who they are. Although the way they go about trying to alter their bodies may look different, the goal for men and women is the same: to try to control feelings by controlling the body and physical appearance; to gain approval and acceptance from others; and to cope with or manage stress, anxiety, and heavy emotions.

In summary, eating disorders are caused by many factors, and not all of them will be present in each person. No two people are exactly the same, so an eating disorder may show up in different ways. The information in this section provides a comprehensive overview of some of the more common causes of eating disorders. Eating disorders are serious issues with serious physical complications. Table 3.1 provides a short overview of physical signs and complications associated with each disorder talked about in this chapter.

## What God Wants for People

Genesis 1:26 confirms that God created each person in his image, with an identity that is both physical and spiritual. Ephesians 1:5 says that Christians have the special privilege of being adopted into God's family. God wants people to know the truth—him. John 8:32 states, "Then you will know the truth, and the truth will set you free." God's truth is that he loves all people unconditionally. He wants people to know that, even when they feel unlovable and worthless, they are worth so much in his eyes. This unconditional love, above everything, builds the foundation for the Christian's life. People who can't accept this love can't accept Christ, others, or themselves, because God is love (1 John 3:16).

Christ wants people to focus on him and to keep their eyes fixed on him. How can you be focused on him when you are anxious and concerned and obsessed with your body and with food? Society says that you need to be thin and beautiful to feel self-worth, but Christ has a different message. He is the source of self-worth; you don't need to find it in superficial, impermanent things. Your relationship with him, not the way you look or how much you weigh, should mean the most to you as a Christian. It's hard to live outside of society's standards! Christ never gave in to that pressure, though. He lived in the world, but he was not "of the world." Your aim is to live like Christ. The ultimate message he sends is that he loves you *unconditionally,* and he wants you to love yourself that way, too.

First Corinthians 3:16 states, "Don't you know that you yourselves are God's temple and that God's Spirit lives in you?" Your body houses his Spirit, so you need to be responsible and take care of your body, to make sure it is healthy enough to do his work. You are, in fact, "created in the image of God" (Genesis 1:27). Your image of a healthy body should be Christ's, not the world's. This doesn't mean that you should make your body an idol. Rather, with the attitude of Christ, replace the lies that the world tells (see Philippians 2:5–11).

The opening chapter of this book and of the Bible establish that God's physical creation was very good. People get deceived, though, into thinking they are weak and ugly—not good. They look for a quick fix and end up like Eve in the Bible. She said to God after

## Table 3.1    Physical Complications of Eating Disorders

| Anorexia nervosa | • Abnormally slow heart rate and low blood pressure, which means that the heart muscle is changing. The risk for heart failure rises as the heart rate and blood pressure levels lower.<br>• Reduction of bone density (osteoporosis), which results in dry, brittle bones<br>• Muscle loss and weakness<br>• Severe dehydration, which can result in kidney failure<br>• Fainting, fatigue, and overall weakness<br>• Dry hair and skin; hair loss<br>• Growth of lanugo (downy hair) all over the body in an effort to keep the body warm |
|---|---|
| Bulimia nervosa | • Electrolyte imbalances that can lead to irregular heartbeats and possibly heart failure and death. Electrolyte imbalance is caused by dehydration and loss of potassium and sodium from the body and is a result of purging behaviors.<br>• Potential for gastric rupture during periods of bingeing<br>• Inflammation and possible rupture of the esophagus from frequent vomiting<br>• Tooth decay and staining from stomach acids released during vomiting<br>• Chronic, irregular bowel movements and constipation as a result of laxative abuse; peptic ulcers and pancreatitis |
| Binge eating disorder | • High blood pressure<br>• High cholesterol levels<br>• Heart disease as a result of elevated triglyceride levels<br>• Secondary diabetes<br>• Gallbladder disease |
| Muscle dysmorphia | • Side effects and complications from steroid use<br>• Side effects from the overuse of protein supplements (e.g., kidney failure)<br>• High risk for injury from long, exhaustive workouts |
| Female athlete triad/ anorexia athletica | • Abnormally slow heart rate<br>• Bone fractures<br>• Amenorrhea (absence of menses)<br>• Osteoporosis and decreased bone density (which cannot be regained)<br>• Fatigue that can inhibit athletic performance and increase risk of injury<br>• Electrolyte abnormalities<br>• Depression |

Adapted from ANRED. Available: www.anred.com/causes.html.

she took the forbidden fruit, "The serpent deceived me, and I ate" (Genesis 3:13). Paul warned people against thinking they're stronger or less gullible than Eve was: "I am afraid that just as Eve was deceived by the serpent's cunning, your minds may somehow be led astray from your sincere and pure devotion to Christ. For if someone comes to you and preaches a Jesus other than the Jesus we preached, or if you receive a different spirit from the one you received, or a different gospel from the one you accepted, you put up with it easily enough" (2 Corinthians 11:3-4). Maybe people put up too easily with media's unrealistic and distorted views of what women and men should look like and become deceived, lose self-esteem, and try to be someone they're not.

Heed Paul's warning, then, in Romans 16:17-19: "I urge you, friends, to watch out for those who cause divisions and put obstacles in your way that are contrary to the teaching you have learned. Keep away from them. For such people are not serving our Lord Christ, but their own appetites. By smooth talk and flattery they deceive the minds of naive people. Everyone has heard about your obedience, so I am full of joy over you; but I want you to be wise about what is good, and innocent about what is evil." Paul says in his letter to Titus that imprisonment to evil should be a thing of the past. He writes: "At one time we too were foolish, disobedient, deceived and enslaved by all kinds of passions and pleasures. We lived in malice and envy, being hated and hating one another. . . . And I want you to stress these things, so that those who have trusted in God may be careful to devote yourself to doing what is good. These things are excellent and profitable for everyone" (Titus 3:3, 8). Take a hard look at how you allow media to shape and imprison your thoughts, emotions, actions, and lifestyle. Pray about how you can glorify God through your body and take pleasure in his good gifts to you.

# Recovery From an Eating Disorder

Because many factors contribute to the development of an eating disorder, and because every person's situation is different, the "best" treatment must be tailored to each individual. The process begins with evaluation by a physician or trained counselor, as eating disorders often coexist with other disorders (Hudson et al., 2007) and require comprehensive interventions targeting "sociolcultural cognitions and behaviours, combined with healthy living education" (Urquhart & Mihalynuk, 2011).

Recovery is a difficult process that can take several months—even years. It takes more than abandoning starving. At minimum it involves

- maintaining a normal or near normal weight;
- in women, resuming normal menstrual periods (not triggered by medication);
- eating a well-balanced diet that includes a variety of foods; and
- reducing irrational fears about different types of food.

Recovering individuals need to work on relationships, too. They need to seek out age-appropriate relationships with family members and others. During recovery, they will begin to realize and become aware of unreasonable cultural demands for thinness; engage in fun activities that have nothing to do with food, weight, or appearance; gain a sense of self; and set realistic goals and plans for achieving them.

Information from ANRED: Anorexia Nervosa and Related Eating Disorders, Inc. www.anred.com.

Men struggling with body image concerns or eating disorders need to put in place a multidisciplined assessment and treatment plan like females do. Getting weight back to normal is a priority. Furthermore, destructive behaviors, such as bingeing, purging, using steroids, and being preoccupied with supplements, need to be reduced (Anderson & Holman, 1997). Developing muscle through a balanced weight-training program is also important. Emotionally, these men may be dealing with substance abuse, alcoholism, or shoplifting, which are some means of feeling good when physical needs are not being met. These men may also need help expressing emotions and exploring their relationships with their fathers (Cumella, 2003; Stein, 2005).

Recovery is a long, hard process. In the book *Eating Disorders in Women and Children*, Lewis refers to the recovery process as a spiritual quest: "It involves a rediscovery of one's connection with their inner-self, others, and nature. . . . Healthy spirituality is the process of learning how to live daily with the tension between our desire for perfection and the reality of our imperfection" (Lewis, 2001, p. 318).

These are some options for treating eating disorders (please refer to table 3.2 for specific treatment goals for the different eating disorders):

## Table 3.2   Specific Treatment Goals for Different Eating Disorders

| | |
|---|---|
| Anorexia nervosa | • Focus on restoring nutritional status, normalizing eating and exercise habits, and altering attitudes toward food and body size.<br>• Concentrate on feelings about body image, weight gain, self-esteem, and identity development. |
| Bulimia nervosa | • Focus on interrupting the binge–purge cycle, normalizing eating patterns, and altering attitudes toward food and body size.<br>• Understand emotional problems and conflicts that may have originally contributed to the bulimic behavior. |
| Binge eating disorder | • Focus on normalizing eating patterns and interrupting the bingeing cycle.<br>• Change attitudes toward food and body size.<br>• Understand emotional problems and conflicts that may have contributed to the bingeing behavior. |
| Muscle dysmorphia | • Normalize eating patterns and exercise habits.<br>• Become aware of cultural demands for unrealistic body ideals.<br>• Engage in activities that have nothing to do with food, weight, or exercise. |
| Female athlete triad/ anorexia athletica | • Normalize eating patterns and exercise habits.<br>• Alter attitudes toward food and body size.<br>• Concentrate on feelings about body image, weight gain, self-esteem, and identity development. |

Information from ANRED. Available at www.anred.com/tx.html.

- Hospitalization to prevent death, suicide, and medical crisis
- **Weight restoration** to improve health, mood, and cognitive functioning
- Medication to relieve depression and anxiety
- Dental work to repair damage and to minimize future problems
- Individual counseling to develop healthy ways of taking control
- Family counseling to change old patterns and create healthier new ones
- Group counseling to learn how to manage relationships effectively
- Nutrition counseling to expose food myths and design healthy meals
- Participation in support groups to break down isolation and alienation

Adapted, by permission, from ANRED, 1999, *Treatment and recovery*. Available: www.anred.com/tx.html.

## Next Steps

Eating disorders and weight preoccupation are serious and sometimes even life threatening. If you know someone struggling with an eating disorder, please review the Guide for Family and Friends of a Person With Food and Weight Problems in appendix A. You'll find two short questionnaires in appendix B. Complete them to understand more about your perceptions of food and weight and about some of your own behaviors. The questionnaires are not intended to be used for diagnostic purposes but for educational purposes only. If your answers to the questionnaires tell you to seek the advice of a counselor, pastor, teacher, or physician, please do so. Please remember to be true to yourself. If one or more points in this chapter fit you and your lifestyle, don't hesitate to seek out help.

Remember, facing these issues isn't easy. This quote from George Grinnell in his book *A Death on the Barrens* is encouraging: "Enlightenment is not obtained through knowledge, but through a change in perspective" (1996, p. 64).

## Key Terms

amenorrhea

anorexia athletica

anorexia nervosa

binge eating disorder

bingeing

body dysmorphic disorder (BDD)

body image

bulimia nervosa

dieting

disordered eating

eating disorders not otherwise specified (EDNOS)

female athlete triad syndrome

muscle dysmorphia

osteoporosis

purging

weight preoccupation

weight restoration

## Review Questions

1. Identify five facts about dieting and describe why dieting is so harmful.

2. Identify and describe the four dimensions of body image.

3. Identify four ways to change a negative body image.

4. Identify and describe the three classified eating disorders and the five nonclassified disorders.

5. Describe three factors that can influence or cause eating disorders to develop.

6. How do men and women differ in experiencing body image concerns and eating disorders?

7. What are five of the identified risk factors (medical complications) associated with eating disorders in general?

8. What does God want people to believe about beauty and the body?

9. What are three treatment or recovery goals for a person struggling with each of the following: anorexia, bulimia, binge eating disorder, and muscle dysmorphia?

10. What can you do to help a friend or family member who is struggling with an eating disorder?

# Application Activities

1. **Reflections on the body**

   Look up the verses in the following list and answer the questions about how they relate to body image.

   a. What does Western society say the body needs to look like?

   b. Read 1 Corinthians 6:19–20. To whom does your body belong and why?

   c. Look up Genesis 1:27. According to this verse, what should you see every time you look in the mirror?

   d. See Psalm 139:13–14. What does the psalmist acknowledge in these verses regarding the formation and nature of the body?

   e. If you have frequent negative thoughts about your body size and shape, write them down.

   Questions adapted from Homme's (1999) *Seeing Yourself in God's Image.*

2. **Gift assessment**

   Too often, people focus on negative perceptions of themselves. Complete a gift assessment like the one on the following pages to explore your areas of strength and giftedness.

# Spiritual Gift Inventory

I would like your opinion. I'd like to better understand how God has equipped me for service. One part of my discovery process involves getting feedback from a few people who know me reasonably well. Your thoughts about the way I relate to others will be very helpful. Please take a few minutes to complete the following assessment.

Observations about: _____

Provided by: _____

Relationship: _____

As you read the following descriptions, please indicate to what degree each one describes me. Mark each letter with Y, S, N, or ?. When you're finished, try to decide which three are most descriptive. Indicate your top three choices by placing an X next to the appropriate letter.

**Y:** Yes, it fully describes me.

**S:** It somewhat or slightly describes me.

**N:** No, it doesn't describe me.

**?:** I'm not sure.

a. ____ Developing strategies or plans to reach identified goals; organizing people, tasks, and events; helping organizations or groups become more efficient; creating order out of organizational chaos.

b. ____ Pioneering new projects; serving in another country or community; adapting to different cultures and surroundings; being culturally aware and sensitive.

c. ____ Working creatively with wood, cloth, metal, paints, glass, and so on; working with various kinds of tools; making things with practical uses; designing or building things; working with my hands.

d. ____ Communicating with variety and creativity; developing and using particular artistic skills (such as art, drama, music, photography); finding new and fresh ways to communicate ideas to others.

e. ____ Distinguishing between truth and error and good and evil; accurately judging character; seeing through phoniness or deceit; helping others to see what's right and wrong in situations.

f. ____ Strengthening and reassuring troubled people; encouraging or challenging people; motivating others to grow; supporting people who need to take action.

g. ____ Looking for opportunities to build relationships with people who don't believe in Christ; communicating openly and effectively about my faith; talking about spiritual matters with people who don't believe in Christ.

h. ____ Trusting God to answer prayer and encouraging others to do so; having confidence in God's continuing presence and ability to help, even in difficult times; moving forward in spite of opposition.

i. ____ Giving liberally and joyfully to people in financial need or to projects requiring support; managing money well to free more of it for giving.

j. ____ Working behind the scenes to support the work of others; finding small things that need to be done and doing them without being asked; helping wherever needed, even with routine or mundane tasks.

k. ____ Meeting new people and helping them to feel welcome; entertaining guests; opening my home to others who need a safe, supportive environment; setting people at ease in unfamiliar surroundings.

l. ____ Frequently offering to pray for others; expressing amazing trust in God's ability to provide; showing confidence in the Lord's protection; spending a lot of time praying.

m. ____ Carefully studying and researching subjects I want to understand better; sharing my knowledge and insights with others when asked; sometimes gaining information that is not attainable by natural means.

n.  \_\_\_  Taking responsibility for directing groups; motivating and guiding others to reach important goals; managing people and resources well; influencing others to perform to the best of their abilities.

o.  \_\_\_  Empathizing with hurting people; patiently and compassionately supporting people through painful experiences; helping those generally regarded as undeserving or beyond help.

p.  \_\_\_  Speaking with conviction to bring about change in other people's lives; exposing cultural trends, teachings, or events that are morally wrong or harmful; boldly speaking truth even in places where it may be unpopular.

q.  \_\_\_  Faithfully providing long-term support and nurturing for a group of people; providing guidance for the whole person; patiently but firmly nurturing others in their development as believers.

r.  \_\_\_  Studying, understanding, and communicating biblical truth; developing appropriate teaching material and presenting it effectively; communicating in ways that motivate others to change.

s.  \_\_\_  Seeing simple, practical solutions in the midst of conflict or confusion; giving advice to others who are facing complicated life situations; helping people take practical action to solve real problems.

Thank you for taking the time to complete this assessment. Your opinions are valuable to me in this process, and I deeply appreciate your help.

From P. Walters and J. Byl, 2013, *Christian paths to health and wellness,* 2nd ed. (Champaign, IL: Human Kinetics). Adapted, by permission, from Bruce Bugbee and Don Cousins. *The Network Curriculum Participant Guide,* © 1994, 2005 by The Willow Creek Community Church and Bruce Bugbee and Don Cousins. (2005) The Zondervan Corporation. For additional resources, go to www.brucebugbee.com.

# References

Abramovitz, B.A., & Birch, L.L. (2000). Five-year-old girls' ideas about dieting are predicted by their mothers' dieting. *Journal of the American Dietetic Association, 100*(10), 1157–63.

Ackard, D.M., Neumark-Sztainer, D., Story, M., & Perry, C. (2003). Overeating among adolescents: Prevalence and associations with weight-related characteristics and psychological health. *Pediatrics, 111*(1), 67–74.

Agliata, D., & Tantleff-Dunn, S. (2004). The impact of media exposure on males' body image. *Journal of Social and Clinical Psychology, 1*, 7–22.

Agras, S., Hammer, L., & McNicholas, F. (1999). A prospective study of the influence of eating-disordered mothers on their children. *International Journal of Eating Disorders, 25*, 253–62.

American Psychiatric Association. (2000). *Diagnostic and statistical manual of mental disorders* (5th ed.). Washington, DC: American Psychiatric Association.

American Psychological Association. (2011). *Eating disorders*. www.apa.org/helpcenter/eating.aspx.

Anderson, A. (1992). Eating disorders in males: A special case? In K.D. Bromnell, J. Rodin, & J.H. Wilmore (Eds.), *Eating, body weight, and performance in athletes: Disorders of modern society* (pp. 172–88). Philadelphia: Lea and Febiger.

Anderson, A. (1998). Eating disorders in males: Critical questions. In R. Lemberg & L. Cohn (Eds.), *Eating disorders: A reference sourcebook* (pp. 73–79). Phoenix: Oryx.

Anderson, A., & Di Domenico, L. (1992). Diet vs. shape content of popular male and female magazines: A dose-response relationship to the incidence of eating disorders. *International Journal of Eating Disorders, 11*, 283–87.

Anderson, A.E., & Holman, J.E. (1997). Males with eating disorders: Challenges for treatment and research. *Psychopharmacology Bulletin, 33*(3), 391–97.

ANRED. (1999a). *What causes eating disorders?* www.anred.com/causes.html.

ANRED. (1999b). *Treatment and recovery*. www.anred.com/tx.html.

Baird, A.L., & Grieve, F.G. (2006). Exposure to male models in advertisements leads to a decrease in men's body satisfaction. *North American Journal of Psychology, 8*(1), 115–22.

Barletta, M. (2007). *The Real Story Behind the Success of Dove's Campaign for Real Beauty*. www.marketingprofs.com/7/dove-pro-age-primetime-women-barletta.asp#ixzz29OiPBiVW.

Barnes, P.M., & Schoenborn, C.A. (2003). *Physical activity among adults: United States, 2000: Advance data vitals and health statistics*. Hyattsville, MD: National Center for Health Statistics.

Barthel, D. (1992). Men, media and the gender order when men put on appearances: Advertising and the social construction of masculinity. In S. Craig, *Men, masculinity, and the media: Research on men and masculinities*. Thousand Oaks, CA: Sage.

Bear, M. (2000). *Dieting and weight loss facts and fiction*. National Eating Disorder information pamphlet, Toronto. www.nedic.ca/knowthefacts/dietingfacts.shtml.

Berry, T.R., & Lauzon, L. (2003). A content analysis of fitness magazines. *Avante, 9*(1): 25-33.

Bonci, C.M., Bonci, L.J., Granger, L.R., C.L. Johnson, R.M. Malina, L.W. Milne, et al. (2008). National Athletic Trainers' Association position statement: Preventing, detecting, and managing disordered eating in athletes. *Journal of Athletic Training, 43*(1), 80–108.

Branch, C.H., & Eurman, E.L. (1980). Social attitudes towards patients with anorexia nervosa. *American Journal of Psychiatry, 137*, 631–32.

Braun, D.L., Sunday, S.R., Huang, A., & Kalmi, K.A. (1999). More males seek treatment for eating disorders. *International Journal of Eating Disorders, 25*, 415–24.

Bugbee, B., Cousins, D., & Hybels, B. (1994). *Network: The right people . . . in the right places . . . for the right reasons: Understanding God's design for you in the church*. Grand Rapids, MI: Zondervan Publishing House.

Byl, J. (1999). Spirituality and wellness: Student perspectives. In J. Byl & T. Visker (Eds.), *Physical education, sports, and wellness: Looking to God as we look at ourselves*. Sioux Center, IA: Dordt College Press.

Cash, T.E., & Henry, P.E. (1995). Women's body images: The results of a national survey in the U.S.A. *Sex Roles, 33*, 19–28.

Cash, T.F., Winstead, B.A., & Janda, L.H. (1986). The great American shape-up. *Psychology Today, 30*, 37.

Cook, K.V., & Reiley, K.L. (1991). Eating concerns on two Christian and two nonsectarian college campuses: A measure of sex and campus differences in attitudes towards eating. *Adolescence, 26*, 273–87.

Cumella, E.J. (2003). Examining eating disorders in males. *Behavioral Health Management, 23*(4), 38–41.

Cusumano, D.L., & Thompson, J.K. (2000). Media influence and body image in 8-11-year-old boys and girls: A preliminary report on the multidimensional media influence scale. *International Journal of Eating Disorders, 29*, 37–44.

DeCastro, J.M., & Goldstein, S.J. (1995). Eating attitudes and behaviors of pre- and post-pubertal females: Clues to the etiology of eating disorders. *Physiology and Behaviour, 58*, 15.

EDAP. (2000). *Facts and stats*. www.nationaleatingdisorders.org/information-resources/general-information.php#facts-statistics.

Epling, W.F., & Pierce, W.D. (1988). Activity based anorexia nervosa. *International Journal of Eating Disorders, 7*, 475–85.

Fallon, A.E., & Rozin, P. (1985). Sex differences in perceptions of desirable body shape. *Journal of Abnormal Psychology, 94,* 102–5.

Field, A.E., Austin, S.B., Camargo, C.A., Jr., Taylor, C.B., Striegel-Moore, R.H., Loud, K.J., et al. (2005). Exposure to the mass media, body shape concerns, and use of supplements to improve weight and shape among male and female adolescents. *Pediatrics, 116,* e214–20.

Field, A.E., Camargo, C.A., Jr., Taylor, C.B., Berkey, C.S., Roberts, S.B., & Colditz, G.A. (2001). Peer, parent, and media influences on the development of weight concerns and frequent dieting among preadolescent and adolescent girls and boys. *Pediatrics, 107,* 54–60.

Fulkerson, J.A., Sherwood, N.E., Perry, C.L., Neumark-Sztainer, D., Story, M. (2004). Depressive symptoms and adolescent eating and health behaviors: A multifaceted view in a population-based sample. *Preventative Medicine, 38,* 865–75.

Furnham, A., Badmin, N., & Sneade, I. (2002). Body image dissatisfaction: Gender differences in eating attitudes, self-esteem, and reasons for exercise. *Journal of Psychology, 136*(6), 581–96.

Furnham, A., & Calnan, A. (1998). Eating disturbances, self-esteem, reasons for exercising and body weight dissatisfactions in adolescent males. *European Eating Disorders Review, 6,* 58–72.

Garfinkel, P.E., Garner, D.M., & Goldbloom, D.S. (1987). Eating disorders: Implications for the 1990s. *Canadian Journal of Psychiatry, 32,* 624–31.

Garner, D.M. (1997). The 1997 body image survey results. *Psychology Today, 30,* 30–41.

Gleaves, D.H., Lowe, M.R., Snow, A.C., Green, B.A., & Murphy-Eberenz, K.P. (2000). Continuity and discontinuity models of bulimia nervosa: A taxometric investigation. *Journal of Abnormal Psychology, 109,* 56–68.

Grieve, F.G., Newton, C.C., Kelley, L., Miller, R.C., & Kerr, N. (2005). The preferred male body shapes of college men and women. *Individual Differences Research, 3*(3), 188–92.

Grinnell, G. (1996). *A death on the barrens.* Toronto: Northern Books.

Groesz, L.M., Levine, M.P., & Murnen, S.K. (2002). The effect of experimental presentation of thin media images on body satisfaction: A meta-analytic review. *International Journal of Eating Disorders, 31,* 1–16.

Harrison, K. (1997). Does interpersonal attraction to thin media personalities promote eating disorders? *Journal of Broadcasting and Electronic Media, 41,* 478–500.

Harrison, K. (2000a). Television viewing, fat stereotyping, body shape standards, and eating disorder symptomatology in grade school children. *Communication Research, 27,* 617–40.

Harrison, K. (2000b). The body electric: Thin ideal media and eating disorders in adolescents. *Journal of Communication, 50,* 119–43.

Hasse, H.L., & Clopton, J.R. (2001). Psychology of an eating disorder. In J.J. Robert-McComb (Ed.), *Eating disorders in women and children: Prevention, stress management and treatment.* Boca Raton: CRC Press.

Hausenblas, H.A., & Fallon, E.A. (2006). Exercise and body image: A meta-analysis. *Psychology and Health, 21,* 33–47.

Haworth-Hoeppner, S. (2000). The critical shapes of body image: The role of culture and family in the production of eating disorders. *Journal of Marriage and Family, 62,* 212–27.

Henriksson, B.G., Schnell, C., Hirschberg, A.L. (2000). Women endurance runners with menstrual dysfunction have prolonged interruption of training due to injury. *Gynecol Obstet Invest, 49,* 41–46.

Hill, A.J., & Franklin, J.A. (1998). Mothers, daughters and dieting: Investigating the transmission of weight control. *British Journal of Clinical Psychology, 37,* 3–13.

Hinrichsen, H., Waller, G., & van Gerko, K. (2004). Social anxiety and agoraphobia in the eating disorders: Associations with eating attitudes and behaviors. *Eating Behaviors, 5,* 285–91.

Hobart, J.A., & Smucker, D.R., (2000). The female athlete triad. *American Family Physician, 61*(11), 3357–70.

Hoek, H.W., & van Hoeken, D. (2003). Review of the prevalence and incidence of eating disorders. *International Journal of Eating Disorders, 34,* 383–96.

Homan, K.J., & Boyatzis, C.J. (2010). The protective role of attachment to God against eating disorder risk factors: Concurrent and prospective evidence. *Eating Disorders, 18*(3), 239–58.

Homme, M. (1999). *Seeing yourself in God's image: Overcoming anorexia and bulimia.* Chattanooga: Turning Point.

Hudson, J.I., Hiripi, E., Pope, H.G., Kessler, R.C. (2007). The prevalence and correlates of eating disorders in the National Comorbidity Survey replication. *Biological Psychiatry, 61,* 348–58.

Jones, D.C., Vigfusdottir, T.H., & Lee, Y. (2004). Body image and the appearance culture among adolescent girls and boys: An examination of friend conversations, peer criticism, appearance magazines and the internalization of appearance ideals. *Journal of Adolescent Research, 19,* 323–39.

Kanayama, G., Barry, S., Hudson, J.I., & Pope, H.G., Jr. (2006). Body image and attitudes towards male roles in anabolic-androgenic steroid users. *American Journal of Psychiatry, 163*(4), 697–703.

Klump, K., McGue, M., & Iacono, W.G. (2000). Age differences in genetic and environmental influences on eating attitudes and behaviors in preadolescent and adolescent female twins. *Journal of Abnormal Psychology, 109,* 239–51.

Koyuncu, M., Tok, S.A., Canpolat, M., & Catikkas, F. (2010). Body image satisfaction and dissatisfaction, social physique

adolescent eating disorders. *International Journal of Eating Disorders, 20*, 19–31.

Weltzin, T.E.,Weisensel, N., Franczyk, D., Burnett, K., Klitz, C., &Bean, P. (2005). Eating disorders in men: Update. *Journal of Men's Health & Gender, 2*(2), 186–93.

Wiseman, C.V., Gray, J.J., Mosimann, J.E., & Ahrens, A.H. (1992). Cultural expectations of thinness in women: An update. *International Journal of Eating Disorders, 11*(1), 85–89.

## Suggested Readings

For books written by world leaders in the study of eating disorders, look up the following:

Homme, M. (1999). *Seeing yourself in God's image: Overcoming anorexia and bulimia*. Chattanooga: Turning Point.

McGee, R. (2003). *The search for significance* (Rev. ed.). Nashville: Thomas Nelson.

Mullen, G. (1999). *Why do I feel so down when my faith should lift me up?* Kent, England: Sovereign Work.

Pipher, M. (2005). *Reviving Ophelia: Saving the selves of adolescent girls*. New York: Riverhead.

Pope, H.G., Phillips, K.A., & Olivardia, R. (2002). *The Adonis complex*. New York: Touchstone.

Goodheart, K., Clopton, J.R., Robert-McComb, J.J. (Eds.). (2011). *Eating disorders in women and children: Prevention, stress management, and treatment* (2nd ed.). Boca Raton, FL: CRC Press.

Wolfe, N. (2002). *The beauty myth*. New York: HarperCollins.

Zerbe, K. (1995). *The body betrayed*. Carlsbad, CA: Gurze Books.

## Suggested Websites

**www.anred.com**

Helpful information and resources from Anorexia Nervosa and Related Eating Disorders, Inc.

**www.dove.us/Social-Mission/campaign-for-real-beauty. aspx**

A website for the Dove Campaign for Real Beauty. An initiative to begin a conversation about self-esteem and beauty, where only 2 percent of the women around the world describe themselves as beautiful.

**www.mirror-mirror.org**

Helpful information about eating disorders, from getting help, dealing with recovery, explaining myths and realities, providing a survivor's wall, and including links and additional information.

**www.ncbi.nlm.nih.gov/pmc/articles/PMC2231403/**

The *Journal of Athletic Training* provides a very instructive and helpful position statement on preventing, detecting, and managing disordered eating in athletes.

**www.nedic.ca**

This website is for the National Eating Disorder Information Centre (NEDIC), a Toronto-based nonprofit organization established in 1985 to provide information and resources about eating disorders and weight preoccupation. NEDIC is the result of the concerted efforts of a group of health care providers.

## Twitter

On Twitter, follow @NEDAstaff.

# Weight Control

John Byl

After reading this chapter, you should be able to do the following:

1. Describe how obesity creeps up on people.
2. Calculate and interpret your body mass index.
3. Explain how to maintain a healthy weight.
4. Learn to set a realistic fat-loss goal through making permanent lifestyle changes.

**Few people** in Canada and the United States live their entire lives without being concerned at some point with increased body weight. People may often pray, "Lord give us this day our daily bread." God often provides abundantly. Do you thankfully treasure this gift with care, or do you allow yourself to get carried away and overindulge? In the midst of global interest in poverty and malnourishment, North Americans need to consider why they eat so much. **Obesity** is **pandemic** in Canada and the United States.

Research by Flegal (2002) and Lillis (2011) and their colleagues indicates that *two-thirds* of Americans are overweight or obese. The Canadian Health Measures Survey from 2007 to 2009 (Statistics Canada, 2011) found that 24.1 percent of adults in Canada were obese. In the last two decades the prevalence of obesity has risen by 10 percent in men and 8 percent in women in Canada. North America has 6 percent of the world's population but 34 percent of biomass (the total weight of organisms in a given area). Asia has 61 percent of the world population but 13 percent of biomass. A ton of human biomass corresponds to approximately 12 adults in North America and 17 adults in Asia. If all countries had the BMI distribution of the United States, the increase in human biomass of 58 million tons (52.6 million metric tons) would be equivalent in mass to an extra 935 million people of average body mass and have energy requirements equivalent to that of 473 million adults (Walpole et al., 2012).

Unfortunately, there is no indication that the rate of obesity is slowing. In the United States, the numbers are more daunting with the prevalence of obesity from 2007 to 2009 at 34.4 percent (Shields et al., 2011). In the future, obesity is expected to reverse the centuries-long trend of longer life expectancy (Olshansky et al., 2005). People's life expectancy in one part of the world is reduced because they have too little food, and people's life expectancy in another part of the world is reduced because they eat too much food.

When I was 20 years old, I weighed a healthy 180 pounds (82 kg). Over the next 30 years, I gained approximately 1 pound (0.45 kg) each year until I weighed 210 pounds (95 kg). A gradual increase in weight is called **creeping obesity**. Part of the increase almost always results from decreasing **metabolism**, a process that begins at close to age 30. At 210 pounds I was too heavy and decided to do something about it. My goal was to bike more and work off my extra weight by increasing time spent doing an activity I love. Things were going well until, a few weeks into my new routine, a drunk driver struck me off my bike. I was confined to a wheelchair for a month, used crutches for another month, and used a cane for a few more weeks. I began to slowly regain my mobility. I had double vision for half a year, so I was unable to do any sports. I was gaining almost a pound every two weeks during my recovery, and within six months I weighed 220 pounds (100 kg). I maintained that new weight for the next year and a half. Because of my injuries I was still unable to do vigorous activities, and I slipped into a depression. The doctor prescribed antidepressant medications. Unfortunately,

## Quick Facts About Obesity

Obesity affects 300 million people worldwide.
Consider statistics about Canada:

- Overweight (BMI of 25 to 29.9—BMI is explained later in this chapter) and obesity affect 50 percent of men and 30 percent of women.
- The prevalence of obesity doubled from 1985 to 1999.
- Obesity levels in adults increased 24 percent from 1995 to 1996 and 2000 to 2001.
- Women aged 20 to 34 decreased obesity levels by 9 percent.
- The cost of dealing with obesity in 1997 was estimated at more than $1.8 billion.
- By 2005 this cost was at $1.27 billion in the province of Alberta alone (Moffatt et al., 2011). By 2007 the cost of obesity in Canada was estimated at $4.3 billion (Witkos et al., 2008).

Compare cost of obesity from the United States: "In the United States alone poor diet and physical inactivity are associated with 400,000 deaths per year, and obesity-related medical expenditures in 2003 approximated $75 billion. Obesity is also an emerging problem in middle- and low-income countries, where the health and fiscal costs are likely to be devastating" (Levine et al., 2005, p. 584). Diseases linked to obesity include heart disease, diabetes, and various forms of cancer.

one of the side effects of my medicine was increased appetite. Within two months I had gained another 20 pounds (9 kg) and weighed 239.5 pounds (109 kg). The scale never did cross 240 pounds (109 kg), but I desperately needed to act.

Also on college campuses, depression and anxiety often lead to eating issues. One study concluded that males who are distressed by the transition from high school to university appear more likely to lose weight, whereas well-adjusted males are more likely to gain weight. For females, weight gain is associated with poorer health and preoccupations with weight and eating (Provencher et al., 2009).

My obesity crept up on me over 30 years and was accelerated by a catastrophic event in my life. I have a good friend who let obesity creep up on her during her university years. Early in her college career, she ate differently and reduced her activity level from when she was in high school. She gained only about a pound (0.45 kg) a month during the academic months. That added up to 8 pounds (4 kg) a year, and approximately 32 pounds (15 kg) over four years, though. The balance of energy input and output does not have to be off by much before, over a long period, a person gains or loses a lot of weight. Daily choices determine, in large part, long-term health and well-being.

In a group of 108 male college students, a study was initiated to investigate the transition from high school to university. Various measurements were taken the summer before first-year university and then at the ends of the first and second semesters of college. What measurement numbers went up?

- Students had a significant weight gain (3.0 kg), with significant increases in BMI, body fat, waist circumference, hip circumference, and waist-to-hip ratio.
- Weekly alcoholic drinks and frequency of binge drinking significantly increased.
- Computer and studying time significantly increased.

What measurement numbers stayed the same?

- Energy and nutrient intake did not change.
- Strength training and flexibility training did not change.

What measurement numbers went down?

- Fast aerobic physical activity (sweating for more than 20 minutes) significantly decreased.
- Television time and hours of nightly sleep significantly decreased.

The study concluded that the negative changes to the body measurements are due to decreased physical activity and increased sedentary activity but appear to be unrelated to dietary intake (Pullman et al., 2009).

When people want to lose weight they are really interested in losing fat, not muscle. Some people may have good BMI scores (and have appropriate weights for their heights) but are actually fatter than someone of the same height who is heavier but has more muscle than fat. It's not always wise to use weight to determine fatness. I looked in the mirror and I knew I was fat. However, the best way to determine body fat is to go through **hydrostatic weighing**. Because fat floats and muscle sinks, people who are weighed in water get a very accurate determination of fat mass and muscle mass. However, this approach requires special equipment and takes considerable time to perform. Two simpler weighing methods correlate positively with hydrostatic weighing. One is **skinfold measurements**, in which a skilled technician

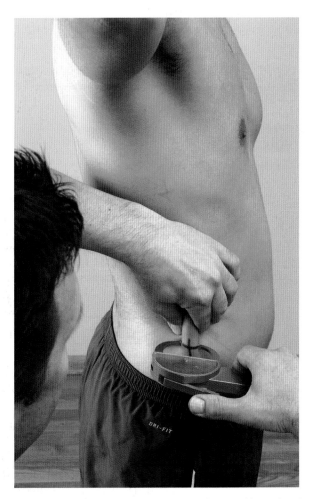

Skinfold measurement devices are to be used by trained technicians.

measures skinfolds at various points on the body. Another simpler method uses various **electrical impedance devices**. The devices measure the resistance of a small electrical charge that is run through the body. Fat has less water in it than muscle does and offers more resistance. By measuring this resistance, a technician can measure body fat. Check with your institution to see if one of these methods of accurately measuring body fat is available to you.

A simpler way to get a fairly close estimate of your body fat is to calculate your body mass index (BMI) and compare yourself to established standards. The Calculating Your Body Mass Index (BMI) sidebar shows how to calculate your BMI. When I calculated a BMI for my height (6 feet 1 inch, or 1.85 m), I was in the obese category. People with muscular bodies will end up with higher BMIs that suggest they have more fat than they actually do. See the websites for the Office of Nutrition Policy and Promotion (2003) and the U.S. Department of Health and Human Services (2012a) for more information on the use of BMI. I think I have more muscle, but I still need to lose weight. I should weigh under 186 pounds, or 85 kilograms, according to the BMI. My initial 40-pound (18 kg) weight loss goal was in the right range. How quickly I got there would depend on my determination and commitment to a healthy weight and lifestyle.

Another way to calculate your health risk from obesity is to see if you are shaped like an apple or a pear (see figure 4.1). People who store extra fat in the abdomen and chest are at a higher risk of developing health problems than those who store extra fat on the hips and thighs (pear shaped). To determine your shape you can calculate your waist-to-hip ratio (WHR). Measure your hip at the widest part and your waist at the smallest part and then divide your waist measurement by your hip measurement. This formula will work the same whether using imperial or metric measurements. For example, if your waist measures 75 centimeters and your hips measure 100 centimeters, divide 75 by 100 and you have a WHR of 0.75. The measurements work for inches as well. For example, if your waist is 30 inches around and your hips are 40 inches wide, you divide 30 by 40 and you have a WHR of 0.75. A WHR more than 0.8 for women or 1.0 for men signals an increased risk of developing weight-related health problems.

## Calculating Your Body Mass Index (BMI)

Weight in pounds ÷ height in inches squared × 703 = BMI or weight in kilograms ÷ height in meters squared = BMI

Here are some examples, using someone 6 feet 1 inch tall (1.85 m).

### Imperial Measurements

235 pounds ÷ (73 in. × 73 in.) × 703 = 31.00

210 pounds ÷ (73 in. × 73 in.) × 703 = 27.71

185 pounds ÷ (73 in. × 73 in.) × 703 = 24.40

### Metric Measurements

107 kilograms ÷ (1.85 × 1.85) = 31.00

95 kilograms ÷ (1.85 × 1.85) = 27.76

84 kilograms ÷ (1.85 × 1.85) = 24.54

### Standards for Men and Women

Underweight is a BMI of less than 18.5.

Normal is a BMI of 18.5 to 24.9.

Overweight is a BMI of 25 to 29.9.

Obese is a BMI above 30.

Information obtained from the U.S. Department of Health and Human Services: Centers for Disease Control and Prevention (2012).

You can find a very helpful BMI calculator at www.bmi-calculator.net. It will automatically calculate your BMI when you type in your weight and height, and it will tell you if you are at an increased health risk.

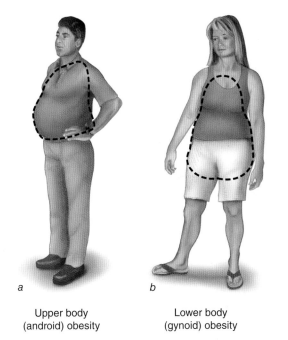

a         b

Upper body
(android) obesity

Lower body
(gynoid) obesity

**Figure 4.1** *(a)* Apple-shaped and *(b)* pear-shaped people.

The implementation of permanent health lifestyle changes is discussed in chapter 2. Seven steps are identified in that chapter for helping you achieve your goals. The remainder of this chapter provides content structured around meeting your weight-control goal. Remember though that reaching and maintaining a desirable weight is a lifelong journey, not a destination. Too often people reduce their caloric intake for a while, reach their target weight, resume their old lifestyle, and soon are back at their unhealthy weight. This yo-yo dieting is not good and tends to lead to weight gain over time—not a permanent and healthy change of balancing proper nutrition and physical activity.

## Step 1: State the Goal

The first step in dealing with being overweight is knowing that you are deeply loved by God, loving yourself enough to make some positive changes in your life, and setting a personal goal to lose fat. My goal was to permanently change my lifestyle by losing about a pound (0.45 kg) a week over 50 weeks. One pound, or approximately a half kilogram, of fat is about 3,500 calories, so I needed to create an imbalance in my **calorie** output and input. I needed to expend 500 calories more than I took in each day for a whole year. To burn 500 calories, I'd need to walk for 90 minutes, eat 7 fewer slices of bread, or do a combination of exercising more and eating less. Perhaps this wasn't a very practi-

cal plan, but I wanted to give it a shot. I knew I had an aggressive goal, and I wanted to complete it in a healthy manner. I know many of the diet plans out there work for some people, but they weren't for me. I mentioned my weight gain to my doctor when I went for a second visit regarding my medications. He said it simply, if somewhat unsympathetically: You gain weight by what you put in your mouth. I was putting too much into my mouth and I needed to reduce it. I also know that eating fewer than 1,000 calories a day isn't helpful for three reasons:

1. The first reason has to do with healthy sustainability.

2. The second reason has to do with viewing God's gifts.

3. The third reason has to do with efficient ways of cutting fat.

## Healthy Sustainability

The first reason to avoid a drastic reduction in calories is that making small lifestyle changes is more sustainable. Eating fewer than 1,000 calories a day would be setting myself up for disaster; the change would be too drastic. I would probably have the willpower to keep up a highly reduced calorie intake for a couple of weeks, but then it would all crash, and I'd probably binge and gain back quickly all the weight I had lost, if not more. Lifestyle changes need to be small, incremental, and sustainable. I wanted not only to lose some weight, but, more important, I wanted also to improve my lifestyle and make permanent changes.

If one wanted to lose weight quickly a person could cut an arm off and probably lose 15 pounds (7 kg). Cutting an arm off is an extreme example about losing weight through means other than a change in lifestyle. It is not about simply losing weight, but doing it in a healthy manner through a positive lifestyle change. But people often look to unhealthy activities like vomiting, diet pills, laxatives, and smoking to cut weight without making permanent lifestyle changes (Al Sabbah et al., 2010), particularly when they are depressed and for some reason even more so for White and Hispanic college or university female students with higher GPAs (Haff, 2009).

What's the best weight-loss strategy—to exercise, to eat fewer calories, or to exercise and eat fewer calories? In one study, males were involved in a 12-week program. The men in the exercising group reduced body weight by 0.3 percent. Those in the group that reduced calories lost 8.4 percent. The group that both reduced calories and exercised lost 11.4 percent. Results for females in a similar program were slightly less (Hagan et al., 1986; Wing et al., 1998). Researchers have determined that combining exercise and calorie reduction is the healthiest and most sustainable route to weight loss, probably because that approach is more achievable than drastically increasing exercise or decreasing calories (Jakicic & Otto, 2006). One of the keys to sustaining weight loss or maintaining a healthy weight appears to be physical activity—and that is totally apart from other health benefits of physical activity.

One of the reasons it is difficult to keep weight off is that a lighter body with less fat requires less energy to maintain. People who have lost weight need to maintain a diet with fewer calories and maintain levels of activity used during weight loss to maintain their body composition at the new, healthier levels (Fogelholm & Kukkonen-Harjula, 2000a; Leibel et al., 1995). People often revert to previous eating and activity levels and consequently return to their previous weight levels, or they regain even more than they'd lost (Fogelholm & Kukkonen-Harjula, 2000b). Permanent lifestyle change comes from making small, positive changes.

## Food Is God's Gift

A second reason to not cut food intake drastically is that to view food as an enemy does not seem a right view of God's good gifts. The Bible states, "For everything God created is good, and nothing is to be rejected if it is received with thanksgiving, because it is consecrated by the word of God and prayer" (1 Timothy 4:4–5). Why should I view as bad something God created as good? God loves everyone (John 3:16). I asked myself, Do I love the me that God loves? Do I love me and others enough to use all of God's blessings (including an abundance of food in North America) for good?

Two diet approaches, the Atkins diet and the Ornish diet, approach weight loss from opposite extremes, but each requires the dieter to avoid or greatly limit some types of food. The **Atkins diet** is high in protein and saturated fat and restricts all carbohydrate. The strength of the Atkins diet is that one feels satiated, or feels full, quite quickly and so consumes fewer calories. However, the Atkins diet contains low levels of antioxidants and may promote osteoporosis and atherosclerosis (Bravata et al., 2003; Reddy et al., 2002). The **Ornish diet**, on the other hand, relies largely on carbohydrate and includes only minimal amounts of animal protein and fat. Growing evidence suggests, though, that a diet containing moderate amounts of beneficial fat and protein (skinless poultry, fish, eggs, and lean cuts of red meat with fat trimmed, cooked slowly with no or very little salt) is a part of a healthy diet (O'Keefe & Cordain, 2004). Not only does eating some meat once a day help a person from a nutritional perspective, but it also helps one feel satiated sooner.

Following an ancient hunter–gatherer diet may improve health, help maintain a healthy weight, and prevent cardiovascular diseases. The hunter–gatherer eating plan includes the following three items (O'Keefe & Cordain, 2004, p. 102):

1. Replacing saturated and trans fat with **monounsaturated fat** and **polyunsaturated fat**

2. Increasing consumption of omega-3 fat from either fish or plant sources such as nuts

3. Eating a diet high in various fruits, vegetables, nuts, and whole grains and avoiding foods with a high **glycemic** load (a large amount of quickly digestible carbohydrate)

The Fundamentals of the Hunter–Gatherer Diet and Lifestyle sidebar provides suggestions for following such an eating plan.

## Cutting Fat

My third reason for not limiting the calories I ate to fewer than 1,000 a day was that, although I was interested in losing weight, I was most interested in losing fat. I had already concluded that the best way to achieve my weight-loss goal would be through a combination of increasing exercise and reducing calories. Muscle tissue burns more calories in daily use than fat does. The more muscular you are, the more calories you burn even when resting. Daily physical exercise is a key to losing and maintaining weight (Wing, 1999).

# Step 2: Assess Your Present Lifestyle

After a month of setting my weight-loss goal I hadn't lost much weight because I hadn't adequately considered the second step of goal setting, assessing my present situation (see chapter 2). I needed to make my goals realistic in the overall context of my personal situation. I asked myself, aside from the medication, what was causing me to choose to eat too much. I was busy with some projects. It was the end of the semester. I was behind in my work. Things at home stressed me. I medicated my stress with trips

## Fundamentals of the Hunter–Gatherer Diet and Lifestyle

- Eat whole, natural, fresh foods; avoid processed and high-glycemic-load foods.
- Consume a diet high in fruits, vegetables, nuts, and berries and low in refined grains and sugars. Nutrient-dense, low-glycemic-load fruits and vegetables such as berries, plums, citrus, apples, cantaloupe, spinach, tomatoes, broccoli, cauliflower, and avocados are best.
- Increase consumption of omega-3 fatty acids from fish, fish oil, and plant sources.
- Avoid trans fat entirely, and limit intake of saturated fat. This means eliminating fried foods, hard margarine, commercial baked goods, and most packaged and processed snack foods. Substitute monounsaturated and polyunsaturated fat for saturated fat.
- Increase consumption of lean protein, such as skinless poultry, fish, and game meats and lean cuts of red meat. Cuts with the words *round* or *loin* in the name usually are lean. Avoid high-fat dairy and fatty, salty, processed meats such as bacon, sausage, and deli meats.
- Incorporate olive oil or non-trans-fatty-acid canola oil into your diet.
- Drink water.
- Participate in daily exercise from various activities (incorporating aerobic and strength training and stretching exercises). Outdoor activities are ideal.

Reprinted from O'Keefe & Cordain, 2004, p. 103.

to the cookie jar and peanut container. Eating food made me feel treated, cared for, even pampered. I was determined to lose weight, but my lifestyle choices didn't help me. I had failed at my first goal, but I was still committed to improving my lifestyle, so I needed to refine my goal. My weight had not gone up (so I was not a complete failure), and I needed to remind myself that weight loss is a journey. I knew that the plan I was making was important because to continue getting fatter would be to increase my risks of cancer, heart disease, type 2 diabetes, high blood pressure, gall bladder disease, psychological

problems, and physical limitations. I had to act with the interest of long-term goals in mind, and physical activity would need to play a role in reaching my long-term goals.

I set two new goals. The first was to accomplish the tasks before me without letting them stress me out, to minimize my involvement in outside projects, and to maintain my weight until I could get on top of things. I figured these three tasks would take about a month to accomplish. My second goal was to lose a pound (0.45 kg) every two weeks for 10 weeks following the period of trying to get my life back in control. I knew

## Increased BMI and Sleep Deprivation

Losing weight is about a lifestyle change. For example, when I am stressed, I sleep less. Research has shown a relationship between sleep and body composition. The research indicates that the fewer hours a person habitually sleeps, from approximately 7.7 hours a night, the higher the BMI score will be. Part of the explanation for increased BMI for short sleepers is that leptin, a hormone that suppresses appetite, is suppressed, and gherlin, a hormone that stimulates appetite, is increased. The result of inadequate sleep is greater appetite. It was hypothesized in this study that "these hormone alterations may contribute to the BMI increase that occurs with sleep curtailment" (Taheri et al., 2004, p. 214). In addition to a greater appetite, those who sleep less also have a preference for fatty and high-calorie foods (Dinges & Chugh, 1997). On the other hand, the more hours a person habitually sleeps, from more than 7.7 hours a night, the higher the BMI score will be. At least two reasons for this increase in BMI scores may exist. Some people may have broken sleep and actually spend more time in bed. But the more likely reason is that when people are in bed they are expending less energy (Taheri et al., 2004). Long sleepers also exercise less (Ayas et al., 2003). For more benefits of sound sleep take a look at chapter 10.

## Fitting in Fitness in Fun Ways

Before I talk about more rigorous activity suggestions, though, it's time to get you into an active mind-set. By that, I mean pursuing a daily lifestyle in which your every choice is the more active alternative. As you go about your day, stand more, walk more, and get outside more! Live with activity in mind. Burning just 100 more calories a day adds up to burning about 3,000 calories a month, or about eight pounds (about four kilograms) a year. Make the important lifestyle choices to seek activity, live by activity, and be nourished by activity. These 11 helpful tips can increase your daily exercise time by 30 to 45 minutes while barely changing your routine:

1. **Frequent flights:** Use stairs at every opportunity at home, school, dorms, or the mall. Welcome the challenge to enhance your fitness by pushing your heart, using your muscles, building your bones, and using extra calories.

2. **Knead some dough?** Try to prepare some of your own foods rather than ordering in. The cost is cheaper so you will save some "dough," the quality will be better, and you will use more calories as you prepare the food.

3. **Walk through writer's blocks.** When you are looking for some creative thoughts for writing, go for a walk. Take along a writing pad and pen or a pocket tape recorder. Let your mind wander, and as your mind comes up with ideas, stop to record them. If you are working on a group project, try walking with your group instead of meeting at the local coffeehouse. You will find the walking stimulating to the brain and therefore academically productive. Your benefits will be in your grades and in your physical health.

4. **Be the fan of the game.** Be a boisterous, clapping, jumping-up-and-down, stamping, laughing cheerleader for your team. If you're at a soccer match, walk up and down the sideline to cheer your team on. The players will appreciate your encouragement, but the physical and emotional release will do even more good for you than for the team you are cheering.

5. **Walk and roll.** When driving somewhere, always bring along some walking shoes, inline skates, or jump ropes. If there is a traffic jam, pull off and release your frustrations with a 10-minute break to explore the area on foot or on skates.

6. **Think on your feet.** Occasionally, read a book while you are walking back and forth across a room.

7. **Walk the talk phone calls.** When you're on a phone call, walk the talk by talking and walking around the room. If you don't have a portable phone, get an extension cord for the phone or headset.

8. **Stretch your computer time.** Too much time at your computer becomes counterproductive. Take some time off and go for a walk, or at least do some occasional stretches.

9. **Add physical activity time during ad time.** When watching television, an advertisement is a signal to get up to do some laundry, make a "walk the talk" phone call, organize some papers, or do some other quick chore. Do not use this time to get a snack or eat. Get off your seat to change the channel instead of using the remote control.

10. **Start a walking bus.** You might not always feel safe walking from home to class or to the store, church, recreation center, or other places. But there is safety in numbers. Try to arrange trips with neighbors and walk together to these places.

11. **Parking lot walks.** Park as far from the building as is safe and reasonable. You'll get more of a walk to the building and back again to your car.

I would have trouble losing weight when I was under stress, but I did not want to get worse.

The semester came to a close, as did other responsibilities. I stopped my involvement in two organizations I was committed to. Guess what? Those organizations continued quite well without me! At the end of a month my weight was still the same, and I was ready to begin the road of cutting weight and cutting fat.

I knew the first bit of weight loss is the easiest, so I thought I'd set a 10-week time period and then reset my goals after that. I was determined to enjoy each morsel of food eaten during three (slightly smaller) balanced meals a day and three nutritious snacks a day, which would include lots of raw vegetables and whole fruits. (Turn to chapter 8, about nutrition, for more information on balanced eating.) To help me enjoy my food I would eat one peanut at a time instead of a handful at a time, and for dinner I would lay my utensil down for a while after every third bite.

I stopped eating on the run and took time to eat each of my meals and snacks, which helped me to reduce stress and enjoy my food. I also tried to avoid eating anything after 8:00 p.m. I committed myself to biking or walking a total of an hour a day to increase my physical activity. Eventually I moved from walking to running three times a week. The exercise benefits me by increasing my muscle mass, improving my cardiovascular system, using up calories, improving my meditative time with God, and reducing my stress. Increasing your physical activity level is essential to losing weight and maintaining weight loss.

Walking is an inexpensive, safe, and technically easy activity for increasing one's activity level. Research by Fogelholm and Kukkonen-Harjula (2000a) found that 25 to 30 minutes of daily walking would improve health, while 35 to 45 minutes of walking each day should lead to further health improvements and also reduce body weight. According to the *2008 Physical Activity Guidelines for Americans*, as well as the Canadian *Physical Activity Guidelines*, 150 minutes of aerobic activity, like brisk walking, is recommended every week (Centers for Disease Control and Prevention, 2011; Public Health Agency of Canada, 2011; U.S. Department of Health and Human Services, 2008). Still other studies note that even though weight might not be significantly reduced by those levels of walking, the activity will improve body composition by decreasing fat and improving muscle mass (Bond et al., 2002; Fox et al., 1996; Irwin et al., 2003). Psychological effects of exercise include appetite regulation and motivation (Mata et al., 2009). As I began to exercise more I increased my self-determination to eat healthier, and I was more motivated to lose weight so I could exercise easier.

In one study, researchers measured the activity levels of people who did not include purposeful exercise into their daily lives. They recruited 10 lean and 10 mildly obese, sedentary volunteers and measured their daily movements two times a second for 10 days. Data analysis showed that the "obese participants were seated for 164 minutes longer per day than were lean participants" (Levine et al., 2005, p. 584). The difference in calories for this activity level was approximately 352 calories a day, the difference between leanness and obesity. This study underlines the importance of more activity throughout the day.

## Step 3: Design a Specific Plan

Designing a specific plan is the third step in setting goals. I found my plan relatively easy to follow when I was at home, even though the people who lived with me had to wait longer for me to finish my meal. I tried to help by eating less, and eventually we came to a nice arrangement. On my calendar I wrote out the days and times and lengths of my runs. I could see certain weeks that might be difficult because of other commitments, and I made some adjustments to those weeks so that I could manage my commitments and still keep up the running. I also signed up for a run each spring and each fall. On those days I was not up to training, I just had to remember the next run. I knew I needed to run or I would not be able to complete the "races"; so I would go out and run. Write out the specific components of your plan in a positive way and make them work. Revisit your plan from time to time to see where you're having difficulties. Revise your plan and you'll succeed.

## Step 4: Predict Obstacles

Predicting obstacles means becoming more self-aware and accepting personal responsibility for actions (Claps et al., 2005). Celebrations, trips, or other unusual food situations were obstacles for me. I needed to be more careful when I ate out and to order salads (without dressing) instead of fries. Eating more slowly and savoring each bite made eating more enjoyable, and I consumed fewer calories. If I had a celebration in the evening I would eat a light snack at mealtime so I didn't arrive at the celebration famished and want to eat everything in sight, putting away too many calories with too little pleasure. It's okay to occasionally use food to celebrate, but food is meant to nourish, not to satisfy unresolved psychological and emotional cravings. Trips, when well planned, gave me an opportunity to see new places in my runs (which often meant running before breakfast so as not to conflict with the activities of the day).

Stress was another major obstacle to achieving my weight-loss goal. It helped knowing that the easy response to stress was for me to open a food container. When the stress came I tried other things, like taking a nap, exercising on my stationary bicycle for 30 minutes, praying, drinking a glass of water, or having a very small snack (and enjoying it). I also tried to let stressors have less effect on me. (Chapter 9 provides information about how to deal with stress in healthy ways.)

For college students the obstacles seem to be such things as personal lack of discipline, social situations, and ready access to unhealthy food. Clearly the obstacles are unique to each person (Greaney et al., 2009).

## Step 5: Plan Intervention Strategies

Making a permanent lifestyle change requires a great deal of time, motivation, and commitment. For that reason, relapse is a formidable risk, especially in the beginning. My fifth step was to design strategies to keep me compliant and to act as motivators toward my goal. I told my wife about my plan and invited her to join in with me, or at least to keep me accountable. The biggest motivator for me was my love for cycling. It felt great to get back on the bike. My extra weight had made climbing hills more difficult, and my heart rate went too high too quickly. Eating less and being more active helps me in my cycling. I'm a numbers person, and watching my heart rate on the heart monitor as I'd bike was motivation enough.

Being able to fit into my clothes again was another motivator. Because I had gained 20 pounds (9 kg) very quickly, I didn't fit into most of my clothes. Fortunately, it was summer and a couple pairs of shorts worked for most occasions. As motivation, I hung one pair of shorts that I used to fit into in my bedroom. I tried them on once a week. At the begin-

ning I could hardly get them on. Six weeks into my plan I could get the shorts on, but I still needed to lose about an inch (2.5 cm) before the clasp would come together. I kept reminding myself I'd get there.

Making life changes isn't easy. Ecclesiastes 10:18 says, "If a man is lazy, the rafters sag; if his hands are idle, the house leaks." I guess the same could be said for caring for the body. The body sags when people are too lazy to care for it. People need to find ways that work for their specific situations as they try to become well. When you eat reasonable portions, more food is available to share with others. Your eating less lets you share more. The prophet Isaiah spoke about this when he wrote, "If you spend yourselves in behalf of the hungry. . . . Your people will rebuild the ancient ruins and will raise up the age-old foundations; you will be called Repairer of Broken Walls, Restorer of Streets with Dwellings" (Isaiah 58:10, 12). Jesus makes this point even more strongly when he argues the people's question: "'Lord, when did we see you hungry or thirsty or a stranger or needing clothes or sick or in prison, and did not help you?' He will reply, 'I tell you the truth, whatever you did not do for one of the least of these, you did not do for me.' Then they will go away to eternal punishment, but the righteous to eternal life" (Matthew 25: 44–46).

For your part, recognize that it's not easy to make permanent lifestyle changes. Avoid quick fixes for decreasing weight, such as smoking, dieting, vomiting, and laxatives. Going for the quick fix is tempting, but it will hurt your health more than help it (Lowry et al., 2000; Middleman et al., 1998; Paxton et al., 2004; Tomeo et al., 1999). Get to know yourself better, and learn what will work for you to make you well.

### Reducing Repetitive-Strain Injury and Building Activity Into Your Lifestyle

- People using computers a lot are encouraged to engage in some stretching, occasionally throughout the day. The Office of Environmental Health and Safety at the University of Virginia offers eight quick and easy stretches you can do at your computer. Hold each stretch for 5 to 10 seconds, involving neck, hand, wrist, forearm, shoulder, upper back, and upper arm stretches. Go to http://ehs.virginia.edu/ehs/ehs.ergo/ergo.stretch.html for more information (Ergonomics, 2012).

- Taking periodic rests and stretching breaks improve productivity. In a study at Cornell University they found that "workers receiving the alerts were 13 percent more accurate on average in their work than coworkers who were not reminded. The more the workers typed, the better their accuracy: the fastest typist made almost 40 percent fewer errors than his counterpart who did not receive the computer alerts" (Lang, 1999).

## Step 6: Assess Compliance With the Plan

The weight scale is the easiest measure for weight loss, so I use it once every couple of weeks to get a sense of my progress. I had used graphs to plot my weight before, but when I got off the projected line I felt I had failed. Now I keep the numbers in my head and keep pushing toward my goal of being more fit for regular living. I focus on enjoying the changes I have made so far. I am not always faithful to myself, but I remind myself that God is faithful and that God's faithfulness is a "shield and rampart" (Psalm 91:4). I need to allow God's Spirit to help me be more faithful. Though I need to keep myself accountable I also need to speak kindly to others and myself, because kind words are "sweet to the soul and healing to the bones" (Proverbs 16:24). I am also reminded about Paul, who wrote, "I have the desire to do what is good, but I cannot carry it out" (Romans 7:18). Like Paul, I am on a journey of loving God through loving myself, by living by his word and Spirit, and making concrete decisions. "For God did not give us a spirit of timidity, but a spirit of power, of love and self-discipline" (2 Timothy 1:7).

Research indicates that the weight scale is still a useful accountability tool for those who are overweight and seeking to lose some weight (Byrne et al., 2003; Klem et al., 1997; McGuire et al., 1999; O'Neil & Brown, 2005; Qi & Dennis, 2000). One study concluded that people who weigh themselves more often than others weigh less and are more successful in losing weight (Jeffrey, 2004).

Weighing can be a problem, though, for those who are not overweight. The scale will encourage them to weigh less and less when they should be weighing more and more. Chapter 3 describes how culture skews a person's self-perception and how the scale can become a weapon of bodily destruction, not an aid toward physical wellness.

Remember that the devil is a deceiver and wants people to live in bondage to the impossible standards of the magazine images. Trying to achieve those standards brings no satisfaction or joy. On the other hand, God created each person uniquely and offers a life of freedom, satisfaction, and joy. Appearance and health are often the two main motivators for weight loss; use either but try to focus on health (Kalarchian et al., 2010). Decide daily which road of wellness to take.

## Step 7: Assess Progress of Your Overall Goal

I know that weight fluctuates significantly from day to day, so I decided to reassess in 10 weeks how close I was to my goal weight. I was successful in my 10-week goal, so I celebrated! Take joy in God's triumphs. Joy is a gift from God (Psalm 4:7) and is medicinal (Proverbs 17:22)—joy will help you in your journey. I then changed my goals to focus on maintaining my lifestyle changes and increasing my activity level. Occasionally I would get on the scale, and my weight decreased by about a pound (0.45 kg) a month. But, more important, I felt like I was getting back in control of my life, had more energy, felt happier, and enjoyed life a lot more. I decided to keep moving forward—to live a life that honors God by offering up my body as a living sacrifice of praise to him (Romans 12:1-2). With thanksgiving, I will enjoy each morsel of food he has provided. I will

 **I Got My Healthy Self Back**

When I was searching through my closet, I found an old pair of jeans I wore just three and a half years ago. Since then I have lost a lot of weight; I had not always been heavy before that, either. How did that weight even come on to my body in the first place? There were lots of factors over time: I gained a few pounds during college and a few more with each pregnancy (three). And then I gained many more as I went through postpartum depression with our youngest child and was on medication that resulted in weight gain. I gained some weight as the result of slight thyroid issues. Finally, I had a miscarriage, which came with significant weight gain in a very short time from medications I needed to restabilize my body.

It's hard to even look at pictures of myself from those years (which is why you see only the "after" picture with the jeans!). I am now 90 pounds lighter, thanks to Weight Watchers, running, cardio, strength training, and healthy eating. I am so thankful to be where I am not only physically but also emotionally and spiritually. I have learned and grown in a good way, and I feel alive and closer to the Lord. Thank you, God!

enjoy each crank of the pedal as I bike up hills more easily than before because I weigh less and am fitter.

## Next Steps

My next steps are to continue to make my goals a reality. In fact, since that time I continued to eat well and exercise more. The smaller adjustments became major lifestyle changes. I took up running, and after completing some shorter races over a couple of years I competed in my first marathon. By then I felt great and had lost 42 pounds (19 kg). That was 24 months ago. I have gained a bit of weight since then so I need to keep at it. However, I have made significant and permanent lifestyle changes that I love.

The next step for you is to get a realistic assessment of your body composition. If you have a healthy body composition and weight, enjoy that and maintain it. If you are too lean and light, eat healthy and allow yourself to look a little fuller. If you are overweight then use the seven steps I used to help bring my weight down. More important than losing weight, though, is significantly improving the quality of your life by having a much healthier body composition and carrying around less excessive and unhealthy fat.

## Key Terms

Atkins diet

calorie

creeping obesity

electrical impedance devices

glycemic

hydrostatic weighing

metabolism

monounsaturated fat

obesity

Ornish diet

pandemic

polyunsaturated fat

skinfold measurements

## Review Questions

1. What is the typical pattern in which most people become overweight?

2. What is the difference between being overweight and having excess fat?

3. What are the seven steps you could take to permanently change your lifestyle to reduce your level of fat (if that's a change you need to make)?

## Application Activities

1. Perform a BMI calculation or other procedure to determine your body fat. What is your level of body fat?

2. Develop a goal for your level of body fat, whether it's to lose fat, gain fat, or maintain your level of fatness:

    a. What is your mission statement? Is this the same as before? If it is different, what did you change and why?

    b. Write down your specific goal in a sentence or two.

    c. In a paragraph or two, assess the behavior and attitudes you are trying to change.

    d. Refine your goal with small, realistic, specific, measurable, and concrete steps.

    e. In a paragraph or two, predict and describe two significant obstacles that prevent you from achieving your goal and describe your plan to overcome those obstacles.

    f. What specific intervention strategies will you have in place to assist you in complying with your plan (the text suggests six strategies in chapter 2)?

    g. How will you evaluate your compliance with your plan?

    h. How will you measure progress in achieving your goal?

# References

Al Sabbah, H., Vereecken, C., Abdeen, Z., Kelly, C., Ojala, K., Németh, Á., et al. (2010). Weight control behaviors among overweight, normal weight and underweight adolescents in Palestine: Findings from the national study of Palestinian school children. *International Journal of Eating Disorders, 43*(4), 326–36.

Ayas, N.T., White, D.P., Al-Delaimy, W.K., Manson, J.E., Stampfer, M.J., Speizer, F.E., et al. (2003). A prospective study of sleep duration and coronary heart disease in women. *Archives of Internal Medicine, 163,* 205–9.

Bond, B.J., Perry, A.C., Parker, L., Robinson, A., & Burnett, K. (2002). Dose-response effect of walking exercise on weight loss: How much is enough? *International Journal on Obesity, 26*(11), 1484–93.

Bravata, D.M., Sanders, L., Huang, J., Krumholz, H.M., Olkin, I., Gardner, C.D., et al. (2003). Efficacy and safety of low-carbohydrate high-protein diets: A systematic review. *Journal of the American Medical Association, 289,* 1837–50.

Byrne S., Cooper, Z., & Fairburn, C. (2003). Weight maintenance and relapse in obesity: A qualitative study. *International Journal of Obesity, 27,* 955–62.

Centers for Disease Control and Prevention. (2011). *How much physical activity do adults need?* www.cdc.gov/physicalactivity/everyone/guidelines/adults.html.

Claps, J.B., Katz, A., & Moore, M. (2005). A comparison of wellness coaching and reality therapy. *International Journal of Reality Therapy, 24*(2), 39–41.

Dinges, D., & Chugh, D.K. (1997). Physiologic correlates of sleep deprivation. In J.M. Kinney & H.N. Tucker (Eds.), *Physiology, stress, and malnutrition: Functional correlates, nutritional intervention* (pp. 1–27). New York: Lippincott-Raven.

Ergonomics--Stretch Breaks. (2012). http://ehs.virginia.edu/ehs/ehs.ergo/ergo.stretch.html.

Flegal, K.M., Carroll, M.D., Ogden, C.L., & Johnson, C.L. (2002). Prevalence and trends in obesity among US adults, 1999–2000. *Journal of the American Medical Association, 288,* 1723–27.

Fogelholm, M., & Kukkonen-Harjula, K. (2000a). Does physical activity prevent weight gain: A systematic review. *Obesity Review, 1*(2), 95–111.

Fogelholm, M., & Kukkonen-Harjula, K. (2000b). Effects of walking training on weight maintenance after a very low-energy diet in premenopausal obese women: A randomized controlled trial. *Archives of Internal Medicine, 160*(14), 2177–84.

Fox, A.A., Thompson, J.L., Butterfield, G.E., Gylfdottir, U., Moynihan, S., & Spiller, G. (1996). Effects of diet and exercise on common cardiovascular disease risk factors in moderately obese older women. *American Journal of Clinical Nutrition, 63*(2), 225–33.

Greaney, M., Less, F., White, A., Dayton, S., Riebe, D., Blissmer, B., et al. (2009). College students' barriers and enablers for healthful weight management: A qualitative study. *Journal of Nutrition Education and Behavior, 41*(4), 281–86.

Haff, D.R. (2009). Racial/ethnic differences in weight perceptions and weight control behaviors among adolescent females. *Youth & Society, 41*(2), 278–301.

Hagan, R.D., Upton, S.J., Wong, L, & Whittam, J. (1986). The effects of aerobic conditioning and/or calorie restriction in overweight men and women. *Medical Science in Sports and Exercise, 18,* 87–94.

Irwin, M.L., Yasui, Y., Ulrich, C.M., Bowen, D., Rudolph, R.E., Schwartz, R.S., et al. (2003). Effect of exercise on total intra-abdominal body fat in postmenopausal women: A randomized controlled trial. *Journal of the American Medical Association, 289*(3), 1323–30.

Jakicic, J.M., & Otto, A.D. (2006). Treatment and prevention of obesity: What is the role of exercise? *Nutrition Reviews, 64*(2), S57–S61.

Jeffrey, R.W. (2004). How can health behavior theory be made more useful for intervention research? *International Journal of Nutrition and Physical Activity.* www.pubmedcentral.nih.gov/articlerender.fcgi?artid=509286.

Kalarchian, M., Levine, M., Klem, M., Burke, L., Soulakova, J., Marsha D. (2010). Impact of addressing reasons for weight loss on behavioral weight-control outcome. *American Journal of Preventive Medicine, 40*(1), 18–24.

Klem, M.L., Wing, R.R., McGuire, M.T., Seagle, H.M., & Hill, J.O. (1997). A descriptive study of individuals successful at long-term maintenance of substantial weight loss. *American Journal of Clinical Nutrition, 66,* 239–46.

Lang, S.S. (1999). When workers heed computer's reminder to take a break, their productivity jumps, Cornell study finds. www.news.cornell.edu/releases/Sept99/computer.breaks.ssl.html.

Leibel, R.L., Rosenbaum, M., & Hirsch, J. (1995). Changes in energy expenditure resulting from altered body weight. *New England Journal of Medicine, 332*(10), 621–28.

Levine, J., Lanningham-Foster, L.M., McCrady, S.K., Krizan, A.C., Olson, L.R., Kane, P.H., et al. (2005, January 28). Interindividual variation in posture allocation: Possible role in human obesity. *Science, 307,* 584–86.

Lillis, J., Hayes, S., Levin, M. (2011). Binge eating and weight control: The role of experiential avoidance. *Behavior Modification, 35*(3), 252–64.

Lowry, R., Galuska, D.A., & Fulton, J.E. (2000). Physical activity, food choice, and weight management practices among US college students. *American Journal of Preventive Medicine, 18,* 18–27.

Mata, J., Silva, M.N., Vieira, P.N., Carraça, E.V., Andrade, A.M., Coutinho, S.R., et al. (2009). Motivational "spillover" during weight control: Increased self-determination and exercise intrinsic motivation predict eating self-regulation. *Health Psychology, 28*(6), 709–16.

McGuire, M.T., Wing, R.R., Klem, M.L., & Hill, J.O. (1999). Behavioral strategies of individuals who have maintained long-term weight losses. *Obesity Research, 7,* 334–41.

Middleman, A.B., Vazquez, I., & Durant, R.H. (1998). Eating patterns, physical activity, and attempts to change weight among adolescents. *Journal of Adolescent Health, 22*(1), 37–42.

Moffatt, E., Shack. L.G., Petz, G.J., Sauvé, J,K., Hayward, K., Colman, R. (2011). The cost of obesity and overweight in 2005: a case study of Alberta, Canada. *Canadian Journal Of Public Health. Revue Canadienne De Santé Publique. 102*(2), 144-8.

Office of Nutrition Policy and Promotion. (2003). Canadian guidelines for body weight classifications in adults. http://preventdisease.com/pdf/weight_book-livres_des_poids_e. pdf.

O'Keefe, J.H., & Cordain, L. (2004). Cardiovascular disease resulting from a diet and lifestyle at odds with our paleolithic genome: How to become a 21st-century hunter-gatherer. *Mayo Clinical Proceedings, 79,* 101–8.

Olshansky, S.J., Passaro, D.J., Hershow, R.C., Layden, J., Carnes, B.A., Brody, J., et al. (2005). A potential decline in life expectancy in the United States in the 21st century. *New England Journal of Medicine, 352,* 1135–37.

O'Neil, P.M., & Brown, J.D. (2005). Weighing the evidence: Benefits of regular weight monitoring for weight control. *Journal of Nutrition Education and Behavior, 37*(6), 319–22.

Paxton, R.J., Valois, R.F., & Drane, J.W. (2004). Correlates of body mass index, weight goals, and weight-management practices among adolescents. *Journal of School Health, 74*(4), 136–43.

Provencher, C., Polivy, V., Wintre, J., Pratt, M.G., Pancer, M.W., Birnie-Lefcovitch, S.M., et al. (2009). Who gains or who loses weight? Psychosocial factors among first-year university students. *Physiology & Behavior, 96*(1), 135–41.

Public Health Agency of Canada. (2011). *Physical activity guidelines.* www.phac-aspc.gc.ca/hp-ps/hl-mvs/pa-ap/03paap-eng.php.

Pullman, A.W., Masters, R.C., Zalot, L.C., Carde, L.E., Saraiva, M.M., Dam, Y.Y., et al. (2009). Effect of the transition from high school to university on anthropometric and lifestyle variables in males. *Applied Physiology, Nutrition & Metabolism. 34*(2), 162–71.

Qi, B.B., & Dennis, K.E. (2000). The adoption of eating behaviors conducive to weight loss. *Eating Behaviors, 1,* 23–31.

Reddy, S.T., Wang, C.Y., Sakhaee, K., Brinkley, L., & Pak, C.Y. (2002). Effects of low-carbohydrate high-protein diets on acid-base balance, stone-forming propensity, and calcium metabolism. *American Journal of Kidney Disease, 40,* 265–74.

Shields, M., Carroll, M.D., & Ogden, C.L. (2011). *Adult obesity prevalence in Canada and the United States.* NCHS data brief, no 56. Hyattsville, MD: National Center for Health Statistics. www.cdc.gov/nchs/data/databriefs/db56.htm.

Statistics Canada. (2011). *Canadian Health Measures Survey: Physical activity of youth and adults.* www.statcan.gc.ca/daily-quotidien/110119/dq110119b-eng.htm.

Taheri, S., Lin, L., Ausstin, D., Young, T., & Mignot, E. (2004). Short sleep duration is associated with reduced leptin, elevated ghrelin, and increased body mass index. *PLoS Medicine, 1*(3), 210–16.

Tomeo, C.A., Field, A.E., & Berkey, C.S. (1999). Weight concerns, weight control behaviors, and smoking initiation. *Pediatrics, 104,* 918–24.

U.S. Department of Health and Human Services. (2008). *2008 physical activity guidelines for Americans.* http://health.gov/paguidelines/pdf/paguide.pdf.

U.S. Department of Health and Human Services. (2012a). *Body mass index.* www.cdc.gov/healthyweight/assessing/bmi/index.html.

U.S. Department of Health and Human Services. (2012b). *Overweight and obesity.* www.cdc.gov/nccdphp/dnpa/obesity.

Walpole, S.C., Prieto-Merino, D., Edwards, P., Cleland, J., Stevens G., & Roberts, I. (2012). The weight of nations: An estimation of adult human biomass. *BMC Public Health, 12,* 439. www.biomedcentral.com/content/pdf/1471-2458-12-439.pdf.

Wing, R.R. (1999). Physical activity in the treatment of the adulthood overweight and obesity: Current evidence and research issues. *Medicine and Science in Sports and Exercise, 31*(suppl.), S547–52.

Wing, R.R., Venditti, E.M., Jakicic, J.M., Polley, B.A., & Lang, W. (1998). Lifestyle intervention in overweight individuals with a family history of diabetes. *Diabetes Care, 21,* 350–59.

Witkos, M., Uttaburanont, M., Lang, C.D., & Arora, R. (2008). Costs of and reasons for obesity. *Journal of the Cardiometabolic Syndrome. 3*(3) 173-6.

## Suggested Readings

For two professional books written by world leaders in the study of obesity, look up the following:

Andersen, R. (2003). *Obesity: Etiology, assessment, treatment, and prevention.* Champaign, IL: Human Kinetics.

Bouchard, C., & Katzmarzyk, P. (2010). *Physical activity and obesity* (2nd ed.). Champaign, IL: Human Kinetics.

# Suggested Websites

www.cdc.gov/obesity/data/trends.html

View a map of the United States showing historical patterns of increasing obesity at this U.S. government website focused on solutions to obesity.

www.cdc.gov/nccdphp/dnpa/obesity

This site from the Centers for Disease Control and Prevention offers information on overweight and obesity.

Three excellent sites offer important information on obesity:

http://origin.phac-aspc.gc.ca/hp-ps/hl-mvs/oic-oac/
assets/pdf/oic-oac-eng.pdf

This 54-page report provides information on the prevalence of obesity in Canada (numbers could be inferred to other areas in North America).

www.naaso.org

For comprehensive information concerning obesity, look at the North American Association for the Study of Obesity website.

www.nature.com/ijo/index.html

The *International Journal of Obesity* provides an international, multidisciplinary forum for the study of obesity. The journal publishes basic, clinical, and applied studies and also features a quarterly pediatric highlight.

Two excellent sites from the U.S. government explain body mass index:

www.cdc.gov/nccdphp/dnpa/bmi/index.htm

This site provides excellent information on BMI, including a BMI calculator. It also includes additional links to such topics as nutrition and physical activity.

www.hc-sc.gc.ca/fn-an/alt_formats/hpfb-dgpsa/pdf/
nutrition/weight_book-livres_des_poids_e.pdf

This helpful article on obesity includes links to such topics as calculating your BMI and guides to healthy eating and physical activity.

www.youtube.com/watch?v = hibyAJOSW8U  or  www.
youtube.com/watch?v = DS6vyTTTfgc&NR = 1

View either one of these videos on YouTube to see how impossible it is even for models to look in their everyday lives like they do on billboards.

www.trendhunter.com/trends/skinny-on-fat

Eight slides based on World Health Organization data on rising world obesity. Poverty and malnutrition remain, but the rich are getting heavier and it is costly.

# Twitter

On Twitter, follow @WeightWatchers, @HarvardHSPH, @DailyHealthTips, @Nutrition_gov, @HealthCanada, and @HHSGov.

# Part III

## Moving Your
# Body

# Cardiorespiratory Assessment and Training

Dianne E. Moroz

After reading this chapter, you should be able to do the following:

1. Understand major benefits of cardiorespiratory fitness.

2. Describe three human energy systems.

3. List and describe the health benefits to an active lifestyle and cardiorespiratory fitness.

4. Define maximal oxygen consumption and explain physiological adaptations that occur with exercise training to increase oxygen consumption.

5. Evaluate your cardiorespiratory fitness using several methods.

6. Design exercise prescriptions for cardiorespiratory endurance.

## Defining Terms

Health and fitness professionals use several terms to describe sustained work that builds the fitness of the heart and lungs. Some of the more common are *aerobic endurance*, *cardiorespiratory capacity*, *cardiorespiratory endurance*, and *cardiovascular fitness*. Most experts use these terms interchangeably to describe the rhythmic movement of larger muscle groups to tax the cardiorespiratory system. For the sake of consistency, the primary term used throughout this chapter is *cardiorespiratory fitness*.

Therefore, I urge you, brothers, in view of God's mercy, to offer your bodies as living sacrifices, holy and pleasing to God—this is your spiritual act of worship. (Romans 12:1)

**I find** this particular scripture to be a powerful reminder of the responsibility to care for God's creation of my fearfully and wonderfully made body. Remember that body, mind, and spirit are a unity, and to respect and care for your body is to honor all that God created in you. Paul explains that caring for your body is a spiritual act of worship in itself—and one that God has shown to be critical to health and functionality.

One very important way to care for your body is through regular activity and exercise. The benefits of exercise that were once speculative are now proven facts. You will see in this chapter that regular exercise improves the way your body functions, improves physical and mental health and performance, and reduces your risk of developing major diseases. This chapter explains cardiorespiratory fitness, illustrates its importance to wellness, and explains how you can plan and implement a fitness regimen. Ideally, exercise will become a part of your lifestyle and ultimately, a part of your identity. It can most definitely be part of your stewardship. "For you have been bought with a price: therefore glorify God in your body" (1 Corinthians 6:20).

But what does it mean to glorify God in your body? I interpret this as keeping your body in optimal health and performance so that you honor God's creation and are a better steward and ambassador of your Christian faith. This is achieved through many avenues discussed throughout this book. Physical activity is undeniably an essential part. Moreover, fitness contributes to all components of wellness. It is men and women's responsibility and pleasure to love, respect, and care for his total creation.

Through most of their existence, people have been physically active as a function of survival. Those who were fittest had a clear advantage in avoiding or surviving predator attacks and in the search and acquisition of food. An overview of anatomy and physiology provides convincing evidence that God designed the body for physical work. More specifically, the human body is designed to sustain continuous low- to moderate-intensity exercise with the capacity for repeated high-intensity bouts of exertion. However, with the onset of the industrial revolution, people have progressively assumed a more sedentary lifestyle. Automation has exacerbated this. In fact, it would seem as though many of the inventions of recent decades have had the sole purpose of reducing physical effort both in the workplace and at home. Electric can openers and mixers, washing machines, automatic staplers and paper hole punchers, escalators, easy-sliding and -closing drawers, and others far too numerous to mention are all modern conveniences that together reduce daily physical effort. Inventions that are critical to the independence of physically challenged people such as automatic car doors and drive-through services present a handicap to the health of the general population. In fact, people have adopted attitudes and behaviors that manifest in a sedentary approach to life. A survey of 2,832 adults aged 20 to 70 years and 1,608 children and adolescents aged 6 to 19 years was conducted in Canada between 2007 and 2009 to determine activity levels of Canadians. All participants wore accelerometers for a full week to determine the amount of time spent in activity and inactivity. On average, adults were sedentary an average of 9.5 hours a day (about 69 percent of their waking hours), while children were sedentary 8.6 hours a day (about 62 percent of their waking hours). For teenagers 15 to 19 years old, the number of sedentary hours in a day was 19! Almost 47 percent of adults exercised less than one day per week. About 53 percent exercised on more than one day per week; however, they accumulated only 30 minutes of moderate to vigorous exercise per week (Statistics Canada, 2011a).

The image of the "couch potato" with the TV controller in hand has become a cliché because it is a truism to which so many can relate. A sedentary lifestyle has been associated with many existing health problems in society, including high stress and stress-related illnesses, osteoporosis, heart disease, diabetes, some cancers, and obesity. Being over-

## Surprised by the Simplicity

I was a full-time physical education student who also worked at a grocery store and had two volunteer jobs. Although other students and professors in my department were running, cycling, playing intramurals, or working out in the weight room, I thought I had no time for that and didn't participate in any activity that wasn't required of my program. A couple of events changed this. The high school I had attended made no mention of caring for the physical body as part of my responsibility to the Lord. Now, I was learning through classes and readings that, indeed, I needed to be a good steward of my body. I was also learning that activity was a large part of wellness. Although I recognized by that point that exercise was valuable, I didn't really think I could do it; I certainly didn't know how to start. That changed one day when, through the suggestion of friends, God led me to a peaceful trail in the woods where I walked for two hours.

weight, a consequence of a sedentary lifestyle and unhealthy eating trends, is associated with a host of diseases, many of which are life threatening. Forty-nine percent of all Canadians are overweight or obese (Statistics Canada, 2011b). North American children are struggling with obesity. In the last 25 years obesity rates tripled in adolescents aged 12 to 17, from 3 percent to 9 percent, with a gruesome cost to health in the form of conditions such as diabetes and heart disease (Statistics Canada, 2011b). In spite of this, there is an improvement in the number of Canadians engaged in at least moderate-intensity activity. The survey found that 52 percent of Canadians aged 12 or older reported that they were at least moderately active in leisure time in 2005, compared to 43 percent in 1996. Furthermore, Canadians increased the amount of time spent in activity aside from leisure. Those spending at least six hours in walking or bicycling for transportation increased from 19 percent in 1996 to 24 percent in 2005 (Statistics Canada, 2007).

As you will read in this chapter, numerous government agencies and health organizations are urging North Americans to become more active. However, you have to keep check of your motives for physical activity. People at times find themselves vulnerable to the pursuit of the lean, sculpted body image valued by modern society and spend hours in the gym driven primarily or purely by vanity. In contrast however, if you care for your physical body because it is God's gift to you, then you show him respect, obedience, and honor. Isn't this what Paul says when he writes to the Romans (Romans 12:1)?

## What Is Cardiorespiratory Exercise?

The term *cardiorespiratory* or *endurance* means that the activity is something that can be done continu-

ously for several minutes or longer like walking, running, and cycling and is not a short-burst activity like sprinting, jumping, or powerlifting. ***Physical activity*** refers to regular and continuous movement. Those who move more by walking, climbing stairs, gardening, and through recreational sports are considered active. There are degrees of activity, and some people move more than others. ***Exercise*** is activity performed with a purpose such as preparing for competition or achieving fitness. *Cardiorespiratory fitness* is the outcome of that exercise when it is performed with the required duration, frequency, and intensity. Achieving cardiorespiratory fitness is discussed later in this chapter.

## Benefiting From Cardiorespiratory Exercise

All forms of physical activity have scientifically proven benefits. None, however, can rival the number of rewards from cardiorespiratory exercise. Numerous health benefits are gained from cardiorespiratory activity and exercise and even more from cardiovascular fitness, a few of which are discussed shortly. I hope that when you are finished reading this section you will be convinced that you are designed to be active because activity, exercise, and fitness benefit your whole being.

### Improving Longevity

People who incorporate exercise into their lifestyles live longer. In turn, sedentary lifestyle and low cardiorespiratory fitness are powerful predictors of premature death (Blair & Lamonte, 2011). A clear, consistent, graded, and inverse relationship exists between cardiorespiratory activity and all-cause mortality. Death rates are lower for those who are active and fit compared to sedentary and unfit. Furthermore, the greater the cardiorespiratory fitness, the lower the risk of mortality (Blair & Lamonte, 2011). This is a consistent and accepted finding in research. Even better is that you don't have to do a lot of exercise to increase longevity. Even a brisk walk 30 to 60 minutes every day is sufficient for expending 1,000 calories per week, which has been shown to decrease mortality rate by a remarkable 20 to 30 percent (Kokkinos et al., 2011). Isaiah once asked God, "Strengthen the feeble hands, steady the knees that give way; say to those with fearful hearts, 'Be strong, do not fear. . . .' Then will the lame leap like a deer, and the mute tongue shout for joy" (Isaiah 35:3-4, 6; see also Romans 15:13; Acts 8:8). Do not be content with weakness but enjoy the strength and joy to move in this world as deer move through the woods.

## Fighting Heart Disease

Heart disease (also known as cardiovascular disease, or CVD) is the process by which substances such as platelets, cholesterol, and fat are absorbed into the walls of the arteries causing a mass (often referred to as plaque) to form that will reduce blood flow or even break off and block a smaller artery downstream. (For a review see Wilmore et al., 2008.) This obstruction blocks the delivery of oxygen to the organ and tissue normally fed by the now blocked artery. This plaque is most dangerous when it occurs in the arteries feeding the heart or the brain where obstruction may result in sudden death from a heart attack or ischemic stroke. You might wonder why a university student should be at all concerned about heart or cardiovascular disease (CVD) since it is generally middle-aged or even senior men and women who have heart attacks and strokes. There are three very important reasons. First, cardiovascular disease (heart and stroke) is the number 2 killer in Canada after cancer (Statistics Canada, 2011c). Second, heart disease can begin in the arteries of someone as young as early teens and progress rapidly or slowly depending largely on lifestyle choices (Arsenault et al., 2012). Third, most risk factors for CVD (factors that cause the development and progression of atherosclerosis) can be modified by lifestyle choices and behaviors under one's control. These risk factors of CVD include hypertension (high blood pressure), dyslipidemia, smoking, physical inactivity, and obesity. If you learn to modify the risk factors in your twenties, you greatly reduce your risk of death from heart disease. Physical activity significantly attenuates each of these risk factors (Ahmed et al., 2012; Wilmore et al., 2008).

## Reducing Hypertension

Hypertension, or high blood pressure, is a risk factor for coronary heart disease. In addition, hypertension independently increases mortality. Hypertension is known as the "silent killer" because it has few, if any, noticeable symptoms and can result in sudden death from a heart attack or stroke. Blood pressure is expressed as a ratio of systolic pressure over diastolic pressure (expressed in mmHg). Normal blood pressure is approximately < 120/ < 80; rising slightly as we age. Systolic pressure is that pressure in the arteries when the heart muscle is contracting, while diastolic is arterial pressure when the heart is relaxing. If either is too high, it indicates there is a clinical condition that could be life threatening. To understand systolic blood pressure, imagine filling a large neck-thick balloon with water gently streaming from a hose. This represents the flow of blood into the heart and through the vessels. Now put a nozzle on that hose at the "jet" setting and try to fill the balloon. You'll most likely damage the balloon. The damage to the artery walls due to the high and turbulent flow is the effect of high systolic blood pressure. While several medications are effective in lowering blood pressure, all have undesirable side effects, such as headaches, dizziness, and fainting. Exercise is a considerable treatment for hypertension. Even one bout of exercise can reduce systolic and diastolic blood pressure by 2 to 9 mmHg for up to 22 hours (Janiszewski & Ross, 2009). In intervention studies that have measured blood pressure before and after an aerobic training program, systolic/diastolic pressure is reduced chronically by about 1 to 12 mmHg (Fagard, 2006; Janiszewski & Ross, 2009). The greatest reduction in blood pressure following exercise is seen in those individuals who need it most, those with hypertension. To put the benefit of exercise in perspective, a reduction in blood pressure of only 2 mmHg relates to a decrease in stroke mortality of 6 percent and a decrease in coronary artery disease of 4 percent (Janiszewski & Ross, 2009).

## Reducing Dyslipidemia

Dyslipidemia is an abnormal amount of **cholesterol** or fat in the blood. Cholesterol greatly contributes to plaque that forms inside arterial walls and can block arteries. Cholesterol, primarily produced in the liver and also taken in through diet, is carried throughout the body by lipoproteins. There are two primary types of lipoproteins: low-density lipoproteins (**LDL-C**) and high-density lipoproteins (**HDL-C**). LDL-C is often referred to as "bad" cholesterol because it carries cholesterol from the liver and circulates it, increasing the likelihood that it will contribute to plaque somewhere along an artery. Conversely, HDL-C is called "good" cholesterol because it retrieves cholesterol from the blood vessels and carries it back to the liver, where it is processed and eliminated from the body. One of the goals of a healthy lifestyle is to increase the HDL-C while decreasing the LDL-C. This is achieved through regular exercise and to a lesser extent, by diet. (For a review see Wilmore et al., 2008.)

The effect of exercise on cholesterol and fat was recently reviewed. Regular exercise sufficient to expend 1,200 to 2,200 calories per week can reduce triglycerides (circulating fat) by 4 to 37 percent and increase HDL-C by 4 to 22 percent (Janiszewski & Ross, 2009). A meta-analysis of research found that 30–60 minutes of moderate exercise three to five times a week reduced triglycerides by 12 percent and increased HDL-C by 4 percent (which represented a .05 mmol/l of blood increase; Carroll & Dudfield, 2004). These effects are quite significant when you consider that even a .025 mmol/l increase in HDL-C can decrease the risk of CVD by about 5 percent (Gordon et al., 1986; Janiszewski & Ross, 2009).

### Reducing Obesity

Chapter 4 explains the increasing levels of obesity in North America. In the last two decades the prevalence of obesity has risen by 10 percent in men and 8 percent in women (Statistics Canada, 2011b). Obesity is associated with many life-threatening conditions such as cardiovascular (heart and stroke) and respiratory disease (e.g., asthma), cancer (uterine, prostate, breast, colon, kidney, pancreas, cervix), and sleep apnea. In addition it is related to numerous health problems such as type 2 diabetes, skin disorders, and bone and joint problems. Physical activity is an excellent way to reduce body fat and to maintain a healthy body weight and composition throughout your life (Ross & Janssen, 2007). Weight loss is directly related to the volume of exercise performed so that the more exercise done, the greater the caloric expenditure, the more weight lost, and the more total fat lost. The American College of Sports Medicine recommends 200 to 300 minutes per week of exercise (burning approximately 2,000 calories per week; Donnelly et al., 2009). Weight loss can be achieved with as little as 200 minutes of exercise per week. To burn 0.45 kilogram (1 lb) of fat per week, one needs to burn 3,500 calories. You can achieve this by exercising between 300 and 400 minutes per week (about 50 minutes per day) at a moderate intensity. Visceral fat, or that fat that is stored around organs in the abdominal cavity, is more dangerous to health than fat stored near the skin (subcutaneous fat). Both are reduced with an exercise program, but exercise causes a greater percentage of visceral fat loss. For example, a 10 percent decrease in body weight with exercise was associated with a 25 percent decrease in subcutaneous fat but a substantially larger 35 percent decrease in visceral fat (Ross & Janssen, 2007).

### Improving Insulin Resistance

When you eat carbohydrate, sugar levels in the blood increase. In response, insulin is released from the pancreas to take that blood sugar up into the muscles and liver, and in this way the blood sugar levels are controlled. If there is not enough insulin or the cells are not sensitive to it, then blood sugar levels remain higher than normal, a precursor for diabetes and a great risk for cardiovascular disease. Type 1 diabetes refers to a low production of insulin, a condition

## How Exercise Helps Reduce Body Weight

1. It burns calories (200–500 calories per 30- to 45-minute session). **Aerobic exercise** burns calories during and after exercise as the metabolic rate slowly returns to rest levels.

2. It increases your resting metabolic rate. A pound of muscle requires more energy for your body to maintain than a pound of fat, which means that each pound of muscle tissue gained will increase basal metabolic rate (BMR). Therefore, you are burning more calories even while resting or sleeping. Furthermore, for the next three days after weight training, resting metabolic rate is increased by about 100 calories per day due to muscle remodeling. This postexercise energy expenditure alone would amount to burning an extra half a kilogram (1 pound) of body weight per month.

3. It leads to increased growth hormone, norepinephrine, and epinephrine, all of which increase fat burning.

4. It promotes healthy attitudes and provides more energy for being active. (Donnelly et al., 2009; Ross & Janssen, 2007; Westcott, 2012)

that begins early in life and is highly genetic. Type 2 diabetes is the resistance (insensitivity) of cells to insulin so the body struggles to reduce blood sugar. While there is a small genetic factor, much of type 2 diabetes is due to lifestyle factors such inactivity, diet, and obesity. Both chronic and acute bouts of exercise improve insulin sensitivity regardless of age, sex, or weight loss. Even one bout of exercise can improve insulin sensitivity by 15 to 24 percent for up to 48 hours postexercise (Janiszewski & Ross, 2009). Regular chronic exercise has an even greater effect independent of weight loss.

### Increasing Activity

In addition to its effect on all these risk factors for CVD, exercise is an independent predictor of death rate from cardiovascular disease. Physical activity has been shown to reduce the death rate from cardiovascular disease. In general, death rates are 50 percent lower in those who are moderately fit compared to unfit (Blair & Lamonte, 2011). Even further protection occurs at higher fitness levels so that the death rate of highly fit persons is 10 to 15 percent lower than that of the moderately fit. The Heart and Stroke Foundation and the Canadian Society for Exercise Physiology recommend a weekly energy expenditure of at least 150 minutes of moderate to vigorous exercise per week in bouts of at least 10 minutes (CSEP, 2011; Heart and Stroke Foundation, 2011).

## Reducing Cancer Risks

Cancer is the leading killer in Canada (Statistics Canada, 2011c). While the odd bout of exercise or even regular low-intensity activity has not been shown to affect death rates from cancer, there is a strong inverse relationship between cardiorespiratory fitness level and cancer mortality. Fitness levels in almost 10,000 Japanese males were measured and divided into equal quarters (quartiles; Blair & Lamonte, 2011). The relative risk of death from cancer for each fitness category compared to the lowest fitness quartile was 79 percent, 46 percent, and 44 percent for the second, third, and fourth quartiles, respectively. Therefore, those who were in the top two fittest quarters were 55 percent less likely to die from cancer than those in the first two quarters. But there was little difference between the two fittest groups, indicating that you don't have to be at the highest fitness level to reap the greatest benefit. Even the second-least-fit group was 20 percent less likely to die from cancer than the least-fit group.

As a young student, you may be asking yourself what all this has to do with you. It's a trademark of youth to feel invincible, an attitude that allows young people to challenge themselves and explore life fully. However, I encourage you to take the preceding risks seriously and reap the benefits of active living that God incorporated into creation, such as offsetting the effects of aging and disease. Would it not be nice to live as Moses did, who was "a hundred and twenty years old when he died, yet his eyes were not weak nor his strength gone" (Deuteronomy 34:7). As you read on, you will also see that regular exercise contributes a great deal to your daily life at any age.

## Improved Sleep

Many students complain that they simply don't get enough sleep or that their sleep is disturbed and they wake up frequently. This is further addressed in chapter 10, but for now it's important to understand that sleep quantity and sleep quality (the amount of time spent in each of the sleep stages) are critical to a healthy mind and body. Poor sleep is associated with physical (obesity, overweight, and related concerns; Beccuti & Pannain, 2011; Leproult & Van, 2010) and psychological (mood, schizophrenia, depression) illness (Balbo et al., 2010). Most of the research has targeted senior populations who have the most trouble sleeping and special sleep disorders. For those suffering from poor sleep, exercise has been shown to improve sleep quantity and quality (Buman et al., 2011). Not much literature exists for young normal people because sleep is not known to be a typical problem in this group. However, one study found that vigorous nighttime exercise (performed 3 to 4 hours before bedtime) may improve sleep quality in young healthy males and females by increasing the duration of sleep spent in the stage that is most restorative, called stage 3 slow-wave sleep (Dworak et al., 2008).

## Improved Mental Health

Anxiety and depression are the most common mental disorders today and affect primarily young adults. A growing body of research investigates the mental benefits of exercise (Barbour et al., 2007; Blumenthal et al., 2007; Deslandes et al., 2009; Kiuchi et al., 2012; Perraton et al., 2010). An article reviewed the effects of chronic and acute exercise on mood (Raglin et al., 2007). Even a single bout of exercise enhances mood and reduces anxiety. Measuring the effects of a single acute bout of exercise is a little tricky because it is usually done by having participants complete a mood questionnaire before and after exercise. Immediately postexercise, especially if that exercise is of a high intensity, people may have poor mood and high anxiety for a few minutes. However, repeated testing shows that after as little as 10 minutes, one can measure profound improvements in mood that last 2 to 4 hours before mood returns to its normal state (Raglin et al., 2007). These mood improvements with a single bout of exercise are seen in healthy people as well as those with emotional disorders. While acute effects of exercise are measured using mood questionnaires, chronic effects of exercise are measured by identifying psychological traits that indicate how someone feels in general so the results are unaffected by transitory events or activities.

For healthy people, exercise appears to offer no additional long-term benefits beyond the immediate postexercise mood enhancement (Raglin et al., 2007). However, those who suffer from mood disorders report reduced anxiety and depression as well as improved feelings of well-being and self-esteem with regular exercise. In fact, some reports suggest that a regular exercise program is as effective as medication and therapy in the treatment of depression (Blumenthal et al., 2007; Perraton et al., 2010). The mechanisms responsible for these results are still unidentified, but different possibilities have been considered (Raglin et al., 2007). Some hypothesize that **endorphins** (which decrease pain and produce feelings of well-being) released during exercise are responsible. The "**runner's high**," a feeling of peace and euphoria reported by long-distance runners, has been attributed to the effects of endorphins. However, research has not reported a correlation between mood and endorphin levels measured following exercise. Furthermore, administration of **naloxone**, a substance that blocks endorphins and thus feelings of euphoria, has produced conflicting results. Most scientists are looking to other possible mechanisms. For example, it has also been suggested that exercise may alter one or more of the neurotransmitters responsible for mood such as norepinephrine, dopamine, or serotonin. Alternatively, an increased body temperature with exercise may increase brain activity and relax muscles. A psychosocial mechanism that has received a good deal of attention is that of distraction, suggesting that exercise offers a significant distraction from the stressors of routine life and offers a new environment, life activity, and sometimes social interaction. Another psychosocial mechanism may be mastery, which suggests that successfully completing a bout of exercise or following a long-term plan improves mood through improved self-efficacy. Further research is required to determine the mechanisms responsible for enhanced mood with exercise and to determine the dose–response relationship. It should be noted that too much exercise can elevate anxiety, depression, and anger as documented in studies of overtraining in serious recreational athletes or higher level athletes (Raglin et al., 2007). The current exercise recommendation for improved mood is moderate-intensity exercise for at least 30 minutes, three times per week (Perraton et al., 2010). Relapse into another depressive episode is reduced with continued exercise.

## Improved Cognition

Regular exercise has been shown to improve cognitive function (i.e., decision making, memory, attention and processing speed, executive function) in children (Hillman et al., 2008; Tomporowski et al., 2011) and adults (Smith et al., 2010). A one-year training program of moderate-intensity exercise for 40 minutes three times per week increased hippocampal volume (a brain structure involved in cognition, specifically executive function) and spatial memory (Erickson et al., 2011). Increases in cognition have been observed even during and after one exercise session (Chang et al., 2012; Kamijo et al., 2007; Kamijo et al., 2009; Lambourne & Tomporowski, 2010).

## Enhancing Immune Function

Regular exercise modulates the immune system to enhance its function (Nieman, 1997; Pedersen & Hoffman-Goetz, 2000; Rhind et al., 1996; Shephard et al., 1994; Walsh et al., 2011; Yakeu et al., 2010). In one study, sedentary males were assigned to either a control group (no exercise) or an exercise group who

### Endurance Without Limits

What are the limits to a human's endurance? If you think it's the Ironman Triathlon in Hawaii, which involves a 2.4-mile (3.8 km) swim, 112-mile (179.2 km) bike ride, and 26.2-mile (41.9 km) run, guess again. Women and men have now completed triple Ironman events. The *Chicago Tribune* reported the story of two men who ran 50 marathons in 50 days in 50 U.S. states (Deardorff, 2006). Fortunately, you only need to be active or exercise moderately to achieve significant benefits to health and well-being.

cycled at 65 to 70 percent $\dot{V}O_2$max for 30 minutes, 4 or 5 days a week for 12 weeks, resulting in a 20 percent increase in $\dot{V}O_2$max. Resting concentrations of natural killer (NK) cells were 22 percent higher and anti-inflammatory lymphocyte counts were up to 44 percent higher after training (Rhind et al., 1996). All subjects performed an acute bout of cycling exercise at 60 percent $\dot{V}O_2$max for 60 minutes before and after the training period (the trained group adjusting absolute workload to accommodate the increase in $\dot{V}O_2$max). Compared to the control group, the trained group showed larger increases in the NK cell count and reduced exercise-induced attenuation of the anti-inflammatory lymphocytes (Rhind et al., 1996). Even a single bout of exercise can cause a rapid and considerable immune response. For example, acute exercise causes an immediate and significant increase in blood neutrophils, which are the first line of defense against bacterial infection (Walsh et al., 2011). The magnitude of the increase is dependent on the dose (both intensity and duration) of exercise. Another important immune function is to reduce low-level systemic inflammation, a whole-body inflammatory activity that is associated with major killers such as CHD as well as other diseases such as dementia. Exercise enhances anti-inflammatory responses both acutely (Walsh et al., 2011) and chronically with training (Yakeu et al., 2010). Even low-intensity exercise increased the anti-inflammatory cytokines and decreased pro-inflammatory cytokines (regulators of inflammatory responses; Yakeu et al., 2010). In fact, several studies show that those who exercise regularly at moderate intensity experience fewer health problems compared to those who are sedentary. However, the inverted U relationship between exercise and immune function has been known for some time (Nieman, 1997; Shephard et al., 1994; Walsh et al., 2011). While immune function is suppressed with inactivity and enhanced with moderate-intensity training, concern has been raised over the suppression of immune function with over-training or even a single bout of exhaustive exercise (Nieman, 1997; Walsh et al., 2011). This has led to the "open window" theory, which suggests that immunosuppression 3 to 72 hours following exercise may allow viruses and bacteria to take hold. This suppression is repeated in those who overtrain, leading to chronically compromised immune function. Thus, while there may be a drop in immune function immediately after exercise, research supports an overall increase in immune function with increased cardiovascular endurance.

# Understanding the Three Energy Systems

Energy, essential for all movement, must be provided continuously for a long period when you walk to school or go for a run or a bike ride. The energy molecule in the body is called **adenosine triphosphate (ATP)**. As the name suggests, ATP is composed of adenosine and three phosphate groups with high-energy bonds between them. When these bonds are broken, energy is released and available for the body to use. The body stores a very small amount of ATP. Therefore, ATP must be continuously produced, especially during exercise. Fat, carbohydrate, and to a lesser extent protein are converted in the body to produce ATP. The faster you can produce ATP, the longer you can work hard or run fast. There are three distinct systems for producing ATP; each provides ATP at a different rate for a different duration (see table 5.1).

Imagine you are an athlete at the starting block in an 800-meter race. The starting gun fires and you fly out of the blocks at an all-out sprint. As you run what happens to your speed? The all-out sprint can be maintained for mere seconds, after which you slow down a little to a fast run. You try hard to maintain this speed, but within two to three minutes you slow down again, this time to a speed you can maintain for the duration of the race. The changes in your

## Table 5.1    **Energy Systems Summary**

| Characteristics | ATP-PC | Glycolytic | Oxidative |
|---|---|---|---|
| Duration of activity | 0–10 s | 11–120 s | More than 2 min |
| Intensity of activity | High | High | Low to moderate |
| Rate of ATP production | Immediate | Rapid | Slow |
| Fuel | Adenosine triphosphate (ATP) | Muscle glycogen and blood glucose | Stored carbohydrate, fat, and protein |
| Oxygen used? | No | No | Yes |

Based on National Strength and Conditioning Association, 2008.

running speed directly reflect the energy systems used to produce ATP as you run. Your initial sprint and subsequent 2-minute high speed running are possible only because you produce ATP quickly using **anaerobic** energy systems. Two systems (glycolytic and **ATP-PCr systems**) compose the anaerobic energy systems and provide most of the energy during the first 2 to 3 minutes of high-intensity exercise; however, ATP production is limited using these systems. Thus, the race must be finished using the aerobic energy system (the third system) that provides energy endlessly but at a slower rate. This explains why your final running speed is a slower pace, perhaps a jog.

## ATP-PCr Energy System

After a high-energy bond between phosphates in ATP is broken, ATP is rebuilt by PCr (phosphocreatine, also known as creatine phosphate) with the help of the enzyme creatine kinase. Consequently, this system is restricted by the amount of stored PCr. During intense exercise, ATP remains high for the first few seconds, but as PCr concentrations decline so does the replenishment of ATP. After 10 to 15 seconds, PCr stores are exhausted and energy must be produced by another system, the **glycolytic energy system**.

## Glycolytic Energy System

The glycolytic energy system, also called the lactic acid system, produces ATP rapidly, but less rapidly than the ATP-PCr system, so you must slow down from the all-out sprint pace. This system uses stored **glycogen**, broken down to **glucose** and released into the blood, and quickly converts it to ATP. The by-product of this process is lactic acid. Lactic acid converts quickly to **lactate** and hydrogen ions, which then accumulate as high-intensity exercise continues. After about two minutes, you must slow down again as you produce energy with the third system, the **oxidative energy system**. Slowing down helps to dissipate lactate faster than it is accumulated.

## Oxidative Energy System

The oxidative energy system can supply an unlimited amount of ATP for long durations but does so more slowly because it depends on oxygen (the anaerobic systems do not use oxygen to produce ATP). The oxidative energy system uses oxygen carried by the blood to convert carbohydrates, fats, and to a lesser extent protein to ATP. Since there is an abundance of oxygen and substrates (fat stores), this system can produce an unlimited amount of ATP continuously but does so slowly. It is, therefore, the dominant

energy system during prolonged endurance-type activities. It is the system you use to produce energy most of the time, whether you are taking notes in lecture or watching television or walking home, and is limited by the availability of oxygen to the working muscles. Therefore, aerobic training forces the body to adapt so that more oxygen is delivered to and used by the exercising muscles. Cardiorespiratory fitness achieved by aerobic training (also known as endurance or cardio training) primarily reflects the performance of the oxidative system.

Because this is a simplified example to explain how the energy systems work, two points need clarification. First, most people are inactive most of their time as they attend lectures, work on the computer, read, and eat meals. They break this pattern occasionally with intermittent periods of exercise and work that call for additional energy resources. This means that people generally use the energy systems in the opposite sequence described in the example earlier. The oxidative energy system is used during most daily activities. The glycolytic and phosphagen systems are employed with the onset of higher-intensity activities such as running for a bus, weightlifting, or running up stairs. Second, the energy systems are not employed in isolation during most activities as in the example. In reality, all three energy systems are available and contribute to the production of work, but in varying proportions. Therefore, exercise physiologists can describe different activities roughly in terms of the percentage of contribution of the aerobic and anaerobic energy systems. Note some of these examples in table 5.2.

# What Is Cardiorespiratory Fitness?

**Cardiorespiratory fitness** (also called aerobic power) is the development of the oxidative energy system and is appropriately defined as the greatest rate of

**Table 5.2  Approximate Percentages of Energy System Contribution**

| Activity | Anaerobic (ATP-PC and glycolytic) | Aerobic (oxidative) |
|---|---|---|
| Tennis | 85% | 15% |
| Soccer | 50% | 50% |
| Basketball | 75% | 25% |
| Volleyball | 90% | 10% |

Adapted from McArdle, Katch, and Katch 2001.

## Using Energy Systems to Design Training Programs

The relative contribution of each energy system to a given sport largely dictates how someone should train for that sport. A marathon runner needs to focus on long-distance cardiorespiratory training to improve the oxidative energy system. A 100-meter sprinter or power lifter must focus on training the anaerobic energy system and will gain little from cardiorespiratory training. The soccer player will need both anaerobic and cardiorespiratory training to perform high-intensity sprints and maintain a high level of performance for long durations.

oxygen utilization in one minute. It is expressed as **maximal oxygen consumption** or $\dot{V}O_2max$ (L/min or ml/kg/min). An increase in cardiorespiratory fitness is an increase in your body's ability to use oxygen. Therefore, the more oxygen your body can *take in* via the cardiorespiratory system, *deliver* to the working muscles via the cardiovascular system, and *use* by the working muscles, the greater your cardiorespiratory fitness.

The mathematical equation for $\dot{V}O_2max$ is as follows:

$$\dot{V}O_2max = HR \times SV \times (a\text{-}\bar{v})O_{2diff}$$

Oxygen use is dependent on two factors: the amount of oxygen you can transport to the working tissues (primarily muscle) and how much of that oxygen the muscles can take up and use. The equation provides a measure of both these factors. First, it provides a measure of how much oxygen is transported to the working muscles using the product of $HR \times SV$. **Heart rate** (HR) is the number of cardiac contractions or beats in one minute. **Stroke volume** (SV) is the amount of blood ejected by the heart in one cardiac contraction or heartbeat. If you multiply heart rate by stroke volume, the product is **cardiac output ($\dot{Q}$)**, which is the volume of blood pumped by the heart in one minute and reflects the amount of blood (and therefore oxygen) transported to the muscles from the heart each minute. Therefore, the $HR \times SV$ part of the equation provides a measure of oxygen delivery to the muscles and tissues. Second, the equation provides a measure of how much oxygen is used by the working tissues. Arteries supply oxygen carried in blood to the muscles and all other tissues in the body, which extract some of that oxygen according to how much they need at that moment. The veins carry the remaining oxygen (whatever wasn't used by the tissues) back to the heart. Therefore, the oxygen used by the tissues is expressed as the arterial-to-venous oxygen difference (**$a\text{-}\bar{v}O_{2diff}$**) or the oxygen in the arteries minus the oxygen in the veins. During exercise, the primary users of the oxygen in the blood are the working muscles. $\dot{V}O_2max$ is therefore expressed as the product of cardiac output and arterial–venous oxygen difference or in simpler terms, the product of the amount of blood (and therefore, oxygen) delivered to the muscles every minute and the amount of oxygen extracted and used by those muscles.

Since fitter people can provide more oxygen faster, they can produce ATP faster and so perform harder exercise longer; the fitter person can run farther faster.

# Evaluating Cardiorespiratory Fitness

The first step in improving your cardiorespiratory fitness is assessing your current condition. Any of the following four tests will give you a good idea of your cardiorespiratory fitness level.

## Resting Heart Rate Test

Typically, trained individuals have lower resting heart rates, and so **resting heart rate** has been used to reflect cardiorespiratory fitness. This is the simplest, fastest way to indicate cardiorespiratory fitness, but it is also the least accurate. Some people have inherently lower or higher than average heart rates independent of training and fitness. Resting heart rate decreases with regular training so it is also often used as a quick check that training programs are effective. Typically, resting HR is lower after a cardiorespiratory training program of several months by 10 beats per minute (bpm) or more. A sedentary person with a typical resting HR of 80 bpm may decrease HR by 1 bpm per week for up to 10 weeks, but many large-scale studies have shown much smaller average changes (5 bpm over 20 weeks of training), and some studies have found no changes in resting HR with training (Wilmore et al., 2008). Many factors may affect resting HR such as diet, temperature, and previous activity. Therefore, it's best to take this measurement in the morning before getting out of bed. *Complete the first application activity at the end*

## Cardiorespiratory Fitness: (Surprisingly) Important Even in Hockey and Basketball

Cardiorespiratory fitness is regarded as the most valuable fitness component. Clearly, this type of fitness improves performance in long-duration, less-intense exercise such as swimming, cycling and running, and endurance sports like soccer. Less obvious is that cardiorespiratory fitness also has a significant role to play in team sports that appear to be primarily anaerobic. Consider hockey, where shifts are 20 to 40 seconds of mostly all-out bursts followed by equal or longer rest periods, or basketball, with similar repeated bouts of anaerobic sprints and jumps. Cardiorespiratory fitness improves the ability of the athlete to recover between shifts or anaerobic bursts. It improves stamina throughout the duration of the game. Although the hockey player's shift is only seconds long, using anaerobic more than aerobic power for his or her shift, the aerobically fit hockey player with a higher cardiorespiratory fitness will be less fatigued in the third period than his or her untrained counterpart.

*of this chapter to get an accurate measure of your resting heart rate.*

## Maximal Oxygen Consumption Tests

A much better estimate of aerobic fitness is a direct measurement of maximal oxygen consumption, or $\dot{V}O_2$max. To measure this directly, however, requires the use of very expensive and sophisticated lab equipment. The gold standard test measures oxygen uptake by the evaluation of gas concentrations in expired air during a graded exercise test where workload on some ergometer such as a treadmill or cycle increases by the same amount every one to two minutes. This is the type of test used to assess fitness in elite athletes. For most people, this is unavailable. Fortunately, numerous simple and inexpensive tests estimate $\dot{V}O_2$max. *Try one of the three field tests at the end of the chapter to estimate your $\dot{V}O_2$max: the 3-minute step test, 1.5-mile (1.92 km) run test, and the 12-minute walk/run test.*

A larger person will require more oxygen simply because he or she is bigger and has more tissue, regardless of whether the person is fit. For this reason, $\dot{V}O_2$max is normally expressed per kilogram of body weight (ml/kg/min) instead of just liters per minute.

## Discouraged After Your Aerobic Assessment? Consider This . . .

How did you fare in your **cardiorespiratory assessment**? If you feel discouraged by lower-than-expected results, there is good news: you have the potential to make dramatic changes to your aerobic fitness level in a relatively short time. Healthy adults can reach an excellent level of fitness, according to the standards presented in the assessment section, typically in six to eight months of training, and you will see benefits within a few weeks! Furthermore, you don't have to run as hard as you can to experience improvement. If you follow the recommendations outlined later, you'll start off slowly and adapt to higher exercise loads in small, manageable steps. Refer to chapter 2 to review steps to take to make permanent lifestyle changes.

If you completed the cardiorespiratory test with little difficulty, congratulations! You've probably already been doing some type of aerobic activity. If you're not quite in the excellent group, you don't have far to go. With just a little extra push in terms of intensity or time, you'll be there. If you are already where you want to be, you need only a small investment of time for maintenance.

## What to Expect From Training

The benefits you achieve from training depend largely on your approach. For some, increasing activity is their only goal. As mentioned earlier in this chapter, this is enough to achieve several health benefits, such as improved mood, weight management, and reduced risk of heart disease. For others, cardiorespiratory fitness and some muscle fitness is their primary goal. With cardiorespiratory fitness come additional health benefits such as greater insulin sensitivity, reduced risk of cancer, better weight management, and of course, improved performance in a variety of sports. Improvements in

# Physiological Adaptations That Increase Oxygen Consumption

Cardiorespiratory training results in physiological adaptations that improve health and sport performance. Highly trained endurance athletes may have oxygen uptake values higher than 85 ml/kg/min, compared to values in the middle 30s for the untrained adult. The following physiological adaptations collectively produce the ability to increase oxygen consumption and produce ATP.

- **Increased maximal ventilation:** The maximal capacity for airflow and oxygen diffusion increases due to endurance training. Maximal ventilation (amount of air inspired or expired in a minute) increases as a result of an increased tidal volume (volume inspired and expired during a normal breath) and an increased breathing rate. Highly trained endurance athletes may have ventilations in excess of 220 L/min, compared to the untrained adult at 120 L/min. Endurance training can easily increase ventilation to about 160 L/min (Wilmore et al., 2008).

- **Heart size increases:** The heart is made of a specialized cardiac muscle that responds to training by getting bigger (hypertrophy) and stronger so that the muscular wall of the heart is thicker in athletes compared to their sedentary counterparts (Fagard, 1996; Pluim et al., 2000). This means that the heart is a stronger, more effective pump. Furthermore, there are two cavities (called the right and left ventricles) in the heart that fill with blood before that blood is ejected when the heart contracts. When the heart muscle contracts, blood is forced out of the right ventricle to the lungs and from the left ventricle to the aorta, which distributes blood to the head, neck, and rest of the body (excluding the lungs). Following training, the cavity size of the left ventricle in particular enlarges, allowing for a greater blood volume to be distributed via the aorta with every heartbeat.

- **Increased stroke volume:** As the heart's dimensions change in response to training, it becomes more effective and efficient at pumping blood. The combination of larger ventricular chambers and a stronger, larger cardiac muscle mass means that there is more blood filling the heart and that blood is more effectively pumped out of the heart to the rest of the body so that less blood is left in the ventricles. After endurance training, stroke volume is greater during rest and during both submaximal and maximal exercise.

- **Greater blood flow:** Since muscles require more oxygen during exercise, blood flow must be increased. One way that the body responds to demands for greater blood flow is by increased **capilarization**, or the sprouting of new capillaries (small blood vessels) to carry blood within working tissues. Existing capillaries also are more open to flow in a trained muscle. With increased density and dilation of capillaries, the transit time and distance from the blood vessel (capillaries) to the muscle cell is less, so more oxygen is available for the working muscles. Additionally, **blood volume** is increased by small increases in red blood cells and much larger increases in plasma volume, resulting in a lower blood viscosity and, therefore, improved blood flow. In other words, small increases in the number of red blood cells and large increases in plasma volume lower blood viscosity, which improves blood flow.

- **Increased density of myoglobin, mitochondria, and oxidative enzymes:** Aerobic training causes structural changes within muscle that permit greater oxygen metabolism. One resulting adaptation is that the amount of muscle **myoglobin** increases. Myoglobin is the oxygen-binding compound in muscle, similar to hemoglobin in the blood, that stores oxygen and carries it to the mitochondria within the muscle cell. **Mitochondria**, which are the organelles in muscle that house the oxidative energy system within the muscle, increase in number, size, and efficiency. Furthermore, enzymes such as succinate dehydrogenase and citrate synthase that are key to oxygen metabolism increase in number and density.

All of these physiological changes are the body's way of responding to increased demands for oxygen. Collectively they have a dramatic effect on the amount of oxygen your body can use and, probably more important to you, the amount of work you're able to perform. Of equal or greater importance for most people is that many of these changes have a direct impact on health.

The design of the body and its capacity to perform and respond to exercise and other healthy lifestyle choices always amazes me. These examples just noted demonstrate clearly how humans are truly fearfully and wonderfully made, that the body responds relatively quickly to improvements in activity levels. Furthermore, there is a forgiveness clause in humanity's creation since these physiological improvements occur at all ages, and it's never too late to start exercising!

## There Is No Magic Potion to Health

People endlessly seek quick fixes and magic potions that will bring instant energy, weight loss, and improved performance at school, work, and sports. But God created humans with a requirement to "live by the spirit" (Galatian 5:16) with self-discipline and patience in accordance with the fruits of the spirit (Galatians 5:22, 23). Only then can the true and lasting gifts of a healthy mind, body, and soul be enjoyed.

cardiorespiratory fitness are general such that gains made in one mode of exercise are transferred to performance in another mode. So, for example, if you train by running, you will improve performance while cycling, in-line skating, or in any sport or activity that uses the oxidative energy system. For athletes trying to achieve their highest attainable $\dot{V}O_2$max, the training program should be specific to that sport. For example, cyclists will achieve greater gains if their continuous and interval training involves cycling versus running.

Cardiorespiratory fitness is affected by genetics, sex, age, body composition, and training. Thus, at some point during a continuous training program, you will reach your genetic cap. That is, given your genetics, body composition, age, and sex, you will not be able to improve fitness further, at which point maintenance will become your primary goal. Genetics explain between 25 percent and 50 percent of the individual variation in $\dot{V}O_2$max. Furthermore, there is a genetic component to the capacity for improvement. Persons in the same training program will show different gains in $\dot{V}O_2$max. In 1999, a large-scale study (HERITAGE study; Bouchard et al., 1999) was designed to determine the individual responses and the genetic component of variables, including $\dot{V}O_2$max, that typically respond to aerobic training. Over 700 sedentary people made up of families of a natural mother and father and three or more of their children trained three times per week for 20 weeks at an initial training intensity of 55 percent for 35 minutes and progressing to 75 percent for 50 minutes per day. Participants showed an average improvement in $\dot{V}O_2$max of 18 percent, with some improving by 50 percent! Improvement also depends on initial fitness level, with the least fit making the greatest gains. Your peak cardiorespiratory fitness can be attained within 8–18 months of training (Wilmore et al., 2008).

There may be occasional setbacks along the journey, but remember the apostle Paul, who recognized this when he wrote, "I have the desire to do what is good, but I cannot carry it out" (Romans 7:18). Thankfully there is a power (the Holy Spirit) that transcends human strength and bears the fruit of goodness. Do good, be active, and do it through the power of God's Spirit.

Once you have achieved your highest $\dot{V}O_2$max, you can improve performance for years by exercising at progressively higher percentages of your $\dot{V}O_2$max. Your performance increases because you can work at a harder level even though your $\dot{V}O_2$max stays the same. That is, you are running faster at a pace equivalent to 80 percent $\dot{V}O_2$max than a pace equivalent to 65 percent. Competitive runners, for example, will run at a pace just under that which causes an accumulation of lactate. Remember that at higher intensities of exercise, when you need ATP faster than can be provided by the oxidative system, you recruit the lactate system, which produces lactate along with ATP. When lactate starts to accumulate it interferes with muscle contraction and limits exercise. Training at progressively higher percentages of $\dot{V}O_2$max improves the body's ability to buffer lactate, and therefore, you can work at higher intensities, or run faster, without accumulating lactate.

## Outlining an Aerobic Exercise Prescription

The acronym **FITT (frequency, intensity, time or duration, and type)** is commonly used as a means of understanding the components of a training program and developing strategies for increasing cardiorespiratory fitness.

- Frequency
- Intensity
- Time
- Type

## Continuous Training

Continuous training is continuous exercise with no rest. It is a popular approach to aerobic exercise for runners, cyclists, and cross-country skiers who like to enjoy the outdoors by exercising. The intensity of this exercise can vary as does the duration. The low- to midintensity exercise for long durations became known as long, slow distance (LSD) training. High-intensity training is typically performed either in intervals (discussed later) or shorter, less frequent training sessions.

## Frequency

Aerobic or endurance activities can be done every day with no ill effects. Consider athletes training for a marathon or the Tour de France who train hours almost every day. In fact, the recommendation by all health organizations (e.g., cancer societies, Health Canada, Heart and Stroke) is that people perform some exercise almost daily. How often you exercise is a function of the intensity and duration of your exercise, with harder and longer workouts performed less often. In order to achieve fitness gains, it must be performed a minimum of three times per week on nonconsecutive days. Exercising three times a week for 30 minutes on alternating days is sufficient **frequency** to build cardiorespiratory fitness in most people if the intensity is high enough. As your aerobic fitness improves, you may want to increase the number of sessions to between four and six per week. Increased frequency has some advantages.

Age is another consideration when determining frequency. With age, regular daily exercise has even greater health and well-being benefits. Health Canada endorses the recommendations for exercise set by the Canadian Society for Exercise Physiology (CSEP), which suggests that older adults accumulate 150 minutes of moderate to intense activity per week (CSEP, 2011). American College of Sports Medicine (ACSM) recommends 30 to 60 minutes (five days per week) of moderately intense activity totaling 150 to 300 minutes per week or 20-60 minutes of vigorous-intensity exercise (three days per week) (Chodzko-Zajko et al., 2009). With aging will come a natural decline in intensity, and one should reduce the frequency of very intense workouts because they will require longer recovery (even a day or two) and increase the risk of injury and immune suppression. Furthermore, often the mode of exercise must not create any orthopedic stress. Walking, swimming, and cycling are low-impact choices, but of these, only walking will benefit bone mass, which is of primary importance as one ages.

## Intensity

Once a minimum duration (20 to 30 minutes of continuous exercise) and frequency (3 days per week on alternate days) have been achieved, intensity is the most important factor in improving cardiorespiratory fitness. Cardiorespiratory fitness is improved when the systems and tissues in the body are challenged enough by the exercise and the demand for oxygen that they need to adapt to meet that demand. Those adaptations result in improved fitness. If the intensity is too low, the body's systems that are involved in the delivery and use of oxygen in the oxidative energy system are unchallenged and therefore do not adapt, so there is no change in $\dot{V}O_2$max. If the intensity is too high, then the oxidative system cannot provide ATP fast enough, so the anaerobic energy systems are employed instead and no adaptation in the cardiorespiratory system occurs. Most authorities agree that exercise intensity between 50 and 90 percent of $\dot{V}O_2$max cardiovascular exertion will provide a challenge to the body resulting in physiological adaptations that improve $\dot{V}O_2$max. Higher intensities force the oxidative energy system to produce ATP quickly, challenging it further. It's easy to make mistakes in one of two ways. If you don't push yourself hard enough, you won't improve. On the other hand, if you push yourself too hard, you'll be susceptible to exercise-related injuries and overtraining syndrome. So find a challenging but safe exercise zone. There are two simple ways to determine an appropriate zone for aerobic exercise: target heart rate (HR) and rating of perceived exertion (RPE).

### Target Heart Rate Zone

You have probably heard the term *target heart rate* as it relates to aerobic exercise. However, a better phrase is **target heart rate zone**. A "zone" is important because it's nearly impossible to keep the heart rate at one specific rate, such as 173 beats per minute (bpm). Therefore, it's necessary to establish a zone that has some variability.

Target heart rate zone consists of a lower and an upper limit. Within this zone, the body's systems involved in the delivery and use of oxygen are being challenged and therefore adapting, resulting in improved cardiorespiratory fitness. You can calculate your target heart rate zone in different ways, with percent maximum heart rate and percent heart rate reserve being just two.

After you've calculated your target heart rate zone you will need some way of measuring when you are inside and outside of your zone. The best device for accomplishing this is a **heart rate monitor** (see figure 5.1). Most health and fitness products are gimmicks. However, from time to time a product comes along that can seriously aid anyone who exercises. Such is the case with a heart rate monitor.

A heart rate monitor resembles a traditional wristwatch. Wearing the chest strap and watch provides an

# Calculating Target Heart Rate Zone

## Percent Maximum Heart Rate (%HRmax)

There are two steps to determine intensity this way.

1. Determine your estimated maximum heart rate, or EMHR. You do this by subtracting your age from 220. If you're 18 years old, for example, your estimated maximum heart rate would be 202 beats per minute. You can tell from this formula that your maximum heart rate decreases with age.

   After examining heart rate values from 351 studies involving 18,712 subjects, Dr. Hanaka Hirofumi and his colleagues discovered that this iconic fitness formula actually underestimated the true maximum heart rate of adults in those over 40 years old (Tanaka et al., 2001). The reason for this error is that studies used to establish the formula of 220 minus age used predominantly young subjects. Individuals 60 years and older were inadequately represented. Therefore, the scientists established a new formula that considered older subjects.

   208 − (0.7 x age)

   For example, a 50-year-old would have an estimated maximum heart rate of 173 beats per minute (208 − [0.7 x 50]).

2. Then determine the lower and upper limit that falls within a range of a percentage of your estimated maximum heart rate. The aim is to work hard enough to maintain or increase cardiorespiratory function without working to the point of injury or dread of exercise because it is so painful. Exercising at less than 40 percent of maximum heart rate won't provide sufficient cardiorespiratory stress to increase or maintain fitness and health in adults (Garber et al., 2011). ACSM established 55 or 65 percent of maximum heart rate (%HRmax) as the minimum intensity level for aerobic exercise. For young adults who are apparently healthy, 65 to 90 %HRmax is recommended. The ASCM recommends not exceeding 90 %HRmax as the upper limit (Garber et al., 2011).

Here's an example. Sue is 18 years old, so her EMHR is 202 (220 minus age). Her lower limit is 131 beats per minute (202 × 0.65). Her upper limit is 182 beats per minute (202 × 0.90).

## Percent Heart Rate Reserve (%HRR)

The second method for calculating training heart rate zone is using percent heart rate reserve. ACSM recommends a training intensity between 55 percent and 85 percent HHR (Garber et al., 2011). This calculation takes into consideration your maximum heart rate and your resting heart rate. Many of the charts you'll see employ this method. To calculate target HR using HHR use the following equation:

Target HR = (MHR − RHR) × %TI + RHR

MHR = Maximum HR in bpm calculated as 220 − age.

RHR = resting HR in bpm

%TI = training intensity expressed as a percentage (i.e., 50 percent to 85 percent).

For a 20-year-old with a resting HR of 72 bpm, determine the upper and lower limit of his target HR zone.

1. Estimate maximum heart rate (MHR) with the following formula: MHR = 220 − age. Therefore, MHR = 220 − 20 = 200 bpm.

2. Check resting HR after you have been sitting quietly for 15 or 20 minutes and before any caffeinated drinks. This is best done in the morning when you first wake up. Place your index and ring finger on the radial artery on your wrist until you feel the pulse or on the carotid artery on your neck just to the left or right of the trachea. For this example, say the resting HR is 72 bpm.

*(continued)*

**A Run With God**

A lot of people think running must be boring because there is nothing to do but put one foot in front of the other a whole bunch of times. It is exactly the repetitive ease of running that allows runners to do so much else during their runs.

One option is to run with a partner. If you are running so fast you cannot keep up a conversation, you are running too fast. A running partner provides accountability to go on the run, is a guide during the run to keep your speed at a suitable level, and the conversation will make the miles go by very quickly.

When I run on my own I often have a watch on and periodically assess my pace. On longer runs I take along some gels or nutrition bars and eat them as I run. Sometimes I take along a portable mp3 player and listen to music. When running on my own I often use this time to run with God and have a longer conversation with him. This conversation can include a time of prayer for people and situations (and you can spend quite a bit of time in prayer for each item), or it can be a more focused pondering of a scripture text. Sometimes it can be a holy time of simply being in the presence of God and allowing God to speak. Often it is hard for people to find times of quiet, but when one runs for 20 minutes, 40 minutes, an hour, or hours, what a great place to spend time in conversation with God.

In all my runs I am keenly aware of the weather. I try running different routes each time so I see new things. At times I am discouraged by the garbage on the side of the roads, and other times I am delighted to watch a rabbit run by, a deer standing in the woods nearby, the long grass sway in the breeze, or just what other people are up to. I should add that in some very long runs I finish the last portion by just talking to myself and encouraging myself to put one foot in front of the other and make it home or to the finish line. I am never bored while running. I am too busy enjoying the sights and sounds around me, feeling myself train and strain, and enjoying time speaking and listening to God.

---

- Focus your eyes on the horizon, or at least 10 yards (9 m) in front of your feet. Your chin should be parallel with the ground. Feet should be shoulder-width apart.

- Use the heel-to-toe method of walking. Avoid hard impact with the ground. Roll your foot from heel to toe.

## Jogging or Running

No one agrees on how to define the difference between jogging and running. The general consensus is that jogging is just a slower form of running used primarily for cardiorespiratory fitness.

If you're just beginning but want to do more than simply walk, start with the walk/run program in table 5.4. If you want something a little more challenging, you can train for a 5K (3.2 mi) road race. The 12-week program outlined in table 5.5 will ensure that you're prepared to go the distance.

Paul often used running as a metaphor for Christian life (12 times he talks about endurance). People clearly understood running, and it was never referred to in a negative way. Think of the following lines and how understanding persevering at running will help you understand your run with God:

I do not run like someone running aimlessly. (1 Corinthians 9:26)

I wanted to be sure I was not running and had not been running my race in vain. (Galatians 2:2)

You were running a good race. Who cut in on you to keep you from obeying the truth? (Galatians 5:7)

I will be able to boast on the day of Christ that I did not run or labor in vain. (Philippians 2:16)

Let us run with perseverance the race marked out for us. (Hebrews 12:1)

### Running Techniques

Here are some key points on running technique (Hahn, 2011).

- Run tall. Your back should be erect and your head high.

- Your head guides your posture, so look naturally ahead. Some say to look about 9 meters (10 yards) ahead, rather than down at your feet.

- Relax your shoulders and bend your elbows so that your forearms are almost parallel to the ground. When runners get tired, they tend to

## Table 5.5 12-Week Plan for Completing First 5K Run

### Phase I  5K Run Program

| | Monday | Wednesday | Friday |
|---|---|---|---|
| Week 1 | Moderate run*<br>Time: 20 min | Moderate cycle**<br>Time: 30 min | Easy run***<br>Time: 25 min |
| Week 2 | Moderate run<br>Time: 24 min | Moderate cycle<br>Time: 30 min | Easy run<br>Time: 28 min |
| Week 3 | Treadmill run<br>Time: 27 min | Moderate cycle<br>Time: 30 min | Easy run<br>Time: 30 min |
| Week 4 | Moderate run<br>Time: 30 min | Moderate cycle<br>Time: 30 min | Easy run<br>Time: 30 min |

*Moderate run = 70 to 85 percent of estimated maximum heart rate
**Moderate cycle = 70 to 85 percent of estimated maximum heart rate
***Easy run = 60 to 75 percent of estimated maximum heart rate

### Phase II  5K Run Program

| | Monday | Wednesday | Friday |
|---|---|---|---|
| Week 5 | Pace run* 1:15 (min:s)<br>Recover walk**** 1:15<br>10 sets<br>Time: 25 min | Easy run**<br>Time: 40 min | Moderate run***<br>2.0 mi (3.2 km)<br>Timed |
| Week 6 | Pace run 1:30<br>Recover walk 1:30<br>8 sets<br>Time: 24 min | Easy run<br>Time: 45 min | Moderate run<br>2.25 mi (3.5 km)<br>Timed |
| Week 7 | Pace run 1:45<br>Recover walk 1:45<br>7 sets<br>Time: 24:30 min | Easy run<br>Time: 30 min | Moderate run<br>2.5 mi (4 km)<br>Timed |
| Week 8 | Pace run 2 min<br>Recover walk 2 min<br>6 sets<br>Time: 24 min | Easy run<br>Time: 50 min | Moderate run<br>2.75 mi (4.4 km)<br>Timed |

*Pace Run = 85 percent or above estimated maximum heart rate
**Easy Run = 60 to 75 percent of estimated maximum heart rate
***Moderate Run = 70 to 85 percent of estimated maximum heart rate
****Recover Walk = Slow walking

### Phase III 5K Run Program

| | Monday | Wednesday | Friday |
|---|---|---|---|
| Week 9 | Pace run* 1 min<br>Recover walk**** 30 s<br>14 sets<br>Time: 21 min | Easy run**<br>Time: 30 min | Moderate run***<br>3.0 mi (4.8 km)<br>Timed |
| Week 10 | Pace run 1:30 (min:s)<br>Recover walk 45 s<br>10 sets<br>Time: 22:30 min | Easy run<br>Time: 50 min | Moderate run<br>3.2 mi (5 km)<br>Timed |
| Week 11 | Pace run 2 min<br>Recover walk 1 min<br>6 sets<br>Time: 18 min | Easy run<br>Time: 40 min | Moderate run<br>3.2 mi (5 km)<br>Timed |
| Week 12 | Pace run 2 min<br>Recover walk 1 min<br>6 sets<br>Time: 18 min | Easy run<br>Time: 10–15 min | Race day |

*Pace run = 85 percent or above estimated maximum heart rate
**Easy run = 60 to 75 percent of estimated maximum heart rate
***Moderate run = 75 to 85 percent of estimated maximum heart rate
****Recover Walk = Slow walking

tighten the upper body, which drains energy and negatively affects fluid running form. Make sure your shoulders are low and loose and shake them out periodically to ensure that they are not creeping up and tightening. Make sure shoulders don't dip from side to side but remain level.

- Don't clench your fists while running because this can influence tension in your upper body. Arms should swing front to back and not across your body. Elbows should be bent at about a 90-degree angle. Imagine that you're holding an egg in either hand.

### Running Form

Here are some key points to keep in mind on your running form.

- Be careful not to overstride. If you overstride, your head tends to move up and down. This wasted energy distracts from moving efficiently in one direction—horizontally. Your feet should make contact with the ground directly under your body (not in front) and your knee should be slightly bent so that it can absorb the impact.

- Breathe in through your nose and out through your mouth. Develop a rhythm to your breathing, just as you would do for your stride.

- When you approach a hill, shorten your stride. Lift your knees higher and pump your arms more. If the hill is really steep, lean slightly forward.

## Swimming

Swimming is becoming a more popular form of aerobic training; many community pools have several daily time slots just for those swimming laps for fitness. In addition, various water aerobics programs use water as a resistance to movement, which will increase heart rate significantly when you try to move quickly against the water. A combination of water aerobics and laps would make a well-rounded and varied program. Similar to the walk/run program, start slowly and at the lower end of your heart rate zone three times a week and increase intensity and duration and possibly frequency as you progress.

## Cycling

Cycling is a common mode of exercise and activity. Biking while running errands, getting to class, commuting to and from work, and just cruising around town is a great way to increase the amount of activity you do but can also be used for training if it meets the duration and intensity requirements for improving cardiorespiratory fitness. During poor weather, you can continue cycling using a stationary bike or wind trainer.

Indoor stationary cycling (also called Spinning) has been a longtime favorite because there is no impact, and you can do it comfortably while watching television or even reading during a lower-intensity workout. Most gyms now offer Spinning classes several times a week. It has grown in appeal because it is efficient and doesn't involve high impact on the

 **Cycling Is Easy When You Don't Feel Like Exercising**

Even on my most tired days or during afternoons when my energy is low or on days when I just don't feel like exercising, I can always motivate myself to cycle because anyone can sit on a bike, and I know I don't have to pedal really hard to reap the benefits. I envision myself enjoying my music and letting my mind wander as I spin my legs. So I change into my sport clothes, sit on the bike, and start to spin my legs at a speed and gear that are easy. When I feel like it, I pedal a little faster or change the gear to pedal harder. Sometimes I'm off in my own world, and I realize only later that I'm pedaling at a moderate workload without ever having noticed that I've begun to work harder. I always feel a little more energetic when I return and especially satisfied that I accomplished a training session when I could have easily abandoned it. There are other days when I don't feel like exercising but know that I should, and when I go out it feels hard and continues to feel hard. Sometimes I will cycle for a shorter time or at an easier intensity to accommodate this, but I always feel better for having exercised. On these days I remember that Jesus doesn't promise that the road is easy, only that it is worthwhile.

The gateway to life is very narrow and the road is difficult, and only a few ever find it. (Matthew 7:14)

joints, and people of all ages, skills, and fitness levels can participate.

Safety is an important concern for outdoor cyclists. In 2009 in the United States, 630 people died in bicycle incidents (U.S. Department of Transportation, 2010), and 58 died in Canada in 2006 (Vehicular Cycling, 2007). Safety helmets can reduce the risk of death by 85 percent (Unintentional Injury, 2002).

A colleague of mine would not be teaching or writing had he not worn a helmet while bike riding. The research supports the strong connection between the use of helmets and reduced head injuries (Council on Scientific Affairs, 1994; Rivara et al., 2000; Spaite et al., 1991). Statistics indicate that the risk of brain injury and mortality increases by 60 to 88 percent when not wearing a bicycle helmet (Attewell et al., 2001; Thompson et al., 1999). It can be argued that those riding bikes and wearing helmets are safer riders. But when that is factored into the statistics, helmets still reduce injuries by about half (Abu-Zidan et al., 2007).

Here are a few quick reminders for cycling safety:

- When riding outdoors, be sure to wear a helmet. Look for proof that it conforms to the Consumer Product Safety Commission (CPSC) standard for head protection.

- Make yourself visible. Wear reflective clothing if you can. If you can't, remember that drivers see bright pink, yellow, and orange most easily.

- Always follow the rules of the road—stick to the right, stop at stop signs, heed one-way signs, and so on.

Cyclists and cars both have equal rights and responsibilities to obey all traffic laws. It is encouraged by some states, Georgia for example, that car drivers give cyclists three feet of space between the vehicle and bicycle (Georgia Bike Sense, 2012).

## Next Steps

Developing your aerobic capacity will take patience. There are few quick fixes. But be encouraged by the words instructing that those who faithfully and actively "hope in the Lord will renew their strength. They will soar on wings like eagles; they will run and not grow weary, they will walk and not be faint" (Isaiah 40:31; see also Psalm 40:1–3; Psalm 130). "For God did not give us a spirit of timidity, but a spirit of power, of love and of self-discipline" (2 Timothy 1:7). Go for it!

## Key Terms

$a\text{-}\bar{v}O_{2diff}$

adenosine triphosphate (ATP)

aerobic capacity

aerobic endurance

aerobic exercise

anaerobic

ATP-PCr energy system

blood volume

capilarization

cardiac output

cardiorespiratory assessment

cardiorespiratory endurance

cardiorespiratory fitness

cholesterol: HDL-C, LDL-C

endorphins

exercise

FITT

frequency

glucose

glycogen

glycolytic energy system

heart rate

heart rate monitor

lactate

maximal oxygen consumption ($\dot{V}O_2$max)

mitochondria

myoglobin

naloxone

oxidative energy system

perceived exertion

physical activity

resting heart rate

runner's high

stroke volume

target heart rate zone

## Review Questions

1. Explain the differences between an aerobic and anaerobic exercise.

2. List three major benefits of developing cardiorespiratory fitness.

3. Identify three physiological adaptations that result from aerobic exercise.

4. Discuss several health benefits of cardio-respiratory fitness.

5. Apply FITT to describe a training prescription for aerobic exercise.

6. List and describe methods of monitoring exercise intensity.

## Application Activities

1. **Resting heart rate**

Obtaining an accurate resting heart rate is harder than you might think because a lot of preparation is required to get an accurate measurement. The participant should not have eaten or exercised in the previous 3 hours and must lie in a prone position for at least 20 minutes before measuring the resting heart rate. Because of these requirements, most students perform this test after they wake but before getting out of bed in the morning.

If you have a heart rate monitor, simply place the chest strap as recommended by the manufacturer and obtain your heart rate. If you don't have a heart rate monitor, place your forefinger and middle finger on your carotid artery (on your neck) or radial artery (on the inside of your wrist) and count the number of heartbeats in one minute (see figure 5.2a–c). If you are taking this measurement manually, take at least two separate readings. The discrepancy between your readings should

be fewer than four beats. Repeat this process until the discrepancy falls within the acceptable range. Take an average of your readings and compare this to the standards for resting heart rate (see table 5.6).

The following are some common mistakes people make while taking resting heart rate:

- Not taking enough time to become fully rested

- Performing the test in a seated instead of a prone position

- Using the thumb instead of the forefinger for palpation

2. **Three-minute step test**

This test requires you to step up and down on a step that measures 16.25 inches high (41.25 cm) for three minutes (see figure 5.3). Many gymnasium bleachers have a riser height of 16.25 inches. Men step at a rate (cadence) of 24 per minute, while women step at a rate of 22 per minute. This cadence

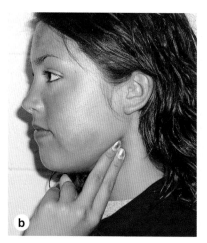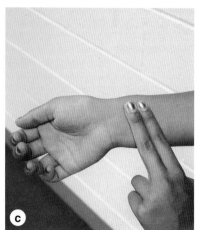

**Figure 5.2**  *(a)* Make sure you use the index or middle finger for taking your pulse; *(b)* measure your pulse at the carotid artery; or *(c)* measure your pulse at the radial artery.

## Table 5.6    Standards for Resting Heart Rate

| Age (years) | 18–25 | | 26–35 | | 36–45 | | 46–55 | | 56–65 | | >65 | |
|---|---|---|---|---|---|---|---|---|---|---|---|---|
| Sex | M | F | M | F | M | F | M | F | M | F | M | F |
| Excellent | 40–54 | 42–57 | 36–53 | 39–57 | 37–55 | 40–58 | 35–56 | 43–58 | 42–56 | 42–59 | 40–55 | 49–59 |
| Above average | 55–65 | 58–67 | 54–64 | 58–67 | 56–65 | 59–68 | 57–65 | 59–69 | 57–67 | 60–68 | 56–65 | 60–69 |
| Average | 66–69 | 68–71 | 65–67 | 68–70 | 66–69 | 69–71 | 66–70 | 70–72 | 68–71 | 69–72 | 66–69 | 70–72 |
| Below average | 70–72 | 72–76 | 69–71 | 72–74 | 70–72 | 72–75 | 72–74 | 73–76 | 72–75 | 73–77 | 70–73 | 73–76 |
| Poor | >73 | >77 | >72 | >75 | >73 | >76 | >75 | >77 | >76 | >78 | >74 | >77 |

Based on YMCA 1989.

should be monitored with the help of a metronome set at 88 for females and 96 for males. A step cycle has four parts: step up with one leg, step up with the other, step down with the first leg, and finally step down with the last leg.

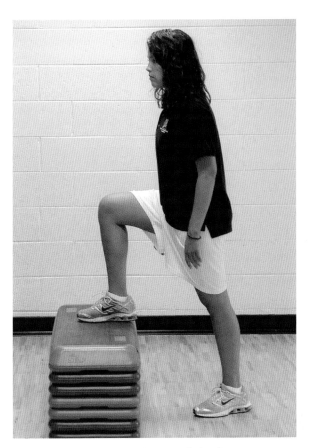

**Figure 5.3** A step test is one of the fastest ways to estimate cardiorespiratory fitness.

At the end of the three minutes, immediately stop, and while standing, find your pulse (you have five seconds to do this). Count your pulse for 15 seconds (from 5 seconds to 20 seconds after exercise). Multiply your count by 4 to determine your heart rate in beats per minute. Then use the appropriate formula to calculate your $\dot{V}O_2$max. Compare your scores to the standards for maximal oxygen consumption to evaluate your cardiorespiratory fitness level (see table 5.7).

Your $\dot{V}O_2$max is determined from the heart rate (HR) immediately after this test by using the following formulas:

For men: $\dot{V}O_2$max (ml/kg/min) = 111.33 – (0.42 × HR)

For women: $\dot{V}O_2$max (ml/kg/min) = 65.81 – (0.1847 × HR)

For example, if a man finished the test with a recovery HR of 144 bpm, then

$\dot{V}O_2$max (ml/kg/min) = 111.33 – (0.42 ×144)

$\dot{V}O_2$max = 50.85 ml/kg/min

The following are some common mistakes people make on this test:

- Having a box or step set at the wrong height
- Stepping either faster or slower than the required cadence
- Not checking the pulse within the 5- to 20-second postexercise period
- Not accurately measuring heart rate

## Table 5.7  Standards for Maximal Oxygen Consumption ($\dot{V}O_2$max)

| Age (years) | 13–19 | | 20–29 | | 30–39 | | 40–49 | | 50–59 | | 60+ | |
|---|---|---|---|---|---|---|---|---|---|---|---|---|
| **Sex** | **M** | **F** | **M** | **F** | **M** | **F** | **M** | **F** | **M** | **F** | **M** | **F** |
| Excellent | ≥51.4 | ≥44.2 | ≥51.4 | ≥44.2 | ≥51.4 | ≥41 | ≥48.2 | ≥39.5 | ≥45.3 | ≥35.2 | ≥42.5 | ≥35.2 |
| Above average | 46.8–51.3 | 38.1–44.1 | 46.8–51.3 | 38.1–44.1 | 46.8–51.3 | 36.7–40.9 | 41.8–48.1 | 33.8–39.4 | 38.5–45.2 | 30.9–35.1 | 35.3–42.4 | 29.4–35.1 |
| Average | 42.5–46.7 | 35.2–38 | 42.5–46.7 | 35.2–38 | 41–46.7 | 33.8–36.6 | 38.1–41.7 | 30.9–33.7 | 35.2–38.4 | 28.2–30.8 | 31.8–35.2 | 25.8–29.3 |
| Below average | 39.5–42.4 | 32.3–35.1 | 39.5–42.4 | 32.3–35.1 | 37.4–40.9 | 30.5–33.7 | 35.1–38 | 28.3–30.8 | 32.3–35.1 | 25.5–28.1 | 28.7–31.7 | 23.8–25.7 |
| Poor | ≤39.5 | ≤32.3 | ≤39.5 | ≤32.3 | ≤37.4 | ≤30.5 | ≤35.1 | ≤28.3 | ≤32.3 | ≤25.5 | ≤28.7 | ≤23.8 |

Data from ACSM 2000; Cooper 1994; Franklin et al. 2000.

### 3. 1.5-mile run test

This test requires you to run 1.5 miles (2.4 km) as fast as possible. Setting an appropriate pace for this test is critical. Ensure that the distance for performing this test measures 1.5 miles. A standard 400-meter track would be ideal (6 laps = 1.49 miles, or add 16 more yards to get 1.5 miles). Warm up before you begin this test.

Start a stopwatch when you begin to run. If someone is monitoring this test, ask him or her to give lap times if you're running on a track, because this helps with pacing. Record the total time to complete the test. Use the following formula to calculate your $\dot{V}O_2$max. Compare your scores to the standards for maximal oxygen consumption in table 5.7 to evaluate your cardiorespiratory fitness level.

For men and women: $\dot{V}O_2$max (ml/kg/min) = 3.5 + 483 ÷ time

Time = time to complete 1.5 miles (2.4 km) in nearest tenth of a minute

For example, if the time to complete the distance was 11:12 (11 minutes and 12 seconds), then the time used in the formula would be 11.2 (12 seconds ÷ 60 seconds = 0.2 minute).

$\dot{V}O_2$max (ml/kg/min) = 3.5 + 483 ÷ 11.2

$\dot{V}O_2$max = 46.6 ml/kg/min

The following are some common mistakes participants make on this test:

- Not warming up sufficiently
- Not pacing correctly

- Forgetting how many laps they have completed

### 4. 12-minute walk/run test

This test requires you to travel as *far* as you can in 12 minutes by walking, running, or using a combination of walking and running. It is important to warm up before you begin this test.

Start a stopwatch when you begin the test. Run if you are able, because this allows you to cover the greatest amount of distance. When 12 minutes have passed, measure the distance traveled. Note that the distance needs to be expressed in meters. To convert yards into meters, multiply yards by 0.9144. For example, 400 yards × 0.9144 = 365.76 meters. Use the formula that follows to calculate your $\dot{V}O_2$max. Compare your scores to the standards for maximal oxygen consumption in table 5.7 to evaluate your cardiorespiratory fitness level.

For men and women: $\dot{V}O_2$max (ml/kg/min) = 0.022351 × (meters covered in 12 minutes) − 11.3

For example, if a person completed 1,463 meters in 12 minutes, then

$\dot{V}O_2$max (ml/kg/min) = 0.022351 × 1,463 − 11.3

$\dot{V}O_2$max = 21.40 ml/kg/min

The following are some common mistakes participants make on this test:

- Not warming up sufficiently
- Not pacing correctly
- Not accurately measuring distance traveled

# References

Abu-Zidan, F., Nagelkerke, N., & Rao, S. (2007). Factors affecting severity of bicycle-related injuries: The role of helmets in preventing head injuries. *Emergency Medicine Australasia, 19*(4), 366–71.

Ahmed, H.M., Blaha, M.J., Nasir, K., Rivera, J.J., & Blumenthal, R.S. (2012). Effects of physical activity on cardiovascular disease. *Am.J.Cardiol., 109,* 288–95.

Arsenault, B.J., Kritikou, E.A., & Tardif, J.C. (2012). Regression of atherosclerosis. *Curr.Cardiol.Rep., 14,* 443–49.

Attewell, R.G., Glase, K., & McFadden, M. (2001). Bicycle helmet efficacy: A meta-analysis. *Accident Analysis and Prevention, 33,* 345–52.

Balbo, M., Leproult, R., & Van, C.E. (2010). Impact of sleep and its disturbances on hypothalamo-pituitary-adrenal axis activity. *Int.J.Endocrinol., 2010,* 1-16.

Barbour, K.A., Edenfield, T.M., & Blumenthal, J.A. (2007). Exercise as a treatment for depression and other psychiatric disorders: A review. *J.Cardiopulm.Rehabil.Prev., 27,* 359–67.

Beccuti, G., & Pannain, S. (2011). Sleep and obesity. *Curr. Opin.Clin.Nutr.Metab Care, 14,* 402–12.

Blair, S.N., & Lamonte, M.J. (2011). Physical activity, fitness, and mortality rates. In C. Buchard, S.N. Blair, & W.L. Haskell (Eds.), *Physical activity and health* (pp. 143–59). Windsor: Human Kinetics.

Blumenthal, J.A., Babyak, M.A., Doraiswamy, P.M., Watkins, L., Hoffman, B.M., Barbour, K.A., et al. (2007). Exercise and pharmacotherapy in the treatment of major depressive disorder. *Psychosom.Med., 69,* 587–96.

Borg, G. (1998). *Borg's perceived exertion and pain scales.* Champaign, IL: Human Kinetics, 47.

Bouchard, C., An, P., Rice, T., Skinner, J.S., Wilmore, J.H., Gagnon, J., et al. (1999). Familial aggregation of VO(2max) response to exercise training: Results from the HERITAGE Family Study. *J.Appl.Physiol, 87,* 1003–8.

Buman, M.P., Hekler, E.B., Bliwise, D.L., & King, A.C. (2011). Moderators and mediators of exercise-induced objective sleep improvements in midlife and older adults with sleep complaints. *Health Psychol. 30*(5): 579-587.

Carroll, S., & Dudfield, M. (2004). What is the relationship between exercise and metabolic abnormalities? A review of the metabolic syndrome. *Sports Med., 34,* 371–418.

Chang, Y.K., Labban, J.D., Gapin, J.I., & Etnier, J.L. (2012). The effects of acute exercise on cognitive performance: A meta-analysis. *Brain Res., 1453,* 87–101.

Chodzko-Zajko, W.J., Proctor, D.N., Fiatarone Singh, M.A., Minson, C.T., Nigg, C.R., Salem, G.J., et al. (2009). American College of Sports Medicine position stand. Exercise and physical activity for older adults. *Med.Sci.Sports Exerc., 41,* 1510–30.

Council on Scientific Affairs American Medical Association. (1994). Helmets and preventing motorcycle- and bicycle-related injuries. *The Journal of the American Medical Association, 272,* 1535–38.

CSEP. (2011). *New Canadian physical activity guidelines.* Canadian Society for Exercise Physiology. www.csep.ca/guidelines.

Deardorff, J. (2006, August 27). Two extremists teach a physical side to faith. *Chicago Tribune.*

Deslandes, A., Moraes, H., Ferreira, C., Veiga, H., Silveira, H., Mouta, R., et al. (2009). Exercise and mental health: Many reasons to move. *Neuropsychobiology, 59,* 191–98.

Donnelly, J.E., Blair, S.N., Jakicic, J.M., Manore, M.M., Rankin, J.W., & Smith, B.K. (2009). Appropriate physical activity intervention strategies for weight loss and prevention of weight regain for adults. *Medicine Science in Sports and Exercise, 41,* 459–71.

Dworak, M., Wiater, A., Alfer, D., Stephan, E., Hollmann, W., & Struder, H.K. (2008). Increased slow wave sleep and reduced stage 2 sleep in children depending on exercise intensity. *Sleep Med., 9,* 266–72.

Erickson, K.I., Voss, M.W., Prakash, R.S., Basak, C., Szabo, A., Chaddock, L., et al. (2011). Exercise training increases size of hippocampus and improves memory. *Proc.Natl. Acad.Sci.USA, 108,* 3017–22.

Fagard, R.H. (1996). Athlete's heart: A meta-analysis of the echocardiographic experience. *Int.J.Sports Med., 17* (Suppl. 3), S140–44.

Fagard, R.H. (2006). Exercise is good for your blood pressure: Effects of endurance training and resistance training. *Clin.Exp.Pharmacol.Physiol., 33,* 853–56.

Foster, C., Florhaug, J.A., Franklin, J., Gottschall, L., Hrovatin, L.A., Parker, S., et al. (2001). A new approach to monitoring exercise training. *J.Strength.Cond.Res., 15,* 109–15.

Franklin, B.A., Whaley, M.H., Howley, E.T., & Balady, G.J. (2000). *ACSM's guidelines for exercise testing and prescription* (6th ed.). Philadelphia: Lippincott Williams & Wilkins.

Garber, C.E., Blissmer, B., Deschenes, M.R., Franklin, B.A., Lamonte, M.J., Lee, I.M., et al. (2011). American College of Sports Medicine position stand. Quantity and quality of exercise for developing and maintaining cardiorespiratory, musculoskeletal, and neuromotor fitness in apparently healthy adults: Guidance for prescribing exercise. *Med.Sci.Sports Exerc., 43,* 1334–59.

Georgia Bike Sense. (2012). *Motorists and cyclists: Sharing Georgia's roads.* http://dot.ga.gov/travelingingeorgia/bikepedestrian/Documents/motorists_cyclists_sharing.pdf.

Gordon, D.J., Knoke, J., Probstfield, J.L., Superko, R., & Tyroler, H.A. (1986). High-density lipoprotein cholesterol and coronary heart disease in hypercholesterolemic men: The Lipid Research Clinics Coronary Primary Prevention Trial. *Circulation, 74,* 1217–25.

Graves, J.E., Martin, A.D., Miltenberger, L.A., & Pollock, M.L. (1988). Physiological responses to walking with hand weights, wrist weights, and ankle weights. *Med.Sci.Sports Exerc., 20,* 265–71.

Hahn, J.U. (2011). The perfect form: Running better, from head to toe. *Runner's World* [Online]. www.runnersworld.com.

Heart and Stroke Foundation. (2011). *Adult needs for physical activity*. Heart and Stroke Foundation [Online]. www.heartandstroke.bc.ca.

Hillman, C.H., Erickson, K.I., & Kramer, A.F. (2008). Be smart, exercise your heart: Exercise effects on brain and cognition. *Nat.Rev.Neurosci., 9,* 58–65.

Hinch, D., & Houston, M. (1987). The effects of replacing endurance running training with cycling in female runners. *Canadian Journal Sport Science, 12,* 131–35.

Janiszewski, P.M., & Ross, R. (2009). The utility of physical activity in the management of global cardiometabolic risk. *Obesity (Silver Spring), 17* (Suppl. 3), S3–14.

Kamijo, K., Hayashi, Y., Sakai, T., Yahiro, T., Tanaka, K., & Nishihira, Y. (2009). Acute effects of aerobic exercise on cognitive function in older adults. *J.Gerontol.B.Psychol. Sci.Soc.Sci., 64,* 356–63.

Kamijo, K., Nishihira, Y., Higashiura, T., & Kuroiwa, K. (2007). The interactive effect of exercise intensity and task difficulty on human cognitive processing. *Int.J.Psychophysiol., 65,* 114–21.

Kiuchi, T., Lee, H., & Mikami, T. (2012). Regular exercise cures depression-like behavior via VEGF-Flk-1 signaling in chronically stressed mice. *Neuroscience, 207,* 208–17.

Kokkinos, P., Sheriff, H., & Kheirbek, R. (2011). Physical inactivity and mortality risk. *Cardiol.Res.Pract., 2011,* 924–45.

Lambourne, K., & Tomporowski, P. (2010). The effect of exercise-induced arousal on cognitive task performance: A meta-regression analysis. *Brain Res., 1341,* 12–24.

Leproult, R., & Van, C.E. (2010). Role of sleep and sleep loss in hormonal release and metabolism. *Endocr.Dev., 17,* 11–21.

Mayo Foundation for Medical Education and Research. (2011). *Proper walking technique*. Mayo Foundation for Medical Education and Research [Online]. www.mayoclinic.com/health/medical/IM02436.

McArdle, W.D., Katch, F.L., & Katch, V. (2001). *Exercise physiology* (5th ed.). Baltimore: Lippincott, Williams & Wilkins.

National Strength and Conditioning Association. (2008). *Essentials of strength training and conditioning* (3rd ed.). Champaign, IL: Human Kinetics.

Nieman, D.C. (1997). Immune response to heavy exertion. *J.Appl.Physiol., 82,* 1385–94.

Pedersen, B.K., & Hoffman-Goetz, L. (2000). Exercise and the immune system: Regulation, integration, and adaptation. *Physiol. Rev., 80,* 1055–81.

Perraton, L.G., Kumar, S., & Machotka, Z. (2010). Exercise parameters in the treatment of clinical depression: A systematic review of randomized controlled trials. *J.Eval. Clin.Pract., 16,* 597–604.

Pluim, B.M., Zwinderman, A.H., van der Laarse, A., & van der Wall, E.E. (2000). The athlete's heart. A meta-analysis of cardiac structure and function. *Circulation, 101,* 336–44.

Raglin, J., Winberg, J.O., & Galper, D. (2007). Exercise and its effects on mental health. In C. Bouchard, S.N. Blair, & W.L. Haskell (Eds.), *Physical Activity and Health* (pp. 247–70). Windsor: Human Kinetics.

Rhind, S.G., Shek, P.N., Shinkai, S., & Shephard, R.J. (1996). Effects of moderate endurance exercise and training on in vitro lymphocyte proliferation, interleukin-2 (IL-2) production, and IL-2 receptor expression. *Eur.J.Appl.Physiol Occup.Physiol, 74,* 348–60.

Rivara, F.P., Thompson, D.C., & Thompson, R.S. (2000). Bicycle helmets: It's time to use them. *British Medical Journal, 321,* 1035–36.

Ross R., & Janssen, I. (2007). Physical activity, fitness, and obesity. In C. Bouchard, S.N. Blair, & W.L. Haskell (Eds.), *Physical Activity and Health*. Windsor: Human Kinetics.

Shephard, R.J., Rhind, S., & Shek, P.N. (1994). Exercise and the immune system. Natural killer cells, interleukins and related responses. *Sports Med., 18,* 340–69.

Smith, P.J., Blumenthal, J.A., Hoffman, B.M., Cooper, H., Strauman, T.A., Welsh-Bohmer, K., et al. (2010). Aerobic exercise and neurocognitive performance: A meta-analytic review of randomized controlled trials. *Psychosom. Med., 72,* 239–52.

Spaite, D.W., Murphy, M., & Criss, E.A., Valenzuela, T.D., Meislin, H.W. (1991). A prospective analysis of injury severity among helmeted and nonhelmeted bicyclists in collisions with motor vehicles. *The Journal of Trauma and Acute Care Surgery, 31,* 1510–16.

Statistics Canada. (2007). *Physically active Canadians*. www.statcan.gc.ca/daily-quotidien/070822/dq070822b-eng.htm.

Statistics Canada. (2011a). *Canadian Health Measures Survey: Physical activity of youth and adults*. www.statcan.gc.ca/daily-quotidien/110119/dq110119b-eng.htm.

Statistics Canada. (2011b). *Canadian Health Measures Survey: Adult obesity prevalence in Canada and the United States*. http://www.statcan.gc.ca/daily-quotidien/110302/dq110302c-eng.htm.

Statistics Canada. (2011c). *Leading causes of death*. www.statcan.gc.ca/daily-quotidien/101130/dq101130b-eng.htm.

Tanaka, H., Monahan, K.D., & Seals, D.R. (2001). Age-predicted maximal heart rate revisited. *J.Am.Coll.Cardiol., 37,* 153–56.

Thompson, D.C., Rivara, F.P., & Thompson, R. (1999). Helmets for preventing head and facial injuries in bicyclists. *Cochrane Database of Systematic Reviews, 4*(1–31).

Tomporowski, P.D., Lambourne, K., & Okumura, M.S. (2011). Physical activity interventions and children's mental function: An introduction and overview. *Prev.Med., 52* (Suppl. 1), S3–9.

Unintentional Injury. (2002). www.health.state.mn.us/strategies/injury.pdf.

U.S. Department of Transportation. (2010). *Traffic safety facts.* www-nrd.nhtsa.dot.gov/Pubs/811363.pdf.

Vehicular Cycling. (2007). *Cyclist fatality trends in Canada.* www.vehicularcyclist.com/fatals.html.

Walsh, N.P., Gleeson, M., Shephard, R.J., Gleeson, M., Woods, J.A., Bishop, N.C., et al. (2011). Position statement. Part one: Immune function and exercise. *Exerc. Immunol.Rev., 17,* 6–63.

Westcott, W.L. (2012). Resistance training is medicine: Effects of strength training on health. *Curr. Sports Med. Rep., 11,* 209–16.

Wilmore, J.H., Costill, D.L., & Kenney, W.L. (2008). *Physiology of Sport and Exercise* (4th ed.). Champaign, IL: Human Kinetics.

Yakeu, G., Butcher, L., Isa, S., Webb, R., Roberts, A.W., Thomas, A.W., et al. (2010). Low-intensity exercise enhances expression of markers of alternative activation in circulating leukocytes: Roles of PPARgamma and Th2 cytokines. *Atherosclerosis, 212,* 668–73.

YMCA. (1989). *Y's Way to physical fitness* (3rd ed.). Champaign, IL: Human Kinetics.

## Suggested Readings

Bishop, J.G. (2010). *Fitness through aerobics* (8th ed.). San Francisco: Benjamin Cummings.

Methodologies for performing all types of aerobic dance exercises are outlined. It illustrates step-by-step exercises, highlights various exercise methodologies, and teaches injury prevention.

Cooper, K.H. (1991). *The aerobics program for total well-being: Exercise, diet, emotional balance.* New York: Bantam.

This book discusses how cardiovascular fitness fits into holistic health.

Foran, B. (2001). *High-performance sports conditioning.* Champaign, IL: Human Kinetics.

Everyone from weekend warrior to competitive athletes can benefit from this guide to aerobic training for athletes.

Lee, B. (2010). *Jump rope training* (2nd ed.). Champaign, IL: Human Kinetics.

Think jumping rope is for grade-school children? Think again. This book shows you how to get an incredible cardiovascular workout in minutes. One of the best things about learning to jump rope for exercise is that you can do it almost anywhere.

Stokes, R., & Trapp, D.E. (2004). *Aerobic fitness everyone* (3rd ed.). Winston-Salem, NC: Hunter Textbooks.

Designed as a textbook for aerobic conditioning and dance, the goal of this book is to teach students to maximize their cardiovascular function.

## Suggested Websites

**www.acsm.com**

The American College of Sports Medicine prepares position papers for exercise and activity recommendations and helpful tips for healthy adults, aging, and special populations.

**www.csep.com**

Visit the Canadian Society for Exercise Physiology website to find the current Canadian national recommendations for activity levels.

**www.fitness.gov**

President's Council on Physical Fitness and Sports. Although the target audience is primarily grade school–age children, a host of health-related material is available.

**www.halhigdon.com**

One of the best sites for beginning to intermediate runners who are running anything from a 5K to marathon road races.

**www.mapmyrun.com**

If you want to plan a running route for a certain distance or find out how far you ran, this is an excellent and free website that helps you make just those calculations. Type in your starting address, click on the starting point, click on the next corner in your route, and you begin to build your route and automatically add up the distance.

**www.phac-aspc.gc.ca/new_e.html**

Canadian guidelines for physical activity and nutrition. A well-designed site with excellent health information.

**www.shapeup.org/shape/steps.php**

Shape Up America: 10,000 steps program. A wealth of walking information targeted toward individuals who are just getting started on a fitness program.

**www.totalimmersion.net**

Instructional swimming material. One of the best resources for learning how to swim efficiently and for long enough to get a cardiovascular workout.

## Twitter

On Twitter, follow @HeartDiseases, @TheHSF, @American_Heart.

# Muscular Strength Assessment and Training

Peter Walters

After reading this chapter, you should be able to do the following:

1. Outline five major benefits of strength training.
2. Understand basic muscle anatomy and physiology.
3. Be able to evaluate muscular strength and muscular endurance.
4. Identify the primary types of resistance training and advantages and disadvantages of each.
5. Perform a beginning strength-training program.
6. List seven guidelines for safe weightlifting.

**The Greek** civilization flourished politically, scientifically, intellectually, and architecturally during the sixth, fifth, and fourth centuries BC. Democracy was invented, astronomy was developed, Plato philosophized, and Sophocles wrote great tragedies. People credited the gods for these successes and held religious festivals to honor them. Athletic competitions, which began as peripheral parts of these celebrations, soon became the main attraction. None was more famous than the ancient Olympic Games (Harris, 1993).

Probably the greatest champion of the ancient Olympics was the wrestler Milo of Croton (Harris, 1966). Born near the end of the sixth century BC, Milo competed until he was more than 40 years old and was the only man ever to win six consecutive Olympic victories. Legend has it that Milo could break a ribbon tied across his brow just by expanding the veins in his forehead. After his victories, Milo reportedly cooked a small bull, ate all of it, and washed it down with nine quarts of wine (Harris, 1966). Unlike Hercules, Milo's mythical hero, Milo achieved his strength through resistance training. **Resistance training** (more commonly called strength training) refers to lifting weights that vary in load, in order to develop increased muscular tone and strength.

The goal of this chapter is not to teach you how to obtain the strength of Milo of Croton. Rather, it is to help you obtain lifelong health benefits, such as reducing your risk of injury, increasing your metabolic rate, pleasantly altering your body shape, and having the strength to act with goodness toward God, others, and yourself. This chapter is for people who are new to strength training, so if you have been intimidated by athletes grunting and groaning, or by the complexity of the equipment you see in most weight rooms, this chapter is for you. By the end of this chapter you'll not only know how muscles function, understand resistance-training terminology, and know how to not get injured while lifting, you will be given an effective, easy-to-follow strength-training program.

The end result of developing strength is not about bulging biceps, bench pressing double your body weight, or even preventing neuromuscular injuries. In the final analysis, strength should bring about goodness—the goodness of God. At times, goodness must be supported by strength.

In his day, Jesus recognized the existence of evil forces whose primary aim was to steal, kill, and destroy any goodness in the lives of the people (John 10:10). Not only did he recognize evil, he moved

 ## World's Strongest Man

Paul Anderson was born in Taccoa, Georgia, on October 17, 1932. He would ultimately become one of the most dominant strongmen in the world. At 5 feet 9 inches (175 cm) and 360 pounds (163 kg), Anderson was the first man to lift 450 pounds (204 kg) from the floor to overhead. Olympic and world champion, Anderson held 18 American and 9 world records. In 1957, Anderson earned the title of world's strongest man from Guinness World Records because he lifted 6,270 pounds (2,844 kg) off the ground (Guinness World Records, 1957).

Paul Anderson speaking to a group of prison inmates.

After achieving stardom, Anderson traveled around the world giving approximately 500 strength exhibitions each year. During his demonstrations, Anderson would lift a platform holding 8 to 10 adult men, hoist a 300-pound (136 kg) dumbbell above this head, and drive a 20-penny nail through a 2-inch (5 cm) board with his bare hands. Such feats are inconceivable to most people. To Anderson, who on some occasions repeated these performances three times in one day, they seemed like child's play. Yet this behemoth of a man concluded every incredible display of strength by simply saying, "They call me the world's strongest man, but I'm telling you that the world's strongest man could not live one day without Jesus Christ" (Jenkins, 1975, p. 110).

powerfully against it. One of the most common miracles that Jesus performed was driving out evil spirits. When a group of religious zealots, called the Pharisees, saw Jesus casting out demons, they said he did this by the power of the "prince of demons" (Beelzebub). Notice Jesus's reply in Matthew 12:24–29:

> Every kingdom divided against itself will be ruined, and every city or household divided against itself will not stand. If Satan drives out Satan, he is divided against himself. How then can his kingdom stand? . . . But if I drive out demons by the Spirit of God, then the kingdom of God has come upon you. Or again, how can anyone enter a strong man's house and carry off his possessions unless he first ties up the strong man?

Not only did Jesus refute their claims on the basis of simple logic, he specifically mentioned strength as a necessary ingredient for this type of goodness. Moving into Satan's territory is just as fierce as claiming gang turf in any urban area of a major city. It's not work for the weak.

The prophet Micah outlines a less confrontational form of goodness in Micah 6:8: "He has showed you, O man, what is good. And what does the Lord require of you? To act justly and to love mercy and to walk humbly with your God."

This goodness sounds softer and more genteel than casting out demons. But if you think justice, mercy, and humility come from being weak, you've probably never tried to help oppressed people receive justice or to walk in humility in a culture that promotes self-promotion. This type of goodness is not only difficult—it is impossible. The apostle Paul recognized this when he wrote, "I have the desire to do what is good, but I cannot carry it out" (Romans 7:18). Men and women should be thankful to have a power (the Holy Spirit) that transcends human strength and bears the fruit of goodness. It is only through God's power that humans can bring about goodness in this world.

# Five Major Benefits of Strength Training

Although you may not have Olympic aspirations, you may have considered pumping iron to shape and firm your body. What you may not know is that lifting weights can also help boost your fat-burning metabolism, develop strong bones, reduce your risk of injury, and can significantly enhance your functional capacity. Many experts list more than a dozen beneficial effects resulting from strength training. In an effort not to overwhelm, this section will detail the following five major benefits of strength training:

1. Shapes your body
2. Helps boost fat-burning metabolism
3. Assists in building strong bones
4. Reduces risk of neuromuscular injury
5. Enhances functional capacity

## Shapes Your Body

A common misconception (and sometimes fear) among women is that if they lift weights, they may end up with muscles like a man's. Actually, women have little to fear. Women do have hypertrophic capacities (see figure 6.1). **Hypertrophy** means muscle enlargement and is the opposite of **atrophy**, or muscle shrinkage. However, women's capacity to enlarge their muscles is much more limited than men's. One of the main reasons for this disparity is hormonal; men have 20 to 30 times more testosterone than women do, as figure 6.2 illustrates (McGlynn & Moran, 1997). High levels of testosterone help create a positive environment for building muscle. Another contributing factor is that although women have the same number of muscles that men have, from birth women have fewer individual fibers

**Figure 6.1** Bev Francis, champion female bodybuilder.

**Minimum and maximum levels of testosterone for women and men**

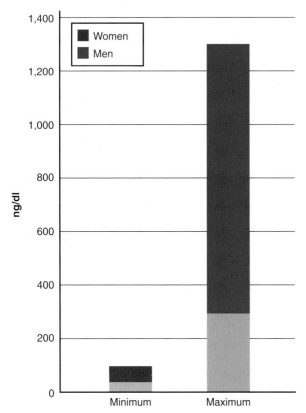

**Figure 6.2**  Men have 20 to 30 times more testosterone than women have.

**Figure 6.3**  Corrie Walters lost 10 pounds (4.5 kg) of fat and gained 4.2 pounds (1.9 kg) of muscle.

(Incledon, 2005). These and other factors contribute to women on average having about half (40 to 60 percent) of the upper-body strength and three-quarters (65 to 85 percent) of the lower-body strength of their male counterparts.

Women who lift weights are much more likely to achieve results like those seen in figures 6.3 and 6.4. These before-and-after photographs depict females who participated in an experimental 16-week resistance-training course. These pictures, rather than figure 6.1, illustrate the more typical **body composition** changes women can achieve through strength training. The average female in this 16-week class lost 11.7 pounds (5.3 kg) of fat while gaining 3.7 pounds (1.7 kg) of muscle. (Body composition changes were measured with a Bodpod, which measures changes in body composition via air displacement. This method of testing body composition is comparable to hydrostatic measures.) This experimental class was required to adhere to a strict regimen of not only resistance training but also of diet. Therefore, these changes are not representative of people who lift weights only.

**Figure 6.4**  Elizabeth Woodson lost 22 pounds of fat (10 kg) and gained 3.8 pounds (1.7 kg) of muscle.

## Helps Boost Fat-Burning Metabolism

Weight training turns the body into a fat-burning machine. Here is how. **Resting metabolic rate (RMR)**, the rate at which the body burns calories when completely inactive, is profoundly affected by the amount of **lean body mass** a person has. Each pound (0.45 kg) of muscle burns 30 to 40 calories per day at rest (Darden, 1995; Westcott, 1994), making it the most metabolically active substance in the body. (By contrast, a pound of fat burns one to two calories per day.) It follows that a person who gains 5 pounds of muscle (2.3 kg) will burn 150 to 200 more calories per day *doing nothing*.

The power of resistance training to affect fat has been well documented. In one study (Westcott, 1994), 72 men and women agreed to exercise for 30 minutes a day, three days a week, for 12 weeks. Twenty-two of the participants spent the entire 30 minutes in cardiovascular exercise. The other 50 participants divided their workouts into 15 minutes of aerobic exercise and 15 minutes of strength training. Table 6.1 shows the changes in body composition for each group.

In a more recent scientific review comparing the effects of fat loss using either high-intensity exercise, namely resistance training, to steady-state aerobic exercise, Dr. Stephen Boutcher, at the University of South Wales School of Medicine, reported that high-intensity strength training was much more effective at lowering fat (Boutcher, 2011).

The average adult between the ages of 30 and 65 loses half a pound (0.2 kg) of muscle per year (Westcott, 1994). This means that if caloric intake is unchanged, adults burn approximately 6,387.5 fewer calories per year (since 0.5 lb. of muscle burns 17.5 calories per day, 1 lb of muscle burns approximately 35, multiplied by 365 days = 6,387.5). No wonder most adults experience creeping obesity, a gain of one or two pounds, or a kilogram, of fat per year as they get older (described in chapter 4).

Figures 6.5 and 6.6 show the changes that occurred in two men who participated in the 16-week

## Table 6.1 Changes in Body Composition as a Result of Strength and Endurance Training

| Exercise | Weight change | Fat | Muscle |
|---|---|---|---|
| Strength + endurance | −8.0 lb (3.6 kg) | −10.0 lb (4.5 kg) | +2.0 lb (0.91 kg) |
| Endurance only | −4.0 lb (1.8 kg) | −4.0 lb (1.8 kg) | +0 lb |

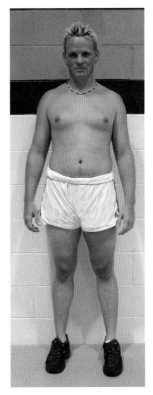

**Figure 6.5** Brandon Lochstampfor lost 16.8 pounds (7.6 kg) of fat.

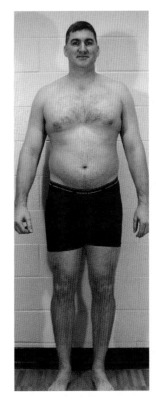

**Figure 6.6** Bob Norris, who started at a body weight of 264.7 pounds (120 kg), lost 39.3 pounds (17.8 kg) of fat.

## Effect of 5,004 Sit-Ups on Abdominal Fat

Dr. Frank Katch and other investigators set out to determine the effect of 5,004 sit-ups on abdominal fat (Katch et al., 1984). After measuring total body fat hydrostatically (underwater) and taking fat biopsies of the abdomen, subscapular, and gluteal regions, 13 men began a progressive sit-up routine for 27 days. As a group, the men performed a total of 5,004 sit-ups. Although cell diameter at all three biopsy sites decreased significantly, the study measured no significant differences in the rate of fat change in the abdominal area compared to the other areas measured (e.g., the gluteal and subscapular).

This study was one more well-designed and controlled investigation that refutes the myth of spot reduction. The theory of spot reduction suggests that by exercising muscles around the region of the body that has too much fat, a person can reduce fat in that spot. For example, a person who wants to burn fat on the thighs would do many exercises that involve the quadriceps and hamstring muscles.

One study that tested this theory in a clever manner involved competitive tennis players. Tennis players exercise their dominant arms much more than their nondominant ones, so if spot reduction were possible, it would be evident among this group. When researchers measured the composition of muscle and fat in both arms, they found that the amount of muscle was significantly different, but there were no significant differences in the amount of fat (Gwinup et al., 1971).

resistance-training experiment cited earlier. The average man in this study, whose aim was to lose fat while building muscle, lost a little more than 1 pound (0.45 kg) of fat per week, or 18.3 pounds (8.3 kg) overall.

## Assists in Building Strong Bones

Most people know that resistance training strengthens muscles, but few realize that it strengthens bones as well. Weight training delays and prevents the loss of bone tissue. Bones consist of hard weblike structures of collagen fibers, calcium, and other minerals; this part of the bone is called the **bone matrix**. The structure of bone matrix leaves gaps in the web, which is filled with bone marrow and blood vessels. **Osteoporosis** (derived from the Greek words for *bone* and *porous*) is the breakdown of the bone mineral web, which makes the bone more vulnerable to compression and shear fractures. This process tends to happen with aging: 55 percent of people over age 50 have low bone density (National Osteoporosis Foundation, 2012). Figure 6.7 illustrates how bone mineral density is affected by osteoporosis (National Osteoporosis Society, 2012).

Although scientists do not completely understand the causes of osteoporosis, its general progression is well-documented. Bones are constantly being broken down and regenerated. In resorption, cells called **osteoclasts** break down bone matrix and release minerals, such as calcium, into the blood. Likewise, cells called **osteoblasts** are responsible for rebuilding the matrix that eventually becomes

mineralized and forms bone (Feng & McDonald, 2011). In young people, the latter process more than compensates for the former, but with age the balance between the two processes becomes more problematic. Bone density peaks between ages 20 and 30, but after this climax there is often a faster rate of bone resorption than growth. The decline is especially apparent in older women because after menopause there is a decrease in the release of estrogen, a hormone that plays a role in inhibiting bone resorption.

Researchers have known that calcium supplements help prevent osteoporosis, but recent research indicates that resistance training may be just as important if not more important than ingesting adequate levels of calcium. In one study, 39 women

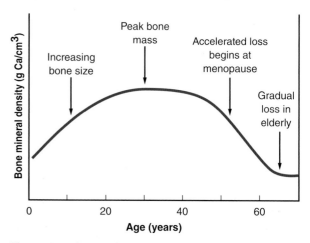

**Figure 6.7**    Bone mineral density begins deteriorating in most people after age 25.

were divided into two groups. Both groups had adequate calcium intake, but the first group did strength training twice a week while the second group did not. After one year, testing revealed that, on average, bone mineral density decreased by 2 percent in the second group but increased by 1 percent in the group that participated in strength training (Dornemann, 1997). Many other studies have shown similar results for women, but a more recent study analyzed the effect of weight-bearing resistance training on the bone density of men. One hundred and eighty men between the ages of 50 and 79 years old were divided into four groups: one that only exercised, one that drank calcium-fortified milk, one that both exercised and consumed fortified milk, and the control group, which did not exercise or drink fortified milk. After 18 months, the results indicated that fortified milk, whether alone or combined with exercise, did not enhance bone mineral density whereas the multicomponent exercise program significantly increased the bone density in the femoral neck and lumbar spine (Kukuljan et al., 2011).

## Reduces Risk of Neuromuscular Injury

Eric Helland, strength and conditioning coach of the Chicago Bulls basketball team, once said, "Without a doubt, the number one reason I want my athletes in the weight room is that it protects them from injury" (personal communication, June 2009). Whether you're a multimillion-dollar sports star or a weekend warrior, resistance training builds not only muscular strength but tendon and ligament stability along with skeletal integrity. This enhancement of muscle, bone, and connective tissue has a dramatic effect on lowering one's chance of injury.

One example of the potency of strength training to reduce injury rates is provided by the widespread struggle with lower-back pain. Lower-back pain is the second most common health problem in the United States, ranking just below the common cold (Wipf & Deyo, 1995). Eight out of ten people will have lower-back pain at some point in their lives (Eidelson, 2006), and one-fourth of U.S. adults report having lower-back pain in the past 3 months (Deyo et al., 2006). Back pain is responsible for more days in the hospital than any other medical condition except childbirth (Reynolds et al., 1990). At any given time, 31 million Americans have lower-back pain; 80 million Americans have recurring back distress (Sharkey, 2002). All this pain and suffering costs individuals, companies, and the entire health care system a significant amount of money. The average

cost for an American with lower-back pain is $6,000 per occurrence. Liberty Mutual Insurance Company, the largest payer of workers' compensation claims, pays out $1 million each day to cover claims from people with lower-back maladies. The total estimated cost of lower-back pain is $20 billion per year (CDC, 2008). These statistics have been used to argue that the lower back is the weakest link in the human muscular chain. Although that is debatable, there is no question that lower-back pain is a serious health care concern.

Although the role of strength training in preventing and treating back injuries is still being investigated, growing evidence suggests that the strength of the lower back plays an important role. One long-term study examined the effect of lower-back strengthening on 50 postmenopausal women. Those who engaged in resistance exercises not only had greater bone mineral density but also experienced far fewer back injuries. In fact, the control group, which did not perform any resistance exercises for the lower back, had 2.7 times more lumbar factures than the strength-training group during an eight-year period (Sinaki et al., 2002). This is only one of the many studies suggesting a relationship between greater lower-back strength and reduced lower-back pain and injury (Seung-Houn et al., 2004; Wheeler, 1995).

Two strength-training exercises that strengthen the lower back and protect it against injury are illustrated in figures 6.8 and 6.9. You can adjust the resistance in the incline back extension (figure 6.8) exercise by simply changing your arm placement. Placing your arms beside the hips is a good place to start because that reduces the amount of resistance you are working against. When your lower back gets stronger, try crossing your arms in front of your chest while performing this movement, which raises your center of gravity and makes the exercise more strenuous.

## Enhances Functional Capacity

Weight training enables harder and longer work. The ability to do physical work is called **functional capacity**. The average person's functional capacity peaks between the ages of 20 and 25, is maintained until about age 30, and then slowly begins to decline. Of the many factors that influence functional capacity, muscular strength is one of the most important. It is impossible to move without contracting a muscle.

An increase in muscular strength—that is, the ability to exert more force—is perhaps the biggest result

**Figure 6.8**    Seated back extension. Lean back so your upper back is in a straight line with your legs.

**Figure 6.9**    Incline back extension. Rise up so your upper back is in a straight line with your legs.

of weight training and the first one you will notice when you begin a training program. Gains happen fastest at the beginning; several studies report a 30 to 40 percent increase in strength after only three months (Westcott, 1994). Weight training benefits people of all ages, too. Participants in a study of people over age 90 on average more than doubled their strength after three months of weight training (Fiatarone, 2002).

People with sedentary desk jobs may think it is not important for them to have muscular strength, but this is far from true. One study showed that participants lost, on average, 30 percent of their neck strength simply by sitting at a desk for eight hours

(Westcott, 1994). Subtle changes like these decrease energy and drain levels of productivity.

To summarize, resistance training has the potential to dramatically alter the shape of one's body, increase metabolic rate, enhance bone mineral density, reduce risk of injury, and increase one's ability to work and play. Do you need any more incentives?

## Basic Muscle Anatomy

To understand muscular strength, it is first necessary to understand the way muscle functions in the body. There are three basic types of muscle. **Cardiac** muscle is found only in the heart and is specialized to produce the powerful contractions that pump blood throughout the body. The contractions of cardiac muscle are not under voluntary control but instead are controlled automatically by the nervous system. **Smooth muscle** is the other type of involuntary muscle and is located in all other muscles not under thoughtful control. Examples include the digestive organs, the blood vessel walls, and the reproductive system organs. **Skeletal muscle** is the third type of muscle and is the only type that is under voluntary control. This muscle is used to produce body movement and is responsible for what is called muscular strength. Skeletal muscle is the type studied in this chapter.

The contractions of all skeletal muscles occur because of microscopic contractions of the cells that make up the muscle. A muscle cell is called a **sarcomere**, and the contraction of each sarcomere is caused by interaction between the two types of protein that run the length of the cell. The thick filament, made of the protein **myosin**, has extensions called heads that attach to the thin filament, made of the protein **actin**. The myosin heads can pull the thin filaments so that the thick and thin filaments slide past each other, making the whole cell shorter. When this process occurs throughout an entire muscle, the muscle itself shortens.

Muscles are made up of cells. These cells are bound to each other to form strands, so that the protein filaments go through the entire strand. Muscle fiber is made up of strands, called **myofibrils**. Whole groups of muscle fibers that are covered by a connective tissue sheath (called **fascia**, as in figure 6.10) make up a muscle.

## Basic Muscle Physiology

All voluntary muscle contractions begin in one place: the brain. Signals originate in the cerebellum, the region at the back of the brain that coordinates movement and balance. From there, the nerve signals pass through the spinal cord until they reach the motor neuron that communicates with the target muscle. A motor neuron conveys signals from the brain and spinal cord to another part of the body to cause a change in that tissue. Each motor neuron has a specific group of muscle fibers that it connects to and communicates with; combined, the motor neuron and muscle fibers are called a **motor unit**. Small motor units allow precise, delicate movements, such as swiveling the eyeballs. Large motor units, like those in the thigh muscles, enable forceful tasks like running or jumping.

The strength of a muscular contraction depends on two things: how many motor units of the muscle were used in the contraction and what type of muscle fibers are recruited. A muscle fiber contracts either 100 percent or not at all, depending on whether that fiber's motor neuron signaled contraction or not. For example, much less force is needed in the biceps to lift a 5-pound weight compared to a 10-pound weight. Yet this difference is not because all of the fibers are half contracted; instead, it is because only half of the muscle fibers are contracted and the rest are not contracted at all. In order to produce stronger contractions, the nervous system recruits more motor units.

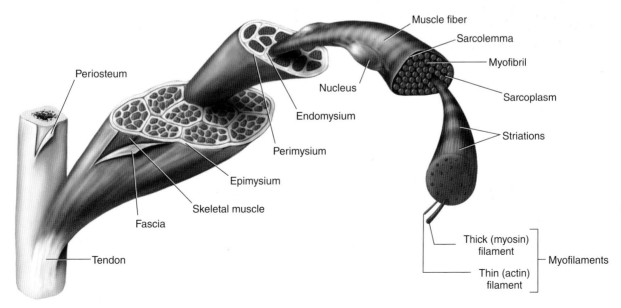

**Figure 6.10** The structure of skeletal muscle.

## Muscle Fiber Types

Three types of muscle fiber are used to do work (see table 6.2). Fast-twitch fibers (also called Type IIB) produce great force and contract very rapidly, but they produce energy anaerobically (without oxygen), which means that they fatigue quickly and cannot sustain contraction for very long. In contrast to these, slow-twitch fibers (also called Type I) produce less force and contract more slowly, but they are much more fatigue resistant because they use oxygen to produce energy, so they can sustain contraction for a long time. The final type of muscle fiber, intermediate-twitch fiber (also called Type IIA), has characteristics in common with both slow- and fast-twitch fibers. Intermediate-twitch fibers use oxygen to produce energy for contraction, but they contract more rapidly than slow-twitch fibers. These three types of fiber are found throughout the body's muscles but in varying concentrations based on the functions of the muscles. For example, the back muscles that enable a person to stand erect do not require great amounts of force, but they do need to be able to sustain contraction for a long time. These muscles are therefore made primarily of slow-twitch fibers.

## Some Major Muscles

While it is important to understand the way muscles work, it is also important to know some of the major muscles you exercise when strength training. Everyone, male or female, has 614 skeletal muscles, but for strength training, you need to be familiar with about a dozen of them. Figure 6.11 identifies each of the muscles you should know.

It is good to know basic muscle anatomy for at least two reasons. First, when performing exercises that target specific muscles groups, it helps to know where you should feel the tension or strain. Even more important, when designing a strength-training program, you want to train all the major muscles of the body. Although it may sound a bit overwhelming to work all major muscles previously described, for simplicity these muscles are grouped into six major body regions. Those body regions and the muscles they include are outlined in table 6.3. At the end of this chapter, you will see how each of these body regions is included in the strength-training program.

## Assessing Muscular Strength

To know how to get to your destination, you first need to know where you are. Any strength-training program should begin with a measurement of your current strength level. Milo, the Greek wrestler cited at the start of this chapter, could carry a newborn calf that weighed from 60 to 90 pounds (27 and 41 kg) the length of the Olympic stadium, which was a little more than 100 meters. Fortunately, things have changed somewhat since Milo's day, and you can assess your ability without bearing barnyard beasts on your back. The application activities throughout this chapter include tests that measure both muscular strength and muscular endurance.

**Muscular strength** is the ability of a muscle or muscle group to generate maximal force, and it is usually tested by trying to lift as much weight as possible one time. Lifting as much weight as possible for one repetition is commonly referred to as a **one-repetition maximum** (1 RM). **Muscular endurance** is the ability of a muscle or muscle group to maintain a contraction or to perform repeated submaximal contractions over an extended period of time. Muscular endurance is usually tested by lifting a submaximal load as many times as possible.

The following five assessment measures test both muscular strength and muscular endurance of various major muscles of the body.

1. **Grip test**

    This test requires you to grip a handheld dynamometer as forcefully as possible with the right hand and then the left hand. Prepare for this test by adjusting the grip bar to fit comfortably within your hand. The second joint of the fingers should fit under the handle of

### Table 6.2    Muscle Fiber Types

|  | Contraction time | Contraction force | Energy efficiency economy | Fatigue resistance |
|---|---|---|---|---|
| Type I | Low | Low | High | High |
| Type IIA | High | High | Low | Low |
| Type IIB | High | High | Low | Low |

Adapted from McArdle, Katch, and Katch 2001.

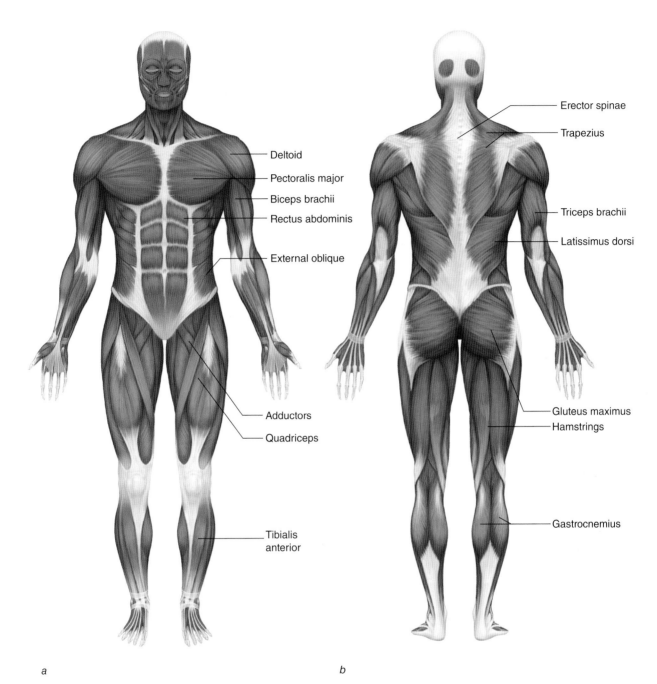

**Figure 6.11** Primary muscles to know for resistance training.

## Table 6.3 Six Primary Body Regions and Corresponding Muscles

| Body region | Primary muscles |
|---|---|
| Legs | Gluteus maximus, quadriceps, hamstrings, adductors, gastrocnemius, tibialis anterior |
| Back | Trapezius, latissimus dorsi, erector spinae |
| Abdominals | Rectus abdominis, external oblique |
| Chest | Pectoralis major |
| Shoulders | Deltoid |
| Arms | Biceps, triceps |

**Figure 6.14** *(a)* Females should perform the push-up test with the lower body supported by the knees. *(b)* Starting position for the men's push-up test. *(c)* Triceps must be at least parallel to the floor.

**Table 6.5  Standards for One-Minute Push-Up Test**

| Age (years) | 15-19 | | 20-29 | | 30-39 | | 40-49 | | 50-59 | | 60-69 | |
|---|---|---|---|---|---|---|---|---|---|---|---|---|
| Sex | M | F | M | F | M | F | M | F | M | F | M | F |
| Excellent | ≥52 | ≥43 | ≥46 | ≥40 | ≥30 | ≥27 | ≥22 | ≥24 | ≥21 | ≥21 | ≥18 | ≥17 |
| Above Average | 40-51 | 35-42 | 35-45 | 31-39 | 22-29 | 20-26 | 17-21 | 15-23 | 13-20 | 11-20 | 11-17 | 12-16 |
| Average | 23-39 | 18-35 | 22-35 | 15-30 | 17-21 | 13-19 | 13-16 | 11-14 | 10-12 | 7-10 | 8-10 | 5-11 |
| Below average | 18-27 | 12-17 | 17-21 | 10-14 | 12-16 | 8-12 | 10-12 | 5-10 | 7-9 | 2-6 | 5-7 | 1-4 |
| Poor | ≤17 | ≤11 | ≤16 | ≤9 | ≤11 | ≤7 | ≤9 | ≤4 | ≤6 | ≤1 | ≤4 | ≤1 |

Data from Cooper-Institute for Aerobics Research 1994.

 **How Many Push-Ups Are Possible?**

Here are some world records for push-ups:

- *Most push-ups in one minute*: 138, by Roy Berger, Canada, 2004 (Guinness Book of World Records, 2011)
- *Most push-ups in one hour*: 3,416, by Roy Berger, Canada, 1998 (Guinness Book of World Records, 2011)
- *Most consecutive (without stopping) push-ups*: 10,507, by Minoru Yoshida, Japan, 1980 (Linster, 1999)
- *Most push-ups in one year*: 1,500,230, by Paddy Doyle, UK, 1988–1989 (Guinness Book of World Records, 2011)

Bend your knees to approximately 90 degrees and place your feet shoulder-width apart. Someone or something will need to keep your feet from moving during this test. Cross your arms and place your hands on your shoulders (see figure 6.15a). Keep your hands in this position throughout the test. Start the one-minute timing device. Curl your abdomen forward, flexing your upper body until your elbows touch your knees (see figure 6.15b). Return to the starting position. This marks the end of one repetition. Repeat this movement as many times as possible in one minute and record the total number of repetitions you complete. Compare your test results to the standards for the one-minute sit-up test found in table 6.6 to evaluate your muscular endurance.

The following are common mistakes made on the one-minute sit-up test:

- Failing to complete the full range of motion (e.g., not touching the elbows to the knees

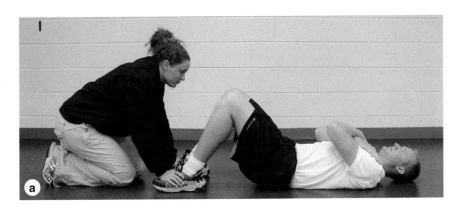

**Figure 6.15**  (a) The beginning position for the sit-up test. (b) Elbows must touch the knees for a complete sit-up to be performed.

### Table 6.6    Standards for One-Minute Sit-Up Test

| Age (years) | 15-19 | | 20-29 | | 30-39 | | 40-49 | | 50-59 | | 60-69 | |
|---|---|---|---|---|---|---|---|---|---|---|---|---|
| Sex | M | F | M | F | M | F | M | F | M | F | M | F |
| Excellent | ≥48 | ≥42 | ≥43 | ≥36 | ≥36 | ≥29 | ≥31 | ≥25 | ≥26 | ≥19 | ≥23 | ≥16 |
| Above Average | 42-47 | 36-41 | 37-42 | 31-35 | 31-35 | 24-28 | 26-30 | 20-24 | 22-25 | 12-18 | 17-22 | 12-15 |
| Average | 38-41 | 32-35 | 33-36 | 25-30 | 27-30 | 20-23 | 22-25 | 15-19 | 18-21 | 5-11 | 12-16 | 4-11 |
| Below average | 33-37 | 27-31 | 29-32 | 21-24 | 22-26 | 15-19 | 17-21 | 7-14 | 13-17 | 3-4 | 7-11 | 2-3 |
| Poor | ≤32 | ≤26 | ≤28 | ≤20 | ≤21 | ≤14 | ≤16 | ≤6 | ≤12 | ≤2 | ≤6 | ≤1 |

Data from Cooper-Institute for Aerobics Research 1994.

or not returning to the starting position)

- Swinging the body to gain momentum
- Removing hands from shoulders
- Lifting the hips off the floor

4. **Bench press (one-repetition maximum; 1RM) test**

This test requires you to lift as much weight as you can for one repetition in the bench press while maintaining proper form. Free weights should be used for this test to be valid, and it is imperative that a spotter be present and alert during the test performance.

Position your body so that your back is on the bench, feet are on the floor, and hands are a little wider than shoulder-width apart on the barbell. Start by removing the weight from the supported uprights to a position in which your arms are fully extended (see figure 6.16*a*).

Lower the bar to your chest (see figure 6.16*b*) and then push it back up until your elbows are fully extended. It is important to start this test using light weight; lifting only the bar without any additional resistance would be a good place to start for most men. Women can begin by bench pressing 5- or 10-pound dumbbells before moving to a barbell. After warming up with a light weight for 8 to 10 repetitions, increase the weight and try to complete only one repetition. Continue increasing the weight

until you can't perform a single repetition at the new weight. Record the highest weight lifted and obtain a body weight measurement. Calculate your bench-press to body-weight ratio using the formula that follows, and compare the result to the standards for the bench press 1RM test in table 6.7.

A ratio of bench press to body weight is determined by dividing the maximum weight lifted in kilograms or pounds by the subject's weight in kilograms or pounds.

For men and women: Bench press (1RM) = maximum weight lifted ÷ body weight

For example, if a person lifts 190 pounds (86 kg) and weighs 185 pounds (84 kg)

Bench press (1RM) = 190 pounds (86 kg) ÷ 185 pounds (84 kg)

Bench press (1RM) = 1.02

The following are some common mistakes made on this test:

- Failing to lower the weight all the way to the chest
- Bouncing the bar off the chest to gain momentum
- Lifting the hips and legs in an effort to gain a mechanical advantage

5. **Leg press (1RM) test**

This test requires you to lift as much weight as you can for one repetition in the leg press

**Figure 6.16** *(a)* Starting position for the bench press test. *(b)* The bar must come in contact with the chest for a successful repetition.

**Table 6.7    Standards for Bench Press (One-Repetition Maximum) Test**

| Age (years) | 15-19 | | 20-29 | | 30-39 | | 40-49 | | 50-59 | | 60-69 | |
|---|---|---|---|---|---|---|---|---|---|---|---|---|
| Sex | M | F | M | F | M | F | M | F | M | F | M | F |
| Excellent | ≥1.48 | ≥0.90 | ≥1.48 | ≥0.90 | ≥1.24 | ≥0.76 | ≥1.10 | ≥0.71 | ≥0.97 | ≥0.61 | ≥0.89 | ≥0.64 |
| Above Average | 1.22-1.47 | 0.74-0.89 | 1.22-1.47 | 0.74-0.89 | 1.04-1.23 | 0.63-0.75 | 0.93-1.09 | 0.57-0.70 | 0.84-0.96 | 0.52-0.60 | 0.77-0.88 | 0.51-0.63 |
| Average | 1.06-1.21 | 0.65-0.73 | 1.06-1.21 | 0.65-0.73 | 0.93-1.03 | 0.57-0.62 | 0.84-0.92 | 0.52-0.56 | 0.75-0.84 | 0.46-0.51 | 0.68-0.76 | 0.45-0.50 |
| Below average | 0.93-1.05 | 0.56-0.64 | 0.93-1.05 | 0.56-0.64 | 0.83-0.92 | 0.51-0.56 | 0.76-0.83 | 0.47-0.51 | 0.68-0.74 | 0.42-0.45 | 0.63-0.67 | 0.40-0.44 |
| Poor | ≤0.93 | ≤0.56 | ≤0.93 | ≤0.56 | ≤0.83 | ≤0.51 | ≤0.76 | ≤0.47 | ≤0.68 | ≤0.42 | ≤0.63 | ≤0.40 |

Adapted from Dwyer and Davis 2005; Data from Institute for Aerobics Research 1994; Data from Franklin 2006.

while maintaining good form. A leg press machine is required for this exam. Data for this exam were originally collected from subjects using a Universal Gym leg press. A comparable leg press, such as the one in figure 6.17, should be used for the test results to be valid.

Sit in the leg press and adjust the seat position so that your knees are bent at a 90-degree angle. Place your feet approximately shoulder-width apart and grasp the handles with your hands (see figure 6.17a). Begin this lift by pushing the foot platform away from your body until your knees are fully extended (see figure 6.17b). Lower the weight to the starting position. This completes one repetition.

As in the bench press, continue adding resistance until you cannot perform a single repetition at the new weight. Record the most weight you pressed for one repetition and obtain an accurate body weight measurement. Calculate your leg-press to body-weight ratio using the following formula, and compare your results to the standards for the leg press test in table 6.8.

A leg-press to body-weight ratio is determined by dividing the maximum weight lifted by the subject's weight.

For men and women: Leg press (1RM) = maximum weight lifted ÷ body weight

For example, if a person presses 250 pounds (113 kg) and weighs 150 pounds (68 kg)

Leg press (1RM) = 250 pounds (113 kg) ÷ 150 pounds (68 kg)

Leg press (1RM) = 1.6

**Figure 6.17**    *(a)* Starting position for the leg press. *(b)* Successful completion of the leg press is when both legs are fully extended.

**Table 6.8    Standards for Leg Press (One-Repetition Maximum) Test**

| Age (years) | 15-19 | | 20-29 | | 30-39 | | 40-49 | | 50-59 | | 60+ | |
|---|---|---|---|---|---|---|---|---|---|---|---|---|
| Sex | M | F | M | F | M | F | M | F | M | F | M | F |
| Excellent | ≥2.27 | ≥1.82 | ≥2.27 | ≥1.82 | ≥2.07 | ≥1.61 | ≥1.92 | ≥1.48 | ≥1.8 | ≥1.37 | ≥1.73 | ≥1.32 |
| Above Average | 2.05-2.26 | 1.58-1.81 | 2.05-2.26 | 1.58-1.81 | 1.85-2.06 | 1.39-1.60 | 1.74-1.91 | 1.29-1.47 | 1.64-1.79 | 1.17-1.36 | 1.56-1.72 | 1.13-1.31 |
| Average | 1.91-2.04 | 1.44-1.57 | 1.91-2.04 | 1.44-1.57 | 1.71-1.84 | 1.27-1.38 | 1.62-1.73 | 1.18-1.28 | 1.52-1.63 | 1.05-1.16 | 1.43-1.55 | .99-1.12 |
| Below average | 1.74-1.90 | 1.27-1.43 | 1.74-1.90 | 1.27-1.43 | 1.59-1.70 | 1.15-1.26 | 1.51-1.61 | 1.08-1.17 | 1.39-1.51 | 0.95-1.04 | 1.30-1.42 | 0.88-0.98 |
| Poor | ≤1.74 | ≤1.27 | ≤1.74 | ≤1.27 | ≤1.59 | ≤1.15 | ≤1.51 | ≤1.08 | ≤1.39 | ≤0.95 | ≤1.30 | ≤0.88 |

Adapted from Dwyer and Davis 2005; Data from Institute for Aerobics Research 1994; Data from Franklin 2006.

The following are common mistakes made on the leg press (1RM) test:

- Failing to fully extend the legs
- Coming out of the seated position during the test to gain a mechanical advantage
- Using the arms to aid in extending the legs

If you're disappointed with your existing strength, consider that one study (ACSM, 1998) found that 40 percent of boys and 70 percent of girls aged 6 to 12 are unable to do more than one pull-up. In fact, the average man can do only one, and the average woman cannot do any. Well over half of all older women cannot lift 20 pounds (9 kg) over their head with one arm (ACSM, 1998). No matter how old or weak you are, you can get much stronger if you commit to a consistent strength-training schedule.

## Types of Strength Training

Today, most people think of dumbbells, barbells, and weight machines when they hear the term *strength training*. Those types of strength-training equipment are used to create four fundamental methods of resistance:

1. Isometric
2. Isokinetic
3. Isotonic
4. Variable resistance

- ***Isometric*** means "equal length" and is a combination of the Greek terms *iso* (same) and *metric* (distance). In isometric exercise, muscles contract without the body moving. The imaginary chair or wall sit is an example of an isometric exercise. During the exercise, a person sits motionless with his or her back against a wall as if sitting upright in a chair, and neither joint angle or muscle length changes. The muscle is contracting without physical movement.

In the 1920s, bodybuilder Charles Atlas popularized the isometric method of strength training, which he called dynamic tension. Atlas promised that even the 98-pound weakling who followed his mail-order program would never again have sand kicked in his face (Atlas, 2012). Few people today train regularly with isometric exercise, though, because it develops strength within a very small range of motion (at most, 20 degrees in each direction from the point of contraction; National Strength and Conditioning Association, 1994).

- ***Isokinetic*** means "equal motion," and again the prefix *iso* means "same." The Greek term *kinetic* refers to movement. The rate of muscular contraction is constant in isokinetic exercise. Isokinetic machines are specially designed so that no matter how hard an exerciser pushes or pulls, the set speed remains constant.

Charles Atlas popularized isometric training.

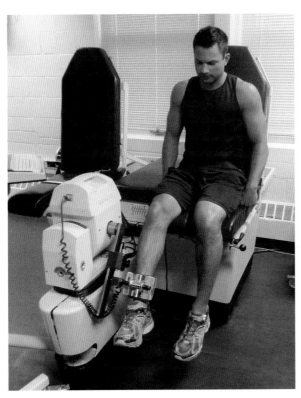

No matter how hard the student contracts his muscles, the isokinetic machine keeps the speed of movement constant.

**Figure 6.18** Attaching bands to the end of a barbell can create variable resistance.

This type of resistance training is most often used by athletic trainers and physical therapists measuring strength or rehabilitating patients from injury.

- *Isotonic* means "equal tension," where force remains constant. Free-weight exercises are good examples of this category. A 50-pound (23 kg) dumbbell, for instance, weighs 50 pounds throughout the lift. Even though the weight stays the same, research shows that the force exerted by the muscles varies because of mechanical advantage and other factors (Fleck & Kraemer, 1997).

- **Variable-resistance** exercises change the resistance to compensate for changes in mechanical advantage. Machines with levers, cams, and pulleys or barbells with bands and chains attached facilitate variable-resistance exercise. For example, during an arm curl the biceps work the hardest when the angle of the elbow is between 80 and 100 degrees, so an exerciser should be able to handle more resistance at the beginning (between 180 and 100 degrees) and at the end (between 80 and 5 degrees) of the movement. The distinct advantage of this method is that muscles have to work harder through a greater range of motion during the contraction as opposed to just the most biomechanically disadvantaged position. Note that in figure 6.18 bands have been attached to each end of

the barbell. As the exerciser is in a squatting position the bands are slack, eliminating any additional force. The importance of this is that most people lose their biomechanical advantage the deeper they squat. As the exerciser moves to a standing position, additional force from the bands is added to the weight of the bar, making the movement more difficult. However, because of the biomechanical advantage, the person is able to complete the movement.

Despite attempts by several researchers to answer the question of whether free weights or machines are better at developing strength, there remains no clear answer. That being said, there are specific benefits to each. Table 6.9 describes these.

## Strength-Training Program

The strength-training program in figures 6.19-6.21 is perfect for people who have never done strength training or who have been lifting weights for less than six months. On average, beginners who complete all three phases of this program as described increase their overall strength by at least 30 percent in three months of training. Although it is meant for beginners, it contains advanced training principles that more experienced lifters can learn from. If you are

## Table 6.9    Comparison of Free Weights and Resistance Machines

| Advantages of free weights | Advantages of resistance machines |
| --- | --- |
| **Cost:** Purchasing a set of free weights is much less expensive than buying most resistance training machines. | **Skill acquisition:** Learning new exercise movements and performing them correctly is accomplished faster because the machine controls the direction of the movement. |
| **Variety:** Barbells, dumbbells, and even the weighted plates themselves can be used for literally thousands of strength-training movements. Machines, on the other hand, generally limit strength-training exercises to particular movement patterns. | **Safety:** Machines are generally safer because spotters rarely are needed to monitor exercises. |
| **Portability:** Free weights can easily be moved from one location to another. | **Speed:** Exercising with machines requires less time because the resistance can be quickly adjusted using a selector pin instead of having to manually change dumbbells or weight plates on both sides of a barbell. |
| **Fit:** People of all ages and sizes can use free weights. One drawback to machines is that they are designed for the average-sized person. Although most of the better resistance machines have some level of adjustment, children and very short or tall adults can have trouble getting into the correct position. | **Focus:** There are a few machine exercises—such as hip abduction, leg extensions, leg curls, and neck exercises—that are extremely difficult to perform with free weights. |
| **Force:** While most machines increase the level of resistance by 10- or 20-pound increments, dumbbells and barbells can be adjusted by as little as 2.5 lbs. | **Variable resistance:** Some machines provide variable resistance. Free weights provide only fixed resistance throughout the range of movement. |
| **Muscle stimulation:** Free weights require balance and therefore use supportive muscles to a greater degree than machines. This for many individuals is the reason free weights are superior to machines. | **Isolation:** By eliminating the need for stabilizing muscles, machines have the advantage of isolating a specific muscle or group of muscles. |

a beginner, this program provides a detailed training plan to follow, and if you are an experienced lifter, examine the components of this program to discover some new ideas.

Take a few minutes to preview the workout program outlined in figures 6.19-6.21. The first thing you may notice is that it seems to be three programs instead of one. There is a good reason for this division: After three to four weeks of repeating the same exercises, most lifters reach a plateau, a period where progress slows dramatically. The world's top athletes frequently change their exercise regimens to counteract the plateau period, and the Westside Barbell Club, located just outside of Columbus, Ohio, provides a good example of this. In 2004, the club had more than 40 members who could bench press in excess of 500 pounds (227 kg; Simmons, 2005). Most gyms would boast if they had one person accomplish such a feat. What is the Westside Barbell Club's secret? Members change their training regimens every two weeks! By systematically changing your strength-training program, you dramatically increase muscle stimulation. The three-phase structure of this training program accounts for this factor with each phase lasting two weeks before starting the next phase.

## Common Questions

You will no doubt have many questions as you examine the training program in figures 6.19-6.21. Therefore, many of the most common questions are addressed in this section.

1. **What should I do if I do not know how to perform the exercises outlined in this workout?**

   If you are unsure how to perform the exercises, ask one of the trainers or supervisors at your facility for assistance.

2. **What if my facility does not have the exercise machines pictured in the workout program?**

## Phase I Strength Training Program

| 1 set/85–100% effort | | | | | Week 1 | | Week 2 | |
|---|---|---|---|---|---|---|---|---|
| 8–10 reps/(2/0/2) repetition speed | | | | | Day 1 | Day 2 | Day 1 | Day 2 |
| **LEGS** Seated leg extension | | | | | Wt. | Wt. | Wt. | Wt. |
| | | | | | Reps | Reps | Reps | Reps |
| **BACK** Lat pulldown | | | | | Wt. | Wt. | Wt. | Wt. |
| | | | | | Reps | Reps | Reps | Reps |
| **BACK** Seated back extension | | | | | Wt. | Wt. | Wt. | Wt. |
| | | | | | Reps | Reps | Reps | Reps |
| **BACK** Abdominal crunch | | | | | Wt. | Wt. | Wt. | Wt. |
| | | | | | Reps | Reps | Reps | Reps |
| **CHEST** Chest press | | | | | Wt. | Wt. | Wt. | Wt. |
| | | | | | Reps | Reps | Reps | Reps |
| **SHOULDERS** Lateral raise | | | | | Wt. | Wt. | Wt. | Wt. |
| | | | | | Reps | Reps | Reps | Reps |
| **ARMS** Arm extension | | | | | Wt. | Wt. | Wt. | Wt. |
| | | | | | Reps | Reps | Reps | Reps |
| **ARMS** Arm curl | | | | | Wt. | Wt. | Wt. | Wt. |
| | | | | | Reps | Reps | Reps | Reps |

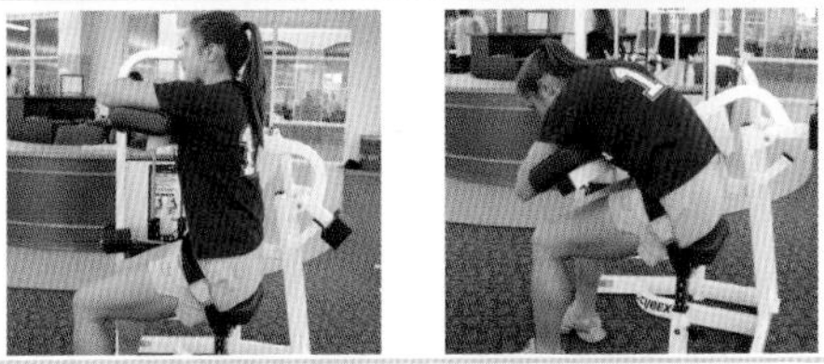

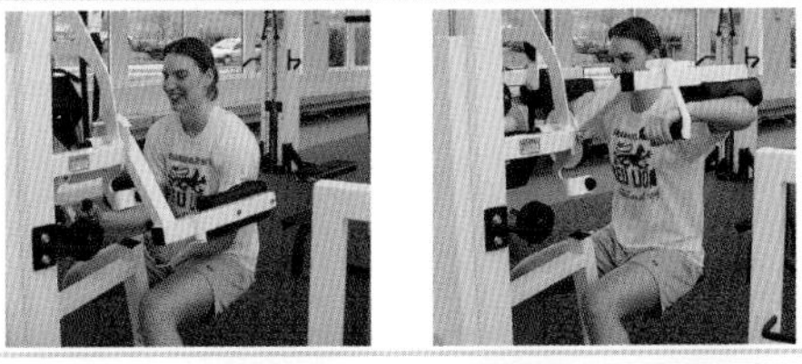

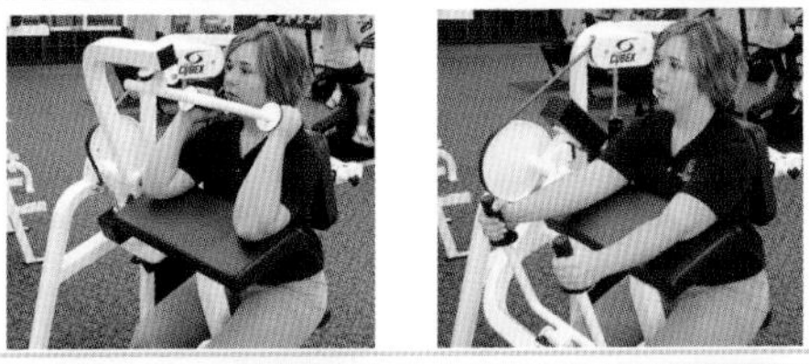

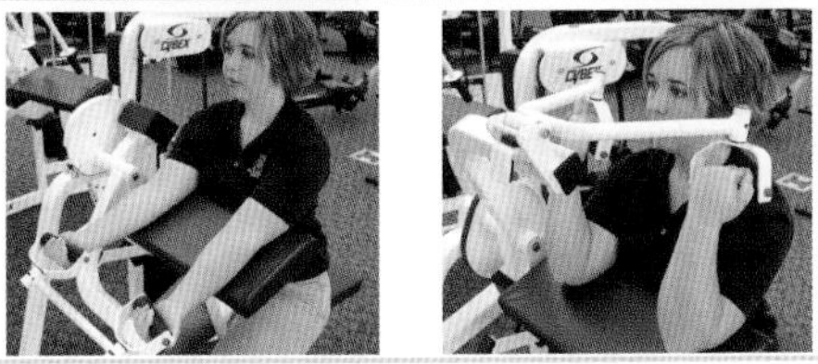

**Figure 6.19** Phase I is composed entirely of machine exercises.

From P. Walters and J. Byl, 2013, *Christian paths to health and wellness*, 2nd ed. (Champaign, IL: Human Kinetics).

## Phase II Strength Training Program

| 1 set/85–100% effort | | | Week 1 | | Week 2 | |
|---|---|---|---|---|---|---|
| **8–10 reps/(2/0/2) repetition speed** | | | Day 1 | Day 2 | Day 1 | Day 2 |
| **LEGS**<br>Leg curl | 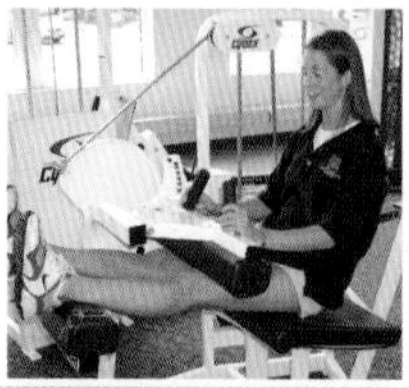 | 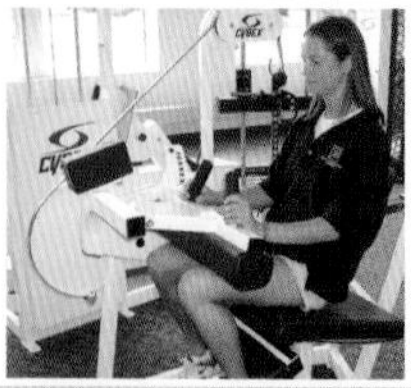 | Wt. | Wt. | Wt. | Wt. |
| | | | Reps | Reps | Reps | Reps |
| **BACK**<br>Seated low row |  |  | Wt. | Wt. | Wt. | Wt. |
| | | | Reps | Reps | Reps | Reps |
| **BACK**<br>Incline back extension |  |  | Wt. | Wt. | Wt. | Wt. |
| | | | Reps | Reps | Reps | Reps |
| **BACK**<br>Seated torso rotation |  |  | Wt. | Wt. | Wt. | Wt. |
| | | | Reps | Reps | Reps | Reps |
| **CHEST**<br>Chest fly |  |  | Wt. | Wt. | Wt. | Wt. |
| | | | Reps | Reps | Reps | Reps |
| **SHOULDERS**<br>Seated overhead press |  |  | Wt. | Wt. | Wt. | Wt. |
| | | | Reps | Reps | Reps | Reps |
| **ARMS**<br>Standing dumbbell curl |  |  | Wt. | Wt. | Wt. | Wt. |
| | | | Reps | Reps | Reps | Reps |
| **ARMS**<br>Triceps cable pushdown |  |  | Wt. | Wt. | Wt. | Wt. |
| | | | Reps | Reps | Reps | Reps |

**Figure 6.20** Phase II combines free-weight and machine exercises.

From P. Walters and J. Byl, 2013, *Christian paths to health and wellness*, 2nd ed. (Champaign, IL: Human Kinetics).

128

## Phase III Strength Training Program

| 1 set/85–100% effort | | | | Week 1 | | Week 2 | |
|---|---|---|---|---|---|---|---|
| 8–10 reps/(2/0/2) repetition speed | | | | Day 1 | Day 2 | Day 1 | Day 2 |
| **LEGS** Incline leg press | | | | Wt. | Wt. | Wt. | Wt. |
| | | | | Reps | Reps | Reps | Reps |
| **BACK** One-arm dumbbell row | | | | Wt. | Wt. | Wt. | Wt. |
| | | | | Reps | Reps | Reps | Reps |
| **BACK** Deadlift | | | | Wt. | Wt. | Wt. | Wt. |
| | | | | Reps | Reps | Reps | Reps |
| **BACK** Hanging leg raise | | | | Wt. | Wt. | Wt. | Wt. |
| | | | | Reps | Reps | Reps | Reps |
| **CHEST** Bench press | | | | Wt. | Wt. | Wt. | Wt. |
| | | | | Reps | Reps | Reps | Reps |
| **SHOULDERS** Standing dumbbell lateral raise | | | | Wt. | Wt. | Wt. | Wt. |
| | | | | Reps | Reps | Reps | Reps |
| **ARMS** Seated alternating dumbbell curl | | | | Wt. | Wt. | Wt. | Wt. |
| | | | | Reps | Reps | Reps | Reps |
| **ARMS** Seated two-arm dumbbell triceps press | | | | Wt. | Wt. | Wt. | Wt. |
| | | | | Reps | Reps | Reps | Reps |

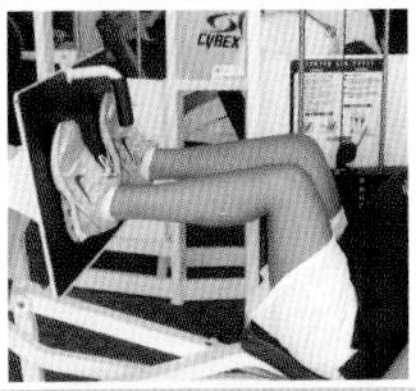

**Figure 6.21** Phase III is almost entirely composed of free-weight exercises.

From P. Walters and J. Byl, 2013, *Christian paths to health and wellness*, 2nd ed. (Champaign, IL: Human Kinetics).

Although your fitness facility or gym may not have the exact piece of equipment illustrated, most likely it will have similar pieces of equipment that provide an appropriate substitute. Ask one of the trainers or supervisors of your facility for suggestions.

3. **Should I complete the exercises in the sequence in which they are listed (from top to bottom)?**

   If possible, it would be a good idea to complete them in this order. The six body regions are ordered from the largest groups of muscles to the smallest. While many (especially men) want to train their arms first, in reality this muscle group is the smallest out of the six by mass. If you train the small muscles first, they become fatigued and less supportive when the larger muscles are exercised. Also, a person's energy level is at the highest at the beginning of a workout and wanes as lifting continues. It takes a lot of energy to train the large muscle groups, and if these groups are exercised last their growth and development will suffer.

4. **Does this workout program target all the major muscle groups?**

   Yes! Novice lifters often make the mistake of focusing on certain body parts while ignoring others. Men usually want to increase muscle and definition in the chest, arms, and abs; women usually want to tone the abdomen, hips, and thighs. The resulting muscular imbalances not only can make you look funny but can increase your chance of muscular injury. For instance, athletes who spend a lot of time on their quadriceps but ignore their hamstrings become more susceptible to leg injuries (Croisier et al., 2008; Ellenbecker et al., 2009).

   In the earlier section on major muscles, you learned the major muscles that can be grouped into six body regions: legs, back, abdominals, chest, shoulders, and arms. Each of these six areas should be included in a balanced strength-training program. Physical disabilities and injuries would of course be important reasons to deviate from this general rule.

   The good news about this program is that all six areas of the body are included, as you can see by the labels above the exercises in each workout phase. If you are designing your own program, it is critical to include each of these six major areas to get a well-balanced

muscular workout. Here is a mnemonic phrase to help you remember the six major body parts: "**l**ittle **b**oys **a**lways **c**atch **s**limy **a**nimals"—legs, back, abdominals, chest, shoulders, arms.

5. **What does "1 set/85–100% effort" mean?**

   You will perform each exercise only once, meaning "1 **set**." When you perform each exercise you will use a resistance requiring approximately 85 to 100 percent of your physical effort.

6. **Why only one set of each exercise?**

   Die-hard lifters might laugh at the idea of doing only one set, but several well-designed studies suggest that one set is virtually as effective as three sets for beginners (Rhea et al., 2002). Researchers at the University of Florida divided a total of 42 male and female beginning lifters into two groups. The first group performed one set of 8 to 12 repetitions on nine different machines; the second group performed three sets. After 13 weeks, there were no significant differences between the two groups in strength, endurance, or body composition (Hass, 2000). As you become more experienced, you will probably want to add additional sets to your exercises. However, if you have been training for fewer than six months, you can cut your workout time by two-thirds (traditional strength-training programs suggest doing three sets of each exercise) and get the same benefit.

7. **What do "repetitions" and "repetition speed" mean?**

   **Repetitions** refer to the number of times you will perform a specific movement pattern for a given exercise. Each movement pattern (repetition) has three parts: the concentric, middle, and eccentric portion. To understand these three parts take a look at the seated leg extension. In this exercise (illustrated in the strength-training program in this chapter), the lifter sits at a machine and raises her legs against resistance (a padded bar that rests against her ankles and is connected to weights) until they extend straight in front of her. This is the concentric phase of the lift, as the quadricep muscle fibers contract and the legs extend. Once the weight is lifted and the legs are extended, the legs are then lowered as the muscles relax. This is the eccentric phase of the lift. Often people think very little about this portion of the lift since it is easier to lower the weight than raise it, but many scientists believe it to be just as important as the concentric phase.

The middle phase, as its name suggests, occurs between the concentric and eccentric phases. However, most individuals think very little of this phase because most people immediately move from the concentric phase to the eccentric phase. But consider again the seated leg extension. Instead of relaxing the muscles and lowering the weight immediately after extending the leg, the lifter holds the leg in the straightened position for 2 seconds before returning the leg to the starting position. The lifter has now created a middle portion of the lift by holding an isometric contraction for 2 seconds. This is a more advanced strength-training technique, but it is easy to learn and increases the effort of the exercise.

**Repetition speed** is written based on these three phases. Take the example of (2/0/2) given in figure 6.19. These numbers represent seconds. The first number is the duration of the concentric phase, the second number the duration of the middle phase, and the last number the duration of the eccentric phase.

8. **How do I determine how much weight to start with?**

For years scientists and physical trainers have promoted a variety of methods to determine how much weight a beginner should lift, typically based on factors like sex and body weight. However, none of these have shown a high degree of reliability. The only fail-safe way to determine your starting weight is individual experimentation. If you have never performed the exercise before, accustom yourself to the movement by performing the exercise without any resistance. This helps your brain and body become familiar with the movement pattern. Next, perform the movement with a very small amount of resistance, or weight, to further ingrain the motor program into your memory. Continue to gradually add resistance (no more than 20 lbs or 9 kg at a time) until you find the weight at which you can perform 8 repetitions while exerting approximately 85 percent effort. You should never begin with 100 percent effort on the first day of your workout for two reasons. First, in your next workout you will be adding repetitions or weight to the exercise. Second, trying to lift too much weight at the begin-

ning often causes people to sacrifice good lifting form. Although in most cases you can hoist a bit more weight by using sloppy technique, poor technique not only fails to stress the muscles properly, but it also exposes the body to injury.

9. **How quickly should I progress?**

The wonderful news for beginners is that the nervous and muscular systems quickly adapt to this new form of stress, so in almost every workout you will be able to increase weight or repetitions. The established progression pattern is to add repetitions one at a time until you reach 10 repetitions. Once you reach 10 repetitions, increase the weight by 5 pounds (2 kg) for all exercises except for the legs. For leg exercises increase the weight by 10 lbs (4 kg). After increasing resistance lower the repetitions to 8.

Here's an example of how this progression works: on the first day of Mark's workout, he discovers that he can lift 85 pounds (38 kg) in the chest press for 8 repetitions. During his next workout he performs 9 repetitions of the chest press at 85 pounds (38 kg). On his next workout he aims to perform 10 repetitions at 85 pounds (38 kg). After successfully performing 10 repetitions of the lift, in his next workout Mark adds 5 pounds (2 kg) of weight (for a total of 90 lbs or 41 kg) and drops his repetitions back to 8. He then continues to increase repetitions at 90 pounds (41 kg) of weight until he reaches 10 reps and then again increases the resistance and decreases the repetitions. This method of progression systematically allows your body to develop strength at an appropriate pace.

10. **How much rest should I take between exercises?**

One to two minutes of rest between exercises is normally recommended.

11. **Should I warm up before beginning each workout?**

Yes. It is a good idea to do a general warm-up (riding a bike, running, stretching) for about five minutes before performing any strenuous exercise. Warming up increases the body's blood flow and prepares muscles to perform work. To take the general warm-up one step further, do a quick *specific* warm-up for each exercise. On the machine you plan to use for your workout, simply adjust the resistance or weight to approximately 50 to 60 percent of the workout load (the weight you plan to lift for

# Should Women Train Differently Than Men?

Women, on average, have two-thirds the strength of men (Lauback, 1976) largely because of hormonal differences. The influence of hormones becomes obvious as children experience puberty. Before puberty, there are essentially no differences in height, weight, body size, lean body mass, and adipose tissue between boys and girls. During puberty, the production of estrogen in girls increases their percentage of body fat, whereas testosterone production in boys increases their bone formation and muscle mass. The net effect of these changes is that men develop more muscle tissue and have taller and wider skeletal frames that support the additional muscle.

These differences suggest to some that men and women should perform resistance training differently. Others believe there is no sensible reason why resistance-training programs for women need to be different than those for men.

Thomas Baechle and Roger Earle, who have written *the* manual for most strength-training professionals, state the following:

> It is a misperception that resistance training programs for women should be different from those for men or that women lose flexibility or develop "bulky" muscles if they train with weights. The only real difference between training programs for men and women is generally the amount of resistance used for a given exercise. (National Strength and Conditioning Association, 2008, p. 152)

Although there may not be physiological differences in men's and women's muscle tissue, there are other factors to consider.

The first is that women generally have different goals for strength training than men. While many men seek muscular strength and size, women desire firmness and muscular definition. These goals should be reflected in strength prescriptions. A second difference is susceptibility to injury. Some studies suggest that females are more susceptible to knee injuries than males (Arendt & Dick, 1995; Baker, 1998). In one NCAA report, female basketball players were six times more likely to incur an anterior cruciate ligament tear than the male players were (National Collegiate Athletic Association, 1994). Review the literature on this controversial issue and develop an informed opinion.

---

one set). Position yourself in the machine and do four to six easy repetitions with this light resistance. This quick warm-up (usually about 30 seconds) adds another layer of protection to your joints and muscles by preparing the body for the lift.

12. **What do I do after I complete all three workout phases?**

    After you finish the last phase, go back to the beginning and repeat each phase again. Just as you did at the beginning of this training program, experiment to determine what weight requires 85 percent effort. Remember the amount of resistance you used during your first phase? You will be amazed at how easy that beginning weight feels now that you are stronger and at how much higher your new resistance level is. After going through the entire program twice (12 weeks), you should experience at least a 30 percent improvement in your overall strength.

## Safety in Strength Training

Resistance training can help you prevent and recover from injuries. But if you are not careful, it may also cause injuries—strains and sprains, bumps and bruises, and perhaps worse. Make sure you follow these six guidelines for weight room safety:

1. **Warm up before you lift.** Warming up increases the amount of blood and oxygen delivered to your muscles, increases the temperature of your muscles and joints, and can enhance your performance by up to 20 percent. Running, biking, and stair climbing are all examples of good warm-up exercises. They increase circulation (blood flow) throughout the entire body.

2. **Always practice proper form.** Don't let your ego endanger your safety by sacrificing form to lift more weight. Here are some general rules regarding lifting form:

- Keep your torso firm and your back straight while doing most free-weight exercises.
- Focus on the muscles being worked rather than the weight or number of repetitions.
- Maintain control of how fast you lift. Force your muscles, not momentum, to move the resistance.

3. **Progress slowly.** Using the progression methods outlined in this chapter allows your body to gradually accommodate increasing levels of stress.

4. **Use the equipment properly.** When you work with barbells, make sure the weight is equal on each side, and always use **barbell collars,** the protective clamps that secure plates on a weightlifting bar.

5. **Use proper breathing technique. Never hold your breath.**

6. **Have someone spot you on potentially dangerous lifts.** Death is rare in the weight room, but when it happens it is usually when people lift alone. A classic example is bench pressing without a spotter. If you are unable to complete a lift, the bar gets stuck at your chest and can slide down to your neck and suffocate you.

## Next Steps

As this chapter concludes, consider once more the story of Milo of Croton. Carrying a 90-pound (41 kg) calf 100 meters, as Milo did at the beginning of his strength training, is good but not an amazing feat of strength. However, the story doesn't end there. Milo carried his calf several days of the week. As the calf grew larger, so did Milo's strength. According to legend, Milo could still carry the calf when it weighed more than 1,000 pounds (454 kg) (Harris, 1993).

Milo was unquestionably the most famous athlete of his day—like LeBron James, Lionel Messi, and Michael Phelps all rolled into one. He won five consecutive victories at the Olympics, six at the Pythian Games, nine at the Nemean Games, and ten at the Isthmian Games. Five times he was also granted the title of *Periodonikes*, or quadruple-crown winner, having won at all four festivals in the same cycle. The Greeks worshiped Milo and erected a statue of him inscribed with the words "Neither god nor man can stand against him" (Harris, 1966). And Milo believed it.

Ironically, Milo's belief in his own invincibility led to his demise. One day, while walking through the forest far from the city, he came upon the stump of a tree that had broken off close to the ground and split down the middle. Allured by the challenge to test his strength, he thrust his hands into the wedge in an attempt to tear the stump in half. However, he failed, and when it closed on his fingers, he was trapped. After the sun set, he was killed by wolves (Harris, 1966).

The story of Milo's rise and fall is a reminder that human strength, no matter how great, will one day come to an end. By contrast, God's might will last forever: "My flesh and my heart may fail, but God is the strength of my heart and my portion forever" (Psalm 73:26). As you build your physical strength, remember the one whose strength will never be exhausted. Keep in mind that most of the principles and methods in this chapter also apply to building spiritual power.

### Never Hold Your Breath While Lifting

Most fitness professionals have two recommendations about breathing: exhale during the most strenuous phase of the lift, and never hold your breath while lifting (National Strength and Conditioning Association, 2008). The first is a good guideline for beginners; however, the second needs to be reconsidered. It is true that holding your breath for an extended time can result in dizziness, disorientation, and even blackouts, but there are some good reasons to hold your breath for brief periods while lifting. Scientific evidence suggests that holding the breath for a brief time has performance and safety advantages (Findley & Keating, 2003; Haykowsky et al., 2001). If someone is asked to pick up a heavy object, he or she will almost always perform what's known as a Valsalva maneuver just before applying force. A Valsalva maneuver is produced by pressing air from the lungs against a closed glottis. When a person does this, the muscles of the abdomen and rib cage contract, creating a rigid torso. This inner rigidity of the torso supports the vertebral column, which in turn can reduce compressive forces on the vertebral disks during a lift (Findley & Keating, 2003; National Strength and Conditioning Association, 2008). This maneuver has a similar effect to wearing a safety belt while picking up a heavy weight. One word of caution: Hold your breath for no more than two seconds (National Strength and Conditioning Association, 2008).

# Key Terms

| | | |
|---|---|---|
| actin | isotonic | osteoporosis |
| atrophy | lean body mass | repetitions |
| barbell collar | motor unit | repetition speed |
| body composition | muscular endurance | resistance training |
| bone matrix | muscular strength | resorption |
| cardiac muscle | myofibril | resting metabolic rate (RMR) |
| fascia | myosin | sarcomere |
| functional capacity | one-repetition maximum (1RM) | set |
| hypertrophy | | skeletal muscle |
| isokinetic | osteoblast | smooth muscle |
| isometric | osteoclast | variable resistance |

# Review Questions

1. Describe five benefits of resistance training.
2. Draw a cross-section of skeletal muscle and add as much detail as possible.
3. Identify five methods of evaluating muscular strength or endurance.
4. Describe four types of resistance training.
5. Define and describe each of the following items in the strength-training prescription: sets, effort, repetitions, repetition speed, rest interval, method of progression.
6. List six safety guidelines for resistance training.

# References

ACSM. (1998). Exercise in physical activity for older adults. *Medicine and Science in Sports and Exercise, 30*(6), 992.

Arendt, E., & Dick, R. (1995). Knee injury patterns among men and women in collegiate basketball and soccer: NCAA data and review of literature. *American Journal of Sports Medicine, 25,* 694–701.

Atlas, C. (2012). *Charles Atlas: The world's most perfectly developed man.* www.charlesatlas.com/about.html.

Baker, M. (1998). Anterior cruciate ligament injuries and female athletes. *Journal of Women's Health, 7,* 343–49.

Baldo, B. (1996). Grip strength testing. *National Strength and Conditioning Association Journal, 18*(5), 32–35.

Behnke, R. (2006). *Kinetic anatomy* (2nd ed.). Champaign, IL: Human Kinetics.

Boutcher, S.H. (2011). High-intensity intermittent exercise and fat loss. *Journal of Obesity.* www.hindawi.com/journals/jobes/2011/868305/cta/.

Canadian Physical Activity, Fitness & Lifestyle Appraisal. (2003). *The Canadian physical activity, fitness & lifestyle appraisal: CSEP's plan for healthy active living* (3rd ed.). Ottawa, Ont.: Canadian Society for Exercise Physiology.

Centers for Disease Control and Prevention. (2008). *Preventing back injuries in health care settings.* http://blogs.cdc.gov/niosh-science-blog/2008/09/lifting/.

Croisier, J-L., Ganteaume, S., Binet, J., Genty, M., & Ferret, J-M. (2008). Strength imbalances and prevention of hamstring injury in professional soccer players. *The American Journal of Sports Medicine, 36*(8), 1469–75.

Darden, E. (1995). *Living longer and stronger.* New York: Berkley.

Deyo, R.A., Mirza, S.K., & Martin, B.I. (2006). Back pain prevalence and visit rates: Estimates from U.S. national surveys, 2002. [Research Support, N.I.H., Extramural]. *Spine* (Phila Pa 1976), *31*(23), 2724–27. doi: 10.1097/01.brs.0000244618.06877.

Dornemann, T.M. (1997). Effects of high-intensity resistance exercise on bone mineral density and muscle strength of 40–50-year-old women. *Journal of Sports Medicine and Fitness, 37*(4), 246–51.

Dwyer, G.B., & Davis, S.E. (2005). *ACSM's health-related physical fitness assessment manual.* Philadelphia: Lippincott Williams & Wilkins.

Eidelson, S. (2006). *Back pain—A universal language.* www.spineuniverse.com/displayarticle.php/article1457.html.

Ellenbecker, T.S., Pluim, B., Vivier, S., & Sniteman, C. (2009). Common injuries in tennis players: Exercises to address muscular imbalances and reduce injury risk. *Strength & Conditioning Journal, 31*(4), 50–58.

Feng, X., & McDonald, J.M. (2011). Disorders of bone remodeling. *Annual Review of Pathology: Mechanisms of Disease, 6*(1), 121–45.

Fiatarone, A. (2002). Exercise comes of age: Rationale and recommendations for a geriatric exercise prescription. *Journals of Gerontology A: Biological Sciences & Medical Sciences, 54*(5), 262–83.

Findley, B., & Keating, T. (2003). Is the Valsalva maneuver a proper breathing technique? *National Strength and Conditioning Association Journal, 25*(4), 52–53.

Fleck, S., & Kraemer, W. (1997). *Designing resistance training programs* (2nd ed.). Champaign, IL: Human Kinetics.

Franklin, B.A. (Ed.). (2006). *ACSM's guidelines for exercise testing and prescription.* Philadelphia: Lippincott Williams & Wilkins.

Gentle, D. (2000). *Some amazing feats of grip strength.* www.bobwhelan.com/history/gripstrength.html.

Guinness World Records. (1957). *Guinness world records 1957.* London: Young.

Guinness Book of World Records. (Ed.). (2011). *Guinness world records 2004.* New York: Bantam.

Gwinup, G., Chelvam, P., & Steinberg, T. (1971). Thickness of subcutaneous fat and activity of underlying muscles. *Annals of Internal Medicine, 74,* 408–11.

Harris, H.A. (1966). *Greek athletes and athletics.* London: Indiana Press.

Harris, H.A. (1993). *Sport in Greece and Rome.* Ithaca, NY: Cornell University Press.

Hass, C. (2000). Single versus multiple sets in long-term recreational weightlifters. *Medicine & Science in Sports and Exercise, 32*(1), 235.

Haykowsky, M., Taylor, D., Teo, K., Quinney, A., & Humen, D. (2001). Left ventricular wall stress during leg-press exercise performed with a brief Valsalva maneuver. *Chest, 119,* 150-154.

Incledon, L. (2005). *Strength training for women.* Champaign, IL: Human Kinetics.

Jenkins, J. (1975). *A greater strength.* Old Tappan, NJ: Revell.

Katch, F.I., Clarkson, P., Kroll, W., & McBride, T. (1984). Effects of sit-up exercise training on adipose cell size and adiposity. *Research Quarterly for Exercise and Sport, 55*(3), 242–47.

Kukuljan, S., Nowson, C.A., Sanders, K.M., Nicholson, G.C., Seibel, M.J., Salmon, J., et al. (2011). Independent and combined effects of calcium-vitamin D3 and exercise on bone structure and strength in older men: An 18-month factorial design randomized controlled trial. *The Journal of Clinical Endocrinology & Metabolism, 96,* 955–63.

Lauback, L. (1976). Comparative muscle strength of men and women: A review of the literature. *Aviation, Space, Environment and Medicine, 47,* 534–42.

Linster, C. (1999). *World record for non-stop push-ups.* www.recordholders.org/en/list/ulysses.html.

McArdle, W.D., Katch, F.I., & Katch, V. (2001). *Exercise physiology* (5th ed.). Baltimore: Williams & Wilkins.

McGlynn, G., & Moran, G.T. (1997). *Dynamics of strength training and conditioning* (2nd ed.). Chicago: Brown & Benchmark.

National Collegiate Athletic Association. (1994). Injury rate for women's basketball increases sharply. *NCAA News, 31,* 9, 13.

National Osteoporosis Foundation. (2012). *Bone Basics: Get the Facts.* www.nof.org/learn/basics.

National Osteoporosis Society. (2012). What is osteoporosis? www.nof.org/learn.

National Strength and Conditioning Association. (1994). *NSCA's essentials of strength training and conditioning.* Champaign, IL: Human Kinetics.

National Strength and Conditioning Association. (2008). *Essentials of strength training and conditioning* (3rd ed.). Champaign, IL: Human Kinetics.

Reynolds, J., Stevenson, M., Rutstein, S., & Conte, S. (1990). *Caring for your low back.* San Bruno, CA: Krames.

Rhea, M., Alvar, R., Burkett, B., & Lee, N. (2002). Single versus multiple sets for strength: A meta-analysis to address the controversy. *Research Quarterly for Exercise and Sport, 73*(4), 485–89.

Seung-Houn, L., Sung-Hwan, Y., & Ji-Han Seo, J.M.A.K. (2004). Development of an exercise program to prevent low back pain using an ergonomic approach. *International Journal of Advanced Manufacturing Technology, 24*(5/6), 381–88.

Sharkey, B. (2002). *Fitness and health* (5th ed.). Champaign, IL: Human Kinetics.

Simmons, L. (2005). The regulation of training. *Powerlifting USA, 22*(7), 32–33.

Sinaki, M., Itoi, E., Wahner, H.W., Wallan, P., Gelzcer, R., Mullan, B.P., et al. (2002). Stronger back muscles reduce the incidence of vertebral fractures: A prospective 10 year follow-up of postmenopausal women. *Bone, 30*(6), 836.

Strossen, R. (2007). *Official list of those certified as closing the No. 4 Captains of Crush gripper.* www.ironmind.com/ironmind/opencms/ironmind/Main/captainsofcrush4.html.

Westcott, W. (1994). *Strength fitness physiological principles and training techniques.* Boston: WCB/McGraw-Hill.

Wheeler, A.H. (1995). Diagnosis and management of low back pain and sciatica. *American Family Physician, 52*(5): 1333–41, 1347-1348

Wipf, J., & Deyo, R. (1995). Low back pain. *Medical Clinics of North America, 79*(2), 231–47.

# Suggested Readings

Baechle, T., & Earle, R. (2012). *Weight training: Steps to success* (4th ed.). Champaign, IL: Human Kinetics.

This easy-to-follow resistance-training manual is a step-by-step approach for those with little to no strength-training background.

Bompa, T., Di Pasquale, M., & Cornacchia, L. (2003). *Serious strength training* (2nd ed.). Champaign, IL: Human Kinetics.

Advanced strength-training principles and programs are described and illustrated.

Delavier, F. (2010). *Strength training anatomy* (3rd ed.). Champaign, IL: Human Kinetics.

If you're curious about which exercises develop particular muscles, this book is for you. A multitude of pictures clearly illustrates the specific musculature trained and most primary strength-training exercises.

Jenkins, J. (1975). *A greater strength*. Old Tappan, NJ: Revell.

This book documents the life of one of the strongest men who ever lived—Paul Anderson. A modern-day "Samson," Anderson has an interesting spiritual journey as well.

National Strength and Conditioning Association. (2008). *Essentials of strength training and conditioning* (3rd ed.). Champaign, IL: Human Kinetics.

This is *the* manual for strength-training professionals or anyone desiring to expand his or her weight-training expertise.

# Suggested Websites

www.acefitness.org
The American Council on Exercise (ACE) site is dedicated to developing personal trainers, but it has some excellent information on strength training for consumers.

www.nsca-lift.org
The National Strength and Conditioning Association site is for personal trainers and strength coaches.

www.teamusa.org/USA-Weightlifting.aspx
The USA Weightlifting site is an excellent source for those interested in recreational or competitive Olympic weightlifting.

www.usapowerlifting.com
The USA Powerlifting site is for those who may be interested in recreational or competitive powerlifting.

# Twitter

On Twitter, follow @acefitness.

# 7

# Flexibility Assessment and Training

Peter Walters

After reading this chapter, you should be able to do the following:

1. Define common flexibility terms.
2. Identify factors that affect flexibility.
3. Understand the benefits of flexibility.
4. Be able to assess your flexibility.
5. Describe five types of flexibility training.
6. Know effective guidelines for improving and maintaining flexibility.

## World's Most Flexible Man?

In the space of seconds, Daniel Browning Smith can fit himself into a box that is 16 inches (66.04 cm) wide, 13.5 inches (55.88 cm) tall, and 19.5 inches (68.58 cm) long, with a total volume of 18 gallons. He can dislocate both arms and legs and rotate his torso 180 degrees. This five-time Guinness World Record holder is commonly known as the "Rubberboy" for his remarkable feats. (Want to see for yourself? Go to www.therubberboy.com; Smith, 2012.)

**The flexibility** that the Rubberboy exhibits is far from average, and you probably do not want such extreme flexibility. However, you may be tired of the frequent tension and stiffness throughout your body and desire an ease and suppleness that flexibility training can help you enjoy. In this chapter, you will learn what flexibility is, what factors affect a person's range of motion, the actual benefits of flexibility (you might be surprised to find out that not all purported benefits are scientifically justified), and methods for enhancing your mobility.

## What Is Flexibility?

**Flexibility** is derived from the Latin *flectere* or *flexibilis*, which means "to bend." Human physical flexibility is commonly defined as the **range of motion (ROM)** that is possible in a joint or group of joints. In the discipline of exercise science, ROM is typically measured using a protractor-like device called a **goniometer**.

Figure 7.1*a* demonstrates the elbow joint of a person who has 180 degrees of extension. Compare this photo to the person depicted in figure 7.1*b* who has only 160 degrees of flexion at the elbow joint. Often injuries are one of the factors contributing to less than normal ROM. At the other extreme is the person depicted in figure 7.1*c* who has 200 degrees of flexion at the elbow joint. A term often used to describe the person in figure 7.1*c* is *double-jointed*. The term is a misnomer, since it does not accurately describe this person's anatomy. Those labeled as double-jointed do not have two joints where normal people have only one.

Two terms that more accurately describe this condition are **hypermobility** or **joint laxity**. Both are used to characterize a condition in which the muscle, connective tissue, and joint capsule surrounding a particular joint are extremely flexible. Generally this is not a condition to be desired. A rare genetic disorder called **Ehlers-Danlos syndrome** (EDS), more specifically EDS type III, is characterized by a defect in the collagen fibers that make up connective tissues. People with this condition are at increased risk for **sprains** (stretch or tearing of a ligament), dislocations, **subluxations** (partial dislocations), and the early onset of osteoarthritis.

So flexibility, which is a measure of a person's range of motion, should fall within a particular range. Humans, and more specifically humans' joints, can suffer from either being too limited or limitless in their range of motion. Most people do not suffer from being too flexible but rather from being inflexible. Fortunately, in most cases this can be corrected by applying a few principles discussed later in this chapter.

## Five Factors That Affect Flexibility

As with most other physical qualities such as strength, cardiorespiratory endurance, and agility, several factors contribute to your level of flexibility:

1. Anatomical
   a. Joint structure
   b. Ligaments and tendons

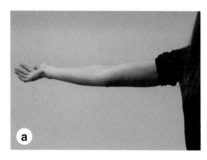 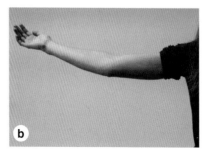 

**Figure 7.1**    *(a)* Elbow extension at 180 degrees, which is a normal range of motion; *(b)* elbow extension at 160 degrees, which is a limited range of motion; *(c)* elbow extension at 200 degrees, which is an excessive range of motion.

c. Muscle elasticity

d. Stretch receptors

e. Other tissues

2. Age

3. Sex

4. Temperature

5. Physical inactivity

As you read through this section, note especially the particular factors that can be influenced by behavior. Those are the ones that you can leverage later to enhance your range of motion.

## Anatomical: Joint Structure

*Joint structure* refers to how the skeleton is designed to connect articulating bones. Figure 7.2 illustrates six major types of joints in the body.

By examining figure 7.2, it is easy to see how just the structure of the joint permits wide-ranging deviations and movement. For example, the elbow is a **hinge joint** and permits movement in only one plane, similar to the way a door swings back and forth on one axis. Contrast that with the shoulder joint, which is a **ball-and-socket joint** that has

360 degrees of rotation in virtually every plane of movement.

## Anatomical: Ligaments and Tendons

Connective tissues, specifically ligaments and tendons, also affect range of motion. A **ligament** attaches one bone to another, whereas a **tendon** connects muscle to bone. Although both of these fibers bend easily, they are not designed to extend. In one classic study, collagen fibers (the primary component of both ligaments and tendons) resisted extending even when loaded with resistance 10,000 times their original weight (Verzar, 1963). When tendons or ligaments are stretched beyond their normal capacity, mechanical weakening results (Rigby et al., 1959; Warren et al., 1971, 1976). So when stretching, the goal is not to stretch tendons and ligaments.

## Anatomical: Muscular Elasticity

Assuming that your bone structure is normal and your ligaments and tendons are healthy, most of the flexibility of your joints is determined by the muscles and their fascia. Unlike tendons and ligaments,

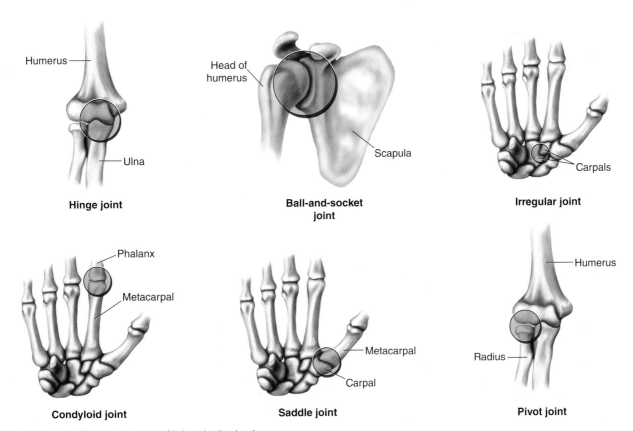

**Figure 7.2** Six major types of joints in the body.

skeletal muscle is designed to extend and contract. There are visual effects of contraction, as when you flex your biceps muscle. Although extension is more difficult to observe, muscles can typically extend to about 150 percent of their resting length (Alter, 2004).

## Anatomical: Stretch Receptors

Two stretch receptors, **muscle spindles** and **Golgi tendon organs**, provide information regarding movement, position, and changes in muscle length and tension. Muscle spindles are located in the center of skeletal muscle and provide feedback to the brain as to muscle length. Golgi tendon organs are located near either end of the muscle fiber within the tendon and are sensitive to changes in muscle length but also respond to increases in muscle tension (Fredette, 2001). Because of these responses, people are attuned to the "edge" of a stretch—the point where the stretch begins to hurt and feel uncomfortable. With training, the sensitivity of these two neurological receptors allows for increased degrees of motion (Magnusson et al., 1996).

## Anatomical: Adipose Tissue

The last anatomical feature is adipose tissue or body fat, which is increasingly becoming a problem for North Americans. Quite simply, excessive amounts of fat get in the way of movement. Overweight people often have great difficulty in bending over to tie shoelaces because abdominal mass impedes movement.

## Age

Children can often perform movements with ease that most adults find nearly impossible. Research into flexibility across the life span suggests that the average person's level of flexibility peaks some time from age 15 to 18. This is generally maintained until the mid-20s, when it begins to decrease (Knudson et al., 2000). One study reported that flexibility in the average person decreases about 20 to 30 percent between 30 and 70 years of age (Kell et al., 2001). One reason for this age-associated decline has to do with **collagen**. Collagen is the primary connective protein in the body. In aging, the body's ability to produce collagen is reduced and the structural components of collagen change, making it more rigid and the body less flexible (Alter, 2004).

## Sex

The average woman is more flexible than the average man (Alter, 2004). Although the reason for this difference is not completely understood, one possible contributor is the hormonal differences between sexes. Women have a unique hormonal makeup that makes stretching during childbirth possible. Some scientists have suggested that this hormonal difference equips women with an enhanced degree of flexibility throughout the entire body (Nieman, 2003).

## Temperature

As connective and muscular tissue temperature rises, stiffness decreases and extensibility increases (Laban, 1962; Noonan et al., 1993; Rigby, 1964). This is one of the reasons it is critical to thoroughly warm up before stretching. Some experts report up to a 20 percent increase in range of motion after warming up (Hoeger & Hoeger, 2011). The now-popular Bikram yoga uses heat to aid in developing increased range of motion in 26 postures (Choudhury, 2007).

## Physical Inactivity

The American College of Sports Medicine has been involved in extensive health- and fitness-related research and supports the notion that active people are usually more flexible than sex- and age-matched inactive people. Studies have also consistently reported a lessening of collagen synthesis for inactive people (Alter, 2004). A type of general logic supports the notion of decreased flexibility with inactivity. Consider perhaps the fastest way to lose joint mobility: joint immobilization. When joints are immobilized after injury in a hard cast, dramatic levels of flexion and extension are lost within a matter of weeks.

The good news is that although there are some factors over which people have little to no control, there are several, such as muscle elasticity, stretch receptors, adipose tissue, temperature, and activity level, that can be controlled and result in significantly increased range of motion.

# Benefits of Flexibility

Many aspects of flexibility remain a mystery. One reason for this is that the number of well-controlled and well-designed studies is woefully lacking, especially when considering the comparative literature on cardiorespiratory fitness, strength training, and weight management. Consequently there is simply not sufficient evidence to support or refute many declarations commonly made about flexibility. Well-meaning trainers, coaches, and other health care professionals frequently encourage athletes and nonathletes to stretch to avoid injury, reduce soreness, enhance performance, and gain a host of other potential advantages. Yet what evidence is there to support these recommendations? This section summarizes the research related to the benefits of flexibility training. The benefits are placed into one of three categories: doubtful, possible, and reliable.

## Doubtful Benefits

This category is reserved for benefits for which there is no scientific support. While applied practitioners are almost always far ahead of scientists when it comes to innovative and unique practices, given time, controlled scientific studies eventually support or refute the numerous anecdotal proclamations of experts in health and fitness. The single benefit placed in this category may be a surprise, since it is one of the benefits most often attributed to stretching: reduced muscular soreness.

If you have muscular soreness after a hard weight-training workout, long run, or rugged bike ride, you could benefit from some mild to moderate stretching. But does stretching really help? Currently there are no well-controlled studies that support the notion (Anderson, 2005; Lund et al., 1998).

You should keep in mind two cautions before tossing this benefit aside completely. First, there are many unanswered questions related to the delayed-onset of muscular soreness (DOMS). Very little is known about why DOMS occurs or how to alleviate it (Armstrong, 2003). In light of the dearth of knowledge surrounding DOMS, perhaps investigators are not asking the right questions or looking in the right locations. Or they simply don't have the sophisticated research instrumentation that helps them uncover the benefits that do exist. Yet, given the current status of science, this is not one well-designed study to support this claim.

## Possible Benefits

This category describes benefits where the jury is still out. Put simply, there is insufficient scientific evidence to either support the characteristic as a benefit or discount it as a waste of time. So consider these metaphorically as "yellow light" areas in which you need to proceed with caution.

### Reduced Risk of Injury

Several studies have suggested that stretching before exercise does not reduce the likeliness of injury. In a review of 361 studies on the impact of stretching on injury rates, investigators concluded that stretching was not significantly associated with the reduction of total injuries (Thacker et al., 2004). More recently,

364 studies were identified, and researchers concluded that only one study suggested that stretching helped reduce injuries (Small et al., 2008). Even more discouraging is that one investigator suggested that stretching before physical activity is more likely to cause injury than to prevent it (Shrier, 2004).

Although this evidence sounds compelling, you should note some key factors before drawing conclusions. First, although many studies were identified in both reviews, only a very small number of them were actually selected for review. In the 2004 review, more than 30 studies were identified as possibilities for analysis, but only 6 were actually included. In the 2008 review, only 7 of the more than 50 study possibilities were included. The primary reason given by investigators in both of these reviews for not including well over 95 percent of the studies was poor design, assessment, and controls. Furthermore, investigators in the 2008 review reported that three out of the seven studies had significant reductions in musculotendinous and ligament injuries despite insignificant reductions in all injury risks (Small et al., 2008). In other words, almost half of the studies in the most current review showed some reduction in injuries. Finally, some experts recognized that although stretching may not have an immediate benefit to injury reduction, they argue that longitudinal data, which have not been thoroughly investigated, would be a better indicator of the effect of stretching on injury rates (Shrier, 2004; Woods et al., 2007).

So there is no consistent relationship between stretching and total number of injuries, a point the U.S. Centers for Disease Control and Prevention summarized well (Thacker et al., 2004). In time and with additional research, a more conclusive answer might be drawn.

### Increased Performance

Former Los Angeles Dodgers baseball manager Tommy Lasorda had his players stretch before and after every workout. Mike Marshall, coach and former Cy Young Award winner, refused to allow time for his players to stretch, believing it to be a complete waste of time. Which expert coach is correct?

In a review, 23 studies on stretching and performance were examined. Twenty-two reported no significant benefit to performance outcomes (Shrier, 2004). In a review on the effect of stretching on strength performance, investigators concluded that it had an acutely negative effect on strength activities (Rubini et al., 2007). Finally, in a study examining the effects of stretching on sprint and jump performances of elite athletes, investigators found that neither static, nor dynamic, nor combinations of those stretching protocols enhanced performance. In one case, **dynamic stretching**, which typically involves stretching while completing repetitive movement patterns, immediately followed by static stretching actually reduced the athletes' sprint performance (Chaouachi et al., 2010).

The weight of the evidence seems to point toward stretching having little to no effect on subsequent physical activity. However, the detrimental effects of stretching reported in the previous studies used protocols that were not representative of a typical warm-up and stretching program used by athletes before competition. For example, studies used stretch treatments of 15 or more minutes for a single muscle group (Choudhury, 2007; Knudson et al., 2000; Rigby et al., 1959), which is a far greater time than what is commonly practiced. In addition, several studies observed performance decrements after stretching when there was no submaximal exercise preceding it (Gulbahar et al., 2006; Knudson et al., 2000; Rigby et al., 1959) or when there were no practice trials of the test activity. Here is an example of how testing procedures were implemented. Participants performed active stretching of a single muscle group for up to 15 minutes. For this example, let's say they focused on their quadriceps. Then without any additional warm-up or practice trials they were asked for maximal exertion in a quad-dominate movement such as vertical jump. Although this research model seems necessary for isolating the influence of stretching, it is possible that the low-intensity exercise and practice components of a warm-up may offset any potential negative effects of stretching. Thus, additional controlled studies need to be performed before a definitive answer can be established.

## Reliable Benefits

While statistically speaking nothing is 100 percent guaranteed, most of the studies in this section report a 95 percent likelihood that stretching will yield the benefits described.

### Helps Maintain ROM at Any Age

The inability to move joints freely can have a profound effect on a person's ability to function. Although you do not likely have reduced functionality as a result of limited ROM, it is not uncommon for older adults to have tremendous difficulty bending over to tie their shoes or squatting down to pick up a piece of paper from the floor. Both of these daily activities require the most flexibility of what would be classified as typical activities in a person's daily routine (Kell et al., 2001). Yet, a host of other lifestyle activities require

significant levels of flexibility that often go unnoticed. Consider that when driving a car, you must be able to turn your head approximately 180 degrees from side to side to have good visibility. Decreases in stride length of 10 to 20 percent will lower leg flexion and extension and result in a much slower walking pace. Insufficient neck, shoulder, and back flexibility not only contribute to poor posture but are believed to lead to increased lower-back pain (Daltroy et al., 1997; Hochschuler & Reznick, 1998; Inlander & Skinner, 1997; Miller & Opie, 1997; Roth & Roehrs, 1996).

In summary, reductions in range of motion can lead adults toward dependency on others for assistance and can expose them to a variety of risks (Warburton et al., 2001). The good news is that at any age, you can enhance and maintain ROM through a systematic flexibility program, and there is a host of scientific evidence to support this claim.

### Reduction in Muscular Tension

Society holds plenty of stress and muscular tension. Approximately one-sixth of the products advertised in a recent sales catalog for the popular retail store Brookstone (2011) are designed to help alleviate stress and muscle tension. Their fall 2011 catalog is titled "Get Over It" and features items such as eye masks, lights, hot and cold wraps, and head-to-toe massagers to help customers "get over" their stress.

Fortunately, people do not need to need to spend $3,000 on a "human touch" massage chair to reduce muscular tension. Simple stretching does this job quite well. In fact, in a classic study, moderate stretching exercises were more effective than prescription medications for reducing muscular tension (DeVries & Adams, 1972).

Much like the need for urination, stress, muscular tension, and stiffness build throughout the day. How wonderful the dissipation of this tension feels after a quick stretch break. Even moderate levels of stretching have been shown to reduce muscular stiffness and tension for as long as one hour (Klinge et al., 1997; Magnusson, 1998; Magnusson et al., 1996). A relatively inexpensive tool for increasing both the enjoyment and benefits of moderate stretching is a foam roller (see Foam Rolling sidebar).

Although you may be a bit disheartened to learn that stretching probably does not or may not produce some of the results you have been told, the fact that stretching can help you maintain your mobility until the day you die or that stretching is not only a low-cost alternative to muscular relaxation but does a better job at relieving muscular tension than many drugs should encourage you to include flexibility training as part of your regular fitness program.

# Foam Rolling: Banish Muscular Knots

"I've got this crick in my neck" or "There's a knot in my leg" are often descriptions of **trigger points**, small nodules of skeletal muscle felt just beneath the skin, typically the size of a pea or small bean. While the exact physiology of these "knots" is unknown, the best way to alleviate a trigger point is through direct pressure, which can be administered by a physical therapist, athletic trainer, or massage therapist. This type of therapy is commonly referred to as **myofascial release** (Travell et al., 1983).

What help can be offered to college students who typically cannot afford the services of a professional therapist? One possible answer is a foam roller. Often called the "poor person's massage," a foam roller acts like a rolling pin rolling out lumps in dough. The foam roller is typically placed underneath a part of the body that needs attention, and body weight is used to exert pressure.

Although there are literally hundreds of positions in which a foam roller can be used, table 7.1 describes six commonly used techniques.

## Table 7.1 Six Fundamental Foam Rolling Movements

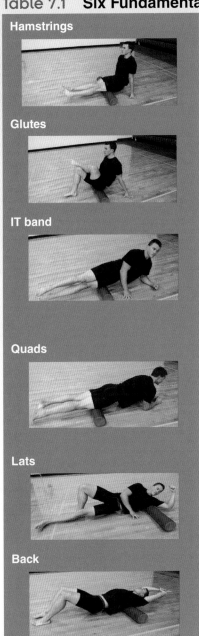

| | |
|---|---|
| **Hamstrings** | Sit on a foam roller with your hands on the floor behind you for support. Begin on the top of the hamstrings and slowly allow the roller to move down the hamstring to just above the knees. Slowly return to the staring position. If you need more pressure cross your right leg over your left and vice versa. If this is too much pressure, try it without crossing your legs. |
| **Glutes** | Sit on a foam roller with your hands on the floor behind you for support and your knees bent. Cross your left leg over your right knee in a figure 4 position, shift your weight slightly to the left, and slowly roll yourself on the foam roll by pushing and pulling the floor with your right foot and left hand. Switch and do the other side as well. |
| **IT band** | The iliotibial band, located on the distal side of the leg, extends from the pelvis to just below the knee. Iliotibial band friction syndrome (ITBS) is a common injury experienced by many runners, cyclists, or hikers. This particular exercise is targeted at both preventing and treating ITBS. Lie on your side with the foam roller under your left hip. From this position, slowly roll your body upward using your hands to pull you along the floor. Continue to just above the knee. Switch and do the other side as well. |
| **Quads** | Place the foam roller under your hips and lie on it so that the foam roll is perpendicular to your body. Use your forearms to pull your body upward so that your quadriceps roll over the foam roll. You can make slight adjustments to the manner in which your quads move over the roller in order to target the inside and outside of your quads as well as the middle. If you need more pressure, cross one foot behind the other. |
| **Lats** | Lie on your side with the foam roller in the pit of your arm. From this position, slowly roll your body forward and backward against the foam roll. Switch and do the other side as well. |
| **Back** | Lie on your back with your knees bent and feet on the floor. Place a foam roller under your back just below your shoulder blades. Move from the shoulder blades to the lower back in a nice slow motion, using your feet for movement pressure. |

Data from Verran 2007.

*(continued)*

*(continued)*

Accomplished runner and author Clint Verran (2007) offers five guidelines for using a foam roller.

1. Roll back and forth across the painful or stiff area for 60 seconds.
2. Spend extra time directly over the knot or trigger point itself.
3. Roll the injured area two or three times a day. For prevention of injuries, two or three times a week is recommended.
4. Avoid rolling over bony areas.
5. Always stretch the area after foam rolling.

Foam rollers come in various sizes. The one depicted in table 7.1 is 6 inches (15 cm) in diameter and 36 inches (0.9 m) in length. You can purchase one of these at many local sporting good stores for less than $20. Try seeing a professional therapist for help with your trigger points for that amount.

## Assessing Your Flexibility

You might have greater-than-normal flexibility in one joint, fairly normal flexibility in a second, and even lower-than-normal flexibility in a third joint. For that reason, any single measure of flexibility may not be a good indicator of your overall flexibility. Therefore, a meaningful flexibility assessment must include more than one joint. In this section, two clinical assessments of flexibility, one for the lower body and another for the upper body, are described.

### Sit-and-Reach

The sit-and-reach test is probably the most popular flexibility test administered. Several valid variations of this test exist (Baltaci et al., 2003; Hui et al., 2000; Lemmink et al., 2003). The ACSM (2009) currently recommends the Canadian trunk forward flexion test (Canadian Physical Activity, Fitness & Life Appraisal, 2003). This test involves measuring forward trunk flexion using the sit-and-reach box.

After warming up, remove footwear. Sit on a flat surface and place the soles of your feet on the front of the sit-and-reach box (as seen in figure 7.3a).

Keeping the legs fully extended and knees locked into position, place your hands one on top of the other and push the metal slider forward as far as possible (see figure 7.3b). While pushing the metal slider forward, refrain from any fast, jerky movements, which not only increase the chance of injury but also can cause inaccurate measurements. To ensure you do not shove the metal slider forward by bouncing, maintain an extended position for a minimum of one second before returning to the starting position. In addition to bouncing forward, other common errors in this test include not taking the time to warm up, flexing the knees while reaching forward, and reaching farther with one hand than the other.

You should have at least three trials in order to determine maximum trunk flexion. Your farthest reach is compared to the standards listed in table 7.2.

The sit-and-reach box used in these photographs has a "zero" point set at 23 centimeters. If your box's zero point is set at 26 centimeters, add 3 centimeters from each value before comparing your scores to the reference norms.

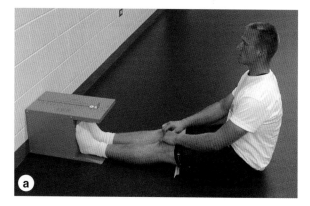
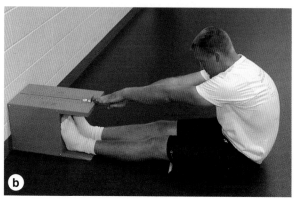

**Figure 7.3** The Canadian trunk forward flexion test using the sit-and-reach box: *(a)* starting position; *(b)* stretching position.

## Table 7.2    Canadian Fitness Standards for Sit-and-Reach

| Age (years) | 15–19 | | 20–29 | | 30–39 | | 40–49 | | 50–59 | | 60 + | |
|---|---|---|---|---|---|---|---|---|---|---|---|---|
| **Sex** | **M** | **F** | **M** | **F** | **M** | **F** | **M** | **F** | **M** | **F** | **M** | **F** |
| Excellent | >39 | >40 | >39 | >40 | >37 | >39 | >34 | >37 | >35 | >37 | >32 | >34 |
| Above average | 33–38.9 | 35–39.9 | 33–38.9 | 35–39.9 | 31–36.9 | 34–38.9 | 27–33.9 | 32–36.9 | 26–34.9 | 30–36.9 | 23–31.9 | 28–33.9 |
| Average | 28–32.9 | 31–34.9 | 28–32.9 | 31–34.9 | 26–30.9 | 30–33.9 | 22–26.9 | 28–31.9 | 22–25.9 | 27–29.9 | 19–22.9 | 25–27.9 |
| Below average | 23–27.9 | 26–30.9 | 23–27.9 | 26–30.9 | 21–25.9 | 25–29.9 | 17–21.9 | 23–27.9 | 15–21.9 | 23–26.9 | 13–18.9 | 21–24.9 |
| Poor | <23 | <26 | <23 | <23 | <21 | <25 | <17 | <23 | <15 | <23 | <13 | <21 |

From *ACSM's guidelines for exercise testing and prescription*, 6th ed.; Data: Canada Fitness Survey. All scores are measured in centimeters.

## Shoulder Rotation

This test requires the participation of at least one other person as a test administrator and the use of an Acuflex III measuring rod. You should gradually warm up by reaching above the head with both arms as high as possible.

While you warm up, the test administrator should measure your biacromial width, which is between the lateral edges of the acromion process (see figure 7.4*a*). The test administrator records your biacromial width to the nearest half inch (the *yellow* scale on the measuring rod).

Next, grip the rod with your right hand using a supinated grip so that the pinky finger is adjacent to the *white* zero point as illustrated in figure 7.4*b*. The validity of this test rests on the assumption that the right hand maintains this position relative to the zero point throughout this test.

Note that the edge of the hand is right next to the *white* zero point in figure 7.4*b*. The administrator places the measuring rod behind your back, and you grip it with your left hand, also using a supinated grip with the arms almost as wide as possible.

The administrator asks you to slowly move the bar from behind the back to overhead (as illustrated in figure 7.5) with elbows locked. This first trial should be done without a lot of difficulty if the grip is wide enough. Now return the bar to behind your back. Repeat this movement, moving the bar from behind the back to an overhead position, narrowing the grip one to two inches with each successful trial. Stop when you are no longer able to perform this movement without undue strain or the ability to keep from bending the elbows. To obtain reach width, the administrator simply records the location of your left hand (from position of the little finger). If, for example, the left little finger is at 42, then your

**Figure 7.4**    *(a)* Measuring biacromial width; *(b)* correct grip to start shoulder rotation test.

**Figure 7.5** Slowly move the bar from behind your back to overhead.

reach width is 42. Now you're ready to calculate shoulder rotation by subtracting the biacromial width from the reach width. For example, if the last successful trial was 42 inches (107 cm) and the biacromial width was 15 inches (38 cm), the shoulder rotation is 27 inches (69 cm) (42 in. − 15 in. = 27 in.; 107 cm − 38 cm = 69 cm). To evaluate your shoulder rotation, compare your results to the standards identified in table 7.3.

As stated at the beginning of this section, flexibility is joint specific and needs to be assessed in more than one location. The two assessments outlined in this chapter serve as a very basic starting point. Eventually you may want to take a more comprehensive assessment such as a Flexitest (Araújo, 2004), which provides a detailed analysis of range of motion in each of the major joints of the body.

Regardless of your assessment outcomes, the good news is that you can maintain or dramatically improve your existing range of motion through training. Specific methods for designing an efficient flexibility program are outlined in the next section.

# Five Types of Stretching

Stretching, a type of physical activity done with the intent of improving range of motion, can be subdivided into five major categories: active, passive, static, ballistic, and proprioceptive neuromuscular facilitation (PNF). Knowing these categories will enable you to increase the variety of your stretching exercises and give you insight into which method of stretching to use for a specific activity or sport.

## Active Force

The first two classifications, active and passive, are not methods typically understood by the general public because they are fundamentally about how force is

## Table 7.3  Standards for Shoulder Rotation

| Age (years) | 15–19 | | 20–29 | | 30–39 | | 40–49 | | 50–59 | | >60 | |
|---|---|---|---|---|---|---|---|---|---|---|---|---|
| Sex | M | F | M | F | M | F | M | F | M | F | M | F |
| Excellent | <15.4 | <10.9 | <15.9 | <7.5 | <19.8 | <13.8 | <22.2 | <16.4 | <27 | <20.5 | <28.9 | <24.7 |
| Above average | 22–15.3 | 15.7–10.8 | 21.6–16 | 14.9–7.4 | 23.2–19.9 | 18.5–13.9 | 26.6–22.3 | 21.5–16.5 | 29.3–27.1 | 23.5–20.6 | 30.5–29 | 30.3–24.8 |
| Average | 25.5–22.1 | 20–15.8 | 25.1–21.7 | 19.5–15 | 26.8–23.3 | 21.6–18.6 | 28.9–26.7 | 24.1–21.6 | 30.5–29.4 | 25.5–23.6 | 32.9–30.6 | 32.3–30.4 |
| Below average | 29–25.6 | 24–20.1 | 27.8–25.2 | 23.6–19.6 | 30.5–26.9 | 25.2–21.7 | 32.6–29 | 26.8–24.2 | 31.4–30.6 | 28.5–25.6 | 34.2–33 | 33.8–32.4 |
| Poor | >29 | >24 | >27.8 | >23.6 | >30.5 | >25.2 | >32.6 | >26.8 | >31.4 | >28.5 | >34.2 | >33.8 |

Adapted from W. Hoeger and S. Hoeger, 1991, *Lifetime physical fitness and wellness: A personalized program*, 2nd ed. (Belmont, CA: Cengage Learning-Wadsworth).

applied to the area being stretched rather than distinguishing a particular method of stretching. However, by understanding their distinctiveness, you can understand the method of force being applied to the joint.

**Active force** is the movement achieved in a joint through self-initiated muscle contraction. Most often this is accomplished by contracting the muscle opposite to the one you are stretching. For example, if you want to stretch the hamstrings, the quadriceps must be contracted, as illustrated in figure 7.6.

In addition to the opposing muscle assisting in elongating various tissues, this method taps into a neurological reflex called reciprocal inhibition. **Reciprocal inhibition** is the cooperation of the neuromuscular system to relax the opposing contracted muscles.

While this type of stretching is based on a sound scientific neuromuscular approach, it has one major shortcoming: Most beginners do not have enough muscular strength to create a necessary force for overloading the stretched tissue to the degree necessary for adaptation to occur. Additional force can be introduced through passive force.

## Passive Force

**Passive force** occurs when something besides contractile muscle stretches tissue. Typically, this something is gravity, a partner, or some type of rope or band. For example, when you stand on your toes on a platform and allow your upper body to flex forward as low as possible, you are allowing gravity to supply additional resistance. If you grasp a cloth strap to flex your upper body even farther, as illustrated in figure 7.7, you are engaged in passive stretching. Because an

outside force is helping you stretch, this type of stretching is sometimes referred to as assisted stretching.

The key to focus on with the first two types of stretching is how the tension (resistance) is applied to the area being stretched. Active force creates a muscular stretch through muscular contractions—typically the opposing muscle to the one being stretched. Passive force, as the term implies, does not employ direct muscular contraction but rather applies force via gravity or the use of ropes and bands, which technically does require a bit of indirect (musculature not associated with the area being stretched) muscular assistance.

## Static Stretching

The next three classifications, static, ballistic, and PNF, all have more traditional movements, particularly the static and ballistic methods. When people talk about stretching, most often they refer to static stretching. **Static stretching** is performed by moving slowly to a lengthened position and then holding that position for a time until finally relaxing the area being stretched.

This slow and controlled method is popular for three reasons. First, the stretches are generally more familiar to the general public. Second, they are thought to be the safest method, and finally, static stretching minimizes the inhibiting influence of muscle spindles. As stated earlier, if a muscle

**Figure 7.6**   One example of active stretching is contracting the quadriceps while stretching the hamstrings.

**Figure 7.7**   Using bands to help engage in passive stretching.

spindle is quickly lengthened or stretched too far, a signal is sent to the central nervous system for the muscle under tension to contract. This contraction inhibits additional range of motion, thus protecting the muscle and connective tissue from damage. While this sensory response is important for daily activity, this activation inhibits your ability to engage in stretching movements.

A key question is how a person communicates to muscle spindles that developmental stretching, as opposed to harmful movement, is being performed. Two factors hold the answer: speed and repetitions. By slowly applying tension via static stretching and repeatedly stretching the same joint, muscle spindles lose their sensitivity to the process of elongation and developmental stretching can occur.

## Ballistic Stretching

**Ballistic stretching** is bouncing, bobbing, rocking, or moving in a pulsing pattern to place a muscle in and out of an elongated position. In the early 1950s, calisthenics (body-weight exercises) and ballistic stretching were popular forms of exercise in physical education classes and military training. Then in the 1970s ballistic stretching lost popularity because it was thought to increase the potential for injury and be less effective than static stretching. Ballistic stretching has regained some momentum, especially among athletes, since neither of these claims has been proven to be scientifically accurate. More recently, it seems that ballistic stretching, especially for those involved in explosive sports, is actually preferred (Shrier, 2004; Young & Elliott, 2001). This is because, according to the most recent reviews, static stretching seems to have a negative effect on subsequent explosive activities such as sprinting and jumping. However, ballistic stretching does not seem to produce the same ill effect.

One consideration to keep in mind is the need for a good general warm-up preceding ballistic movements. In addition, you need to use graduated intensity in ballistic movements. An example of these two principles employed correctly may help. Imagine that a pitcher needs to prepare to throw high-velocity baseballs. Ideally, the pitcher would begin with a 5- to 10-minute general warm-up, such as jogging or cycling. Then the pitcher's body is prepared to begin ballistic movements such as arm circles, illustrated in figure 7.8a-g, or torso twists, illustrated in figure 7.8h-o.

Gradually the speed and intensity of these movements can increase. Now the pitcher is ready to perform the whole throwing motion (with a ball), building up the speed and force of the throw as was done in the ballistic movements. Ballistic stretching after the proper warm-up can be effective, especially if you're involved in activities with high-velocity movement.

## Proprioceptive Neuromuscular Facilitation

**Proprioceptive neuromuscular facilitation (PNF)** is a stretching technique that uses the body's neuromuscular system to enhance range of motion, improve strength, and promote functional progression. PNF was originally developed in the early 1950s by Herman Kabat as a rehabilitation tool for people suffering from musculoskeletal injuries or disabilities (Kabat, 1950, 1955; Levine & Kabat, 1952, 1953). Some studies suggest that this is the most effective method of increasing range of motion (Nieman, 2003).

Among the many methods of PNF stretching, one of the most popular is the contract–relax method. Here's an example of this method when used to stretch the hamstrings: A person lies on the floor with the right leg pulled upward by a partner so that the right hamstring is stretched. After holding that position for 15 to 30 seconds, the partner provides resistance for the person being stretched to execute a 5- to 10-second isometric contraction of the right hamstring. Next, the person being stretched relaxes the right hamstring as the partner actively stretches it. This process of actively stretching and isometrically contracting the muscle is repeated several times so that additional range of motion is achieved.

Several limitations exist for the general population in implementing PNF stretching. First, PNF has an added level of complexity requiring knowledge on sequencing muscular contraction, relaxation, and stretching. Second, performing this type of stretching requires more time. Third, most PNF stretches require the assistance of a partner. Fourth, it generally produces more discomfort during a stretch routine since more tension on the connective tissue is created through muscular contractions. Finally, there is more muscular soreness associated with this method of stretching than any other.

PNF stretching technique is best if used in the context of physical therapy, athletic training, or an advanced strength and conditioning program supervised by a knowledgeable professional.

# Six Guidelines for Maximum Flexibility

No matter the type of stretching you choose, following six guidelines will dramatically affect the outcome of your flexibility work. One additional benefit of following these guidelines is time conservation. Often in training there are points at which additional time and effort add little to improvement outcomes. Perhaps student athletes are willing to spend an extra hour or two per day to get an extra 1 to 2 percent increase in flexibility, but this is just not feasible for most college students. Therefore, these guidelines not only are based on the best science practices but also save time.

## Warm-Up

People are often told to stretch at the beginning of their exercise program; however, this recommendation is ineffective and can lead to injury. In general, heat allows human joints to move more easily and have an increased range of motion. One reason for this is that as muscle temperature rises, the viscous medium within connective tissue changes from a Vaseline-like substance to oil. Furthermore, tissues in the body, such as muscle, elongate more easily as heat increases. Some researchers who examine the extensibility of muscle under various temperatures have reported up to a 20 percent increase in muscle extensibility when moderate heat is applied (Funk et al., 2001).

This evidence suggests that the most optimal time to stretch is after body temperature has risen. With the aim of conserving time, stretch after your workout. This way the training cycle is not broken into segments, and you can allow your body to cool down and stretch at the same time.

**Figure 7.8** *(a-g)* Proper technique for arm circles *(continued)*.

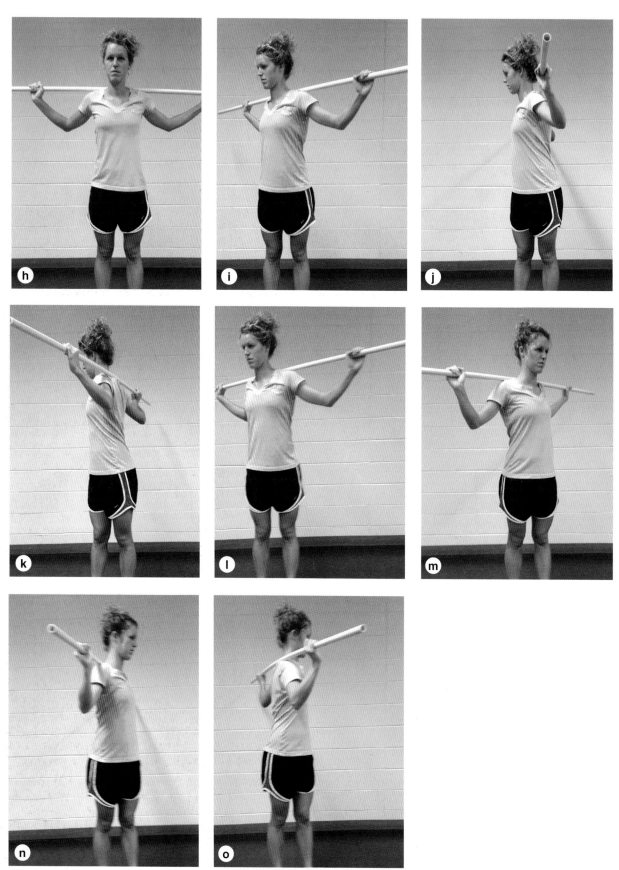

**Figure 7.8** *(continued) (h-o)* Proper technique for torso twists.

## Repetitions

Repetitions have to do with the number of times a particular stretching movement is repeated. For example, two repetitions in the toe touch require you to reach for your toes and, if static stretching is used, hold that position for a few seconds before returning to the starting position. One repetition of the exercise is then complete. You repeat this process to complete two repetitions.

In a series of well-controlled laboratory experiments using animal muscle and tendons, investigators discovered that the greatest change in muscle and tendon length occurs during the first four stretching attempts (Taylor et al., 1990). Even when as many as 10 repetitions were introduced, stretches beyond the fourth repetition did not result in significant increases in length. This knowledge can save you up to 60 percent of the time spent on stretching without significantly compromising the result.

## Intensity

Stretching muscle beyond its existing range of motion is necessary for improvement. Evidence suggests that muscles must be stretched at least 10 percent beyond their resting length for increased range of motion. This 10 percent recommendation is difficult to practically apply, so many scientists have correlated perceived exertions with changes in flexibility. In an applied sense, it is much easier to measure perceived exertion than to measure the percentage of change. John Walter, from the University of Michigan, reported that participants working at intensities from 85 to 100 percent noticed significantly greater flexibility improvements than participants who exerted a 60 percent effort while stretching. Investigators in the study failed to test whether intensities greater than 60 percent but less than 85 percent would yield similar benefits to those seen by the group who stretched at 85 to 100 percent of intensity (Alter, 2004).

Although stretching should produce some discomfort, it should not cause pain. Since discomfort and pain are subjective matters, it is difficult to give an absolute answer about where to draw the line when it comes to stretching intensity. Given the findings in the study just mentioned, perceived exertion greater than 85 percent is currently recommended.

## Time

The time guidelines recommended here refer to the amount of time a particular stretch is maintained or held, not the total amount of time spent completing all stretching exercises. The amount of time a stretching routine will take can easily be calculated by taking the number of movements multiplied by the number of repetitions.

One study (Bandy & Trion, 1994) compared the effectiveness of stretching the hamstrings statically for 15, 30, and 60 seconds. The study revealed that 30- and 60-second increments were more effective at increasing hamstring flexibility than stretching for 15 seconds or not stretching at all. However, the most significant finding of this study was that there were no significant differences between the groups that stretched for 30 and 60 seconds. This finding was further substantiated in a follow-up study (Bandy et al., 1997) that used a similar protocol. Other investigators have reported that stretching as long as 2 minutes does not significantly improve range of motion beyond the level of participants who stretched for only 30 seconds (Grady & Saxena 1991).

One study does seem to dispel the idea that stretching for longer than 30 seconds has little beneficial effect (Feland et al., 2001). In this study participants were randomly divided into three groups: those that stretched for 15, 30, and 60 seconds. Each of the participants stretched five times a week for six weeks. The results indicated that those who stretched for 60 seconds had the greatest increases in ROM. One critical factor to keep in mind is that all participants in this study were 65 years of age or older. The investigators speculated that the longer stretch duration "may have been more beneficial than shorter durations in overcoming the increased muscle stiffness and collagen deposition that accompany the aging process" (Feland et al., 2001 p. 1116).

Although there are a limited number of studies dealing with stretching duration, given the current evidence, the best recommendation for college students is to hold stretches for 30 seconds.

## Frequency

While stretching only twice per week for a minimum of five weeks has been shown to significantly improve flexibility (Baechle, 2008), most experts agree that substantially greater benefits can be obtained by stretching more often (ACSM, 2009). The American College of Sports Medicine recommends stretching five or six times per week, which is the generally accepted norm for flexibility training (ACSM, 2009). Some do recommend higher frequencies for maximal benefits (Apostolopoulos, 2011); however, that recommendation remains unproven through scientific investigation. Therefore until scientific studies suggest that additional frequency significantly increases the rate of ROM extensibility, the guideline established by the American College of Sports Medicine remains the benchmark.

## Breathing

Most people who practice stretches involving torso flexion and extension discover that breathing affects range of motion. Maximum torso flexion can be enhanced after exhaling. Just as letting the air out of an inner tube allows the tube to flex, voiding the diaphragm of air allows the torso greater degrees of movement. Most stretches are directly affected by breathing. All stretches can be indirectly affected by breathing. Inhaling in a slow, rhythmic manner seems to facilitate relaxation, which indirectly affects range of motion.

The only strict guideline related to breathing is to never hold your breath for an extended time while stretching (ACSM, 2009). Holding your breath not only inhibits relaxation but can also cause you to hyperventilate and pass out.

## Stretching Prescription

While it is always a bit tricky to promise results, various studies suggest that the average adult can improve static flexibility from 5 to 20 percent within 4 to 6 weeks of flexibility training (Alter, 2004; Hoeger & Hoeger, 2011). Of course, individual results will vary based on several factors, many of which have already been discussed (sex, age) and some of which have not (existing range of motion, time available to stretch, and motivation). A good thing to keep in mind is that a small investment in time spent stretching can yield significant results.

Often at the beginning of any type of new stretching program there are concerns about the possibility of performing the wrong stretch or stretching incorrectly. It's easy for novices to watch others who have been practicing flexibility training for years and gasp, "That looks dangerous! If I did that I'd break something." For those who feel that way, there are two important considerations to keep in mind.

First, no stretches are contraindicated for all people. *Contraindicated* is a medical term to identify a condition or factor that should be withheld. Beginners need some special consideration when prescribed stretching exercises, but no stretches should be universally blacklisted. However, there are unsafe ways of executing any movement. Everything depends on the individual's needs. Medical writer, Dr. Adele Lubell stated, "There are some stretches that some people can't do, and there are others that some people can do" (Lubell, 1989, p. 191). Dr. Mel Siff, former editor of *Fitness and Sports Review International* presents another way to look at the controversy of supposedly dangerous stretches: "There is generally no such thing as an unsafe stretch or exercise.... There are however unsafe ways of executing any movement for a specific individual at a specific time" (Siff, 1993, p. 128). In some health and wellness textbooks, more time is spent detailing stretches you should not perform rather than ones you should.

The second point is that while it is not recommended for beginners to attempt advanced stretching postures too quickly, almost anyone can perform a variation of advanced stretches. Take, for example the splits, as illustrated in figure 7.9*a*. It would be nearly impossible for a beginner to perform this stretch. However, a beginner can do several variations of this movement, as illustrated in figure 7.9 *b* through *d*.

The routine illustrated in figure 7.10 is a whole-body flexibility workout targeting the major joints of the body as recommended by the American College of Sports Medicine (ACSM, 2009). Notice that each of the stretches in this program uses a rope for assistance. Using a rope allows you to add assistance with minimal effort. You do not have to run out and purchase a rope for this program. A long belt will do. However, having a brightly colored rope in your dorm room not only allows you to perform these stretches with ease but is also a good reminder to do some stretching. The stretches outlined in figure 7.10 are safe for virtually all healthy college-age individuals.

## Next Steps

Though you may not have the flexibility of the Rubberboy (and probably do not want it), maintaining flexibility is a gift that you have some control over. Taking time after a warm-up to stretch various muscles and tendons may enhance your joy of movement, relaxation, and quality of life.

**Figure 7.9** Variations of the splits.

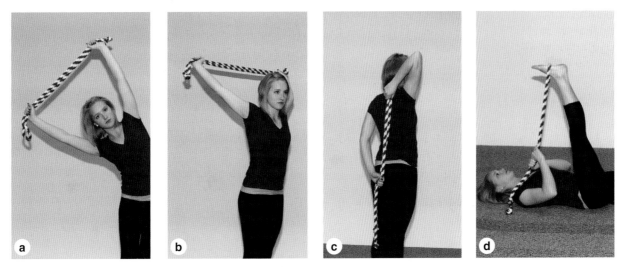

**Figure 7.10** General flexibility exercises *(continued)*.

**Figure 7.10** *(continued)*

## Key Terms

active force

ball-and-socket joint

ballistic stretching

collagen

dynamic stretching

Ehlers-Danlos syndrome (EDS)

flexibility

Golgi tendon organ

goniometer

hinge joint

hypermobility

joint laxity

ligament

muscle spindles

myofascial release

passive force

proprioceptive

neuromuscular facilitation (PNF)

range of motion (ROM)

reciprocal inhibition

sprain

static stretching

subluxation

tendon

trigger points

## Review Questions

1. Define flexibility.
2. List five factors that affect flexibility.
3. List the doubtful, possible, and reliable benefits of stretching.

4. How does a person determine and measure an optimal level of flexibility?
5. How does a person best improve or maintain flexibility?

## Application Activities

1. Perform a sit-and-reach test (or other tests as assigned by your instructor) to determine your back flexibility. Use table 7.2 to compare your score with the norms for your sex and age.

2. Write down your specific flexibility goals in a sentence or two.

    a. In a paragraph or two, assess the behavior and attitudes you are trying to change to improve your flexibility.

    b. Refine your goal with small, realistic, specific, measurable, and concrete steps.

    c. In a paragraph or two, predict and describe two significant obstacles that might prevent you from achieving your flexibility goal and describe your plan to overcome those obstacles.

    d. How will you measure progress in achieving your flexibility goal?

## References

ACSM. (2009). *ACSM guidelines for exercise testing and prescription*. Baltimore: Williams & Wilkins.

Alter, M.J. (2004). *Science of flexibility* (2nd ed.). Champaign, IL: Human Kinetics.

Anderson, J.C. (2005). Stretching before and after exercise: Effect on muscle soreness and injury risk. *Journal of Athletic Training, 40*(3), 218–20.

Apostolopoulos, N. (2011). *MicroStretching*. www.microstretching.com/nikos.php.

Araújo, C.G.S.d.A. (2004). *Flexitest: An innovative flexibility assessment method*. http://catdir.loc.gov/catdir/toc/ecip041/2003006317.html.

Armstrong, R. (2003). [Kinesiology seminar: what we know about DOMS after 20 years] Wheaton, IL..

Baechle, T. (2008). *Essentials of strength training and conditioning* (3rd ed.). Champaign, IL: Human Kinetics.

Baltaci, G., Un, N., Tunay, V., Besler, A., & Gerçeker, S. (2003). Comparison of three different sit and reach tests for measurement of hamstring flexibility in female university students. *British Journal of Sports Medicine, 37*(1), 59.

Bandy, W.D., Irion, J.M., & Briggler, M. (1997). The effect of time and frequency of static stretching on flexibility of the hamstring muscles. *Phys. Ther. 77*, 1090–96.

Bandy, W.D., & Trion, H.O. (1994). The effect of time on static stretch of the flexibility of the hamstring muscles. *Phys. Ther. 74*, 845–52.

Brookstone. (2011). *Fall 2011*. Oakbrook, IL: Brookstone.

Canadian physical activity, fitness & lifestyle appraisal. (2003). *The Canadian physical activity, fitness & lifestyle appraisal : CSEP's plan for healthy active living* (3rd ed.). Ottawa, Ont.: Canadian Society for Exercise Physiology.

Chaouachi, A., Castagna, C., Chtara, M., Brughelli, M., Turki, O.,Galy, O. Charmari, K. & Behm, D.G. (2010). Effect of warm-ups involving static or dynamic stretching on agility, sprinting, and jumping performance in trained individuals. *Journal of Strength & Conditioning Research, 24*(8), 2001–11.

Choudhury, B. (2007). *Bikram yoga : The guru behind hot yoga shows the way to radiant health and personal fulfillment*. New York: Morrow.

Daltroy, L.H., Iversen, M.D., Larson, M.G., Lew, R., Wright, E., Ryan, J., Zwerling, C., Fossel, A.H., & Liang, M.H. (1997). A controlled trial of an educational program to prevent low back injuries. *The New England Journal of Medicine, 337*(5), 322–28.

DeVries, H.A., & Adams, G.M. (1972). EMG comparison of single doses of exercise and meprobamate as to effects of muscular relaxation. *American Journal of Physical Medicine, 51*, 130–41.

Feland, J.B., Myrer, J.W., Schulthies, S.S., Fellingham, G.W., & Measom, G.W. (2001). The effect of duration of stretching of the hamstring muscle group for increasing range of motion in people aged 65 years or older. *Phys. Ther., 81*(5), 1110–17.

Fredette, D. (2001). Exercise recommendations for flexibility and range of motion. In J.L. Roitman (Ed.), *ACSM resources manual* (4th ed.). Philadelphia: Lippincott Williams & Wilkins.

Funk, D., Swank, A.M., Adams, K.J., & Treolo, D. (2001). Efficacy of moist heat pack application over static stretching on hamstring flexibility. *Journal of Strength & Conditioning Research, 15*(1), 123–26.

Grady, J.F., & Saxena, A. (1991). Effects of stretching the gastrocnemius muscle. *J. Foot Surg. 30*(5), 465–69.

Gulbahar, S., Sahin, E., Baydar, M., Bircan, C., Kızıl, R., Manisalı, M., Akalin, E., & Peker, O. (2006). Hypermobility syndrome increases the risk for low bone mass. *Clinical Rheumatology, 25*(4), 511–14.

Hochschuler, S., & Reznick, B. (1998). *Treat your back without surgery: The best non-surgical alternatives for eliminating back and neck pain*. Alameda, CA: Hunter House.

Hoeger, W. & Hoeger, S. (2011). *Lifetime physical fitness and wellness : A personalized program* (12th ed.). Belmont, CA: Cengage Learning-Wadsworth.

Hui, S. S. C., & Yuen, P. Y. (2000). Validity of the modified back-saver sit-and-reach test: a comparison with other protocols. / Validite du test sit-and-reach modifie: comparaison avec d'autres protocoles. *Medicine & Science in Sports & Exercise, 32*(9), 1655-1659.

Inlander, C.B., & Skinner, P. (1997). *Backache: 51 ways to relieve pain.* New York: St. Martin's Press.

Kabat, H. (1950). Central mechanisms for recovery of neuromuscular function. *Science, 112*(2897), 23–24.

Kabat, H. (1955). Analysis and therapy of cerebellar ataxia and asynergia. *Archives of Neurology & Psychiatry, 74,* 375–82.

Kell, R.T., Bell, G., & Quinney, A. (2001). Musculoskeletal fitness, health outcomes and quality of life. *Sports Medicine, 31*(12), 863–73.

Klinge, K., Magnusson, S., Simonsen, E., Aagaard, P., Klausen, K., & Kjaer, M. (1997). The effect of strength and flexibility training on skeletal muscle electromyographic activity, stiffness, and viscoelastic stress relaxation response. *The American Journal of Sports Medicine, 25*(5), 710–16.

Knudson, D.V., Magnusson, P., &McHugh, M. (2000). *Current issues in flexibility fitness.* Washington, DC: President's Council on Physical Fitness and Sports Research Digest.

Lemmink, Koen A. P. M., Kemper, Han C. G., de Greef, Mathieu H. G., Rispens, Piet, & Stevens, Martin. (2003). The Validity of the Sit-and-Reach Test and the Modified Sit-and-Reach Test in Middle-Aged to Older Men and Women. [Article]. *Research Quarterly for Exercise & Sport, 74*(3), 331-336.

Laban, M. (1962). Collagen tissue: Implications of its response to stress in vitro. *Archives of Physical Medicine and Rehabilitation, 43*(9), 461–65.

Levine, M. G., & Kabat, H. (1952). Cocontraction and Reciprocal Innervation in Voluntary Movement in Man. *Science (New York, N.Y.), 116*(3005), 115-118.

Levine, M.G., & Kabat, H. (1953). Proprioceptive facilitation of voluntary motion in man. *Journal of Nervous and Mental Disease, 117,* 199–211.

Lubell, A. (1989). Potentially dangerous exercises: Are they harmful to all? *Physician Sports Med, 17*(1), 187–92.

Lund, H., Vestergaard-Poulsen, P., Kanstrup, I.L., & Sejrsen, P. (1998). The effect of passive stretching on delayed onset muscle soreness, and other detrimental effects following eccentric exercise. *Scandinavian Journal of Medicine & Science in Sports, 8*(4), 216–21.

Magnusson, S.P. (1998). Passive properties of human skeletal muscle during stretch maneuvers: A review. *Scandinavian Journal of Medicine & Science in Sports, 8*(2), 65–77.

Magnusson, S.P., Simonsen, E.B., Aagaard, P., Sørensen, H., & Kjaer, M. (1996). A mechanism for altered flexibility in human skeletal muscle. *The Journal of Physiology, 497*(Pt. 1), 291–98.

Miller, R., & Opie, C. (1997). *Back pain relief: A comprehensive pain management program.* Santa Barbara, CA: Capra Press.

Nieman, D. (2003). *Exercise testing and prescription: A health-related approach.* Boston: McGraw Hill.

Noonan, T.J., Best, T.M., Seaber, A.V., & Garrett, W.E. (1993). Thermal effects on skeletal muscle tensile behavior. *American Journal of Sports Medicine, 21*(4), 517–22.

Rigby, B. (1964). The effect of mechanical extension under thermal stability of collagen. *Biochimica et Biophysica Acta, 79,* 634–36.

Rigby, B., Hirai, J., Spikes, J., & Eyring, J. (1959). The mechanical properties of rat tail tendon. *Journal of General physiology, 43*(2), 265–83.

Roth, T., & Roehrs, T.A. (1996). Etiologies and sequelae of excessive daytime sleepiness. *Clin Ther, 18*(4), 562–76.

Rubini, E.C., Costa A.L., & Gomes, P.S. (2007). The effect of stretching on strength performance. *Sports Med., 37*(3), 213–24.

Shrier, I. (2004). Does stretching improve performance? A systematic and critical review of the literature. *Clinical Journal of Sport Medicine, 14*(5), 267–73.

Siff, M. C. (1993). Soft tissue biomechanics and flexibility. *Fitness and Sports Review International, 28*(4), 128.

Small, K., Naughton, L.M., & Matthews, M. (2008). A systematic review into the efficacy of static stretching as part of a warm-up for the prevention of exercise-related injury. *Research in Sports Medicine: An International Journal, 16*(3), 213–31.

Smith, Daniel. (2012). *Rubberboy.* www.therubberboy.com.

Taylor, D.C., Dalton, J.D., Seaber, A.V., & Garrett, W.E. (1990). Viscoelastic properties of muscle-tendon units. The biomechanical effects of stretching. *American Journal of Sports Medicine, 18*(3), 300–309.

Thacker, S.B., Gilchrist, J., Stroup, D.F., & Kimsey, C.D., Jr. (2004). The impact of stretching on sports injury risk: A systematic review of the literature. *Medicine & Science in Sports & Exercise, 36*(3), 371–78.

Travell, J.G., Simmons, D.G., & Simmons, B.D. (1983). *Myofascial pain and dysfunction: The trigger point manual.* Baltimore: Lippincott Williams & Wilkins.

Verran, C. (2007, January/February). The almost magical foam roller. *Running Times Magazine.*

Verzar, F. (1963). Aging of collagen. *Scientific American, 208*(4), 104–17.

Warburton, Darren E. R., Gledhill, Norman, & Quinney, Arthur. (2001). The Effects of Changes in Musculoskeletal Fitness. *Canadian Journal of Applied Physiology, 26*(2), 161-216.

Warren, C.G., Lehmann, J.F., & Koblanski, J.N. (1971). Elongation of rat tail tendon: Effect of load and temperature. *Archives of Physical Medicine and Rehabilitation, 52*(10), 465-474.

Warren, C.G., Lehmann, J.F., & Koblanski, J.N. (1976). Heat and stretch procedures: An evaluation using rat tail tendon. *Archives of Physical Medicine and Rehabilitation, 57*(3), 122–26.

Woods, K., Bishop, P., & Jones, E. (2007). Warm-up and stretching in the prevention of muscular injury. *Sports Medicine, 37*(12), 1089–99.

Young, W., & Elliott, S. (2001). Acute effects of static stretching, proprioceptive neuromuscular facilitation stretching, and maximum voluntary contractions on explosive force production and jumping performance. *Research Quarterly for Exercise & Sport, 72*, 273–79.

## Suggested Readings

Alter, M.J. (2004). *Science of flexibility* (3rd ed.). Champaign, IL: Human Kinetics.

Consult sections of interest (sciences of, clinical considerations of, principles of, anatomy of, and specific sport applications of flexibility) in this book to gain a greater understanding of flexibility.

Anderson, B. (2010). *Stretching: 30th anniversary revised edition*. Bolinas, CA: Shelter Publications.

One of the most popular fitness books in the world, this book provides a summary of 200 different stretches with routines and stretching programs for over 20 sports.

Nelson, A.G., & Kokkonen J. (2007). *Stretching anatomy*. Champaign, IL: Human Kinetics.

See inside every stretch—and maximize flexibility. *Stretching Anatomy* will arm you with the knowledge to increase range of motion, supplement training, enhance recovery, and maximize efficiency of movement. You'll also gain a detailed understanding of how each stretch affects your body.

## Suggested Websites

**www.bath.ac.uk/ ~ masrjb/Stretch/stretching_1. html#SEC1**
The University of Bath site includes nine chapters by Bradford Appleton, dancer and martial artist, at the University of Bath.

**www.gsu.edu/ ~ wwwfit/flexibility.html**
Georgia State University Exercise and Physical Fitness page has photographs of a model doing 10 common stretches.

**www.nia.nih.gov/health/publication/exercise-physical-activity-your-everyday-guide-national-institute-aging/sample-2**
The National Institute on Aging at the U.S. National Institutes of Health provides general guidelines and illustrates (some animated) stretches from the chapter on stretching.

**www.rice.edu/ ~ jenky/stretch.html**
The Rice University Sports Medicine website gives advice about flexibility and illustrates stretches.

# Part IV

# Understanding Your Behaviors

# Nutritional Health and Wellness

Peter Walters

After reading this chapter, you should be able to do the following:

1. Outline the digestive process.
2. Describe the function of six major categories of nutrients.
3. Understand the fundamental principles and strategies for healthy eating.
4. List the benefits and challenges of being a vegetarian.
5. Appreciate the value of fasting.

**From the** time of creation God provided people with food. One of the first things God said to Adam and Eve is "I give you every seed-bearing plant on the face of the whole earth and every tree that has fruit with seed in it. They will be yours for food" (Genesis 1:29). Later in the New Testament Paul uses food as an example and states that "everything God created is good, and nothing is to be rejected if it is received with thanksgiving" (1 Timothy 4:3–4).

Food was meant to sustain but from time to time also to enliven celebrations. Think of the psalmist's words: "He makes grass grow for the cattle, and plants for people to cultivate—bringing forth food from the earth: wine that gladdens human hearts, oil to make their faces shine, and bread that sustains their hearts" (Psalm 104:14–15). Consider Jesus, whose first miracle was turning water into wine at a wedding feast (John 2). God knows that good food and drink can be part of the joy in celebrating with God's triumphs: seeing, feeling, and expressing celebration in God's victories. It is a response often shared in a festive manner with others. Joy is not a simple add-on in the Christian life but is listed significantly as the second fruit of the spirit. Food can occasionally be an important part of a joyful and filled life (Psalm 30:11; 126:1–2; Jeremiah 31:13; Romans 15:13; Acts 8:8). Proverbs even makes a comparison with joy and feasting: "The cheerful heart has a continual feast" (15:15). Christians celebrate the Lord's Supper with food and drink. In the consumption of common bread and wine God's loving sacrifice, in which his flesh was torn and his blood poured out, is remembered. Food and drink are essential ingredients of the most sacred of Christian sacraments.

God has given men and women food to sustain and to use for occasional festive celebrations. Let me suggest a word of caution and one of encouragement. The caution is that at times people eat to suppress emotional issues; they are not at peace. During these times, it is important to get to the core issue disturbing your peace because God wants to bless humanity with peace (Numbers 6:24–26; Psalm 121). Part of peaceful living is living justly (Romans 2:10; 14:17–19; 1 Corinthians 7:15; 1 Peter 3:11; James 2:16) and with love for oneself and others. My encouragement is for you to use food in a loving way. Love for oneself and others means enjoying the gift of food in a balanced manner by eating neither too little nor too much and by being deeply committed to ensuring that all people of this world have food (Matthew 25:37–46).

## Nutritional Habits of College Students

One longitudinal study conducted by Tufts University (Food Service Director, 2002) found that 59 percent of college freshmen's diets change for the worse after leaving home. You are on your own to know and choose foods that meet your daily requirements. Based on demographically segregated nutritional surveys, it seems that the average college student is not making some of the best choices related to diet. See figure 8.1, which identifies the most common

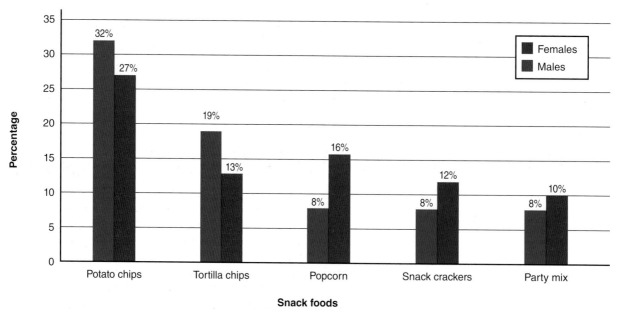

**Figure 8.1**  Comparison by sex of what college students snack on the most.

foods the average male and female college students snack on.

This chapter on **nutrition**, the science of food and how it affects the body, helps you make educated decisions about the food you consume so that you can enjoy the benefits of nutritional adequacy. The first step in this process is to understand how the food you consume gets broken down and absorbed by the body. Next comes an overview of the approximately 40 essential nutrients your body needs. These nutrients are grouped into six major categories. The focus then shifts to the implementation of nutritional principles and strategies that ensure nutritional adequacy. Finally, two specific nutrition challenges are discussed: fasting and being a vegetarian.

## Digestive System

The **digestive system** operates as an assembly line in reverse, taking whole foods and breaking them down into their chemical components. This system is essentially a tube—some 27 feet (8 m) of continuous organs that carry food through the body from mouth to rectum, removing needed nutrients all the while (see figure 8.2). This tube is called the **alimentary canal**, or the gastrointestinal tract. The digestive system is essentially involuntary, meaning that once a person swallows, it runs on "autopilot." Think about it: When you swallow a mouthful of food, do you have to tell your throat, stomach, and intestines what to do with it?

With the help of the circulatory system, the digestive system gets the right amount of water, protein, fat, carbohydrate, vitamins, and minerals to each of the 100 trillion cells in the body and then picks up waste products for disposal and elimination on its return trip, all without conscious thought.

Digestion begins in the mouth. When you take a bite of food, your teeth and tongue begin to mechanically break it down into smaller units. Saliva not only bathes your food with water but also contains **digestive enzymes**, molecules that facilitate the breakdown of food particles into smaller molecules that can be absorbed into the blood and cells. When the chewed food has been reduced to a soft, moist mass called a **bolus**, your tongue pushes it to the back of your mouth where it is swallowed. For the fraction of a second it takes to swallow, your respiratory tract is closed so that food does not enter the lungs, and you can neither breathe nor talk. Swallowing is the end of the voluntary part of digestion; the rest is involuntary. For the next two or three seconds after swallowing, the bolus travels down the **esophagus** to the **stomach**. This process is called **peristalsis**,

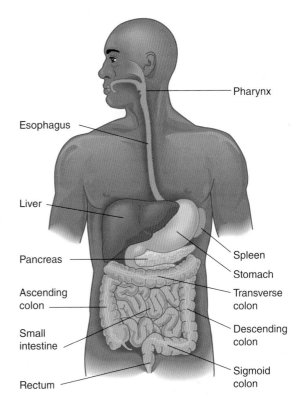

**Figure 8.2** The digestive system is approximately 27 feet (8 m) long.

Labels: Pharynx, Esophagus, Liver, Pancreas, Ascending colon, Small intestine, Rectum, Spleen, Stomach, Transverse colon, Descending colon, Sigmoid colon

## Understanding Ulcers

Most ulcers are located in the **duodenum** and are known as **duodenal ulcers**. Ulcers located in the stomach are called **gastric ulcers**, and those in the esophagus are called **esophageal ulcers**. Regardless of location, the pain from an ulcer is most often caused when the mucous lining fails to protect the underlying tissues. The cause of ulcers is often mistakenly attributed to poor diet, smoking, or stress. However, in reality over 90 percent of ulcers are caused by one factor—the overabundance of helicobacter pylori bacteria (H. pylori). The bacteria interfere with the production of the mucous lining and leaves the lining of the stomach unprotected from hydrochloric acid. Fortunately, in most cases this harmful bacterium can be managed through medical treatment.

in which muscular contractions of the esophagus squeeze the bolus from mouth to stomach.

A circular muscle called the **esophageal sphincter** divides the esophagus and the stomach. When you swallow, this muscle relaxes, forming an opening through which food can pass. The rest of the time it is closed, to keep food from moving in the opposite direction. It is the first of several muscular valves that regulate the passage of food. The stomach, as seen in figure 8.2, is located just below the diaphragm. This saclike structure is shaped like a capital J when empty and like a boxing glove when full. When food is present, the stomach expands and contracts about three times per minute to churn food and bathe it in **gastric juices**. These are fluids secreted by thousands of glands in the stomach lining; they consist of water, **hydrochloric acid**, and more digestive enzymes. Hydrochloric acid not only breaks down food but also kills many of the harmful microorganisms found within. The gastric juices are so potent that the stomach would literally digest itself, except that it has a mucous lining, a coating that protects the tissues of the stomach from damage. See more information in the Understanding Ulcers sidebar.

About one hour after a meal, food processed by the stomach, now a semifluid mass of food and gastric juices called **chyme**, begins to pass a little bit at a time through the **pyloric sphincter**, a circular muscle valve that divides the stomach and the small intestine. Most digestion and absorption occur in the small intestine. This narrow, twisting tube, about 1 inch (2.5 cm) in diameter and 20 feet (6 m) long, fills most of the lower abdomen. For three to six hours, peristalsis (the rhythmic, squeezing contraction of muscles in the tissue of the small intestine) moves the chyme through the intestines. In the intestines, more enzymes are added to the chyme to further digest the food. Bile, secreted by the liver, breaks down fat, and pancreatic enzymes break down sugar and protein. Now the majority of nutrients can be absorbed into the bloodstream to supply the needs of the body's cells. What remains unabsorbed—a watery residue of indigestible food and digestive juices—passes by peristalsis through the large intestine, where it spends the next 12 to 24 hours. The large intestine is about 2.5 inches (6.4 cm) in diameter and 5 to 6 feet (1.5 to 1.8 m) long and is shaped like an inverted U. It performs several important functions: It absorbs water (about 1.6 gallons or 6.1 L daily) and contains good bacteria that promote the breakdown of undigested materials. What remains is now called feces, which is moved by peristalsis toward the **rectum**, the final 6 to 8 inches (15 to 20 cm) of the alimentary canal. The rectum stores feces until elimination.

# Six Major Nutrient Groups

The body uses nutrients for growth, maintenance, and repair and needs to take in about 40 varieties to function properly. Nutrients can be grouped into six categories: carbohydrate, protein, lipid (fat), water, vitamins, and minerals (see table 8.1).

These six nutrients are further classified according to size and energy. Carbohydrate, protein, and fat are **macronutrients** because they make up the bulk of your diet. Vitamins and minerals are **micronutrients** because they are required in much smaller amounts. For example, the average person consumes about 2.5 gallons (9.5 L) of food and water per day, but only an eighth of a teaspoon of that is vitamins and minerals. This does not mean that vitamins and minerals are unimportant. The ignition key is only a small part of a car, but it's hard to get the car started without it! A deficiency in $B_{12}$, just one of the eight B vitamins, can result in anemia, hypersensitive skin, and degeneration of peripheral nerves resulting in paralysis (Whitney & Rolfes, 2012). You may have noticed the omission of water as a macronutrient. People definitely need a large supply of water; however, water is a micronutrient because it does not contain energy.

Food energy is measured in calories. You may recall from high school chemistry that a **calorie** is the amount of energy necessary to raise the temperature of one kilogram of water by one degree Celsius. When discussing nutrition and exercise, however, *calorie* usually means **kilocalorie**, 1,000 calories, or the

## Table 8.1  Primary Functions of the Six Major Nutrients

| Nutrient | Primary functions |
| --- | --- |
| Water | Dissolves and carries nutrients, removes waste, and regulates body temperature |
| Protein | Builds new tissues, antibodies, enzymes, hormones, and other compounds |
| Carbohydrate | Provides energy |
| Fat | Provides long-term energy, insulation, and protection |
| Vitamins | Facilitate use of other nutrients; involved in regulating growth and manufacturing hormones |
| Minerals | Help build bones and teeth; aid in muscle function and nervous system activity |

amount of energy necessary to raise the temperature of 1 liter of water by 1 degree Celsius. To avoid confusion, when *calorie* is used in this text it will be used in the conventional manner.

The energy nutrients are carbohydrate, protein, and fat; the nonenergy nutrients are water, vitamins, and minerals.

## Carbohydrate

**Carbohydrate** is fuel for the body and brain and comes in three types: **simple carbohydrate**, com-plex carbohydrate, and **fiber**. Simple carbohydrate is further divisible into **monosaccharides**, which contain only one type of sugar—such as **glucose** (blood sugar), **fructose** (fruit sugar), and **galactose** (milk sugar)—and **disaccharides**, which are made up of glucose combined with another sugar. The three primary disaccharides are **maltose**, **lactose**, and **sucrose**; what most people mean by *sugar*. Complex carbohydrate, or starch, is a **polysaccharide**, which contains long chains of glucose molecules bonded together. Because the body must break these bonds to release the chemical energy stored in them,

---

### Nutrient Density

The phrase *empty calories* is used to describe high-sugar, low-nutrient foods. Foods containing an abundance of nutrients relative to the energy they provide are said to have "packed calories." In either case, the determination is made through a method known as **nutrient density**, which calculates the nutritional value of food compared to the number of calories it contains.

Figure 8.3 illustrates a comparison of the nutrient density of a typical 12-ounce (355 ml) soft drink and 8 ounces (240 ml) of nonfat milk.

To calculate the nutrient density of any food, divide the amount of a selected nutrient by the calories the food provides. For example, an 8-ounce (240 ml) glass of orange juice contains 125 milligrams of vitamin C and 111 calories, and a generic brand of orange drink usually contains 84 milligrams of vitamin C and 128 calories for the same serving size. Divide 125 milligrams by 111 calories to calculate a nutrient density of 1.12 for vitamin C in the serving of orange juice, and divide 84 milligrams by 128 calories to calculate a nutrient density of 0.65 for vitamin C in the serving of orange drink.

Orange juice contains twice the nutritional power of vitamin C in a typical orange drink. Although there is a significant difference in the amount of vitamin C, there are even more dramatic variations of other nutrients. Orange juice is a packed-calorie food because it contains more than 5 times the magnesium, 7 times the folate, and 18 times the vitamin A of a typical orange drink.

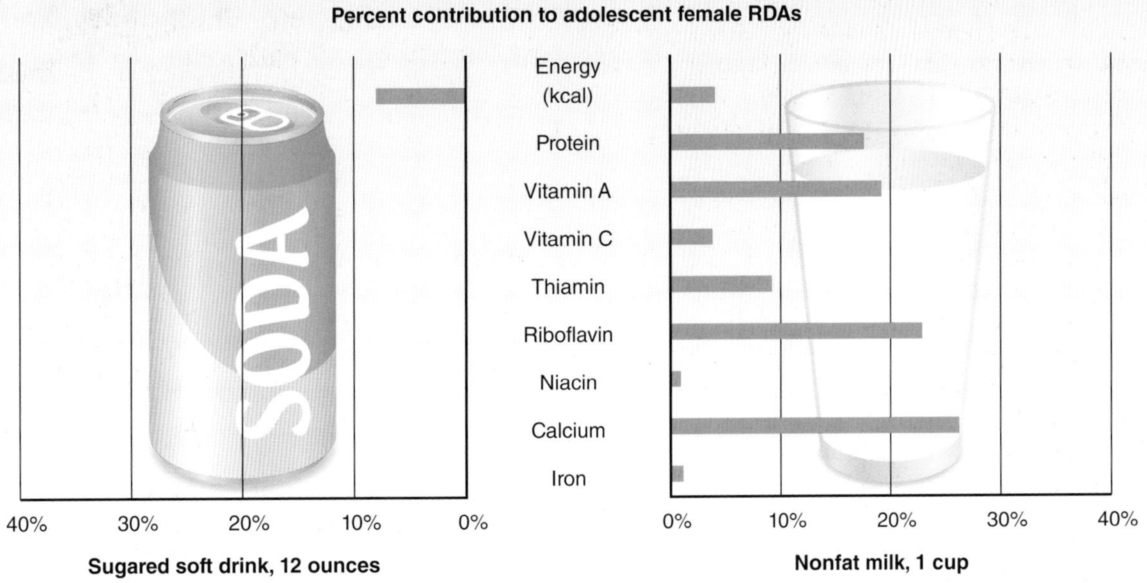

**Percent contribution to adolescent female RDAs**

**Sugared soft drink, 12 ounces**          **Nonfat milk, 1 cup**

**Figure 8.3**   A comparison of the nutrient density of a 12-ounce (355 ml) soft drink to a 1-cup (240-ml) serving of nonfat milk.

complex carbohydrate takes longer to digest and therefore allows for a more sustained energy release than simple carbohydrate does. In some cases these bonds cannot be broken down by human digestion, as is the case with fiber. Unlike animals, humans lack the necessary enzymes to break down the energy in fiber. Fiber comes in two types: soluble and insoluble. **Soluble fiber** dissolves in water to form a gel, and it can help lower blood cholesterol and control blood sugar levels. **Insoluble fiber** does not dissolve, and it can help prevent constipation and other bowel disorders. Each of the three types of carbohydrate and their subcategories and primary functions are listed in table 8.2.

The 2010 dietary guidelines published by the U.S. Department of Health and Human Services (HHS) and the U.S. Department of Agriculture (USDA) recommend that 45 to 65 percent of total calorie intake come from carbohydrate—at least 130 grams of carbohydrate per day (U.S. Department of Agriculture and U.S. Department of Health and Human Services, 2010). This minimum is required to supply the brain with an adequate amount of glucose. It is a fairly moderate recommendation, considering that the average American adult male consumes 220 to 330 grams and the average American adult female consumes 180 to 230 grams of carbohydrate daily (Institute of Medicine, 2002). According to the Institute of Medicine (2002), an agency that works with HHS and the USDA to establish nutritional guidelines, an adequate intake of fiber is 14 grams for every 1,000 calories.

### Table 8.2   Categories and Functions of Carbohydrate

| Carbohydrate | Subcategories | Primary sources |
| --- | --- | --- |
| Simple | Monosaccharides, disaccharides | Processed sugar, fruit, dairy |
| Complex | Polysaccharides, starches | Breads, fruits, vegetables, nuts, legumes |
| Fiber | Soluble, insoluble | Bran, vegetables, fruits, nuts, oats, legumes |

 **Is Sugar Bad for You?**

No, sugar is not bad for your health. Sugar is in fruits, grains, vegetables, and nearly everything you eat. And the chemical structure of "refined" sugar is no different from that of "natural" sugar. Despite what you may have heard, the only proven health risk of sugar is tooth decay (U.S. Department of Health and Human Services, 2005). The problem is quantity. Virtually all major health organizations currently recommend reducing the amount of sugar in the diet because, according to the USDA, the yearly sugar intake of the average American has continually risen over the last 99 years, from 4 pounds (1.8 kg) in 1900 to 180 pounds (41 kg) per person in 2009 (Whole Vegan, 2012; see figure 8.4).

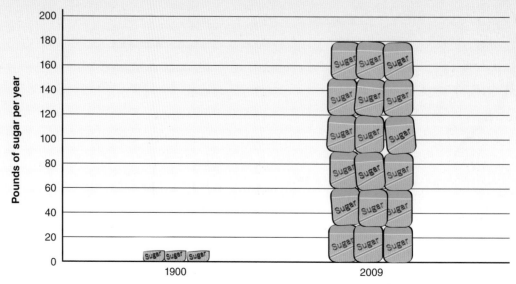

**Figure 8.4**   Change in average annual intake of sugar per person in the United States.

## Terms for the Carbohydrate Conscious

Low-carbohydrate diets come into fashion periodically. In a 2004 survey, 30 to 40 million American adults (16 percent of the adult population at the time) said they were trying to control their weight by counting grams of carbohydrate instead of calories. Manufacturers introduced 930 low-carbohydrate foods in the United States between 1999 and 2004 (Consumer Reports, 2004). Three relatively new terms—*glycemic index*, *glycemic load*, and *net carbohydrate*—have crept into the vocabulary of those who are carbohydrate conscious.

Low-carbohydrate diets are based, in part, on the effect that carbohydrate has on blood sugar and insulin levels, which rise and fall after the consumption of carbs. Some foods have a quick and dramatic effect on glucose and insulin levels, while others have a slower, more moderate effect. **Glycemic index** (GI) is one measure of how foods affect the level of blood sugar. GI is determined by consuming 50 grams of carbohydrate from a particular food and measuring the effect on blood sugar during the two hours after consumption. The resulting value is compared to an index in which a reference food (most often glucose) is given a 100-point value. High-GI foods have a measure greater than 70, foods with a value between 55 and 69 are considered intermediate, and those below 55 are considered low. Table 8.3 illustrates the glycemic index of some common foods.

A more comprehensive list of glycemic measures can be found in "International Tables of Glycemic Index and Glycemic Load Values," an article published in the *American Journal of Clinical Nutrition* (Powell et al., 2002).

Foods high in sugar and low in fat generally elevate blood sugar and insulin rapidly. Large, chronic doses of insulin outputs have been found to be related to a sluggish feeling, calories burned at a reduced rate, increased hunger, elevated blood triglycerides, increased fat synthesis and storage, and increased risk for developing diabetes (Miller, 2003).

### Table 8.3 Glycemic Index and Load for Various Foods

|  | Serving size | Glycemic index | Carbohydrate (g) | Glycemic load |
|---|---|---|---|---|
| Apple | 1 medium | 38 | 22 | 8 |
| Baked beans | 1 cup (253 g) | 48 | 54 | 26 |
| Banana | 1 medium | 55 | 29 | 16 |
| Chocolate | 1 oz (28 g) | 49 | 18 | 9 |
| Honey | 1 tsp (5 ml) | 73 | 6 | 4 |
| Ice cream | 1 cup (132 g) | 61 | 31 | 19 |
| Milk, nonfat | 1 cup (240 ml) | 32 | 12 | 4 |
| Milk, whole | 1 cup (240 ml) | 27 | 11 | 3 |
| Orange | 1 medium | 44 | 15 | 7 |
| Potato chips (crisps) | 1 oz (28 g) | 54 | 15 | 8 |
| Potato, baked | 1 cup (227 g) | 85 | 57 | 48 |
| Spaghetti | 1 cup (140 g) | 41 | 40 | 16 |
| Vanilla wafers | 5 cookies | 77 | 15 | 12 |
| White bread | 1 slice | 70 | 10 | 7 |
| Whole-wheat bread | 1 slice | 69 | 3 | 9 |

Adapted from Powell, Holt, and Brand-Miller 2002.

*(continued)*

*(continued)*

One major drawback of the glycemic index is that the values are based on the consumption of 50 grams of carbohydrate rather than on a typical serving size. You would have to consume more than 4 cups (950 ml) of whole milk to get 50 grams of carbohydrate. Only 2 ounces (56 g) of jellybeans, however, have 50 grams of carbohydrate. As a result, many health professionals look at **glycemic load**, which takes into account the glycemic index along with the actual amount of carbohydrate consumed (Donatelle, 2006). To calculate the glycemic load, multiply the carbohydrate grams by the glycemic index and then divide by 100. A small bagel that contains 30 grams of carbohydrate would be multiplied by the glycemic index (72) and divided by 100 to result in a glycemic load of 22:

$$(30 \times 72) \div 100 = 22$$

Most consumers simply count the number of grams of carbohydrate they consume rather than look at glycemic index tables or calculate the glycemic load of their diets. Therefore, many manufacturers are doing everything they can to lower the grams of carbohydrate in the food they sell.

One recent strategy has been to use the term **net carbohydrate** (commonly called net carbs). Although the term has no agreed-on definition, it generally refers to the total grams of carbohydrate per serving minus the grams of sugar alcohols and fermentable fiber. These sugar alcohols (erythritol, hydrogenated starch hydrolysates, isomait, lactitol, maititol, mannitol, sorbitol, xylitol) are not digested in the small intestine but instead pass to the large intestine where they are digested by fermentation. They do not elevate blood sugar and insulin levels nearly as much as regular sugar does.

Manufacturers are subtracting these particular types of carbohydrate because they do not have as much absorbable energy as regular carbohydrate does. They do contain calories, however, ranging from 0.2 calorie to 3 calories per gram—nearly as much as a normal carbohydrate.

What can science offer regarding the effectiveness of low-carbohydrate diets? One of the few long-term studies indicates that low-carbohydrate dieters lose weight faster than low-fat dieters (Foster, 2003). But although the low-carbohydrate dieters lost an average of 8.4 pounds (3.8 kg) more than the low-fat dieters did during the first six months, the gap between the two groups narrowed to a statistically insignificant amount by the end of a year.

Why do low-carbohydrate diets work? Since carbohydrates retain water, much of the initial weight loss in a low-carbohydrate diet is the body retaining less water. A study that tracked the calorie consumption of low-fat and low-carbohydrate dieters reported that during a six-month trial the low-carbohydrate dieters cut an average of 189 more calories per day than the low-fat dieters did (Samaha, 2003). This reduction is more than enough to account for the extra 8.4 pounds (3.8 kg) that low-carbohydrate dieters lost in the study cited earlier. Despite all the impressive terminology, weight management always seems to come back to balancing calorie intake and expenditure.

## Protein

Nothing can match protein's power for physical growth and repair. **Protein** is made up of **amino acids**, which are the building blocks of cell membranes, muscle tissues, and enzymes. There are 20 amino acids, 9 of which are essential. Foods that contain all nine, such as meat, eggs, and dairy products, are called **complete proteins**. Americans get about 70 percent of their protein from these animal products. Most fruits, grains, and vegetables, with the notable exception of soy, are incomplete proteins.

Although it contains four calories per gram, protein is not usually a major source of energy—rarely does it contribute more than 10 percent of daily caloric expenditure. An exception to this rule is for people such as marathon runners who train exceptionally hard while on a low-calorie diet. In this case the body begins to draw on protein stored in muscle tissue for energy (Sharkey, 2002).

Most American adults get between 14 and 18 percent of their calories from protein, thus falling well within the range of the 10 to 35 percent recommended by the *Dietary Guidelines for Americans 2010*

(U.S. Department of Agriculture and U.S. Department of Health and Human Services, 2010).

One of the ongoing debates among coaches and athletes is whether those who participate in vigorous sports and exercise need additional protein. Although the available research does not provide a definitive answer concerning the exact amount of protein a particular athlete needs, the weight of the evidence does suggest that individuals involved in vigorous physical activity can benefit by increasing dietary protein beyond the recommended dietary allowance (RDA) suggestion of 0.8 to 1.0 grams per kilogram of body weight. Existing science seems to indicate that endurance athletes can benefit from dietary intake of 1.2 to 1.6 grams of protein per kilogram of body weight, and strength athletes should get 1.6 to 1.8 grams per kilogram of body weight (American College of Sports Medicine, 2000; Lemon, 1995).

To illustrate how to calculate protein needs, consider the case of a 140-pound (63.6 kg) college-age male who wants to gain muscle weight. The RDA for this male is between 51 and 64 (63.6 kg multiplied by 0.8 and 1.0) grams of protein per day. However, based on the evidence concerning protein and strength training, he should consume between 102 and 115 (63.6 kg multiplied by 1.6 and 1.8) grams of protein per day.

## Fat

Despite its reputation, **fat** is a vital ingredient in a healthy diet. Besides being the most energy-rich nutrient (nine calories per gram), fat is needed to transport vitamins A, D, E, and K; conduct nerve impulses efficiently; and cushion vital organs. It also serves as a thermal regulator and makes up a large portion of bone marrow and brain tissue. People like fat because it enhances the flavor and texture of food.

There are three primary types of fatty acids: **saturated fat**, **monounsaturated fat**, and **polyunsaturated fat**. Although most of what you eat contains a mixture of all three types, usually one type predominates. For example, margarine has between 40 and 75 percent polyunsaturated, 10 to 50 percent saturated, and 5 to 25 percent monounsaturated fatty acids. Therefore, it is classified as a polyunsaturated fat (see table 8.4).

The average American consumes too many calories from added fat. Currently, Americans are 180 percent over the limit for calories from both solid fats and added sugars and are 10 percent over the limit for saturated fat. The latest guidelines regarding dietary fat recommend consuming 20 to 35 percent of calories from fat, of which 10 percent or less comes from saturated sources (U.S. Department of Agriculture and U.S. Department of Health and Human Services, 2010).

## Vitamins

Most **vitamins** and minerals are measured in milligrams (a thousandth of a gram) or micrograms (a millionth of a gram) instead of in grams because humans need only very small doses to maintain health. Even so, a prolonged deficiency in just one of the many vitamins can lead to severe health effects. For example, the deficiency of vitamin $B_1$ (thiamine) results in a disease called beriberi that produces

## Table 8.4 Grams of Fatty Acids Per 100 Grams of Food Weight

|  | Saturated | Monounsaturated | Polyunsaturated |
|---|---|---|---|
| Coconut oil | 85 | 6.6 | 1.7 |
| Butter | 54 | 20 | 2.6 |
| Palm oil | 45 | 42 | 8 |
| Margarine | 16 | 21 | 41 |
| Soybean oil | 15 | 23 | 57 |
| Olive oil | 14 | 70 | 11 |
| Corn oil | 13 | 25 | 58 |
| Safflower oil | 10 | 13 | 72 |
| Rapeseed oil | 7 | 57 | 32 |

Each fat is classified according to its most predominant fatty acid.

## Nuts: A Healthy Fat?

"A handful a day may help reduce the risk of heart disease" is the claim boldly written on some new peanut containers, but should you try to include nuts in your daily diet? This new health claim is among the first to be permitted by the Food and Drug Administration in the United States because more than 30 studies have indicated that nuts help reduce cholesterol levels. Nuts are relatively good sources of vitamin E and are rich in monounsaturated fat and soluble fiber, both of which tend to lower LDL (bad) cholesterol.

During one controlled trial, researchers randomly assigned 27 people with high cholesterol to eat almonds daily for a month as part of various low-fat diets. The study, published in the American Heart Association journal *Circulation* (Jenkins et al., 2002), found that almonds reduced LDL cholesterol by as much as 9.4 percent. In two large-population studies from Harvard University, people who ate nuts often had lower risks of sudden cardiac death and heart attacks than those who rarely or never ate nuts (Albert et al., 2002).

Adding a handful of nuts to your diet is a good idea. Note that this particular claim is allowed on package labels for almonds, peanuts, pecans, pistachios, hazelnuts, walnuts, and some pine nuts. It cannot be used on labels for Brazil nuts, cashews, macadamias, and some other pine nuts, which have a bit too much saturated fat.

---

general fatigue, muscular atrophy, paralysis, and eventual heart failure. Insufficient levels of folic acid (another B vitamin) increase the risk of neural tube defects such as spina bifida, which can result in the spinal cord's protruding from the spinal column of a newborn. Vitamins are critical to blood coagulation and the production of energy, hormones, enzymes, and antibodies.

Vitamins are classified according to the substrate they are soluble in. Vitamin C and the B-complex vitamins are water-soluble vitamins. Vitamins A, D, E, and K are fat soluble. Fat-soluble vitamins are stored in the liver and fatty tissues of the body and are eliminated at a slower rate than water-soluble vitamins. Thus, water-soluble vitamins need to be consumed and replaced more regularly. A mnemonic phrase to help you remember the fat-soluble vitamins is "all dogs eat kittens." After you have memorized the fat-soluble vitamins, you can simply remember that all the rest are water soluble (see table 8.5). You may think it would be simpler to remember that vitamins C and the B-complex vitamins are water soluble, but there are eight B vitamins.

Table 8.6 identifies symptoms associated with vitamin deficiencies and excess along with foods that contain substantial amounts of each vitamin people need.

## Minerals

**Minerals** are in many ways the linchpins to health. Although relatively simple, a linchpin is paramount in its supportive role. The same is true of minerals. Minerals are present in all living cells and maintain the body's delicate acid and base balances, enable muscular contraction to occur, and aid in the production of both hormones and enzymes.

Table 8.7 lists the major functions and food sources of all of the major minerals and some of the trace minerals and the symptoms associated with excesses and deficiencies.

Minerals are classified as major or **trace minerals**. The body needs more than five grams a day of the major minerals, which include sodium, potassium, calcium, phosphorus, magnesium, sulfur, and chlorine. Trace minerals (the body needs fewer than five grams a day of these) include iron, iodine, copper, fluorine, and zinc. Although 31 minerals have been found in the human body, only 24 are currently known to be essential.

### Table 8.5    The 13 Essential Vitamins

| Fat soluble | Water soluble |
| --- | --- |
| A | $B_1$ (thiamin) |
| D | $B_2$ (riboflavin) |
| E | $B_3$ (niacin) |
| K | Biotin |
| | Panothenic acid |
| | $B_6$ |
| | Folate |
| | $B_{12}$ |
| | C |

## Table 8.6　Fat-Soluble and Water-Soluble Vitamins

| Fat-soluble vitamins | Major functions | Important sources | Signs of deficiency | Effects of megadoses |
|---|---|---|---|---|
| Vitamin A | Maintains eyes, vision, skin, linings of the nose, mouth, digestive and urinary tracts; immune function | Liver, milk, butter, cheese, carrots, spinach, cantaloupe, other orange or dark green vegetables or fruits | Night blindness, dry skin, increased susceptibility to infection, loss of appetite, anemia, kidney stones | Headache, vomiting, diarrhea, dryness of mucous membranes, vertigo, double vision, bone abnormalities, liver damage, increased risk of miscarriage and birth defects, convulsions, coma, respiratory failure |
| Vitamin D | Aids in calcium and phosphorus metabolism, promotion of calcium absorption; develops and maintains bones and teeth | Fortified milk and margarine, fish liver oils, butter, egg yolks, exposure to sunlight | Rickets (bone deformities) in children; bone softening, loss, and fractures in adults | Calcium deposits in kidneys and blood vessels, causing irreversible kidney and cardiovascular damage |
| Vitamin E | Protects and maintains cellular membranes | Vegetable oils, whole grains, nuts and seeds, green leafy vegetables, asparagus, peaches | Red blood cell breakage and anemia, weakness, neurological problems, muscle cramps | Relatively nontoxic but may cause excess bleeding or formation of blood clots |
| Vitamin K | Blood clotting; maintains bone metabolism | Greens, cereals, fruits, meats, milk products | Hemorrhage | Jaundice, inability to clot |

| Water-soluble vitamins | Major functions | Important sources | Signs of deficiency | Effects of megadoses |
|---|---|---|---|---|
| Vitamin $B_1$ (thiamin) | Converts carbohydrate into usable forms of energy; maintains appetite and nervous system function | Yeast, whole-grain and enriched breads and cereals, organ meats, liver, pork, lean meats, poultry, eggs, fish, beans, nuts, legumes | Beriberi (symptoms include edema or muscle wasting, mental confusion, anorexia, enlarged heart, abnormal heart rhythm, muscle degeneration and weakness, nerve changes) | None reported |
| Vitamin $B_2$ (riboflavin) | Energy metabolism; maintains skin, mucous membranes, and nervous system structures | Dairy products, whole-grain and enriched breads and cereals, lean meats, poultry, green vegetables, liver | Cracks at corners of mouth, sore throat, skin rash, hypersensitivity to light, purple tongue | None reported |
| Vitamin $B_3$ (niacin) | Converts carbohydrate, fat, and protein into usable forms of energy; essential for growth; supports skin, nervous system, and digestive health | Eggs, chicken, turkey, fish, milk, whole grains, nuts, enriched breads and cereals, lean meats, legumes | Pellagra (symptoms include weakness, diarrhea, dermatitis, inflammation of mucous membranes, mental illness) | Flushing of the skin, nausea, vomiting, diarrhea, changes in metabolism of glycogen and fatty acids, low blood pressure |

*(continued)*

**Table 8.6** *(continued)*

| Water-soluble vitamins | Major functions | Important sources | Signs of deficiency | Effects of megadoses |
|---|---|---|---|---|
| Biotin | Energy metabolism use; synthesizes fat, amino acids, metabolism | Widespread in foods | Abnormal heart action, muscle pain, fatigue, weakness | None reported |
| Panothenic acid | Used in energy metabolism | Widespread in foods | Vomiting, insomnia, fatigue | Water retention (uncommon) |
| Vitamin B$_6$ (pyridoxine) | Enzyme reactions involving amino acids and the metabolism of carbohydrate, fat, and nucleic acids | Green leafy vegetables, eggs, poultry, whole grains, nuts, legumes, liver, kidney, pork | Anemia, convulsions, cracks at corners of mouth, dermatitis, nausea, confusion | Neurological abnormalities and damage, depression, loss of reflexes, weakness, restlessness |
| Folate | Amino acid metabolism; synthesizes RNA and DNA; synthesizes new cells | Green leafy vegetables, yeast, oranges, whole grains, legumes, liver | Anemia, gastrointestinal disturbances, decreased resistance to infection, depression | Diarrhea, reduction of zinc absorption, possible kidney enlargement and damage |
| Vitamin B$_{12}$ | Synthesizes red and white blood cells; other metabolic reactions | Eggs, milk, meat, liver | Anemia, fatigue, nervous system damage, sore tongue | None reported |
| Vitamin C | Maintains and repairs connective tissue, bones, teeth, and cartilage; promotes healing; aids in iron absorption | Peppers, broccoli, spinach, brussels sprouts, citrus fruits, strawberries, tomatoes, potatoes, cabbage, other fruits and vegetables | Scurvy (weakening of collagenous structures resulting in widespread capillary hemorrhaging), anemia, reduced resistance to infection, bleeding gums, weakness, loosened teeth, rough skin, joint pain, poor wound healing, hair loss, poor iron absorption | Urinary stones in some people, acid stomach from ingesting supplements in pill form, nausea, diarrhea, headache, fatigue |

**Table 8.7  Essential Major Minerals and Trace Minerals**

| Major minerals | Major functions | Important sources | Signs of deficiency | Effects of megadoses |
|---|---|---|---|---|
| Sodium | Body–water balance, acid–base balance, nerve function | Salt, soy sauce, salted or cured foods, table and sea salt | Muscle weakness, loss of appetite, nausea, vomiting; sodium deficiency is rarely seen | Edema, hypertension in sensitive people |
| Chloride | Aids in digestion; regulates water in body | Salt, cured foods, pickles | Muscle cramps, apathy, poor appetite | Vomiting |
| Potassium | Nerve function and body–water balance | Squash, lima beans, tomatoes, bananas, milk, meats | Muscular weakness, nausea, drowsiness, paralysis, confusion, disruption of cardiac rhythm | Irregular heartbeat, heart attack |

**Table 8.7** *(continued)*

| Major minerals | Major functions | Important sources | Signs of deficiency | Effects of megadoses |
|---|---|---|---|---|
| Calcium | Maintains bones and teeth, blood clotting; maintains cell membranes; controls nerve impulses and muscle contraction | Milk and milk products, tofu, fortified orange juice and bread, green leafy vegetables | Stunted growth in children, bone mineral loss in adults | Nausea, vomiting, hypertension, constipation, urinary stones, calcium deposits in soft tissues, inhibition of absorption of certain minerals |
| Phosphorus | Energy formation, component of teeth and bones | Milk, chicken, seeds, nuts, salmon | Nausea, weakness, confusion, loss of bone calcium | Muscle spasms |
| Magnesium | DNA and protein synthesis, blood clotting, muscle contraction, ATP production | Cheese, sesame seeds, almonds, halibut, spinach, yogurt | Neurological disturbances, impaired immune function, kidney disorders, nausea, weight loss, growth failure in children | Nausea, vomiting, central nervous system depression, coma; death in people with impaired kidney function |
| Iron | Component of hemoglobin (carries oxygen to tissues), myoglobin (in muscle fibers), and enzymes | Lean meats, legumes, enriched flour, green vegetables, dried fruit, liver; absorption is enhanced by the presence of vitamin C | Iron-deficiency anemia, weakness, impaired immune function, cold hands and feet, gastrointestinal distress, pale appearance | Iron deposits in soft tissues, causing liver and kidney damage, joint pains, sterility, and disruption of cardiac function |
| Zinc | Enzyme reactions, including synthesis of proteins, RNA, and DNA; wound healing; immune response; ability to taste | Whole grains, meat, eggs, liver, seafood (especially oysters) | Growth failure, reproductive failure, loss of appetite, impaired taste acuity, skin rash, impaired immune function, poor wound healing, night blindness | Vomiting, impaired immune function, decline in serum HDL levels, impaired magnesium absorption |
| Iodine | Regulates energy production and growth, component of thyroid hormone | Iodized salt, milk, seaweed, seafood, bread | Goiter, mental retardation, hearing loss, and growth failure in newborns | Pimples, goiter, decreased thyroid function |
| Selenium | Antioxidant with vitamin E | Seafood, meat, eggs, grains | Muscle pain and tenderness, heart failure, Keshan disease (impairs the structure and function of the heart) | Hair and fingernail loss, weakness, irritability |
| Copper | Metabolizes iron; aids in brain development and use of glucose, cholesterol, and immunity | Bread, potatoes, beans, nuts, seeds, seafood (especially oysters) | Seizures, anemia, growth retardation | Wilson's disease (accumulation of copper in kidneys and liver), tremors, liver disease |

*(continued)*

**Table 8.7**  *(continued)*

| Major minerals | Major functions | Important sources | Signs of deficiency | Effects of megadoses |
|---|---|---|---|---|
| Manganese | Forms body fat and bone (specifically builds cartilage) | Wheat germ, pineapple, blackberries, tea, sweet potatoes, broccoli | Impairs energy metabolism, produces bone abnormalities | Toxicity is a greater threat than deficiency. Irritability, hallucinations, severe lack of coordination |
| Fluoride | Promotes calcium growth; inhibits bacterial activity on tooth surface; inhibits tooth decay and loss of tooth enamel | Water, mouthwash, toothpaste | Tooth decay | Fluorosis (mottled discoloration and pitting of tooth enamel) |
| Chromium | Aids in use of glucose, energy metabolism | Liver, whole grains, meat, beer, wine, legumes | Weight loss, poor glucose control | Skin and kidney damage |
| Molybdenum | Aids in oxygen transfer from one molecule to another | Dried beans, grains, dark green vegetables, milk | Rapid heartbeat, nausea, vomiting, coma | Joint pain, growth failure, anemia, gout |

## Antioxidants

**Free radicals** are released during metabolism and are stimulated by pollution, smoking, radiation, and stress. Free radicals run throughout the body attacking cells in the brain, heart, bloodstream, and immune system. **Antioxidants** help minimize the damage caused by these free radicals. Vitamins are among the most powerful antioxidants, along with carotenoids, flavonoids, and selenium.

## Water

Although it contains no energy or vitamins and trace amounts of minerals, water is the most important nutrient in the body. Despite its lack of nutritional value, water is necessary for the absorption of vitamins, minerals, and nutrients in food. It is also used for energy production, temperature regulation, and waste elimination. It lubricates joints, helps with digestion, and contributes to sweat production. The body is 50 to 70 percent water (exactly how much depends on age and body composition). Muscle contains a higher concentration of water than many other tissues do—right around 70 percent. Therefore, males, who proportionally have greater muscle mass than females do, have more water. Greater muscle mass is also why a young adult has more water than a senior citizen.

Many brands and varieties of bottled water are on the market, but the evidence seems to indicate that none of them is significantly safer or healthier than regular tap water. A study by a consumer advocacy group found that, of the 1,000 bottles and 103 brands tested in the United States, about one-third were contaminated with bacteria, arsenic, or synthetic organic chemicals, and at least one-fourth were drawn directly from the tap (Natural Resources Defense Council, 1999). In the final analysis, the FDA concluded that bottled water, on average, was not safer or more pure than regular tap water. Despite this, 1 in 15 American households spends between 250 and 10,000 times more for water by choosing to purchase bottled water (U.S. Food and Drug Administration, 1999).

It is difficult, but not impossible, to drink too much water. Most of the time the body will eliminate through urination the water it does not need. Most people who drink too much water are simply inconvenienced by frequent trips to the bathroom. But in rare cases, too much water can lead to serious consequences. At the 2000 Houston Marathon, for example, 21 runners developed a condition known as **hyponatremia** (low sodium levels in the blood due to overconsumption of water). Of those runners, 14 had to be hospitalized (Mulvihill, 2001). If left untreated, hyponatremia can lead to death. Although there are other causes, the primary reason people develop

## Death by Dehydration

If someone wanted to lose weight very rapidly, vigorous exercise (especially in the heat) without rehydrating would be one way of accomplishing that objective. It is also very dangerous. In 1977, three collegiate wrestlers died of dehydration while trying to make it into a lower weight category for competition (Sharkey, 2002). An average-sized person has about 11 gallons (41.63 L) of water in his or her body when fully hydrated. During vigorous exercise, a person can lose 1 pint (0.47 L) to a little over a gallon (3.78 L) of water per hour. If a person were losing one-half gallon (1.89 L) of water per hour, it would take less than six hours to reach a fatal level of water loss (see table 8.8).

### Table 8.8  Effects of Water Loss

| Percentage of water loss in the body | Physical effect |
| --- | --- |
| 1 | Thirsty |
| 5 | Slight fever |
| 8 | Glands stop producing sweat, skin turns blue |
| 15 | Trouble walking |
| 20 | Death |

this condition is that they limit their sodium intake while consuming large amounts of water. Combined with long periods of exercise, typically lasting four or more hours, this creates a serious sodium deficiency. Take these steps to avoid the condition (Clark, 2003):

- Eat salty foods the week before a long-distance endurance event.
- Stop drinking water during exercise if your stomach is sloshing.
- During extended exercise (exercise that lasts more than four hours) in the heat, consume a sport drink that contains sodium.

If you are not getting enough water, however, your body will let you know through thirst. A rough, one-size-fits-all recommendation is eight cups (1.9 L) per day. You can get a more accurate recommendation by dividing your body weight in pounds by two. That number is how many ounces of water you should drink per day. (So if you weigh 140 pounds, you should drink 70 ounces of water, or a little over 2 liters.) Perhaps the simplest method to use to evaluate whether you're getting enough water is to check the frequency of urination and color of your urine. When you are urinating frequently and the color of your urine is pale yellow, you are probably well hydrated (Clark, 2003). This method may be less accurate if you take vitamin supplements because they can darken the color of your urine. Keep in mind that these recommendations do not take into account two very important variables: heat and activity level. If you are working hard in a hot climate, you will need to consume significantly more water.

## Nutrition Guidelines and Principles

The year 1929 marked the beginning of the Great Depression, the longest and worst economic downturn in the history of the modern industrialized world. During that time, when families lost their entire life savings in a couple of days, and when up to a quarter of the workforce was unemployed, Americans had to stand in the government bread lines to stay fed. Out of concern for vitamin and mineral deficiencies, the United States federal government publicized the dietary guidelines shown in figure 8.5, graphically represented by a circle containing seven food groups.

By the 1950s and '60s, those deficiencies were no longer a problem, but concern was growing about declining levels of physical fitness, especially among children. In 1956, President Eisenhower founded the President's Council for Physical Fitness and Sports to encourage schoolchildren to strive for particular fitness objectives. A major element of the program was nutrition; the campaign's slogan was "Food for Fitness."

During these decades, the U.S. Department of Agriculture revised the dietary guidelines and reduced the seven food groups to "the basic four" (see figure 8.6).

The four basic food groups persisted, with slight modifications, until the introduction of the Food Guide Pyramid in 1992. In addition to reclassifying food into six groups, the pyramid recognized that people need more servings of some food groups than of others (see figure 8.7). For example, it recommended 6 to 11 daily servings of bread and cereals but only 2 or 3 of meat and dairy. This is the model that most of today's college students were taught in school. Since then, however, the model has been changed to make it more accessible and understandable for the layperson. In the new system, called MyPlate, relative portions of each food group are shown as divisions of a dinner plate (see figure 8.8).

This new system grew out of the extensive review of nutrition science literature and research for the *Dietary Guidelines for Americans*, first published in 1980. Since its first publication, it has been revised every five years. Its ultimate goal is to enable healthy eating and physical activity in Americans by providing current, accessible information regarding nutritional and physical health. Because of the significance of many recent discoveries, a new food guide system was developed to better reflect these findings. The MyPlate system, released in 2010, was developed as a culmination of work on the part of the U.S. Department of Agriculture

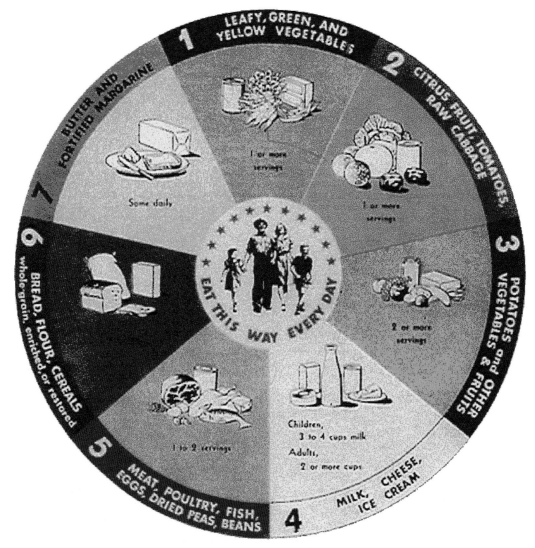

**Figure 8.5** The first graphical representation of dietary recommendations by the U.S. Department of Agriculture, circa 1940.

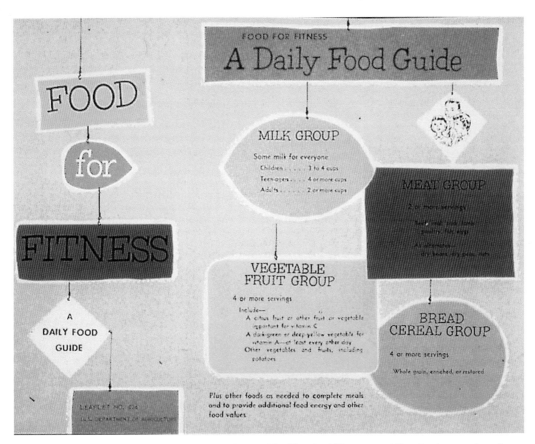

**Figure 8.6** "Food for Fitness" was the President's Council for Physical Fitness and Sports slogan when the council was first created in 1956 by President Eisenhower.

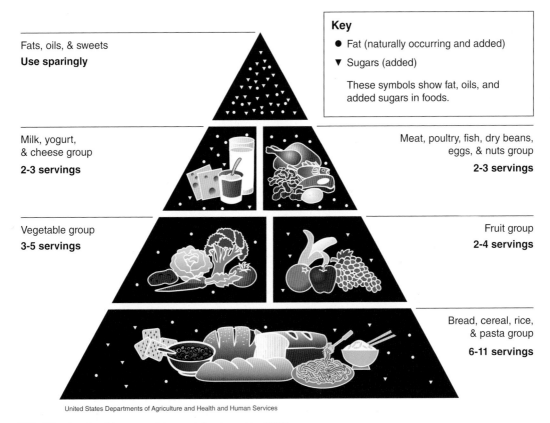

United States Departments of Agriculture and Health and Human Services

**Figure 8.7** The food guide pyramid was introduced in 1992.

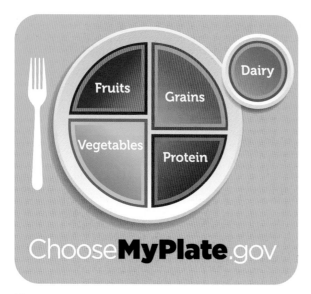

**Figure 8.8**    MyPlate reflects a culmination of work by the U.S. Department of Agriculture and the U.S. Department of Health and Human Services.

and the U.S. Department of Health and Human Services.

## Three Principles to Remember in MyPlate

MyPlate is based on three principles developed by the current edition of *Dietary Guidelines for Americans*: foods to increase, foods to decrease, and balancing calories (U.S. Department of Agriculture, 2007, www. choosemyplate.gov). Though fairly extensive, its recommendations are summarized here.

1. **Foods to increase.** "Foods to increase" include fruits and vegetables: these two food groups should make up at least half of your plate. Such foods also include the following:

   - Whole grains (at least half of total grain intake)
   - Milk (nonfat or 1 percent)
   - Potassium, fiber, and Vitamin D—all areas of concern in the U.S. population. These can be found in vegetables, whole grains, and milk products.

2. **Foods to decrease.** "Foods to decrease" are foods high in fat, sodium (salt), and processed sugars; for example, drink water instead of sugary sodas.

   - Sodium (2,700 mg per day or less)
   - Saturated fats (10 percent or less of daily caloric intake)

   - Calories from solid fats (fats at room temperature, such as beef, butter, and shortening) and added sugars
   - Refined grains (look for the word *enriched* on nutrition labels), especially refined grains that contain solid fats, added sugars, and sodium

3. **Balancing calories.** The primary idea here is to balance the amount of energy consumed with that being expended. In real life no one exactly balances his or her energy every day. However, the cumulative effect of either a caloric deficit or excess will present itself in either weight loss or gain.

   - Generally, Americans consume too many calories, leading to adverse health effects.
   - In MyPlate, proportionality is communicated by the varying sizes of the food group quadrants. This size difference is meant to suggest that a person should eat more foods from the larger wedges and fewer from the smaller.

## Balance and Homeostasis

**Balance** is the core fundamental underlying each of the guidelines recommended in the *Dietary Guidelines for Americans*. Homeostasis is critical for that balance to be achieved. **Homeostasis** describes the ability of the body to maintain healthy, steady conditions in spite of changes in the external environment. Fortunately, God has equipped human bodies with mechanisms that do a tremendous amount of the homeostatic work, without people even noticing it. If you get out of bed in the morning and go for a 20-minute jog, your heart rate, blood pressure, and respiration rate respond to the challenge. If you cut your finger, your blood and skin cells jump into action to stop the bleeding and restore the wounded tissue. When you lie down at night, your body instinctively moves through four stages of sleep to restore mental, emotional, and physical stability.

Although many homeostatic regulations function involuntarily, the choices people make can either help or hinder the process. By wearing more or fewer clothes, you assist the thermoregulatory system in maintaining a core body temperature of about 98 degrees Fahrenheit (37 degrees Celsius). By bathing you assist the largest organ of the body, the skin, with the removal of dead epithelial cells. By choosing to go to bed and get up at approximately the same time each day, you help the body establish a strong internal circadian rhythm. The diet choices you

## No Wonder People Are Getting Larger

In as little as two decades, portion sizes have tripled in caloric value in some cases (see table 8.9). This rapid expansion has led to a corresponding epidemic growth in obesity. Little wonder that one of the fastest shrinking minorities in America is people at a healthy body weight.

**Table 8.9    Changes in Portion Sizes From 1985 to 2005**

| Food item | Calories per portion | |
| --- | --- | --- |
| | **1985** | **2005** |
| Bagel | 140 calories (3 in. [7.6 cm] diameter) | 350 calories (6 in. [15.2 cm] diameter) |
| Fast-food cheeseburger | 333 calories | 590 calories |
| Spaghetti and meatballs | 500 calories (1 cup of spaghetti with sauce and 3 small meatballs) | 1,025 calories (2 cups of spaghetti and 3 large meatballs) |
| Bottle of soda | 85 calories (6.5 oz [29.6 ml]) | 250 calories (20 oz [591.5 ml]) |
| Fast-food french fries | 210 calories (2.4 oz [70.1 ml]) | 610 calories (6.9 oz [204.1 ml]) |
| Turkey sandwich (10 inches) | 320 calories | 820 calories |

Adapted from National Heart, Lung, and Blood Institute, 2010, *Portion distortion quiz.* Available: http://hp2010.nhlbihin.net/portion/portion. cgi?action=question&number=1.

make have enormous impact on your physical homeostasis. Homeostasis is the central idea in the principle of moderation. Dietary moderation is striving for nutritional adequacy as opposed to deprivation or overconsumption.

Nutritional moderation is an idea as old as the scriptures. Notice what God said to the nation of Israel during the time he supernaturally fed them in the Egyptian wilderness.

"Each one is to gather as much as he needs. Take an omer for each person you have in your tent." The Israelites did as they were told; some gathered much, some little. And when they measured it by the omer, he who gathered much did not have too much, and he who gathered little did not have too little. Each one gathered as much as he needed. (Exodus 16:16–18)

This principle is seen again in the New Testament teachings of Jesus when he fed the 5,000 (John 6:1–14). After taking a boy's lunch of five barley loaves and two fish, he miraculously multiplied that small amount of food until, as verse 11 says, "each person had their fill." Then verse 12 says, "And when they had eaten their fill, he told his disciples, 'Gather up the leftover fragments, that nothing may be lost.'"

Gathering and consuming the amount of food that you need, not less and not more, are God's prescription not only for trusting in his faithfulness but cooperating with how he created man and woman.

It seems that whatever pattern God establishes for his creation's goodness, humans in their brokenness can misconstrue. Regarding nutritional moderation, consider the number of college students who choose to willfully deprive their bodies of essential nutrients in order to fit into cultural norms of beauty. On the other hand is the epidemic of obesity in America among young people and adults. The apostle Paul describes enemies of the cross as those who have made a "god of their stomach" by consuming food with reckless abandon (Philippians 3:18–19). Even though gluttony is mentioned more often than tithing in the Bible, it is not a very popular topic in most churches. This has not always been the case. Thomas Aquinas, in the second century, joined other spiritual leaders by placing gluttony in the list of the seven most deadly sins (Pegis, 1997).

Learning how to eat with nutritional moderation, or adequacy, is a central theme of this chapter. Although the concept is simple, its practical application is quite complex and can easily get out of balance. For example, sailors in the fifteenth century suffered from a disease that in its most mild form caused their gums to inflame and start to bleed and in its most severe form led to death. The disease was scurvy and was caused by a deficiency of vitamin C. Vitamin E, which is necessary for proper neural and muscular functioning, can cause excessive bleeding if taken too much. An excess amount of protein causes increased calcium loss and kidney stones, but too little leads to muscles' wasting. Death can be caused not only by dehydration but also by drinking too much water. There are approximately 40 essential nutrients your body must have, and each one of those needs to be consumed in the right amount. The right amount of each of those nutrients varies depending on a person's age, sex, size, activity level, and ethnicity.

## Your Personal Plate

The real power of MyPlate is realized when you go to the U.S. Department of Agriculture's website, put in your individualized information, and receive a personalized report. The first step is to log on to the site at www.choosemyplate.gov. The webpage is illustrated in figure 8.9.

This home page displays lots of interesting information you can explore later, but for right now go to the toolbar at the top of the page and click on "SuperTracker & Other Tools." Select "SuperTracker" from the drop-down list of choices, and when you come to the next webpage, select the "SuperTracker" hyperlink in the paragraph shown. When the new page

resolves, go to the upper right-hand corner and select "Create Profile." You may then enter your name, age, height, weight, sex, and activity level. To illustrate this process, I will enter data for a hypothetical person—Jacinda—an 18-year-old female college freshman who is physically active 30 to 60 minutes most days of the week (see figure 8.10). In addition, her body weight is 142, and her height is 5 feet, 7 inches (if you want to enter these values, you may).

After entering your personalized information and creating a username, as I have done for Jacinda, click "Submit to View Your Plan." When the next page loads (this may take a few moments), "My Coach Center" appears. You can scroll down and select the icon labeled "My Top 5 Goals." Here you can select a maximum of five fitness and nutrition goals that are specifically tailored to your body type and activity level (see figure 8.11).

You will also see a bar at the top of the "My Top 5 Goals" page containing the date, physical activity target, and daily calorie limit. Jacinda's calorie estimate is 2,200 calories per day. The recommendation notes that this figure is only an estimate that needs to be monitored to determine accuracy. In other words, if Jacinda begins carefully consuming 2,200 calories per day and begins to lose weight, the formula used to calculate her caloric expenditure may be underestimating her requirements. On the other hand, if she begins to gain weight, her caloric requirements may be overestimated. Although minor adjustments may

**Figure 8.9**    Home page for ChooseMyPlate.gov.

**Figure 8.10**   Personalize your plate by age, sex, and activity level.

**Figure 8.11**   Personalized recommendations are part of MyPlate.

be necessary, this formula used by the Institute of Medicine should come close to accurately estimating calorie needs (Institute of Medicine, 2002).

To the right of this estimate are specific recommendations for food from each of the five food groups: grains, vegetables, fruits, milk, and meat and beans. The new MyPlate no longer uses the term *serving* because

that led to confusion about how much a serving actually is. For one person, a serving of breakfast cereal may be more than two cups; for another it may be fewer than one. For additional assistance with food portions, the new system gives several general recommendations for common sizes in each of the five food groups. The target daily amount for each of the

**Figure 8.12**    Information on each food group can be individually selected.

*For those less familiar with cups and ounces, you can easily convert these measures to metric by multiplying ounces by 28.34 to get grams and cups by 236.58 to get milliliters.

five groups is listed on the screen, but you can click on "More Info" for a detailed explanation of the food groups in relation to your plan (see figure 8.12).

After selecting "More Info," notice that under "Tips" for Grains is a recommendation that nearly half the grains you eat should be whole grains. According to the National Health and Nutrition Examination Survey (NHANES), which measures consumption norms, Americans are currently consuming most of their grains from refined sources (National Health and Nutrition Examination Survey, 2002). Refined grains are processed in such a way that many of the nutrient-rich vitamins and minerals have been removed. For this reason most nutrition experts recommend limiting the amount of highly refined and processed foods in one's diet.

After Grains you will see your recommendations for Vegetables. Notice the variety of colors and types that are listed. The *Dietary Guidelines for Americans, 2010,* states that the average intake of vegetables in the United States is lower than recommended, contributing to the public health concern for deficiencies in nutrients such as fiber, calcium, potassium, and vitamin D (U.S. Department of Agriculture and U.S. Department of Health and Human Services, 2010). Be adventurous and try a vegetable you have not eaten before—you will be surprised with how many colorful and tasty options there are.

Another personalized recommendation to take note of is the number of teaspoons of oil and the amount of empty or discretionary calories you should aim to take in each day. Jacinda needs six teaspoons of oil per day. Oils, like vegetable, canola, and corn, are liquid at room temperature. Most oils, with the exception of coconut and palm oils, are high in monounsaturated and polyunsaturated fat and low in saturated fat and cholesterol. Six teaspoons of oil may seem like a lot, but it is easy to pour this amount or more on a simple salad. Moderate your personal intake and know what oils are used to prepare the food you eat.

Finally, at the top of your Plan, you will see a recommendation for **empty calories**. An empty calorie, or a **discretionary calorie**, is a new concept in the revised food guide. These calories are like luxuries. Before you spend them you need to understand exactly how they are calculated. Back to Jacinda. She has been given a dietary plan based on 2,200 calories, of which 266 calories are discretionary. It is important to realize that the 266 discretionary calories are included in the 2,200-calorie allotment. Health experts who designed MyPlate are assuming that your food choices within each of the five food groups will be low in added fat and sugar. If Jacinda consistently follows her plan in each of her food selections, her intake per day should be around 1,934 calories. Now she has 266 calories left to "spend" on options such as these:

- Eat more foods from any food group.
- Eat higher-calorie forms of foods—those that contain solid fat or added sugar. Examples are whole milk, cheese, sausage, biscuits, sweetened cereal, and sweetened yogurt.
- Add fat or sweeteners to foods. Examples are sauces, salad dressings, sugar, syrup, and butter.
- Eat or drink items that are mostly fat, calorie sweeteners, or alcohol, soda, wine, and beer.

## Canadian Food Guide

As you might expect, most industrialized countries have developed recommendations and visual graphics to help their citizens make wise nutritional choices. Figure 8.13 shows the webpage for Canada's Food Guide recommendations. Similar to MyPlate, a personalized dietary plan is recommended after demographic information and particular food selections are identified.

Here is a summary of the dietary guidelines for Canadians (Health Canada, 2012):

- Enjoy a variety of foods from the four food groups (vegetables and fruit, grain products, milk and alternatives, and meat and alternatives).
- Include a small amount (2–3 Tbsp) of unsaturated fat each day.

- Make sure that at least 50 percent of your total grain intake is from whole grains.
- Reduce sodium intake.
- Drink skim, 1 percent, or 2 percent milk every day.
- Have meat alternatives such as beans, lentils, and tofu often.
- Satisfy your thirst with water.

You can usually find information about a particular country's nutrition habits and recommendations by doing a Google search for that country's dietary guidelines. If you choose to compare the models in this chapter to others, you will most likely find that there are many more similarities than differences. Whether you are Canadian, German, French, American, or from another country, letting national guidelines direct your decisions on nutrition is one way to ensure you are getting all the nutrients your body needs. As you practice using food guides like the ones discussed in this chapter you will soon be able to categorize foods according to the nutrient group, accurately estimate serving sizes, and evaluate menu selections according to their nutritional contribution. Using these tools will not only expand your knowledge but will also improve your health.

## Vegetarian Alternative

Interest in vegetarian cuisine has dramatically risen, as evidenced by changes in restaurants and on college

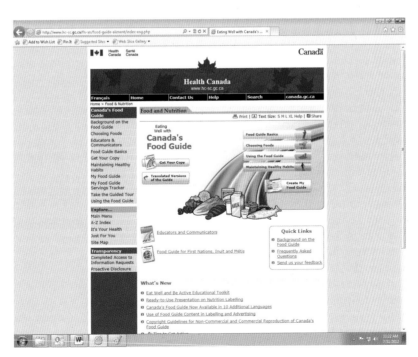

**Figure 8.13**   Canada's Food Guide.

campuses. A survey by the National Restaurant Association found that 20 percent of its customers wanted a vegetarian option (Wardlaw & Hampl, 2007). In another study, 15 percent of college students said they selected vegetarian options at lunch or dinner on any given day (Johnston & Sabate, 2006). It would be erroneous to conclude that one in every nine college students is a vegetarian just because someone is interested in vegetarian cuisine. The study shows, however, that curiosity about the background, rationale, and method of vegetarian consumption is significant. About 9 million Americans (4 percent of the total population) identify with one of the four vegetarian classifications identified in table 8.10 (Vegetarian Resource Group, 2012).

## Background

Historically, vegetarianism has been linked with philosophies and religions. Around 600 BC, the prophet Daniel, along with three of his friends, refused to eat meat from the king of Babylon's table in order to obey God's Old Testament law (Daniel 1:5–21). In the sixth century BC, Pythagoras advocated a meatless diet for its physical health and its ecological, religious, and philosophical benefits (Johnston & Sabate, 2006). Traditional Hindus and Trappist monks adopt vegetarian diets as a practice of their faith. However, most vegetarians today (with notable exceptions such as Seventh-Day Adventists) do not list religious faith as the rationale for their diet. Two of the most common reasons given now are health and ecology.

## Rationale

Numerous studies show that the death rates from cardiovascular disease, hypertension, cancer, type 2 diabetes, and obesity are lower for vegetarians than for nonvegetarians (Berkow & Barnard, 2005; Gardner, 2005; Hu, 2003; Johnston & Sabate, 2006; Lejeune, 2005; Newby, 2005). The lower rates of death and disease may be due in part to the fact that vegetarian diets tend to be lower in saturated fat and cholesterol and higher in complex carbohydrate, dietary fiber, folate, vitamin C, vitamin E, carotenoids, and phytochemicals (Leitzmann, 2005). The lower incidence of chronic disease is not solely due to the diet of vegetarians but to the fact that they tend to be more educated, more physically active, wealthier, and more health conscious than nonvegetarians (BBC News, 2006; Gale et al., 2006; Millet & Dewitte, 2007).

It also makes sound ecological sense to eat primarily plant foods because food sources require different amounts of energy for their production. The least amount of energy is needed to produce grains—about one-third of the caloric output (total amount of calories harvested) is spent to produce each calorie of grain. Animal products, however, require 10 to 90 calories for each calorie of edible food (Whitney & Rolfes, 2012). Figure 8.14 illustrates how much less fuel vegetarian diets require than meat-based diets.

Around 40 percent of the world's grain products are currently used to raise meat-producing animals, and although some of these grain products are inedible for humans, most of them are consumable (Wardlaw & Hampl, 2007). Eating for ecological reasons is wise.

## Planning a Vegetarian Diet

Vegetarians who include milk and egg products in their diets can meet recommendations for most nutrients almost as easily as nonvegetarians can. However, people who follow a strict vegetarian diet consisting exclusively of plant products need to pay more careful attention to obtain the right amount of nutrients. Getting enough protein is not the problem that it was once thought to be for vegetarians. Studies show that those on plant-based diets are unlikely to develop protein deficiencies if their energy intakes are adequate (Whitney & Rolfes, 2012). At the forefront of nutritional concerns for vegans (strict vegetarians) are potential deficiencies of vitamin D, vitamin $B_{12}$, iron, zinc, and calcium (Johnston & Sabate, 2006). With a little planning, however, vegans can compensate for these deficiencies (see table 8.11).

Some slight modifications to the MyPlate food plan allow vegetarians to consume sufficient nutrients (see table 8.12).

## Table 8.10    Four Major Vegetarian Subgroups

| Group | Dietary restrictions |
| --- | --- |
| Vegan | Strictest vegetarian; diet consists of plant foods only |
| Lacto-vegetarian | Diet consists of plant and milk products |
| Ovo-vegetarian | Diet consists of plant and egg products |
| Lacto-ovo-vegetarian | Diet consists of plant, milk, and egg products |

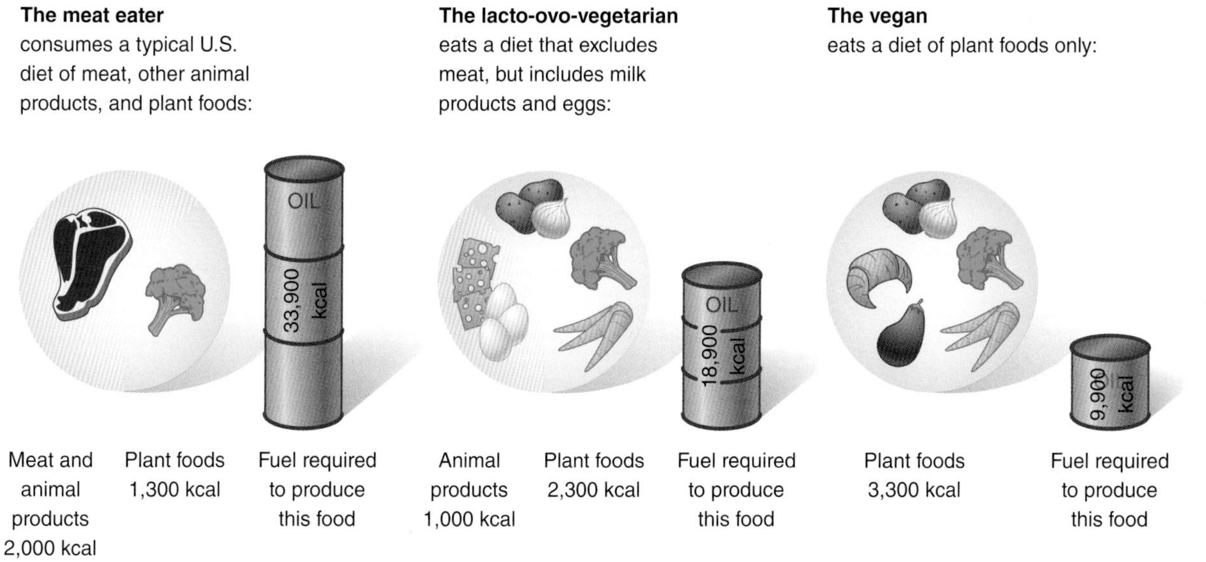

**The meat eater**
consumes a typical U.S. diet of meat, other animal products, and plant foods:

**The lacto-ovo-vegetarian**
eats a diet that excludes meat, but includes milk products and eggs:

**The vegan**
eats a diet of plant foods only:

| Meat and animal products 2,000 kcal | Plant foods 1,300 kcal | Fuel required to produce this food | Animal products 1,000 kcal | Plant foods 2,300 kcal | Fuel required to produce this food | Plant foods 3,300 kcal | Fuel required to produce this food |

**Figure 8.14** Amounts of fuel required to feed individuals consuming food from three different sources, each providing 3,300 calories a day. Note that the fossil fuels necessary to produce each of these diets are based on U.S. conditions.

## Table 8.11  Food Sources of Potential Dietary Pitfalls for Vegetarians

| | |
|---|---|
| Vitamin D | Vitamin D–fortified products like ready-to-eat cereals, soy or rice milk, or from a supplement. One other nondietary solution is to spend 5 to 15 minutes a day in the sun. |
| Vitamin B$_{12}$ | Fortified foods such as ready-to-eat-cereals, soy beverages, meat substitutes, special yeast products, and from supplements |
| Iron | Whole grains, dried fruits, green leafy vegetables, nuts and seeds, beans, soy, and fortified breads and breakfast cereals |
| Zinc | Whole grains, nuts, beans, and soy products |
| Calcium | Legumes, dark green leafy vegetables, nuts, fortified orange juice, soy milk, tofu, bread, and other foods |

For more information on consuming a vegetarian diet, visit the websites listed at the end of the chapter.

# Fasting

In the book *Celebration of Discipline*, Richard Foster writes the following:

The list of [b]iblical personages who fasted reads like a Who's Who of scriptures: Moses the lawgiver, David the king, Elijah the prophet, Esther the queen, Daniel the seer, Anna the prophetess, and Paul the apostle. (Foster, 1998, p. 48)

Pastor and author Mark Buchanan notes the following (Buchanan, 2006, p. 36):

You can't read very far in any direction in the Bible without realizing that fasting was part of the natural rhythm of life for the people of God. They expected and planned to fast as naturally as they expected and planned to eat. To them, fasting was woven into the rhythm of life like day and night, summer and winter, sowing and reaping, waking and sleeping. There were times you ate and times you fasted.

Although Jesus resisted the Pharisees' rigid rules regarding fasting, he fasted himself and indicated that fasting was expected of his followers, particularly after his ministry on earth was completed.

When you fast, do not look somber as the hypocrites do, for they disfigure their faces to show men they are fasting. I tell you the truth, they have received their reward in full. But when you fast, put oil on your head and wash your face, so that it will not be obvious to men that

### Table 8.12    Modifications to MyPlate Food Group Serving Requirements for Vegetarians

| Group | Lacto-vegetarian | Vegan | Key nutrients supplied |
|---|---|---|---|
| Grains | 6–11 | 8–11 | Protein, thiamin, niacin, folate, vitamin E, zinc, magnesium, iron, and fiber |
| Beans and other legumes | 2–3 | 3 | Protein, vitamin B$_6$, zinc, magnesium, and fiber |
| Nuts, seeds | 2–3 | 3 | Protein, vitamin E, and magnesium |
| Vegetables | 3–5 (include one dark green or leafy variety daily) | 4–6 (include one dark green or leafy variety daily) | Vitamin A, vitamin C, and folate |
| Fruits | 2–4 | 4 | Vitamin A, vitamin C, and folate |
| Milk | 3 | — | Protein, riboflavin, vitamin D, vitamin B$_{12}$, and calcium |

This meal plan is based on a diet of 1,600 to 1,800 calories per day and contains about 75 to 100 grams of protein.

Adapted by permission from G. Wardlaw and J. Hampl, 2007, *Perspectives in nutrition,* 9th ed. (New York: The McGraw-Hill Companies), 261. © The McGraw-Hill Companies.

you are fasting, but only to your Father, who is unseen; and your Father, who sees what is done in secret, will reward you. (Matthew 6:16–18)

They said to him, "John's disciples often fast and pray, and so do the disciples of the Pharisees, but yours go on eating and drinking." Jesus answered, "Can you make the guests of the bridegroom fast while he is with them? But the time will come when the bridegroom will be taken from them; in those days they will fast." (Luke 5:33–35)

Clearly, the Bible supports fasting, but going without food for a long time does bring some negative health effects. Following are a number of wellness concerns associated with long-term fasting:

- Decreased metabolic function
- Decreased mental activity
- Increased muscle wasting
- Decreased bone mineral density
- Increased risk for menstrual dysfunction
- Potential for fueling disordered eating

A classic nutritional deprivation study was first published in the book *The Biology of Human Starvation* (Keys, 1950). In the study, Dr. Ancel Keys carefully documented the effects of chronic energy restriction on a group of 32 men. The experiment mimicked the starvation among prisoners of war in World War II. For six months, the caloric intake of the men was cut in half. As you might expect, each subject had signifi-

cant weight loss. Yet in addition to weight reduction, several other psychosocial concerns emerged. The men grew increasingly depressed, self-centered, and apathetic, losing interest in almost everything except food. The men began reporting an extreme preoccupation with food. They spent their days talking about the flavor and texture of food. Before meals they chatted about food preparation and taste. At night the men dreamed about food. They became increasingly protective of the food that they were rationed, secretly stowing away morsels for later consumption. As the experiment continued, the men became increasingly isolated, withdrawing from people with whom they had previously shared friendships. Six of the men developed character neuroses, while two others developed mild psychoses. Although extreme in duration, this study provides a revealing window into the physiological and psychological hardship of extreme starvation.

In light of biblical admonitions and scientific evidence, is it advisable to fast? Do some research and form an opinion about whether the scientific evidence is strong enough to warrant the discontinuation of fasting.

There are no specific rules for fasting, but here are five scriptural motives for fasting:

- To hear from God (Acts 13:2)
- To intercede for others (Psalm 35:13)
- As an act of repentance (Joel 1:13–14)
- For strength and direction (Acts 14:23)
- As an act of worship (Luke 2:37)

## Next Steps

A lot of ground is covered in this chapter, and it ends as it started with a warning about extremes. Some view the Dietary Guidelines, Dietary Reference Intakes, and the meal plan at www.ChooseMyPlate.gov as the "right" way to eat. Others see the information in this chapter as another bombardment of messages from nutrition experts who cannot seem to go two weeks without announcing yet another food that causes cancer. These reactions occupy two extremes: dogged adherence and mindless neglect.

At first glance, dogged adherence seems superior. Unwavering commitment to a detailed dietary regimen was en vogue when Jesus walked the planet. The dietary system included more than 200 laws designed to prevent disease and demonstrate to the world that the Israelites were set apart by God. Yet it was Jesus who caused a stir by breaking many of these sacred dietary regulations. He gathered food when he was not supposed to, dined with inappropriate company, and consumed foods and drink so freely that his critics called him a glutton and drunkard (Matthew 11:19). Jesus simply refused dogmatic adherence to the "dietary line."

The other extreme is disregard for any level of discipline, structure, or order. People become too tired of counting grams of fat, number of calories, and ounces of water, so they decide to follow the mantra "Let us eat and drink, for tomorrow we die" (1 Corinthians 15:32).

Is there a better way? Indeed there is. In his letter to his young apprentice Timothy, Paul talks about how to guard against extremes:

> The Spirit clearly says that in later times some will abandon the faith and follow deceiving spirits and things taught by demons. Such teachings come through hypocritical liars, whose consciences have been seared as with a hot iron. They forbid people to marry and order them to abstain from certain foods, which God created to be received with thanksgiving by those who believe and who know the truth. For everything God created is good, and nothing is to be rejected if it is received with thanksgiving, because it is consecrated by the word of God and prayer. (1 Timothy 4:1–5)

In an interview published in *Christianity Today*, John Stott comments about this portion of Paul's letter to Timothy (Stott, 1996, p. 24):

> Paul avoids both extremes: Asceticism is a rejection of the good gifts of the good Creator. Its opposite is materialism—not just possessing material things, but becoming preoccupied with them. In between asceticism and materialism is simplicity, contentment, and generosity, and these three virtues should mark all of us.

Living between the extremes is wonderful advice for your nutritional health.

## Key Terms

alimentary canal

amino acids

antioxidants

asceticism

balance

bolus

calorie

carbohydrate

chyme

complete proteins

complex carbohydrate

digestive enzyme

digestive system

disaccharides

discretionary calorie

duodenal ulcers

duodenum

empty calories

esophageal sphincter

esophageal ulcer

esophagus

fat

fiber

free radicals

fructose

galactose

gastric juices

gastric ulcer

glucose

glycemic index

glycemic load

homeostasis

hydrochloric acid

hyponatremia

insoluble fiber

kilocalorie

lactose

macronutrients

maltose

micronutrients

minerals

monosaccharides

monounsaturated fat

net carbohydrate

nutrient density

nutrition

peristalsis

polysaccharides

polyunsaturated fat

protein

pyloric sphincter

rectum

saturated fat

self-controlled

simple carbohydrate

soluble fiber

stomach

sucrose

trace minerals

vitamins

## Review Questions

1. Describe how nutrition imbalances affect the world people share (environment, economy, culture, religion, and health).

2. Diagram the digestive system.

3. Identify the specific contributions each of the six major nutrients makes to health.

4. Using MyPlate or Canada's Food Guide, outline a healthy diet for an 18-year-old female who is getting less than 30 minutes of vigorous activity each day.

5. What changes would you need to make in the diet you developed in the answer to the previous question if that individual were a vegetarian?

## Application Activities

1. Search for the dietary guidelines of a country other than the United States. Compare and contrast the guidelines of your chosen country to those offered by MyPlate.

2. Assess your existing diet by going to www.choosemyplate.gov/supertracker-tools/supertracker.html.

3. Outline a dietary plan in line with the personalized recommendations at www.choosemyplate.gov/.

4. Test your ability to interpret food labels by completing the following activity.

# Four Key Questions You Should Answer When Reading Food Labels

Examine figure 8.15 and try to answer the next few questions before proceeding.

1. How many servings and calories are in this box of macaroni and cheese?
2. Which nutrients, if any, should I limit and which should I be sure to obtain?
3. What is relevant about the food label footnote?
4. How can I tell if a % Daily Value is high or low?

U.S. Food and Drug Administration, 2012.

| Nutrition Facts | |
|---|---|
| Serving Size 1 cup (228g) Servings Per Container 2 | |
| **Amount Per Serving** | |
| Calories   250 | Calories from Fat 110 |
| | % Daily Value* |
| **Total Fat** 12g | 18% |
| Saturated Fat 3g | 15% |
| Trans Fat 3g | |
| **Cholesterol** 30mg | 10% |
| **Sodium** 470mg | 20% |
| **Total Carbohydrates** 31g | 10% |
| Dietary Fiber 0g | 0% |
| Sugar 5g | |
| **Protein** 5g | |
| Vitamin A | 4% |
| Vitamin C | 2% |
| Calcium | 20% |
| Iron | 4% |

Footnote

| * Percent Daily Values are based on a 2,000 calorie diet. Your Daily Values may be higher or lower depending on your calorie needs. | | |
|---|---|---|
| | Calories  2,000 | 2,500 |
| Total Fat | Less than 65g | 80g |
| Sat Fat | Less than 20g | 25g |
| Cholesterol | Less than 300mg | 300mg |
| Sodium | Less than 2,400mg | 2,400mg |
| Total Carbohydrate | 300g | 375g |
| Dietary Fiber | 25g | 30g |

**Figure 8.15**   Typical food label for macaroni and cheese.

From U.S. Food and Drug Administration, 2012.

**1. How many servings and calories are in this box of macaroni and cheese?** Serving size is one of the easiest items to overlook when examining a food label. Many people assume that nutritional values represent the entire contents of a package or container. If you made that assumption with a package of macaroni and cheese, you would be underestimating the calorie and nutritional content by 50 percent.

*(continued)*

*(continued)*

More important than the serving size printed on the box is the actual quantity of food you eat. This is what determines your calorie consumption. A general guide to the low-, moderate-, and high-calorie foods follows:

- 40 calories or fewer is considered low,
- 100 calories is considered moderate (5 percent of total intake), and
- 400 calories is considered high (20 percent of total intake).

These values are based upon a 2,000-calorie diet.

**2. Which nutrients should I limit and which should I be sure to obtain?** Four nutrient values need to be limited: saturated fat, trans fat, cholesterol, and sodium. The goal is to get no more than 100 percent of the daily values for these nutrients each day. There is not a reference daily value for trans fat, but experts recommend limiting the amount of trans fat in your diet as much as possible. Studies show that trans fat is highly correlated with an increased risk of heart disease because it increases blood cholesterol levels by altering the way cholesterol is removed from the blood. Therefore, the Institute of Medicine recommends keeping the intake of trans fatty acids to an absolute minimum (Institute of Medicine, 2002).

Consumers can use the food label not only to help them limit particular nutrients but also to encourage the intake of nutrients often neglected in the diet such as dietary fiber, vitamin A, vitamin C, calcium, and iron.

**3. What is relevant about the food label footnote?** The footnote points out that the percent daily values are based on a 2,000- or 2,500-calorie diet. In addition, a "less than" column reminds consumers to be careful of overconsumption of some nutrients.

**4. How can I tell if a % Daily Value is high or low?** Foods that contain 5 percent or less of a person's daily values are considered low. On the other hand, foods that contain 20 percent or more of a person's daily values are considered high. You can use this 5/20 guide as a quick reference to nutrient quantity.

# References

Albert, C.M., Gaziano, J.M., Willett, W.C., & Manson, J.E. (2002). Nut consumption and decreased risk of sudden cardiac death in the physicians' health study. *Archives of Internal Medicine, 162*(12), 1382.

American College of Sports Medicine. (2000). Position paper: Nutrition and athletic performance. *Journal of the American Dietetic Association, 100,* 1543–56.

BBC News. (2006). *High IQ link to being vegetarian.* http://news.bbc.co.uk/2/hi/health/6180753.stm.

Berkow, S.E., & Barnard, N.D. (2005). Blood pressure regulation and vegetarian diets. *Nutrition Reviews, 63*(1), 1–8.

Buchanan, M. (2006). *The rest of God: Restoring your soul by restoring Sabbath.* Waco, TX: Word.

Casey, John. (2012). *The hidden ingredient that can sabotage your diet.* www.webmd.com/diet/features/the-hidden-ingredient-that-can-sabotage-your-diet.

Clark, N. (2003). *Sports nutrition guidebook* (3rd ed.). Champaign, IL: Human Kinetics.

Consumer Reports. (2004, June). The truth about low-carb foods. *Consumer Reports, 12.*

Donatelle, R. (2006). *Access to health* (9th ed.). San Francisco: Pearson.

Food Institute Report. (2002). When, why, and on what are college students snacking? *The Food Institute Report, 4.*

Food Service Director. (2002). Freshmen college student dining habits. *Food Service Director, 15*(3), 1.

Foster, G. (2003). A randomized trial of low carbohydrate diet for obesity. *New England Journal of Medicine, 348*(21), 2082–90.

Foster, R.J. (1998). *Celebration of discipline: The path to spiritual growth.* San Francisco: Harper.

Gale, C.R., Deary, I.J., Schoon, I., Batty, G.D., & Batty, G.D. (2006). IQ in childhood and vegetarianism in adulthood: 1970 British cohort study. *British Medical Journal, 334*(7587), 245.

Gardner, C.D. (2005). The effect of a plant-based diet on plasma lipids in hypercholesterolemic adults. *Annals of Internal Medicine, 142,* 725–33.

Hales, D. (2005). *An invitation to health* (11th ed.). Belmont, CA: Wadsworth.

Health Canada. (2012). *Canada's food guide.* www.hc-sc.gc.ca/fn-an/alt_formats/hpfb-dgpsa/pdf/food-guide-aliment/view_eatwell_vue_bienmang-eng.pdf.

Hu, F. (2003). Plant-based foods and prevention of cardio-vascular disease: An overview. *American Journal of Clinical Nutrition, 78*(Suppl.), 544S.

Institute of Medicine. (2002). *Dietary reference intakes for energy, carbohydrate, fiber, fat, fatty acids, cholesterol, protein, and amino acids.* Washington, DC: Institute of Medicine.

Jenkins, D.J., Kendall, C.W., Marchie, A., Parker, T.I., Connelly, P.W., Qian, W., et al. (2002). Dose response of almonds on coronary heart disease risk factors: Blood lipids, oxidized low-density lipoproteins, lipoprotein(a), homocysteine, and pulmonary nitric oxide: A randomized, controlled, crossover trial. *Circulation, 106*(11), 1327–32.

Johnston, P.A., & Sabate, J. (Eds.). (2006). *Nutritional implications of vegetarian diets.* Philadelphia: Lippincott Williams & Wilkins.

Keys, A.B. (1950). *The biology of human starvation.* Minneapolis: University of Minnesota Press.

Lejeune, M.P. (2005). Additional protein in-take limits weight regain after weight loss in humans. *British Journal of Nutrition, 93,* 281–89.

Leitzmann, C. (2005). Vegetarian diets: What are the advantages? *Forum of Nutrition, 57,* 147.

Lemon, P. (1995). Do athletes need more protein and amino acids? *International Journal of Sports and Nutrition, 5,* S39–61.

Levine, Z. (2012). *Nathan's hot dog eating contest a buffet for the senses.* http://southbrunswick.patch.com/topics/ Nathan%2527s + Famous + Hot + Dog + Eating + Contest.

Miller, B.J. (2003). Glycemic load and chronic disease. *Nutritional Review, 61*(5), S49.

Millet, K., & Dewitte, S. (2007). IQ and vegetarianism: Non-conformity may be hidden driver behind relation. *British Medical Journal, 334*(7589), 327–28.

Mulvihill, K. (2001). *Runners beware: Too much water can be dangerous.* www.womenrunners.com/training_ hyponatremia.htm.

National Health and Nutrition Examination Survey. (2002). Report: National health and examination survey. www. cdc.gov/nchs/nhanes.htm.

National Heart, Lung, and Blood Institute. (2010). *Proportion distortion quiz.* http://hp2010.nhlbihin.net/portion/ portion.cgi?action = question&number = 1.

Natural Resources Defense Council. (1999). *Bottled water: Pure drink or pure hype?* New York: NRDC.

Newby, P.K. (2005). Risk of overweight and obesity among semivegetarian, lactovegetarian, and vegan women. *American Journal of Clinical Nutrition, 81,* 1267.

Pegis, A. (Ed.). (1997). *Basic writings of St. Thomas Aquinas.* Indianapolis: Hackett.

Pimentel, D. (1980). *Food, energy, and the future of society.* Boulder, CO: Associated University Press.

Powell, K.F., Holt, S., & Brand-Miller, J. (2002). International tables of glycemic index and glycemic load values. *American Journal of Clinical Nutrition, 62,* 5–56.

Samaha, F. (2003). A low carbohydrate as compared with a low-fat diet in severe obesity. *New England Journal of Medicine, 348*(21), 2074–81.

Sharkey, B. (2002). *Fitness and health* (5th ed.). Champaign, IL: Human Kinetics.

Spurlock, Morgan. (2012). 30 Days. http://www.tv.com/ shows/30-days/

Stott, J. (1996). Basic Stott: An interview by Roy McCloughry. *Christianity Today, 40*(1), 24.

U.S. Department of Agriculture and U.S Department of Health and Human Services. (2012). *Choose MyPlate. gov.* http://www.choosemyplate.gov/supertracker-tools/ supertracker.html.

U.S. Department of Agriculture and U.S. Department of Health and Human Services. (2010, December). *Dietary guidelines for Americans, 2010* (7th ed.). http://health.gov/ dietaryguidelines/2010.asp.

U.S. Department of Agriculture. (2007). *MyPlate.* www. choosemyplate.gov.

U.S. Department of Health and Human Services. (2005). *Dietary Guidelines for Americans, 2005.* http://www.health. gov/dietaryguidelines/.

U.S. Food and Drug Administration. (2012). How to understand and use the nurtition facts label. www.fda.gov/Food/ ResourcesForYou/Consumers/NFLPM/ucm274593.htm.

U.S. Food and Drug Administration. (1999, July/August). *Water sold state to state safe to drink.* Washington, DC: United States Food and Drug Administration.

Vegetarian Resource Group. (2012). How often do Americans eat vegetarian meals? And how many adults in the U.S. are vegetarians? www.vrg.org/blog/2012/05/18/how-often-do-americans-eat-vegetarian-meals-and-how-many-adults-in-the-u-s-are-vegetarian/.

Wardlaw, G., & Hampl, J. (2007). *Perspectives in nutrition* (9th ed.). New York: McGraw-Hill, 42.

Whitney, E.N., & Rolfes, S.R. (2012). *Understanding nutrition* (13th ed.). Belmont, CA, Wadsworth.

Whole Vegan. (2012). *Refined Sugar History.* www. wholevegan.com/refined_sugar_history.html.

# Suggested Readings

Byrd-Bredbenner, C., Moe, G., Beshgetoor, D., & Berning, J. (2012). *Wardlaw's perspectives in nutrition* (9th ed.). Boston: McGraw-Hill.

This text places special emphasis on the application of nutrition principles in everyday life by exploring the health consequences of their practice.

Duyff, R. (2012). *ADA: Complete food and nutrition guide* (4th ed.). Chicago: American Dietetic Association.

This comprehensive book from the American Dietetic Association is packed with simple, practical tips and flexible guidelines to help you choose nutritious, flavorful, and convenient foods that suit your needs and lifestyle—no matter your age or stage of life.

Selkowitz, A. (2005). *The college student's guide to eating well on campus* (Rev. ed.). Bethesda, MD: Tulip Hill Press.

Targeted toward college students, this guidebook describes how to avoid gaining "the freshman fifteen" and how to make healthy food choices while in college.

Sizer, F., & Whitney, E.N. (2011). *Nutrition concepts and controversies: MyPlate update* (12th ed.). Belmont, CA: Wadsworth/Thomson.

The biological foundations of nutrition are covered without assuming any previous knowledge. This textbook helps students gain a nutritional background to assist them in making healthy food choices.

Whitney, E.N., & Rolfes, S.R. (2012). *Understanding nutrition* (13th ed.). Belmont, CA: Wadsworth/Thomson.

This student-focused textbook presents the major concepts in nutrition, including the body's use of nutrients and diet planning throughout the life cycle.

# Suggested Websites

www.eatright.org

Website for the American Dietetic Association, one of the most respected sources of dietary information in the United States.

www.choosemyplate.gov

Detailed information about dietary guidelines for Americans.

www.fda.gov/food/labelingnutrition/default.htm

A detailed description of what U.S. food labels mean.

www.fda.gov/Food/ResourcesForYou/Consumers/NFLPM/ucm274593.htm

U.S. Food and Nutrition Center site with food guide information for various ethnic and cultural groups.

www.hc-sc.gc.ca/fn-an/food-guide-aliment/index-eng.php

Canada's Food Guide, with dietary reference intakes, healthy weights, nutrition labeling, food programs, and resources.

www.health.gov/dietaryguidelines

Website provides 2010 dietary guidelines for Americans.

www.ivu.org

Website supported by the International Vegetarian Union.

www.nal.usda.gov/fnic/foodcomp/search

Search the USDA nutritional database to find the nutritional contents of a particular food.

www.vrg.org

An informative website on vegetarianism by the Vegetarian Resource Group.

# Twitter

On Twitter, follow @TeamNutrition and @MyPlate.

# Emotional Health and Wellness

Peter Walters • Doug Needham • Bud Williams

After reading this chapter, you should be able to do the following:

1. Appreciate the mind–body connection.
2. Learn the ABCs of stress.
3. Identify how stress can help or hinder.
4. List three principles for becoming stress hardy.
5. Identify the primary symptoms and causes of depression.
6. Learn strategies for treating depression.
7. Understand the fundamental factors that contribute to happiness.

**Intelligence quotient** (IQ) has long been considered a leading predictor of a person's potential for achievement. More recently, psychologists have determined that a different type of intelligence, called emotional intelligence or emotional quotient (EQ), makes an even greater difference in personal and professional success than IQ does (Goleman, 1995).

According to the author of the international best-seller *Emotional Intelligence*, Dr. Daniel Goleman of Harvard University, EQ involves the ability to know and manage one's own emotions and recognize the emotional states of others. More than a decade of research has shown that people with these skills are more productive at work and happier at home. They're also less prone to stress, depression, and anxiety, and they bounce back quicker from serious illnesses (Goleman, 1995; Goleman et al., 2002; Matthews et al., 2002).

According to Dr. Travis Bradberry, who has surveyed more than 500,000 men and women about their emotional intelligence, only 36 percent can accurately identify their emotions when they occur. Approximately 70 percent reported not being able to handle stress effectively, and only 15 percent said they felt respected by others at work (Bradberry, 2003). A survey of more than 1,000 students attending Christian colleges across America found that the "ability to communicate feelings" ranked dead last among their relational abilities (Walters et al., 2006). The students—both male and female—rated themselves better at listening, self-understanding, honesty, conflict resolution, assertiveness, and trustworthiness than at being able to communicate feelings.

The good news is that, while IQ barely budges over a lifetime, you can boost your emotional intelligence. Psychologist John Mayer, of the University of New Hampshire, is one of the pioneers in EQ research. He likens emotional intelligence to skill in algebra (Hales, 2007). Mayer suggests that just as people can learn to solve algebraic equations through a step-by-step process, they also can learn the skills that enhance emotional intelligence.

This chapter teaches theoretical principles and specific skills to expand emotional aptitude in two specific areas, stress and depression. A Kansas State study conducted over a 13-year period reported that mental health issues on college campuses changed between 1988 and 2001. At the beginning of the study most students were seeking help with relational challenges; stress and anxiety topped the list toward the end of the study (Benton et al., 2003). According to the National College Health Assessment survey (2006), which involved 47,202 students from 74 campuses across the United States, 15 percent of students reported being diagnosed with depression, up from 10 percent in 2000.

Stress and depression are major health issues for students, and they can become serious if left untreated. This chapter teaches you to understand, detect, and know how to get help for these common issues.

Much of this chapter focuses on "heavy" emotions, but it does conclude with a discussion about happiness. Several scientific studies have identified traits that are likely to increase happiness. The results of those studies are explored.

## Stress and the Mind–Body Connection

Canadian medical researcher Hans Selye was examining the effects of an ovarian extract that had recently been isolated in a group of laboratory rats. During the testing Selye noticed that the rodents' adrenal glands had enlarged, their immune glands had shrunk, and their stomachs had developed bleeding ulcers (Sapolsky, 2004). Selye was alarmed by these results, but he didn't want to jump to conclusions so he repeated the study. The second time he included a control group that had been injected with a neutral saline solution instead of the extract. To his amazement, the rats in the control group developed the same symptoms. Wracking his brain for another explanation, Dr. Selye realized that he wasn't exactly adept at handling the rats. As he tried to inject them, they would often squirm out of his grasp and he would have to chase them around the lab with a broom. The poor creatures were seriously stressed out! Further experiments confirmed this hypothesis, and Selye extended it beyond rats. His prediction—that sufficient levels of stress can cause physical illness in humans—has since been thoroughly investigated and upheld by a new brand of medical research called **psychoneuro-immunology (PNI)**, the study of the mind's healing and harmful effects on the body (Sapolsky, 2004).

Many studies report the negative and positive consequences related to varying states of mind. In one study college students were tested for salivary IgA (S-IgA), an antibody that fights infection, five days before, the day of, and two weeks after final exams. The results showed that their S-IgA levels were lowest on the days of the exams (Brain Mind Bulletin, 1989), suggesting a compromised immune system. In another study with S-IgA, researchers induced positive moods among their participants by asking them to imagine a situation in which they experienced "care and compassion." When researchers measured levels during these positive states, they found increased S-IgA (Rein et al., 1995).

Mind–body medicine has flourished recently because Americans report higher levels of stress than ever before. According to one survey, 75 percent of U.S. adults feel "great stress" at least one day a week, and some feel it almost daily (American Institute of Stress, 2002). Adults aren't the only ones feeling more stress. The Cooperative Institutional Research Program reports that students, specifically college freshmen in the United States, are feeling more overwhelmed than ever before (Sax, 1999). According to their findings, almost one-third (30.2 percent) of first-year students described themselves as "frequently overwhelmed." That may sound normal for freshmen, but the revealing part of this data is that the percentages increased over time. Figure 9.1 illustrates that from 1985 to 1999 the number of first-year students who said they were frequently overwhelmed doubled (Sax, 1999).

How stressed are you? It is easy to underestimate your stress level and overestimate how much you can endure. The stress test in the application activities at the end of this chapter can help you identify your existing stress load, or you can take the fun test in the Quick Stress Test Sidebar.

## The ABCs of Stress

A common definition of **stress** is any specific or non-specific response of the body to any demand made upon it. This definition is quite broad. To gain a better

### Quick Stress Test

You are under too much stress if

- there are teeth marks on your textbooks;
- you don't have an ulcer, you have a black hole;
- you put posters on your walls to cover your fingernail scratches; or
- you fall asleep counting things on your to-do list.

understanding of exactly what stress is, one needs to analyze it more specifically. Noted psychologist Dr. Albert Ellis and colleagues (1997) did just that. Ellis stated that at least three components, what he called the ABCs of stress, must exist for stress to occur (see figure 9.2).

## A = Activating Events

An **activating event**, or **stressor**, is any event or condition that triggers a stress response. Thomas Holmes, psychiatrist at the University of Washington School of Medicine, and Richard Rahe, a scientist for the United States military, were some of the first to scientifically examine stressors (Holmes & Rahe, 1967). They explored the medical records of 5,000 patients who had recently suffered illness. Then they asked the

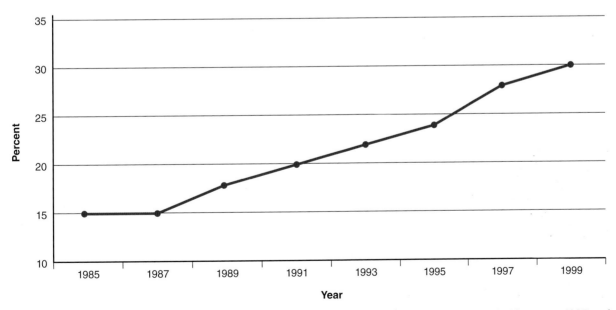

**Figure 9.1** The percentage of college freshmen reporting being "frequently overwhelmed" doubled between 1985 and 1999.

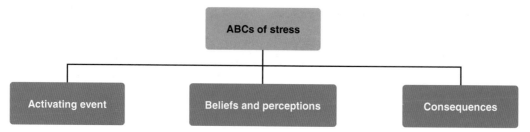

**Figure 9.2**  Three ingredients essential for stress to occur.

patients whether they had experienced any stressful life events preceding their illness. If so, patients were then asked to rate the severity of that stressful event (measured on a 100-point scale). What they reported was a positive correlation between stressful events and illness. In other words, as stress increases so does illness. Table 9.1 presents the results of their research.

As you can see, death of a spouse was considered the most stressful life experience. It is also interesting to note that events generally viewed as positive and enriching, such as getting married, receiving a job promotion, and entering retirement, rank fairly high as stressors. If you can't relate to many of the life changes identified by Holmes, a scale specific to college students was adapted from Holmes' original work and is listed in table 9.2 (Anderson, 1972).

Life changes are only one of three categories of stressors. The second is catastrophes. Natural disasters, war, rape, assault, torture, and other like events can so traumatize people that they later develop **posttraumatic stress disorder (PTSD)**. People with this condition tend to have vivid nightmares or flashbacks in which they relive the awful experience again and again. Epidemiologists report that most people will experience a traumatic event in their lives and that up to 25 percent of them will develop PTSD (Kessler, 2000).

The third category, less intense but still important, is what researcher Richard Lazarus terms "daily hassles" (Lazarus & Folkman, 1984). After questioning many adults, he concluded that most people identify relatively minor annoyances as their main sources of stress and tension. These are some of the more common daily hassles:

- Misplacing and losing things
- Dealing with troublesome people
- Concern over physical appearance
- Anxiety over financial matters
- Feeling overwhelmed by too many things to do

What is stressing you out? The following list identifies how 1,077 students from Christian colleges ranked their leading stressors (Walters et al., 2006).

1. **Academic work:** Men and women both rated the tension of keeping up with academic responsibilities significantly higher than any other life stressor. Perhaps this is no surprise given the primary task of students.

2. **Future concerns:** These include choosing a major, fears about how successful they will be in college, finding a soul mate, and determining a career.

3. **Spiritual matters:** This stressor seems to be unique to students attending private Christian institutions. Specific issues in this category include determining personal beliefs, establishing consistency of spiritual disciplines, experiencing a crisis of beliefs, and feeling inferior to people who seem to have a better relationship with God than they have.

4. **Interpersonal relationships:** College is a unique time of relational transition. Students leave the familiar family environment—not just for the day but for weeks and months at a time—and venture off into new relationships. Dealing with roommates and peers with different perspectives and trying to maintain a balance between social involvement and academic success can be challenging.

5. **Financial matters:** College is expensive. According to the U.S. Department of Education, the average annual cost in 2010 of a four-year private-college education was $36,993 (Goldstein, 2010). Over four years, tuition, room, and board totals well over $100,000—not exactly "small change."

Examining exposure to life changes, catastrophic events, and daily life hassles can help identify potential stressors. But it is important to remember that the same event may affect people in different ways. For example, one person might find driving home from work very stressful, while another might find it relaxing. A person's beliefs and perceptions about those events have an enormous effect on how stress is internalized and expressed.

## Table 9.1    Intensity of Common Stressful Events

| Life change units | Event | Life change units | Event |
|---|---|---|---|
| 100 | Death of spouse | 29 | Change in responsibilities at work |
| 73 | Divorce | 29 | Son or daughter leaving home |
| 65 | Marital separation | 29 | Trouble with in-laws |
| 63 | Jail term | 28 | Outstanding personal achievement |
| 63 | Death of close family member | 26 | Spouse begins or stops work |
| 53 | Personal injury or illness | 25 | Change in living conditions |
| 50 | Marriage | 24 | Revision of personal habits |
| 47 | Fired at work | 23 | Trouble with boss |
| 45 | Marital reconciliation | 20 | Change in work hours or conditions |
| 45 | Retirement | 20 | Change in residence |
| 44 | Change in health of family member | 19 | Change in recreation |
| 40 | Pregnancy | 19 | Change in church activities |
| 39 | Sex difficulties | 18 | Change in social activities |
| 39 | Gain of new family member | 17 | Mortgage or loan for lesser purchase (car, TV, and so on) |
| 39 | Business readjustment | 16 | Change in sleeping habits |
| 38 | Change in financial state | 15 | Change in number of family get-togethers |
| 37 | Death of close friend | 15 | Change in eating habits |
| 36 | Change to different line of work | 13 | Vacation |
| 35 | Change in number of arguments with spouse | 12 | Christmas |
| 31 | Mortgage or loan for major purchase (e.g., home) | 11 | Minor violations of the law |
| 30 | Foreclosure of mortgage or loan | | |

Adapted from *Journal of Psychosomatic Research, 11,* T. Holmes and R. Rahe, The social readjustment rating scale, pp. 213–218. Copyright 1967 with permission from Elsevier.

## B = Beliefs or Perceptions

The following well-known story illustrates that the way a person construes or interprets an event affects the response to it:

On an airplane flying from New York to Boston, a middle-aged man was quickly losing patience with the family next to him. The two toddlers were standing in their seats, crawling around on the floor, making a lot of noise, and otherwise misbehaving. Their mother, however, was doing nothing to control them. She just sat staring blankly into space, oblivious to the commotion. Finally, unable to take it anymore, the man demanded, "Lady, can't you do something about your kids?" Startled, as if awakened from a deep sleep, she quickly reprimanded her children, fastened them in their seats, and gave them toys to occupy them. Then she turned to the man sitting next to her and quietly apologized. "I'm sorry, sir. I guess I was distracted. Three hours ago I received a phone call and was told that my husband had been seriously injured in an automobile accident. They said to

**Table 9.2    Intensity of Common Stressful Events Among College Students**

| Life change units | Event (adapted for college students) | Life change units | Event (adapted for college students) |
|---|---|---|---|
| 87 | Death of a spouse | 50 | Change to a different line of work |
| 77 | Marriage | 50 | Change to a new school |
| 77 | Death of a close family member | 48 | Major change in social activities |
| 76 | Divorce | 47 | Major change in responsibilities at work |
| 74 | Marital separation | 46 | Major change in the use of alcohol |
| 68 | Death of a close friend | 45 | Revision of personal habits |
| 68 | Pregnancy or fathering a child | 44 | Trouble with school administration |
| 65 | Major personal injury or illness | 43 | Work at a job while attending school |
| 62 | Fired from work | 42 | Trouble with in-laws |
| 60 | Broken marital engagement or steady relationship | 42 | Change in residence or living conditions |
| 58 | Sex difficulties | 41 | Change in or choice of a major field of study |
| 58 | Marital reconciliation | 41 | Change dating habits |
| 57 | Major change in usual type and/or amount of recreation | 40 | Outstanding personal achievement |
| 57 | Major change in self-concept or self-awareness | 38 | A lot more or a lot less trouble with your boss |
| 56 | Major change in the health of a family member | 36 | Major change in church activities |
| 54 | Engaged to be married | 34 | Major change in sleeping habits |
| 53 | Major change in financial state | 33 | Trip or vacation |
| 52 | Mortgage or loan for purchase of less than $10,000 | 30 | Major change in eating habits |
| 50 | Enter college | 26 | Major change in the number of family get-togethers |
| 50 | Gain of new family member | 22 | Found guilty of minor violations of the law |
| 50 | Major conflict in or change in values | | |

Reprinted from G.E. Anderson, 1972, *College schedule of recent experience* (Fargo, ND: North Dakota State University).

get there as soon as I could because he might not make it."

Knowing about that phone call changed the gentleman's characterization of the woman from her being a negligent mother to her being a grieving spouse. This may not have completely eliminated the gentle-

man's frustration, but it probably helped him be more understanding of the situation.

Most people respond to stressors without thinking about how their perceptions and beliefs affect them. As people develop and mature, the environment and experiences mold their beliefs. At a certain point, however, beliefs about self, others, and the world begin to solidify, and rather than think afresh about every new event, people respond based on previous experiences and interpretations of them. Increasingly, people see what they believe, rather than believe what they see.

Albert Ellis said that the space between stimulus (activating event) and response (consequences) determines how effectively a person deals with stress. Thought patterns, attitudes, and worldview can either help a person remain calm and joyful or create a life filled with anxiety and tension. This section quickly explores four thought patterns that can destroy serenity and one that can restore it.

Just a handful of beliefs can chain you to the dungeon of distress. Dr. Burns, psychologist and author of the best-selling book *The Feeling Good Handbook*, identifies several of what he calls common forms of "distorted thinking" (Burns, 1989). Here are some of his examples:

1. **All-or-nothing thinking:** Looking at things in absolute, black-and-white categories.
2. **Mental filtering:** Dwelling on the negatives and ignoring the positives.
3. **Emotional reasoning:** Reasoning from how you feel. "I feel lousy, therefore things are lousy."
4. **Labeling:** Identifying with your shortcomings. Instead of saying, "I made a mistake," you tell yourself, "I'm a jerk, a fool, a loser."

You may find this list uncomfortably familiar. It describes self-destructive thinking that typically results in inner turmoil and tension-filled relationships. The good news is that it's possible to change thought patterns. Psychologists call this **cognitive restructuring**, or **reframing**. Sometimes it takes a little creativity to reframe a stressful event, but it can be done, as the following story illustrates:

> After being away from her parents for almost three months with no communication, Julie, a college freshman, sent a letter home. In her letter she described that a fire burned down her dorm during the second week of school. She was hospitalized with minor burns, but nothing too serious. Because of the fire she was forced to relocate off campus where she met her new boyfriend. He had dropped out of college the previous year but had found work at a local convenience store. Unfortunately, she found out two days ago that she is pregnant. Julie signed the letter and included a postscript to "see other side." On the back side of the letter she said that nothing on the other side was true, but she was failing Biology 231. (Cialdini, 2000)

Now that's reframing! But is cognitive reconditioning just being thankful that, even though something didn't go as planned, the results weren't as bad as they could have been? That sounds like just another version of positive thinking, where you try to look on the bright side. Reframing really does mean something different for a disciple of Christ. Jesus said, "The truth will set you free" (John 8:32). Scripture is filled with biblical examples that help combat common distortions. A few are listed here:

1. **All-or-nothing thinking:** Scripture teaches that although people were created in the image of God, they possess a nature that opposes him. Even after someone makes a definite choice to submit to Christ, a paradoxical state of holy and unholy intentions and behavior exists. The apostle Paul describes this struggle in Romans 7:21–25. People are a mixed bag, wanting to do what's right but often falling short.

2. **Mental filtering:** It would have been hard not to laugh along with Abraham and Sarah at God's promise to give them a child (Genesis 17:17, 18:12). Sarah was well past childbearing years and Abraham was about to reach the century mark. Yet despite the impossibility of their circumstances, scripture records that Abraham believed God and eventually received the son he was promised.

3. **Emotional reasoning:** Imagine you are in a small boat in the middle of the night. Waves from a raging storm are swamping your tiny vessel. The boat is beginning to sink. You have no life vest, and if the ship goes down you most assuredly will drown. After bailing water with all your might, you realize your best efforts are fruitless; the boat is sinking. Can you relate to the disciples' emotional outcry—"Don't you care if we drown?"—to their sleeping leader who led them into the eye of the storm (Mark 4:35–40)? Jesus got up and rebuked the wind and his followers for their emotional, rather than spiritual, reasoning.

4. **Labeling:** John the Baptist is locked in a prison cell waiting—waiting until Herod will eventually have his head on a platter. John begins to question if Jesus really is the true Messiah. Plagued by his doubts, he finally asks one of his followers to go ask Jesus if he really is who he says he is. Jesus's response is amazing. First he tells John's messenger of the works he is doing. Then he says, "I tell you, among those born of women there is no one greater than John" (Luke 7:28a). If you wonder if Jesus labels his children as doubters and disbelievers when they honestly question the truth, he doesn't.

These examples are just a sampling of how thinking from a broader worldview can significantly alter the impact of events that one typically sees from a negative perspective.

### C = Consequences

Whether or not the response is logical, the body reacts almost immediately when the brain registers a potential threat. Walter Cannon, noted physiologist at Harvard Medical School, was the first to use the term *fight-or-flight response* for the physiological changes that occur when danger is perceived (Cannon, 1932). Researchers have learned much about how the body responds to stressors since Cannon's original observations. Now they know the nervous system activates the endocrine system to release a number of stress-related hormones. Some of the more notable are cortisol, epinephrine, and nonepinephrine. These hormones are responsible for the host of physiological responses to stress, some of which include the following:

- Pupils dilate to admit extra light for more sensitive vision.
- Mucous membranes of the nose and throat shrink, while muscles force open passages to allow easier airflow.
- Secretion of saliva and mucous decreases, intestinal muscles stop contracting, and digestion is halted.
- Bronchi dilate to allow more air into lungs.
- The liver releases sugar into the bloodstream to provide energy from muscles and the brain.
- The bladder relaxes. Emptying the bladder contents reduces excess weight, making it easier to flee.

- Endorphins are released to block distracting pain.
- Hearing becomes more acute.
- Heart rate and stroke volume increase blood flow.
- The spleen releases more red blood cells to meet an increasing demand for oxygen and to replace any blood loss from injuries.

As uncomfortable and strange as these symptoms may seem, they are essential for survival. Without them humans would be ill prepared for life-threatening emergencies. The problem is that people often mistake annoyances and frustrations for major emergencies.

## Pros and Cons of Stress

Is stress good or bad? The answer is complex. Stress is one of the biggest contributors to a broader phenomenon, **arousal**. *Arousal* simply means a state of physiological and emotional activation (Weinberg & Gould, 2011). Because stress is highly related to arousal, it's possible to make some cautious inferences to stress by examining arousal.

### Drive Theory

One of the first relevant discoveries related to arousal was its positive impact on performance: The greater the arousal, the greater the performance. Originally, scientists thought that the relationship was linear. This was known as the **drive theory** and is illustrated in figure 9.3 (Hill, 1957; Spence & Spence, 1996).

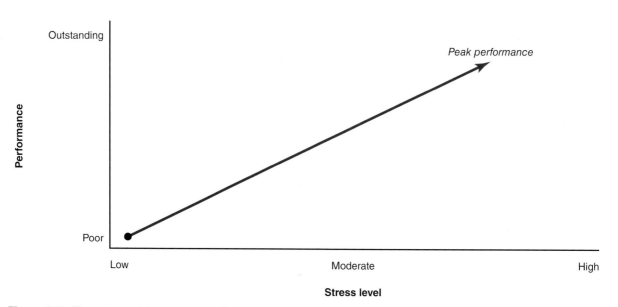

**Figure 9.3** The relationship between performance and the stress level according to the drive theory.

## Inverted-U Theory

Later studies clearly demonstrated that the relationship between arousal and performance was *not* always linear. Two researchers, Yerkes and Dodson (1908), reported that arousal does enhance performance but only up to a certain level. There is a point at which continual increases in arousal decrease, rather than increase, performance. They illustrated this in what is commonly referred to as the **inverted-U theory** of arousal. As you can see in figure 9.4, low to moderate levels of arousal enhance performance, but extremely high levels of arousal decrease performance.

## Individual Zones of Optimal Functioning

More recently, another model concerning arousal and performance has received considerable attention. It is called the **individualized zones of optimal functioning (IZOF)**. Yuri Hanin, a noted Russian psychologist, suggested that people have a zone of optimal arousal, rather than a specific point of optimal arousal as presented in the inverted-U model (Hanin et al., 1986). Hanin also argued that the optimal level of arousal doesn't always occur at the midpoint of the continuum but instead varies from individual to individual. That is, some individuals have a zone of optimal functioning at the lower end of the continuum, some in the midrange, and others at the upper end. Figure 9.5 illustrates this hypothesis, which has since been supported by other investigators (Gould & Tuffey, 1996).

These models don't tell the whole story, though, because they only deal with the effects of arousal over a very short period of time. What happens when you are chronically aroused? Consider some modern examples: You're frustrated at your inability to avoid procrastination, distressed over a relational conflict that seems impossible to resolve, or discouraged because you continually fall short of living a life pleasing to God. Imagine what it would be like to live with issues such as these for weeks, months, or even years. Persistent stress can become debilitating.

## When Stress Turns Ugly

Hans Selye, introduced at the beginning of the chapter, proposed a three-stage model, the **general adaptation syndrome (GAS)**, describing how people deal with chronic stress (see figure 9.6).

1. The first stage is the alarm reaction, the fight-or-flight response already described. Here homeostasis, or a state of equilibrium, is disrupted.

2. In the second resistance stage, the body seeks to self-correct, drawing on available resources to restore equilibrium.

3. Exhaustion, the final stage, occurs if equilibrium can't be regained.

Unrelieved or unmanaged stress eventually destroys a person. Dr. Fred Goodwin of the National Institute of Mental Health says that humans have a fairly robust capacity to withstand even massive

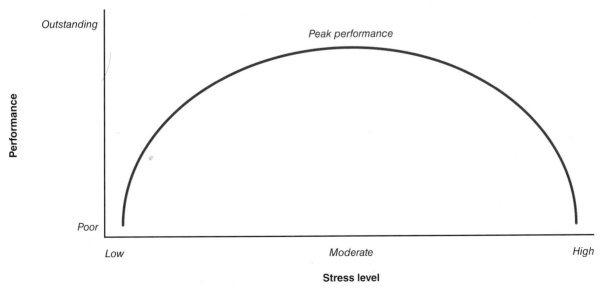

**Figure 9.4**    The inverted-U model of the relationship between performance and stress level.

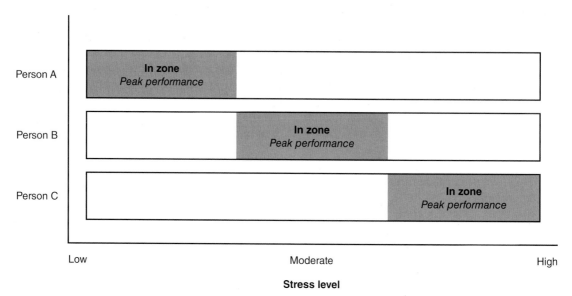

**Figure 9.5** The individualized zones of optimal functioning theory of the relationship between performance and stress level.

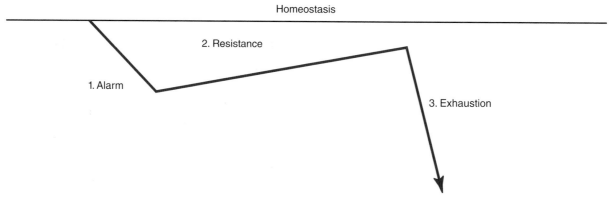

**Figure 9.6** Sustained stress eventually results in exhaustion.

doses of acute stress. The downfall is the inability to mobilize for recurrent stressful episodes (Greenberg, 2002). Legendary U.S. World War II general George Patton stated Goodwin's conclusions more succinctly: "Fatigue makes cowards of us all" (Miner & Rawson, 1997, p. 189). The most challenging life experiences are stressful situations not quickly resolved. Parenting a child with a severe birth defect, caring for a friend who has mental illness, or loving an aged spouse who has Alzheimer's disease are examples of the challenges that require deep inner strength. Those challenges slowly erode even the best intentions.

So here's the question again: Is stress good or bad? The simple answer is that stress can be helpful up to a point, but if it's too intense or prolonged, trouble can occur. Therefore, it's a good idea to have some strategies and techniques to manage stress even during the most troubling times.

## Managing Stress

Various studies in Canada have highlighted the enormous cost of managing stress.

- According to the Canadian Mental Health Association, about 20 percent of the average company's payroll goes toward dealing with stress-related problems, such as absenteeism, employee turnover, disability leaves, counseling, medicine, and accidents (Canadian Mental Health Association, 2006).

- Health Canada reported that "work–life conflict"—stress that arises when work and family clash—costs Canadian business $4.5 billion to $10 billion a year (Health Canada, 2006).

- Mental health problems—stress, depression, and addiction—are a $50-billion-a-year drain on Canada's economy, according to the corporate-sponsored

# Is There Such a Thing as "Righteous Worry"?

Jesus's disciples knew that worry was not his way. During one hillside chat, Christ told his followers,

Do not worry about your life, what you will eat or drink; or about your body, what you will wear. Is not life more important than food, and the body more important than clothes? Look at the birds of the air; they do not sow or reap or store away in barns, and yet your heavenly Father feeds them. Are you not much more valuable than they? Who of you by worrying can add a single hour to his life? (Matthew 6:25–27)

He repeats this admonition as he foresees a time in which his followers will be rejected by their communities, disowned by family, and arrested for being a follower of "the way":

Whenever you are arrested and brought to trial, do not worry beforehand about what to say. Just say whatever is given you at the time, for it is not you speaking, but the Holy Spirit. (Mark 13:11)

Not only did Jesus warn against worry, he exemplified the antithesis of worry during crisis. The boat he and his disciples were in was sinking, and he was sound asleep (Matthew 8:23–25). An angry mob was ready to stone a woman to death, and Jesus calmly wrote in the sand, dispersing the crowd (John 8:1–11). Before a Roman judge who claimed to have the power to crucify or release Jesus, Christ calmly refused to reply to accusations or questions (Mark 15:3–5).

Clearly, Jesus had enormous inner peace during times of testing. On the other hand, some events and circumstances seemed to weigh heavily on his heart. Perhaps the most dramatic example came right before his trial: While praying on the Mount of Olives, he "sweat as if it were great drops of blood" (Luke 22:44).

In addition to stories of Jesus, scripture records how the apostle Paul seemed frequently concerned and at other times anxious. In a lengthy record of his specific difficulties, Paul concludes by acknowledging his daily pressure:

I have worked much harder, been in prison more frequently, been flogged more severely, and been exposed to death again and again. Five times I received from the Jews the forty lashes minus one. Three times I was beaten with rods, once I was stoned, three times I was shipwrecked, I spent a night and a day in the open sea, I have been constantly on the move. I have been in danger from rivers, in danger from bandits, in danger from my own countrymen, in danger from Gentiles; in danger in the city, in danger in the country, in danger at sea; and in danger from false brothers. I have labored and toiled and have often gone without sleep; I have known hunger and thirst and have often gone without food; I have been cold and naked. Besides everything else, I face daily the pressure of my concern for all the churches. (2 Corinthians 11:23–28)

In Paul's letter to the Church at Philippi, he foresees that his anxiety will be alleviated by the safe return of Epaphroditus:

But I think it is necessary to send back to you Epaphroditus, my brother, fellow worker and fellow soldier, who is also your messenger, whom you sent to take care of my needs. For he longs for all of you and is distressed because you heard he was ill. Indeed he was ill, and almost died. But God had mercy on him, and not on him only but also on me, to spare me sorrow upon sorrow. Therefore I am all the more eager to send him, so that when you see him again you may be glad and I may have less anxiety. (Philippians 2:25–28)

What is your reaction? I can almost hear your reply: "It's okay to be concerned, but not worried." One of the problems with that response is that worrying means feeling or experiencing concern. What, then, is your distinction between being worried and concerned? Here are some other questions to consider as you grapple with this issue:

When does concern transfer into worry?

Is it ever appropriate to worry?

What does worry say about your faith in God and concern for his agenda?

## Reality Checks

Everyone can benefit from an occasional reality check. When you need one, ask yourself the following questions:

- How important will this current situation be a year from now?
- On a scale of 1 to 10, 10 being a worldwide catastrophe, where do I rate my problem?
- What difference will this make when I am standing before God in heaven?

Viewing your crisis from a larger perspective has a way of diminishing its effect.

Global Business and Economic Roundtable on Addiction and Mental Health (Riga, 2006).

Given the high cost of treating individuals living in the exhaustion phase of Selye's model, people's learning effective stress management techniques would not only increase serenity but save money. Here is an abbreviated list of some of the low-cost, more popular stress management methods:

- **Deep breathing.** Take a deep breath, inhaling through your nose. Hold the air you have inhaled for five to seven seconds before slowly exhaling. As you release your breath, focus not only on exhaling all your air but also on releasing muscle tension. Repeat three or four times. It is amazing how something this simple can have a dramatic effect on acute levels of stress. Musicians and athletes have used this technique for years to quiet their nerves before a concert or sporting event.

- **Refocus.** Continuing to brood over unpleasant, uncontrollable situations only increases your anxiety. Refocusing your mind on "whatever is true, whatever is noble, whatever is right, whatever is pure, whatever is lovely, whatever is admirable" (Philippians 4:8) is a pathway out of the dark valleys of the mind. Refocusing your thoughts sounds easier than it actually is, but a change of mind can liberate you from the chains of anxiety, fear, doubt, and discouragement. See The Power of Refocusing sidebar.

- **Exercise.** Exercise actually increases physical stress (at least temporarily). Yet, after the body responds to the initial increase in heart rate, blood

 ## The Power of Refocusing

Tom had been dating Emily for two years. During that time his love for and commitment to her had grown to a point that he was convinced she was "the one." Tom had tried hard to follow God's will as he related to Emily socially, physically, and spiritually. One day, though, Emily sheepishly told Tom she didn't have peace about their relationship. She quickly added that it wasn't anything Tom had done; it was simply an unsettled feeling she couldn't shake. After another week, she told Tom she couldn't see him anymore. Tom was floored. In his words, "It was like a divorce."

Tom was consumed with questions:

- What could I have done differently?
- What's wrong with me?
- How did I miss God's leading?
- What is the future of this relationship?

From the moment he got up in the morning until he went to bed at night, Tom couldn't think about anything other than his broken relationship with Emily. He continued to attend class, but he merely occupied a seat because his mind was on his pain. Two weeks passed, and assignments and papers were beginning to pile up. Because he was so hurt, all Tom's conversations were about Emily. About three weeks after the breakup, one of Tom's friends bluntly said, "You've got to get on with your life. You can't change your circumstances, but you can change your reaction." That was the moment the light began to dawn. Although it was hard, Tom began trying to replace thoughts of Emily with scripture, schoolwork, and other social relationships. Looking back on this event, Tom acknowledged, "The power of taking responsibility for your thoughts is the path of deliverance."

pressure, and energy expenditure, the floodgates of stress fly open. Exercise pulls the plug on stress. Researchers have discovered that even mild forms of exercise substantially reduce an individual's stress level. Ornstein and Sobel (1989) reported that walking one mile at a moderate pace significantly lowered participants' anxiety levels. The cathartic effect of exercise has a long and robust history both in the United States and internationally. A nursing faculty at a university in Thailand reported that regular exercise cut in half the levels of stress that 102 Thai women reported before engaging in a regular exercise routine (Sunsern, 2002).

- **Prayer.** Prayer is the most commonly used form of complementary and alternative medicine in the world (Hales, 2007). However, only in recent years has science launched rigorous investigations into the effect prayer has on health.

Praying directly to a higher power affects both the quality and quantity of life, claims Dr. Harold Koenig, director of Duke University's Center for the Study of Religion/Spirituality and Health. It boosts morale; lowers agitation, loneliness, and life dissatisfaction; and enhances ability to cope in men, women, the elderly, the young, the healthy, and the sick (Koenig, 2007). Furthermore, Koenig found in one study that almost half of the patients cited religion (and often prayer, as an expression of religion) as the most significant factor in helping them cope with the stress associated with illness (Koenig et al., 1988).

In a national survey, 35 percent of Americans prayed over health concerns. Of that 35 percent, 75 percent were praying for personal wellness and 22 percent were praying for alleviation of specific medical conditions. Among those who prayed because of a medical condition, 69 percent found prayer very helpful (McCaffrey, 2004).

- **Humor.** Dr. Richard Blonna, professor of community health at William Paterson University, says, "It is physiologically impossible to be stressed when you are laughing. Laughter creates a physiological state that is incompatible with stress" (Blonna, 2005, p. 166). Mounting evidence from the scientific community confirms Solomon was right when he said "a cheerful heart is good medicine" (Proverbs 17:22). For more than two decades Norman Cousins, editor of the *Saturday Review of Literature*, wrote about how humor not only helped him fight off life-threatening illness but helped hundreds of others as well. Professor Keith Karren and colleagues argue in their book *Mind/Body Health* that, similar to the "runner's high" caused by a release in endorphins while running, a "laughter high" likewise exists (Karren et al., 2002).

Three of the most important humor skills are to

- see the absurdity in difficult situations,
- take yourself lightly while taking your work seriously, and
- have a disciplined sense of joy (Metcalf & Felible, 1992).

## Becoming Stress Hardy: Serious Stress Management

Everyone wants to be an overcomer but would prefer not to encounter obstacles along the way. Instead of trying to limit and manage stressful situations, maybe it would be beneficial to spend some time discovering how to increase the capacity to withstand and even thrive in stressful situations. To borrow from agriculture, how can a person become more **stress hardy**? Used to describe plants, *hardy* means capable of surviving unfavorable conditions. Used to describe people, *stress hardy* means capable of keeping cool under pressure (Kobasa, 1979).

During the late 1970s and early 1980s, United States federal deregulation caused a great upheaval in the telecommunications industry, and thousands of people lost their jobs. Dr. Susan Kobasa from the University of Chicago was studying managerial and employee behavior at AT&T during this time. She reported that most employees acted like hunted animals, frantically trying any means they could think of—company politics, verbal harassment, threats of litigation—to avoid getting laid off. A few, however, remained calm and optimistic. They kept their job performance consistent and even encouraged and organized focus groups with their colleagues to brainstorm for positive solutions. Kobasa coined the term *stress hardy* to describe the latter group of employees.

Even more incredible and heroic examples of stress hardiness come from people who have been persecuted for their faith. In AD 168, Roman authorities arrested the well-known bishop Polycarp of Smyrna, who had studied under the apostle John:

"Swear by Caesar," demanded the hostile Roman proconsul. "Take the oath and I will release you. Curse Christ!" The bishop stood firm. "Eighty-six years have I served the Lord Jesus Christ, and He has never once wronged me," he said. "How can I blaspheme the King who has saved me?"

"I have wild beasts ready to tear you to pieces if you do not change your mind," said the proconsul. "Let them come, for my purpose is unchangeable," the old man replied. Unmoved by any threats, and unwilling to renounce his Savior, Polycarp was sentenced to be burned alive. As the Roman guards were about to nail him to the stake, he told them,

*(continued)*

memory, learning, sexuality, and aggression; thus it plays a role in several mental disorders (Hales, 2007). Although this branch of science is relatively new, it holds promise to thousands of people who have neurological and chemical imbalances.

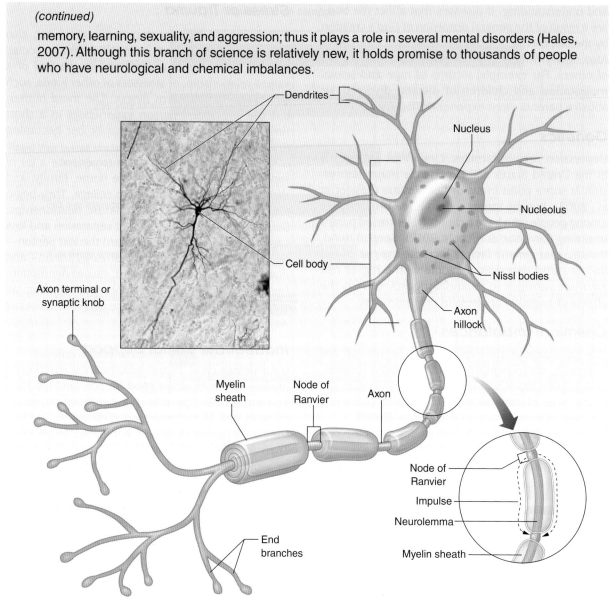

**Figure 9.8**   The anatomy of neurons.

support can intensify their condition, particularly in women. Counselors often train these people in social skills to help break the cycle.

### Negative and Irrational Thoughts

- "I'm a total failure unless I am liked by every significant person in my life."
- "It's horrible when things don't turn out the way I want them to."
- "If I'm not sure about an upcoming event, I must worry about it."
- "Unless I'm competent at everything, I'm worthless."

Irrational, pessimistic, and self-defeating thoughts like these can cause depression and keep it going once it starts. Depression makes people likely to think negatively about themselves ("I am unattractive and unlovable"), their world ("Nobody cares about me") and their future ("I'll never find a spouse or a job, and I'll never be happy"; Beck, 1970; Sacco & Beck, 1995). Depressed people will assume the worst possible outcome in any situation (catastrophizing), assume that because one event turned out badly others will too (overgeneralizing), and believe that they are to blame for anything bad that happens around them, even when they aren't responsible (personalizing; Beck, 1967). They think, irrationally, that they can do nothing to improve a bad situation, so they shouldn't even bother trying. This attitude is called learned helplessness (Seligman, 1974).

When you receive a low grade on a test, do you attribute it to your own stupidity, to insufficient study time, to an incompetent teacher, to unfair test questions, or to something else? What determines your response, other than the simple facts of the matter, is **attribution**, or the meaning you ascribe to the events and circumstances that occur in life (McFarland & Miller, 1994). A person prone to depression will tend to attribute a poor grade to his or her own ineptitude and believe that he or she will continue to fail for a long time and in many other areas. A person not prone to depression might take a more optimistic view of the event and consider it an isolated incident, the result of a bad day (Abramson et al., 1978; Jacobson et al., 1996). Events themselves are not depressing; what is important is how you handle them. Perfectionism, the habit of tying your self-worth to unachievable goals, can easily make you depressed.

Where do such thoughts come from? Some sources might include examples set by parents and other authority figures, early life rejection, and a lack of understanding of God's truth.

## Treatment

Only 30 percent of clinically depressed people seek professional help. The rest are either too embarrassed to go to a "shrink" or think that the symptoms will disappear on their own. Sometimes the symptoms do go away. If you have them for more than two weeks, however, it's best to seek professional help. Even if your condition is mild, without treatment you run the risk of sinking into a deeper state. Other people's efforts to cheer you up can improve a bad mood, but they can't cure clinical depression. The sooner you get help, the better your chances for a quick and complete recovery. If you are having suicidal thoughts, seek *immediate* professional help. Most colleges have staff members who are trained to deal with these issues.

The goals of any treatment program for depression are

- to improve your mood;
- to improve your ability to function normally at home, at school, and at work;
- to improve your overall quality of life; and
- to prevent a relapse.

Before you undergo a treatment program, have your symptoms evaluated by a professional to make sure they are genuinely the result of clinical depression, not just a bad mood, grief, or another condition. The most effective therapy combines medication and counseling, though either one alone can sometimes be enough. Psychiatrists and physicians can prescribe medication; psychiatrists, clinical psychologists, licensed professional counselors, and social workers can perform counseling. Christians may feel most comfortable with Christian counselors who incorporate scripture and prayer into the process.

### Medication

Antidepressants are designed to correct imbalances in the neurotransmitters implicated in depression (Geddes & Butler, 2002). They restore functioning to predepression levels; they do not alter your personality. The newer ones, such as Prozac, Paxil, Zoloft, Lexapro, and Celexa, work for most adults. Though they are equally effective, their side effects vary widely (Geddes & Butler, 2002), so discuss with a professional which one is best for you. Don't start or stop taking medication without supervision because the consequences may be very unpleasant.

Medications that decrease psychiatric symptoms have brought relief to millions of people. About half of all Americans will take a psychiatric drug at some point in their lives (Hales, 2007). This statistic includes people suffering from depression, anxiety, sleeping difficulties, eating disorders, alcohol or drug dependence, impaired memory, or other disorders that disrupt the intricate chemistry of the brain. Psychiatric drugs are now among the most widely prescribed drugs in the United States (Hales, 2007).

The vast majority of antidepressants are designed to correct chemical imbalances in the body (Geddes & Butler, 2002). A new generation of more precise and effective psychiatric drugs has increased the success rate of treating mental disorders significantly. How significantly? About 70 percent of people treated with antidepressants report feeling better within 6 to 10 weeks (Hales, 2007).

Although pharmacological advances have been made, it is important to keep in mind that every individual is unique and that pharmacology is not an exact science. Therefore, it may take several trials to determine the appropriate drug and dosage to treat a specific person's depression. Furthermore, humans are in a constant state of change. This means that any pharmaceutical drug needs to be monitored and in many cases adjusted to meet the ever-changing biology of the body.

### Counseling

The most effective form of counseling for depression, with a success of rate of 65 to 85 percent, is called **cognitive-behavioral therapy** (Clarke et al., 2003; Cuijpers, 1998; Marcotte, 1997). Based on the theory that irrational or pessimistic thoughts and actions cause and subsequently intensify depression, it aims to replace those bad habits with good ones. For instance, instead of saying to himself, "I failed this test, so I will fail all my tests," that client will be taught to say, "I failed this test, so I'll study harder and do better on the next one." If he lacks supportive relationships, he may be trained in social skills. If he is anxious, he may be taught relaxation techniques.

In **rational-emotive therapy**, the counselor directly and often confrontationally challenges the client's negative thoughts in an attempt to convince her that they should be rejected because they do not make sense (Ellis, 1962). A less confrontational means to the same end is to lead the client to discover that her thoughts are unjustified and to reformulate them in a healthier way.

Many Christian counselors prefer those techniques because the counselors view a person's beliefs, either negative or positive, as an integral part of spiritual life (Backus & Chapian, 1980; Crabb, 1977). Spiritual directors or counselors often refer to these beliefs as faith. Regardless of terminology, the ideas help provide answers to these big questions of life: Who created the universe? Why am I here? Where am I going? Faith also helps explain the smaller, more personal questions about identity, success, and failure. Inevitably, at the root of human actions and attitudes, a set of beliefs exists that people embrace to be true. Spiritual mentors see the need to root out illogical, untrue, and harmful beliefs about others and self as an essential part of personal growth.

## What to Do
## If You Are Depressed

Medication and counseling take a few weeks to take effect. While you wait, these steps may help you manage. They may also help prevent a relapse after your treatment ends.

1. **Keep God central.** Pray and ask God for help. You will always need him to strengthen you, but you will especially need him when you are depressed. Trust that no matter how badly you feel, he has not abandoned you. He has promised, "Never will I leave you; never will I forsake you" (Hebrews 13:5). Try to understand your depression as an opportunity for spiritual growth. If it is a result of guilt, remember God's unconditional love and forgiveness. If it is a result of perfectionism, learn to find your self-worth in who you are in God. Pray for the people who are

standing with you during this hard time; they will need strength, patience, wisdom, and understanding.

2. **Maintain a positive attitude.** First, as hard as it is, try to be optimistic. When negative thoughts occur, fight them. "Positive thinking is . . . grounded in the conviction that life is embraced by God's unconditional grace" (Ellens, 1999, p. 885). Never give up hope that your condition will improve. Trust that the Lord has better things in store for you.

3. **Focus on what you *can* still do and don't worry about what you can't.** Don't let yourself sink into self-pity or feelings of worthlessness. Accept the fact that your energy and productivity are lower than normal, and work within your limits. If you can, cut back on your course load at school or on your hours at work. Don't define the meaning of your life or your worth as a human being in terms of how much you can accomplish. Remember that God doesn't expect more of you than you can do, and he doesn't love you for your achievements.

4. **Don't make any major life changes.** Major life changes are difficult and stressful to cope with when you are well; when you are depressed, they can be overwhelming and aggravate your condition.

5. **Get support from friends and family.** Don't be ashamed that you are depressed, and don't be embarrassed to ask for help. Jesus commands that Christians bear one another's burdens. Doing so is a blessing and a privilege.

If someone you know is depressed, pray. Be available. Spend some quiet time with him or her. Respond with kindness and understanding, not with blame or condemnation. Don't offer too much advice, but encourage your friend to get professional help—*especially* if he or she is contemplating suicide (see Suicide sidebar).

# Happiness
# and Life Satisfaction

Historically, mental health professionals have primarily focused on what is wrong. The goal has been to help anxious, depressed, and paranoid people reach a state of normalcy. As Dr. Martin Seligman, past president of the American Psychological Association, said, "We wanted to help people move from a minus five to a zero" (Wallis, 2005, p. A2). Now, a new breed of mental health practitioners and scientists are examining the conditions that contribute to **happiness** and well-being. New questions are being asked: "How do we get people from a zero to a plus five?" (Wallis, 2005, p. A2). Here are some of the findings.

Supportive prayer with God and others is extremely important.

## Suicide

According to official records, about 30,000 Americans commit **suicide** every year (Centers for Disease Control and Prevention, 2004). Experts believe, however, that the actual number is higher because many suicides are misreported as accidents. Furthermore, this figure does not include unsuccessful suicide attempts.

Suicide is the eighth leading cause of death among Americans as a whole and the third leading cause of death among Americans aged 15 to 24. Between 7 and 8 percent of high school students attempt it, and about 10 percent of high school and college students seriously consider it (Mazza, 1997).

Depression, more than any other factor, increases a person's likelihood of attempting suicide (Angst et al., 1999). Between 50 and 70 percent of people who commit suicide clearly satisfy the criteria for clinical depression. More than 90 percent of adolescents who commit suicide have a known psychological disorder at the time of their deaths, and more than half of them have had it for more than two years (American Academy of Child and Adolescent Psychiatry, 1998). Half of the teenagers who take their own lives have depression (Hales, 2007).

### Warning Signs of Suicide

The circumstances surrounding each suicide are different, but there are several common warning signs. People who talk about suicide are more likely to attempt it (Marttunen et al., 1998). People who end up taking their own lives drop hints of this during conversation; so if you hear someone threatening suicide, take the threat seriously. The biggest warning sign, however, is a previous suicide attempt. About 40 percent of people who successfully commit suicide have tried it in the past (Zametkin et al., 2001). The statistic is between 50 and 80 percent in the case of adolescents (Shafii et al., 1985). If the circumstances that pushed a person to attempt suicide have not been dealt with, it is likely that the person will try to attempt suicide again (Blumenthal & Kupfer, 1988; Stevens, 2001). Other warning signs include preparing a will, giving away treasured items,

*(continued)*

*(continued)*

and showing a morbid interest in death or the afterlife. Suicides are often preceded by seriously stressful or traumatic experiences, such as the loss of something or someone important, rejection by others, the end of a romantic relationship, humiliation, arrest, or dismissal from work or school. Sometimes few or no warning signs are present, as is the case with most adolescent males who have been publicly humiliated (Marttunen et al., 1998). People are more likely to commit suicide if they lack the social support and personal resources to help them cope (Blumenthal & Kupfer, 1988; Stevens, 2001).

### What to Do If Someone You Know Is Suicidal

After a loved one takes his or her life, family and friends are often plagued with questions like these:

- Where did things go wrong?
- Why didn't I pick up on this sooner?
- What should I have done differently?

There are no easy answers to those questions. However, there are practical suggestions for when you are in the company of someone who may be suicidal:

1. **Take suicidal talk seriously.** Don't minimize pain or glibly assure the person that "everything will work out" because that communicates you don't understand or appreciate her pain. If you are unsure whether the person is serious about ending it all, ask directly.

2. **Someone who is suicidal may think that no one cares; you must show him you do.** Genuine listening and concern from others make people less likely to commit suicide; but indifferent, angry, or shaming responses can increase the possibility.

3. **Determine why the person is considering taking her life.** Often she will have many problems, but one that is especially significant. Encourage her to identify and clarify that key issue. Then suggest rational solutions to it. Help her to see that suicide is an irrational solution—and not the only possible one (review the discussion of cognitive therapy). Capitalize on any doubts, fears, or hesitations she may have about it.

4. **Strongly urge the individual to seek professional help.** Your loving concern is no substitute for professional help. Just because you talk the person out of suicide once doesn't mean the problem is over. Anything that has driven a person to consider suicide is a deep and serious issue that cannot be solved overnight.

5. **As you work through these steps, remember to incorporate your faith.** As a Christian, you maintain deep convictions about the sanctity of life, a source of abiding and sustaining hope, and a God who listens to prayer and is able to comfort and heal people.

Christians throughout the ages have consistently believed that deliberately taking one's own life is wrong; life is a gift from God, and only he has the right to end it. Though Job suffered and longed for death, he never considered suicide. (He did wish that he had never been born.) As M. Scott Peck says in the first line of his book *The Road Less Traveled*, "Life is difficult" (Peck, 1976, p. 1). Although this truth is inescapable, God promises that, in the midst of the pain, he is present (Psalm 23).

---

## World Happiness

Dr. Edward Diener, psychologist at the University of Illinois, was chief investigator for one of the largest global studies on happiness ever conducted (Diener et al., 1995). More than 100,000 surveys were conducted in 55 countries representing a combined population of 4.1 billion people. A large subset of this data, 18,032 responses, came from college students. Figure 9.9 identifies countries with the highest measures of subjective well-being, and figure 9.10 lists the lowest.

## Prescription for Happiness: Fact or Fiction?

Before identifying the traits that characterize people reporting the highest levels of happiness, it's time to bust some myths about what brings happiness.

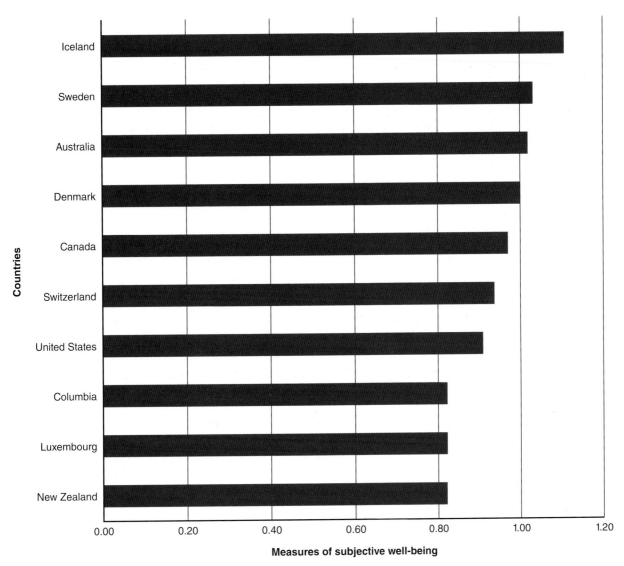

**Figure 9.9** Top 10 countries for measures of subjective well-being.

## Myth 1: Money

There is a positive relationship between income and happiness, but rich people on average are only slightly happier than those with a more average income. According to research by Diener and others, money contributes most substantially to personal happiness when people move from poverty to having adequate funds (Diener et al., 1995). At the point basic needs are met, additional income does little to increase a sense of satisfaction. Since the end of World War II, income has almost tripled in the United States (after controlling for inflation), and house size has more than doubled. Americans currently have the most buying power of anyone in the world. Yet, if you were to chart the number of Americans who report being "very happy" during the same time, the line would be as flat as a table top (Easterbrook, 2005).

## Myth 2: Education

Neither a good education nor a high IQ paves the road to happiness. Two researchers at the University of Amsterdam tested their hypothesis that schooling and IQ positively affect health and happiness. Individuals in their study who had a higher intelligence and increased education had a greater-than-average propensity for health, although it did not affect happiness (Hartog & Oosterbeek, 1997). Ernest Hemingway said, "Happiness in intelligent people is the rarest thing I know."

## Myth 3: Youth

If you were to find the fountain of youth, you might be forever young, but it wouldn't guarantee happiness. In fact, older people consistently rate their satisfaction with life higher than young adults do (Wallis,

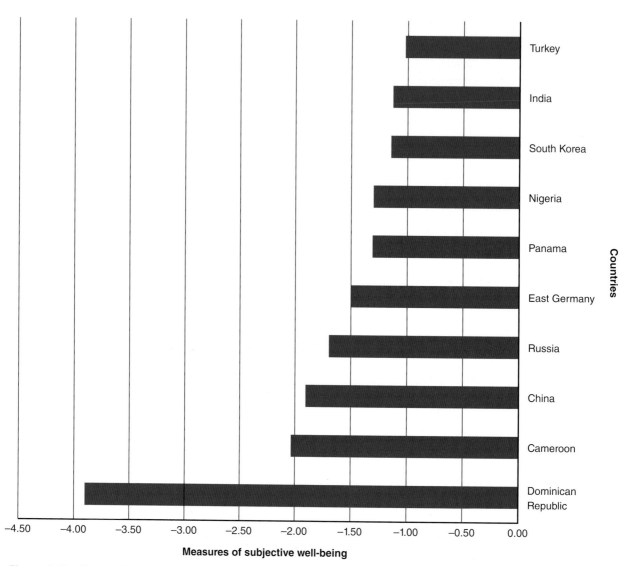

**Figure 9.10**   Bottom 10 countries for measures of subjective well-being.

2005). Older adults are less prone to dark moods. According to a survey by the Centers for Disease Control and Prevention, young adults aged 20 to 24 are sad on an average of 3.4 days per month, compared to 2.3 days for people aged 65 to 74 (Centers for Disease Control and Prevention, 2005).

### Myth 4: Weather

Studies show that warm, sunny days can enhance one's mood, but there is no evidence that weather has a more permanent effect on happiness (Sanders & Brizzolara, 1982). People who live in southern California may think they are happier than those living in the American Midwest—but when controlling for age, sex, income, education, and social connectedness, this is simply not true (Wallis, 2005).

## Reality: What Is the Source of Happiness?

What factors do predict life satisfaction? What characteristics do people with the highest levels of happiness have in common? An argument could be presented for a number of variables, but, by virtue of the quantity and quality of the evidence, love and faith should be on everyone's short list.

### Strong Social Relationships

The degree to which relationships affect happiness is evident in the answers to some probing questions. *Time* magazine asked three such questions in a poll of 1,000 American adults (Wallis, 2005). Figures 9.11 and 9.12 and table 9.3 show the responses.

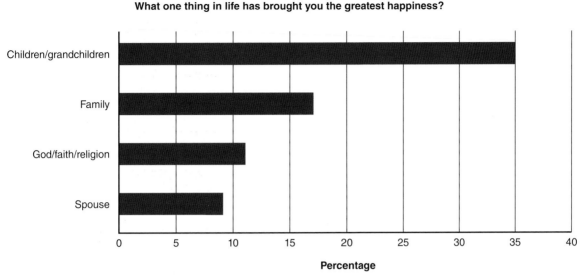

**What one thing in life has brought you the greatest happiness?**

**Figure 9.11**   The top four responses reflect two values: family and faith.

Table 9.3    **What Are Your Major Sources of Happiness?**

| Responses | Percentage of those surveyed selecting this response |
| --- | --- |
| Relationships with my children | 77% |
| Friends | 76% |
| Contributing to the lives of others | 75% |
| Relationship with spouse/partner | 73% |
| Degree of control over life and destiny | 66% |
| Things I do during leisure activity | 64% |
| Relationship with parents | 63% |
| Spiritual life | 62% |
| Holidays | 50% |

Adapted from Wallis 2005.

In a survey of 222 college students, psychologists found the "happiest" 10 percent, as determined by six rating scales, shared one distinctive characteristic: a rich and fulfilling social life. Almost all were involved in rewarding relationships with family and friends and were committed to spending time with them. Although many were involved in romantic relationships, that was not a prerequisite for fulfillment. The happiest students spent the least time alone, and their friends rated them highest on good relationships (Diener & Seligman, 2002).

### Spiritual Faith

Recently, interest in spirituality and well-being has exploded. Before 1982, approximately 100 scholarly articles on the relationship between religion and health were published in academic journals. Twenty years later, from 2000 to 2002, that figure reached 1,000 (Paul, 2005). Clearly defined patterns are emerging from the rapidly expanding research that strongly suggest religion is not just beneficial for the soul. Religious people are less depressed, less anxious, and less suicidal than the nonreligious. They are better able to cope with crises like illness, divorce, and bereavement.

**Do you often do anything in the following to improve your mood?**

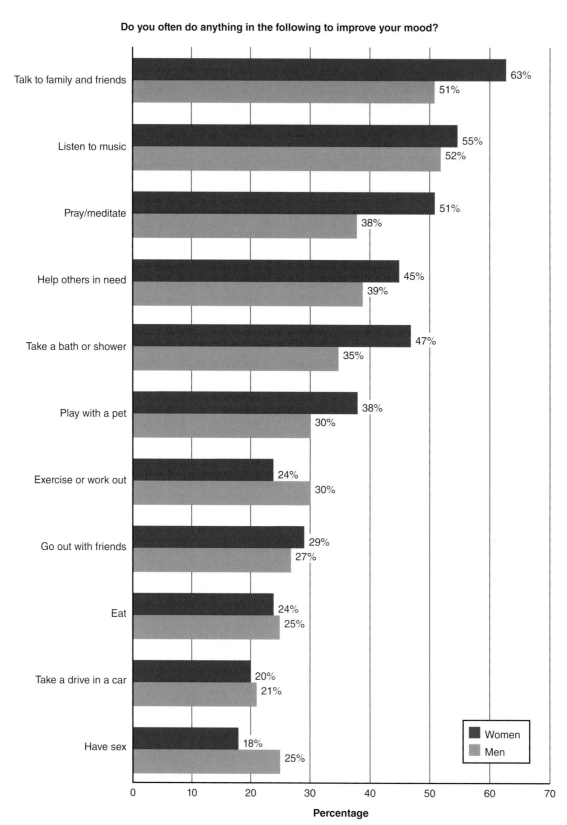

**Figure 9.12** When people want to feel better temporarily, they turn to friends, family, and faith.

Additionally, faith seems to boost a person's overall feelings of fulfillment. Michael McCullough, associate professor of psychology and religious studies at the University of Miami, said that in a comparison of individuals with equivalent levels of depression, "The more religious person will be a little less sad" (Paul, 2005, p. 46). Studies show that the more a person attends church services, reads scripture, and prays, the better he or she will score on measures of happiness—specifically, frequency of positive emotions and overall sense life satisfaction (Paul, 2005). When Jesus said, "I have come that they may have life, and have it to the fullest," he meant it (John 10:10).

## Next Steps

You have covered a broad range of emotional territory in this chapter. Beginning with the exposed cliff edges of anxiety, you moved into the dark caverns of depression. Finally, you scaled the mountain to catch a glimpse of happiness. As is true of most journeys, you've caught only a glimpse of what each of these emotions can teach. As you continue, you no doubt will return to each of these three places in a deeper and more intensive manner. Until then, perhaps you can consider some of the "travel suggestions" outlined in this chapter that will make your return visit less confusing and more insightful.

## Key Terms

activating event, or stressor

all-or-nothing thinking

arousal

attribution

clinical depression

cognitive–behavioral therapy

cognitive restructuring, or reframing

deep breathing

depression

drive theory

emotional reasoning

fight-or-flight response

general adaptation syndrome (GAS)

happiness

individualized zones of optimal functioning (IZOF)

inverted-U theory

labeling

mental filtering

posttraumatic stress disorder (PTSD)

psychoneuroimmunology (PNI)

rational–emotive therapy

stress

stress hardy

suicide

## Review Questions

1. Identify the primary branch of science investigating the mind–body connection.

2. Describe the ABCs of stress.

3. Diagram three current models of how stress affects performance.

4. Identify three primary types of stressors.

5. Describe three traits of a stress-hardy person.

6. List six potential factors that may fuel depression.

7. Identify four action steps for treating depression.

8. List three warning signs of suicide.

9. List the two strongest predictors of happiness.

## Application Activities

1. Stress test

   The assessment in the following form was designed by Dr. Archibald Hart, author of *Adrenaline and Stress* (1998). It can quickly help you identify your stress load.

## Stress Assessment

Assign each question a number according to the following scale. When you are finished, add up your numbers and look at the key that follows.

**0**: I seldom or never feel this way.

**1**: I sometimes (once a month or so) feel this way.

**2**: I often (more than once a month) feel this way.

**3**: I almost always feel this way.

1. Do you feel moody in the morning and have difficulty getting up? ____

2. Do you experience slight fevers, signs of the flu, a sore throat, or tender lymph nodes? ____

3. Are mornings the worst time of your day, with evenings being better? ____

4. Do you fall asleep easily but wake early without being able to fall asleep again? ____

5. Have you ever found yourself staring at a computer monitor, keyboard, or book, barely able to keep your head from dropping? ____

6. Do you feel mentally sluggish, confused, and unresponsive? ____

7. Has your short-term memory worsened, and do you have trouble concentrating? ____

8. Has your daily activity dropped to below half of what it was before? ____

9. Are your emotions relatively blunted, and do you often feel apathetic? ____

10. Does your body ache all over, as if it is weaker than it used to be? ____

11. When you exercise, do you feel debilitated for more than 12 hours afterward? ____

12. Does your work stress you out to the point that you want to escape from it? ____

13. Do you get headaches? ____

14. Do you find yourself desperately wanting to avoid being with other people? ____

15. Are you more impatient, irritable, nervous, angry, or anxious than you used to be? ____

*Total score*: ____

If your score is . . .

**Below 12:** Your fatigue is within normal limits. Cut back on unnecessary stress wherever you can and improve your sleeping habits (see chapter 10).

**12 to 22:** You have type 1 fatigue, which is temporary and not serious. You can reverse it by lowering your stress level, taking a vacation or sabbatical, or increasing your rest and sleep time. If these things don't help, consult a professional.

**23 to 32:** You have type 2 fatigue, which is longstanding and serious. A simple short break will not relieve it. You are suffering from chronic stress, depletion of adrenaline, and most likely a compromised immune system. You probably need to make a major lifestyle change and get professional help.

**Above 33:** You have type 3 fatigue, which is a "disease state." You are at risk for serious depression, hormonal imbalances, and physical illnesses such as chronic fatigue syndrome. You *must* get professional help.

From P. Walters and J. Byl, 2013, *Christian paths to health and wellness*, 2nd ed. (Champaign, IL: Human Kinetics). Adapted, by permission, from A.D. Hart, 1998, *Adrenaline and stress* (Waco, TX: Word).

## 2. Building an effective to-do list

Creating a to-do list fundamentally involves two activities: listing and prioritizing. The first step is to think about everything that you would like to or must accomplish in a week. Despite your best intentions, you won't be able to make this list exhaustive; simply do the best you can. As other items come to mind you can add them to your list later.

After listing each item, the next step is to prioritize them. One tried and true method for doing that involves letters and numbers.

First, go through your list and place an A beside the items you absolutely *must* get done during the week. Place a B next to items that *need* to get done but not necessarily during the week. Finally, Cs go beside items you would *like* to get done at some time.

Now go back to all your As and prioritize them (with numbers) according to how important and urgent each is. Item A1 is, by definition, the most important and urgent you have to accomplish. Begin working here before going on to the next item, A2. You may find yourself at the end of the day being able to mark only one or two items off your list. Don't be discouraged by this because you have accomplished the most important and time-sensitive task.

# References

Abramson, S.Y., Seligman, M.E.P., & Teasdale, J.D. (1978). Learned helplessness in humans: A critique. *Journal of Abnormal Psychology, 87,* 49–74.

American Academy of Child and Adolescent Psychiatry. (1998). Summary of the practice parameters for the adolescent and treatment of children and adolescents with depressive disorders. *Journal of the American Academy of Child and Adolescent Psychiatry, 37,* 1223–39.

American College Health Association. (2011). *National College Health Assessment.* www.acha-ncha.org/data_highlights.html.

American Institute of Stress. (2002). *America's #1 health problem.* www.stress.org.

American Psychiatric Association. (2000). *American Psychiatric Association: Diagnostic and statistical manual of mental disorders* (4th ed.). Washington, DC: American Psychiatric Association.

Anderson, G.E. (1972). *College schedule of recent experience.* Fargo: North Dakota State University.

Angst, J., Angst, F., & Stassen, H.H. (1999). Suicide risk in patients with major depressive disorder. *Journal of Clinical Psychiatry, 60,* 57–62.

Backus, W., & Chapian, M. (1980). *Telling yourself the truth.* Minneapolis: Bethany Fellowship.

Beck, A.T. (1967). *Depression: Clinical, experimental, and theoretical aspects.* New York: Harper & Row.

Beck, A.T. (1970). *Depression: Causes and treatment.* Philadelphia: University of Pennsylvania Press.

Benton, S.A., Robertson, J.M., Tsent, W.C., Newton, F.B., & Benton, S.L. (2003). Changes in counseling center client problems across 13 years. *Professional Psychology, Research and Practice, 34*(1), 66–74.

Birmaher, B., Ryan, N.C., Williamson, D.E., Brent, D.A., Kaufman, J., Dahl, R.E., Perel, J, & Nelson, B. (1996). Childhood and adolescent depression: A review of the past 10 years. *Journal of the American Academy of Child and Adolescent Psychiatry, 35*(11): 1427-1439.

Blonna, R. (2005). *Coping with stress in a changing world.* Boston: McGraw-Hill.

Blumenthal, S.J., & Kupfer, D.J. (1988). Overview of early detection and treatment strategies for suicidal behavior in young people. *Journal of Youth and Adolescence, 17,* 1–23.

Bradberry, T.G.J. (2003). *The emotional intelligence quickbook: Everything you need to know.* San Diego: Talentsmart.

Brage, D., & Meredith, W. (1994). A causal model of adolescent depression. *The Journal of Psychology, 128,* 455–68.

Brain Mind Bulletin. (1989). Princeton study: Student stress lowers immunity. *Brain Mind Bulletin, 14,* 1, 7.

Burns, D. (1989). *The feeling good handbook.* New York: Penguin.

Canadian Mental Health Association. (2006). *Stress at work.* www.cmha.ca/bins/index.asp.

Cannon, W. (1932). *The wisdom of the body.* New York: Norton.

Centers for Disease Control and Prevention. (2004). *Suicide: Fact sheet.* www.cdc.gov/ncipc/factsheets/suifacts.htm.

Centers for Disease Control and Prevention. (2005). *National center for injury prevention and control.* www.cdc.gov/ncipc/wisqars.

Cialdini, R. (2000). *Influence: Science and practice.* Boston: Allyn & Bacon.

Clarke, G.N., DeBar, L.L., Lewinsohn, P.M., Kazdin, A.E., & Weisz, J.R. (2003). Cognitive-behavioral group treatment for adolescent depression. In A.E. Kazdin & J.R. Weisz (Eds.), *Evidence-based psychotherapies for children and adolescents* (pp. 120–34). New York: Guilford Press.

Crabb, L. (1977). *Effective biblical counseling.* Grand Rapids: Zondervan.

Crespian, T., & Becker, J. (1999). Effects of time management practices on college grades. *Journal of Educational Psychology, 83,* 405–10.

Cuijpers, P. (1998). A psychoeducational approach to the treatment of depression: A meta-analysis of Lewinsohn's coping with depression course. *Behavior Therapy, 29,* 52–65.

DC Talk. (1999). *Jesus freaks.* Tulsa: Albury.

Diener, E., Diener, M., & Diener, C. (1995). Factors predicting the subjective well-being of nations. *American Psychological Association, 69*(5), 851–64

Diener, E., Ng, W., Harter, J., & Arora, R. (2010). Wealth and happiness across the world: Material prosperity predicts life evaluation, whereas psychosocial prosperity predicts positive feeling. *Journal of Personality and Social Psychology, 99,* 52–61.

Diener, E., & Seligman, M.E.P. (2002). Very happy people. *Psychological Science, 13*(1), 81–84.

Draper, E. (1992). *Draper's book of quotations for the Christian world.* Wheaton, IL: Tyndale House.

Easterbrook, G. (2005, January 17). The real truth about money. *Time, 165,* 32–34.

Ellens, J.H. (1999). Positive thinking. In D.G. Benner & P.C. Hill (Eds.), *Baker encyclopedia of psychology and counseling* (2nd ed., pp. 885–86). Grand Rapids: Baker.

Ellis, A. (1962). *Reason and emotion in psychotherapy.* Secaucus, NJ: Prentice-Hall.

Ellis, A., Gordon, J., Neenan, M., & Palmer, S. (1997). *Stress counseling.* New York: Springer.

Frankl, V. (1984). *Man's search for meaning.* New York: Touchstone.

Garrett, B. (2003). *Brain and behavior.* Belmont, CA: Wadsworth.

Geddes, J., & Butler, R. (2002). Depressive disorders. *Clinical Evidence, 7,* 867–82.

Goldstein, J. (2010). *Average sticker price for a private college: $36,993 a year.* www.npr.org/blogs/money/.

Goleman, D. (1995). *Emotional intelligence.* New York: Bantam.

Goleman, D., Boyatzis, R.E., & McKee, A. (2002). *Primal leadership: Realizing the power of emotional intelligence.* Boston: Harvard Business School Press.

Gould, D., & Tuffey, S. (1996). Zones of optimal functioning research: A review and critique. *Anxiety, Stress and Coping, 9,* 53–68.

Greenberg, J. (2002). *Comprehensive stress management* (7th ed.). Boston: McGraw-Hill.

Hales, D. (2007). *An invitation to health* (12th ed.). Belmont, CA: Wadsworth.

Hanin, Y.L., Spielberger, C.D., & Diaz-Guerrero, R., (1986). State-trait anxiety research on sports in the USSR. In C.D. Spielberger & R. Diaz-Guerrero (Eds.), *Cross-cultural anxiety* (vol. 3, pp. 45–64). New York: Hemisphere/Harper & Row.

Hart, A.D. (1998). *Adrenaline and stress.* Waco, TX: Word.

Hartog, J., & Oosterbeek, H. (1997). *Health, wealth, and happiness: Why pursue a higher education?* Amsterdam: Unpublished manuscript.

Health Canada. (2006). *Impact of work-life conflict.* www.hc-sc.gc.ca/index_e.html.

Hill, W.F. (1957). Comments on Taylor's drive theory and manifest anxiety. *Psychological Bulletin, 54*(6), 490–93.

Holmes, T., & Rahe, R. (1967). The social readjustment rating scale. *Journal of Psychosomatic Research, 11,* 213–18.

Jacobson, N.S., Dobson, K.S., Truax, P.A., Addis, M.E., Koerner, K., & Gollan, J.K. (1996). A component analysis of cognitive-behavioral treatment for depression. *Journal of Consulting and Clinical Psychology, 64,* 295–304.

Johnson, S. (1993). *Who moved my cheese?* New York: Penguin Putnam.

Kalat, J.W. (2001). *Biological psychology* (7th ed.). Belmont, CA: Wadsworth.

Karren, K.J., Hafen, B.Q., & Smith, N. (2002). *Mind/body health: The effects of attitudes, emotions, and relationships* (2nd ed.). San Francisco: Benjamin Cummings.

Kessler, R.C. (2000). Posttraumatic stress disorder: The burden to the individual and to society. *Journal of Clinical Psychiatry, 6,* 4–12.

Kessler, R.C., Berglund, P., Demler, O., Jin, R., Merikangas, K.R., & Walters, E.E. (2005). Lifetime prevalence and age-of-onset distributions of DSM-IV disorders in the National Comorbidity Survey replication. *Arch Gen Psychiatry, 62*(6), 593–602. doi: 10.1001/archpsyc.62.6.593

Kobasa, S. (1979). Stressful life events, personality, and health: An inquiry into hardiness. *Journal of Personality and Social Psychology, 37,* 1–11.

Koenig, H. (2007). Personal interview with Diane Hales. In D. Hales, *An invitation to health* (pp. 53). Belmont, CA: Thomson.

Koenig, H., Kvale, J., & Ferrel, C. (1988). Religion and well-being in later life. *The Gerontologist, 28*(1), 18–27.

Lazarus, R., & Folkman, S. (1984). *Stress, appraisal, and coping.* New York: Springer.

Levinson, D.F., & Nichols, W.E. (2012). *Major depression and genetics.* http://depressiongenetics.stanford.edu/mddandgenes.html.

Lewinsohn, P.B. (1974). A behavioral approach to depression. In R.J. Friedman & M.M. Katz (Eds.), *The psychology of depression: Contemporary theory and research* (pp. 157–78). Washington, DC: Winston-Wiley.

Marcotte, D. (1997). Treating depression in adolescence: A review of the effectiveness of cognitive-behavioral treatments. *Journal of Youth and Adolescence, 26,* 273–84.

Marttunen, M.J., Henriksson, M.M., Isometsa, E.T., Helkkinene, M.E., Aro, H.M., & Lonnquist, J.K. (1998). Completed suicides among adolescents with no diagnosable psychiatric disorders. *Adolescence, 26,* 669–81.

Matthews, G., Zeidner, M., & Roberts, R. (2002). *Emotional intelligence: Science and myth.* Cambridge, MA: MIT Press.

Mazza, J.J. (1997). School-based suicide prevention programs: Are they effective? *School Psychology Review, 26,* 382–97.

McCaffrey, A.M. (2004). Prayer for health concerns: Results of a national survey on prevalence and patterns of use. *Archives of Internal Medicine, 164*(8), 858–62.

McFarland, C., & Miller, D.T. (1994). The framing of relative performance feedback: Seeing the glass as half empty or half full. *Journal of Personality and Social Psychology, 66,* 1061–73.

Metcalf, C.W., & Felible, R. (1992). *Lighten up: Survival skills for people under pressure.* New York: Perseus.

Miner, M., & Rawson, H. (1997). *American heritage dictionary of American quotations.* New York: Penguin.

National College Health Association. (2006). *National College Health Assessment.* www.acha-ncha.org/data_highlights.html.

National Institute of Mental Health. (2012). Depression. http://www.nimh.nih.gov/health/publications/depression/complete-index.shtml.

New York Times Business. (2003). *Bestseller list.* www.nytimes.com/pages/business/index.html.

Ornstein, R., & Sobel, D. (1989). *Healthy pleasures.* Reading, MA: Addison-Wesley.

Paul, P. (2005, January 17). The power to uplift. *Time,* A46–48.

Peck, M.S. (1976). *The road less traveled.* New York: Simon & Schuster.

Pettingale, K.W., Morris, T., Greer, S., & Haybittle, J.L. (1985, March 30). Mental attitudes to cancer: An additional and prognostic factor. *The Lancet,* 750.

Publishers Weekly. (2004). *Bestsellers.* www.publishersweekly.com/bestsellerslist/1html?channel = bestsellers.

Rein, G., Atkinson, M., & McCraty, R. (1995). The physiological and psychological effects of compassion and anger. *Journal of Advancement in Medicine, 8,* 87–105.

Riga, A. (2006, February 27). Business awakes to the cost of stress. *The Gazette,* 16.

Sacco, W.P., & Beck, A.T. (1995). Cognitive theory and therapy. In E.E. Beckham & W.R. Leber (Eds.), *Handbook of depression* (2nd ed., pp. 95–104). New York: Wiley.

Sanders, J.L., & Brizzolara, M.S. (1982). Relationships between weather and mood. *Journal of General Psychology, 107*(1), 155.

Sapolsky, R. (2004). *Why zebras don't get ulcers* (3rd ed.). New York: Henry Holt & Co.

Sax, L. (1999). *The American freshman.* Los Angeles: Cooperative Institutional Education Research Institute.

Seligman, M.E.P. (1974). Depression and learned helplessness. In R.J. Friedman & M.M. Katz (Eds.), *The psychology of depression: Contemporary theory and research.* Washington, DC: Winston-Wiley.

Shafii, M., Carrigan, S., Whittinghill, J.R., & Derrick, A. (1985). Psychological autopsy of completed suicide in children and adolescents. *American Journal of Psychiatry, 142,* 1061–64.

Spence, J.T., & Spence, K.W. (1996). The motivational components of manifest anxiety: Drive and drive stimuli. In C.D. Spielberger (Ed.), *Anxiety and behavior.* New York: Academic Press.

St. James, E. (1994). *Simplify your life.* New York: Hyperion.

Stevens, L.M. (2001). Adolescent suicide. *Journal of the American Medical Association, 286,* 31–94.

Sunsern, R. (2002). Effects of exercise on stress in Thai postmenopausal women. *Health Care for Women International, 23*(8), 924–32.

Wallis, C. (2005, January 17). The new science of happiness. *Time, 165*(3), A4–9.

Walters, P., Gustafson, J., Williams, B., & Carlson, K. (2006). *What your students are really thinking.* Paper presented at the Christian Society of Kinesiology, Sport, and Leisure. Boston.

Weinberg, R., & Gould, D. (2011). *Foundations of sport and exercise psychology* (5th ed.). Champaign, IL: Human Kinetics.

Wilmore, J., & Costill, D. (2004). *Physiology of sport and exercise* (3rd ed.). Champaign, IL: Human Kinetics.

Yerkes, R.M., & Dodson, J.D. (1908). The relation of strength of stimulus to rapidity of habit-formation. *Journal of Comparative and Neurological Psychology, 18,* 459–82.

Zametkin, A.J., Alter, M.R., & Yemini, T. (2001). Suicide in teenagers. *Journal of American Medical Association, 286,* 3120–25.

## Suggested Readings

Burns, D. (1999). *The feeling good handbook.* New York: Penguin.

This best-selling book describes common mental distortions that can destroy your sense of well-being. Methods for combating these distortions are outlined.

Frankl, V. (2006). *Man's search for meaning.* New York: Touchstone.

Frankl, imprisoned in a Nazi concentration camp, describes the concept that man's deepest driving force is to search for meaning and purpose in life.

Goleman, D. (2006). *Emotional intelligence* (10th anniversary ed.). New York: Bantam Books.

This book describes the five crucial skills of emotional intelligence and shows how they determine one's success in relationships, work, and even physical well-being.

Johnson, S., & Blanchard, K. (1998). *Who moved my cheese?* New York: Penguin Putnam.

An analogy of mice and mankind, this book describes how people must "move with the cheese" in their ever-changing environment.

Mackenzie, A., & Nickerson, P. (2009). *The time trap: The classic book on time management* (4th ed.). New York: American Management Association.

This classic book has time-tested methods and principles for effectively managing your time.

Peck, M.S. (2003). *The road less traveled* (25th anniversary ed.). New York: Simon & Schuster.

The author discusses how discipline and love make up the essential emotional framework for spiritual and psychological health.

## Suggested Websites

**www.apa.org**

The American Psychological Association is the largest psychological association in the world. It is primarily dedicated to assisting mental health care professionals, yet it has a multitude of helpful resources for the general public.

**www.nimh.nih.gov**

A resource provided by the National Institute of Mental Health for information on all aspects of mental health, including stress and depression.

**www.save.org**

SAVE: Suicide Awareness Voices of Education is an organization dedicated to increasing public awareness of depression and suicide.

## Twitter

On Twitter, follow @NIMHgov, @afspnational, and @CAMHnews.

# 10

# Sleep Habits and Wellness

## Peter Walters

After reading this chapter, you should be able to do the following:

1. Understand the scope of sleep deprivation.
2. List the causes and effects of sleep deprivation.
3. Understand how sleep is regulated and basic sleep architecture.
4. Recognize how much sleep you need.
5. Learn how to improve your quality of sleep.
6. Explore a biblical view of rest and sleep.

**In January** 1959, Peter Tripp, the flamboyant and fame-seeking New York City disc jockey for WMGM Radio, was determined to shatter the world record for sleeplessness and gain national attention in the process. His goal: a 200-hour "wakeathon" to raise money for the March of Dimes (Bullman & Milne, 1998; Coren, 1996). An energetic entrepreneur as well as a smooth talker, Tripp had invented both the Top 40 playlist and the radio talk show. He was arguably the most popular DJ alive. Tripp hoped that this stunt would make him the topic of dinner table conversations from coast to coast.

Because no one knew the effects of eight days without sleep, Tripp was urged to seek professional supervision during the challenge. He casually agreed to allow Dr. Floyd Cornelison from Jefferson Medical College in Philadelphia and Dr. Louis West from the University of California to monitor his health during the eight sleepless days. Dr. West had previously worked with American pilots who were captured during the Korean War and tortured with sleep deprivation. Having seen their permanent cognitive damage and alterations in personality, he urged Tripp not to go through with the challenge. Tripp, however, considered national fame worth the risk and insisted on following through with his plan.

On January 20, Tripp began. Confidently broadcasting from a glass booth in the middle of Times Square, he announced his plan to break the world record for number of consecutive hours without sleep. Tripp began broadcasting with his usual charm, but as the hours went on, drowsiness settled in. The radio station staff had to constantly prod him to stay awake between broadcasts and medical tests.

After 48 hours, Tripp's mood changed dramatically. He became irritable and easily angered, even swearing at the barber he had known and loved for years. On day 3 Tripp's cognitive abilities began to decline. His usual fast-paced chatter became slow and cumbersome, he could not concentrate on simple tasks, and he could not remember things he should have been able to recall with ease. Even worse, he began to have mental delusions, such as imagining a rabbit running loose in the broadcasting booth.

After five days, the delusions became more bizarre and more frequent, and, by day seven, Tripp could no longer remember where he was. Somehow, Tripp managed to stay awake through the eighth day despite the deep concern of his medical staff. After the final broadcast, Tripp went to bed and slept for 24 hours straight. When he awoke, he appeared to be refreshed and calm, the keeper of the new world record of 201 sleepless hours. But the long-term consequences of eight nights without sleep had yet to emerge. Soon, his wife perceived a change in his demeanor, and his attitude became sour and argumentative; eventually, after their fights became all too frequent, they divorced. The ratings of Tripp's radio show began to drop as his listeners also noticed the difference in his personality. For the rest of his life, Tripp wandered from town to town and job to job, unable to establish himself. Peter Tripp gained the title he had hoped for, but he lost much more than he could have ever imagined at the outset of the challenge (Bullman & Milne, 1998; Coren, 1996).

Though an extreme example, Peter Tripp is proof that maintaining a regular sleep schedule is imperative to cognitive, emotional, physical, and relational health. Too often, students dismiss sleep as a dispensable activity. Who has time to sleep when there are people to see and studying to do? In reality, getting the proper amount of sleep only enhances life and the activities it demands of us.

# Importance of Rhythms, Cycles, and Sleep

Creation is filled with rhythms and cycles. The daily cycle of photosynthesis allows plants to flourish and produce food. Every water droplet is part of a hydrologic cycle. Conception is possible because of the menstrual cycle. Three weeks after conception, the new embryo's heart begins a cardiac cycle that is maintained until death. These cycles are often so automatic that their presence is hardly noticed, yet human existence is maintained by these subtle rhythms. Many of these cycles operate under autonomic control. Sleep, however, is one cycle under voluntary control. Although a person may feel tired, the ultimate decisions to go to bed and to arise are up to the individual.

For many college students, living away from home for the first time is exciting, especially as they have the freedom to choose when and how long to sleep. This freedom has consequences, however. The most critical factor in making it to an 8:00 a.m. class is not remembering to set the alarm or even having the willpower to get out of bed but, rather, the time the student went to bed the night before. The level of emotional stability, mental alertness, and physical stamina is largely affected by the choices you make. This chapter helps you learn about the ever-important cycle of sleep and how your choices pertaining to it affect many aspects of daily life and well-being.

# Chronic Sleep Deprivation

Not many people take sleep deprivation to the extreme that Peter Tripp did, but recent studies show that the *majority* of Americans today are consistently sleep deprived (Murphy & Delanty, 2007). This was not always the case. In fact, in many unindustrialized countries today, most people get around 10 hours of sleep. It is only in the past 150 years that people in the West have lived with such little sleep. After the invention of the light bulb, people suddenly had the ability to be awake and active after sunset, and this gradually changed the amount of time they spent sleeping. This new ability to freely control sleeping habits without being limited by nature marked the beginning of the emerging sleep deprivation epidemic. Often, people are unaware of sleep deprivation, and "the fact that nearly everyone is chronically sleep deprived has led to an acceptance of less than ideal daytime alertness as normal" (Dement & Vaughan, 1999, p. 231). One sleep expert even claims, "If we operated machinery the way we are now operating the human body, we would be accused of reckless endangerment" (Moore-Ede, 1993, p. 36).

**Sleep deprivation** is the lack of adequate sleep for the needs of the body and mind. Occasional sleep deprivation is an inevitable part of human existence. Emergency phone calls in the middle of the night, academic and work deadlines, and various other stressors can all periodically deprive people of the sleep they need. The problem occurs when these occasional events become regular.

**Chronic sleep deprivation** occurs when one *consistently* does not get sufficient sleep. Although the level of deprivation may be relatively minor (30 to 60 minutes per night), scientists now know that accumulated sleep deficits have major consequences on one's emotional, mental, and physical well-being and can accumulate to form something called a "sleep debt." Monetary credit serves as a good analogy to what occurs in the body with insufficient sleep. After borrowing money, most credit card companies have what they call a "grace period." This time of grace is typically a 25- to 30-day period during which borrowers can repay loans with no penalty. If loans are not repaid during the grace period, charges are assessed to the borrower. The same idea holds true for sleep. The body typically gives a grace period dependent on the level of sleep withdrawal, or the sleep one misses. In general, larger withdrawals accompany shorter grace periods. If a person does not repay his or her **sleep debt**, the accumulated sleep lost due to various conflicts (poor sleep habits, sickness, and sudden awakenings due to environmental factors or other causes), penalties are assessed. These penal-

ties, essentially the effects of sleep deprivation, are discussed in a later section.

# Are You Sleep Deprived?

The sleep deprivation quiz, devised by the Stanford University Center for the Diagnosis and Treatment of Sleep Disorders, is a simple way to assess sleep deprivation (Maas, 1999).

### Sleep Deprivation Quiz

Answer yes or no to the following five questions *based on your behavior over the last six months.*

1. Do you frequently fall asleep if given a sleep opportunity? (A *sleep opportunity* is defined as at least 10 minutes in a cool, dark, and quiet environment.)
2. Do you frequently need an alarm clock to wake up?
3. Do you frequently catch up on sleep during weekends?
4. Do you frequently take naps during the day?
5. When you wake up, do you feel tired most mornings?

From P. Walters and J. Byl, 2013, *Christian paths to health and wellness*, 2nd ed. (Champaign, IL: Human Kinetics). Adapted from POWER OF SLEEP by James B. Maas, copyright © 1999 by James Maas (New York: Harper Collins), 19.

### Notes on These Sleep Deprivation Questions

1. This question may be hard for you to answer, especially if your day is so busy that you rarely have sleep opportunities. But if the mere thought of 10 minutes in a cool, dark, and quiet room seems very appealing to you, chances are you may need them!
2. Forty-six percent of American adults answer yes to this question (National Sleep Foundation, 1995). Figure 10.1 identifies the frequency with which adults, 18 years of age and older, reported needing an alarm clock to wake up. An alarm clock is an artificial way to wake up and disturbs natural sleep rhythms. After a restful night of sleep, your sleep will become progressively lighter until you wake up automatically—a healthier and more pleasant way to get yourself out of bed.
3. According to the National Sleep Foundation (2001), more than half of adults sleep longer on weekends than on weekdays.
4. More than half of surveyed college students report napping during the day (National Sleep Foundation, 2001). Adults take fewer naps

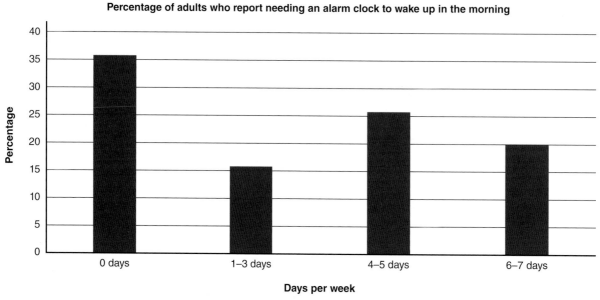

**Figure 10.1**    Approximately 46 percent of adults use an alarm clock to wake up 4–7 days a week.

than children do for the simple reason that sleeping on the job is generally frowned upon.

5. That is, do you wake up feeling refreshed, or do you need a tow truck to drag you out of bed? This has nothing to do with whether or not you consider yourself a "morning person." *Refreshed* doesn't mean eager to do jumping jacks or to solve complex academic problems but rather the feeling of being rested and rejuvenated by your night's sleep. More than half of young adults answer yes to this question—that is, they do not feel refreshed in the morning.

If you answered yes to two or more of the questions, you need more sleep. This puts you in a category with two-thirds of the U.S. population (National Sleep Foundation, 2001).

## Sleep Thieves

Your ancestors got 10 hours of sleep each night on average. Today the average is less than 7 hours (see figure 10.2). What really needs to be explained is the three-hour drop in the average hours of sleep per night, one hour of which was lost in just the last 30 years. This section highlights some of the most common sleep thieves.

## Academic Workload and Life

Being a student is a time-consuming role. In many ways, it is as demanding as a full-time job. Colleges and universities in the United States make few apologies for

burdening their undergraduates with workloads that give them little time for rest. It seems, however, that it is not just studies that keep students up late at night. Approximately 60 freshmen enrolled in a health and wellness course at one college were asked the following question: "What are three things you are doing besides going to bed and getting a sufficient night's rest?" Students then listed their three "sleep thieves" (Walters, 2009). After combining responses, the most popular sleep thief was socializing with friends. Homework came in second place, and technology took third, specifically the Internet (Facebook, e-mail, Skype) and cell phones (primarily text messaging). Of particular interest is the third sleep thief—Internet and cell phones. This category did not exist a short time ago; now students rank it as the one of the top three reasons they are losing sleep. Perhaps there is a correlation between the decline of sleep in the last 10 years and the amount of time spent using social technology. This correlation requires further study; regardless, it appears that schoolwork is not entirely responsible for the late nights of many students. Part of the decline in sleep must be attributed to the personal decisions made to socialize, either in person or through social networking. It is no surprise that students are some of the most sleep deprived. Studies at Cornell University (Maas, 1998) and five Christian colleges (Walters, 2005) found that the average student sleeps only 6.1 hours per night (see figure 10.3). This is significantly less than the general population (see figure 10.4). As a student, it is important to understand the necessity of sleep and make every effort to fit in a full night's rest as often as possible.

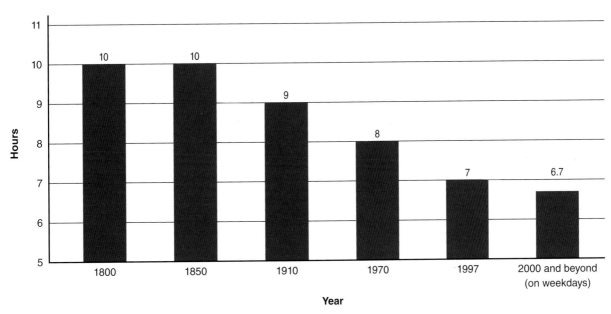

**Figure 10.2**   Average hours of sleep Americans get per night by year.

### ⟳ Sunday Spent in the Library

Do you ever feel like there is so much to be done that you simply cannot accomplish it all? If so, you are not alone. In a recent collegiate health survey, over half of all students polled (54%) reported feeling overwhelmed by all they had to do within the previous two weeks (American College Health Association, 2011).

The term *24/7* has not been in the vernacular that long, but students know what it means from experience. Ask the college student who eats lunch in less than 18 minutes while pecking away at a laptop and talking with a friend on a cell phone how it's going. Most likely, you will hear a response like "Wiped out!" or "Exhausted!"

It is interesting to observe some of the more common ways college students respond to this apparently universal problem. Drowning underneath an ocean of papers, class assignments, and projects, many students say they just need to "work harder." Maybe that reflexive response is what led a large group of students at one Christian college to petition college administrators to open the college library on Sundays. This petition gained momentum from irate community members who were upset over the fact that their public library was being overtaken on Sundays by students from the college, desperate to study.

What does this kind of behavior say about the way that Christian college students live their lives? Maybe it says that they are very serious about academic rigor and intellectual excellence. On the other hand, it may mean that they have jumped aboard the twenty-first-century treadmill, leaving little time for solitude, reflection, and spiritual renewal.

## Work

Data from the National Sleep Foundation (NSF) reveal a strong correlation between the number of hours a person works and the number of hours he or she sleeps (see figure 10.5). Forty-five percent of adults polled in 2001 said they were sleeping less in order to be more "productive" (National Sleep Foundation, 2001). In a more recent poll almost a third of all employees reported that their work schedule did not allow for them to get adequate rest. In some professions, such as transportation, the results were even more disturbing. Almost 47 percent of train conductors and 37 percent of aircraft pilots reported insufficient sleep due to their work schedule (National Sleep Foundation, 2012).

## Ignorance

Any recipe for a healthy lifestyle must include at least these three ingredients: exercise, diet, and rest.

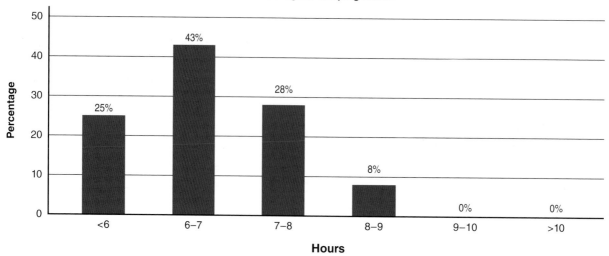

Figure 10.3   Only 8 percent of college students report sleeping 8 or more hours per night.

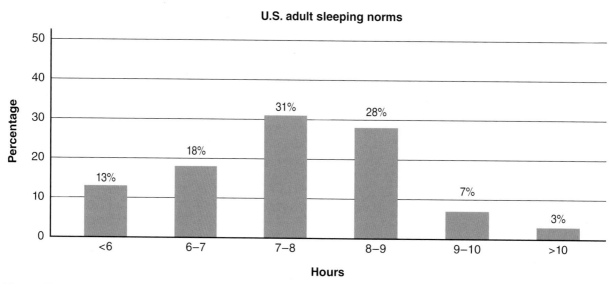

Figure 10.4   In contrast to college students, 38 percent of American adults receive an average of 8 or more hours of sleep per night.

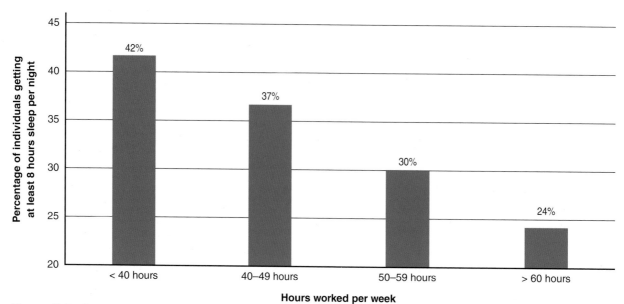

Figure 10.5   Percentage of workers who get 8 hours or more of sleep per night.

## Test Your Sleep IQ

In a 1999 survey by the National Sleep Foundation, 83 percent of American adults failed the following sleep quiz (National Sleep Foundation, 1999). Take it and see how you do. You may be surprised.

### Sleep IQ

True or false?

1. During sleep, your brain rests. _____

2. You cannot learn to function normally with one or two fewer hours of sleep a night than you need. _____

3. Boredom makes you feel tired, even if you have had enough sleep. _____

4. Resting in bed with your eyes closed cannot satisfy your body's need for sleep. _____

5. Snoring is not harmful as long as it doesn't disturb others or wake you up. _____

6. Everyone dreams every night. _____

7. The older you get, the fewer hours of sleep you need. _____

8. Most people don't know when they are sleepy. _____

9. Raising the volume of your radio will help you stay awake while driving. _____

10. Sleep disorders are due mainly to worry or psychological problems. _____

11. The human body never adjusts to a night shift. _____

12. Most sleep disorders go away even without treatment. _____

From P. Walters and J. Byl, 2013, *Christian paths to health and wellness*, 2nd ed. (Champaign, IL: Human Kinetics). Adapted from National Sleep Foundation, 1999, *The sleep quiz* (Washington, DC: National Sleep Foundation).

### Answers to Sleep Quiz

*1. False.* Though your body rests, your brain does not. While you sleep, your brain prepares you for mental alertness and peak functioning the next day, especially during the REM (rapid eye movement) phase.

*2. True.* The need for sleep is biologically encoded. Although children need more sleep than adults, how much sleep any individual needs is genetically determined. Adults need an average of 8 hours of sleep to function at their best, but many need more than that. You can teach yourself to sleep less but not to need less sleep.

*3. False.* People usually do not feel tired when they are active, but when they take a break from activity or feel bored they may notice that they are sleepy. The main cause of sleepiness is sleep deprivation. Boredom does not cause sleepiness but merely reveals it.

*4. True.* Sleep is as necessary to your health as food and water, and rest is no substitute for it. When you don't get the sleep you need, your body builds up a sleep debt that can only be repaid with sleep.

*5. False.* Snoring may indicate the presence of a life-threatening sleep disorder called **sleep apnea.** People with sleep apnea snore loudly and awaken repeatedly during the night gasping for breath. These repeated disturbances are brief and are not full awakenings; as a result, 90 percent of people with sleep apnea remain unaware that they have a serious disorder. Instead, the body wakes up only enough to bring the sleeper out of deep sleep and into the lighter stages. This prevents the sleeper from getting adequate REM sleep and leads to severe daytime sleepiness,

*(continued)*

*(continued)*

which increases the risk of accidents and heart problems. See the Common Sleep Disorders section later in the chapter for further discussion of sleep apnea.

6. *True.* Most people do not remember their dreams, but everyone dreams at night. Dreams are most vivid during REM sleep.

7. *False.* Sleep needs remain constant throughout adulthood. Older people often awaken more frequently and sleep less during the night, but they tend to make up for it with naps during the day. Sleep difficulties are *not* a normal or inevitable part of aging, although they are too common. If poor sleeping habits, pain, or other health conditions make sleeping difficult, a physician can help.

8. *True.* Researchers have seen thousands of people answer no to the question, "Are you sleepy?" and then fall asleep as soon as they are given the opportunity!

9. *False.* If you're having trouble staying awake while driving, the only short-term solution is to pull over to a safe place and take a short nap or have a caffeinated drink. Doing both—for example, drinking coffee and then napping before the caffeine kicks in—may be even better. Studies show that loud music, gum chewing, and open windows all fail to keep sleepy drivers alert. The only long-term solution is to start out well-rested after a good night's sleep. Driving while sleepy has been shown to be even more dangerous than driving while intoxicated, so try to avoid it as much as possible (Kuo, 2001).

10. *False.* Most people who report **insomnia** (difficulty falling asleep or staying asleep) give stress as the reason. But stress only accounts for a fraction of sleep disorders, which have a variety of causes. Sleep apnea, for instance, is caused by the obstruction of the airway during sleep. Narcolepsy, which causes severe daytime sleepiness and sudden sleep attacks, appears to be genetic. The causes of restless legs syndrome, a disorder that causes uncomfortable sensations in the legs that are only relieved temporarily by motion, are unknown.

11. *True.* Human beings, like all other living things, have **circadian rhythms** that affect when they feel alert and when they feel sleepy (see the Sleep Regulation section later in the chapter). These rhythms are set by the cycle of daylight. During travel across time zones, your body quickly adjusts because the light cycle changes; but if you work a night shift, your body never fully adjusts because this cycle does not change. No matter what shift you work, even if you have been working it for years, you will feel sleepy between midnight and 6:00 a.m. and will have trouble sleeping during the day. If you have to work nights, however, avoid caffeine during the last half of your shift, stay away from alcohol and stimulating activities before you go to bed, and block out as much light and noise as you can when going to sleep.

12. *False.* Sleep disorders must be treated. Unfortunately, many people who have them do not realize they are problems that *can* be treated. The cure may be surgical, pharmacological, behavioral (for example, going to sleep and waking up at the same time every day, scheduling naps, or losing weight), or a combination of these. Untreated sleep disorders can ruin your quality of life, your performance at work, and your relationships with others.

---

Much has been written about the first two. More than 3,000 books, not to mention magazine articles, are in print on diet alone. Yet very little has been written about rest, recovery, or sleep. For instance, in 10 North American health and wellness textbooks, less than 2 percent of the content was devoted to the topic (Walters, 2000). As a result, North Americans know very little about sleep: why they need it, when to get it, how to do it, and how much is required. In fact, many of these people are sleep deprived and don't even know it! This ignorance is anything but bliss; instead, it keeps many people miserable.

## Effects of Sleep Deprivation

Peter Tripp's experiences are a fairly accurate case study of the consequences of sleep deprivation. Sleep deprivation generally occurs in stages, revealed by the symptoms characteristic of each one. The six symptoms of sleeplessness are the following:

1. General fatigue
2. Emotional irritability
3. Cognitive impairment
4. Physical impairment

5. Psychosis

6. Death

## General Fatigue

The first symptom of sleep deprivation is a general feeling of drowsiness and a lack of energy. Peter Tripp exhibited this symptom, not surprisingly, within a day of the start of the wakeathon. Though he broadcasted his show as energetically as ever, during breaks his assistants had to constantly force him to stay awake.

According to one study, in less than a century there has been almost a 60 percent increase in the number of people who report feeling tired in the morning and sluggish throughout the day (Pasztor, 1996). Temporary fatigue does not permanently affect health, but the real danger is that it dramatically increases the chances of getting in a car accident.

- The U.S. National Highway Safety Administration estimates that approximately 100,000 accidents, 71,000 injuries, 15,000 deaths, and $12.5 billion in monetary losses per year are directly attributable to drowsy drivers (National Sleep Foundation, 2007).

- According to the National Transportation Safety Board, fatigue is the number one factor detrimentally affecting the ability of pilots (Pasztor, 1996).

- Sleep-related crashes are most common in young people, who tend to stay up late, sleep too little, and drive at night. A study by the state of North Carolina found that 55 percent of such crashes involved people aged 25 or younger (National Sleep Foundation, 2007).

The good news is that fatigue is easily dealt with. One study indicated that alertness increased by approximately 25 percent with just one additional hour of sleep (Leung & Becker, 1992).

## Emotional Irritability

People with sleep deprivation are more prone to depression, irritability, anger, frustration, and anxiety (Stickgold et al., 2004). Peter Tripp certainly showed this and even lost his temper with his favorite barber so badly that he brought the barber to tears. Research has also shown that good emotional memories are reinforced and bad ones dampened during certain phases of sleep, causing a general boost in mood. A 2005 National Sleep Foundation poll investigated the relationship between sleep and the emotional health of teenagers (National Sleep Foundation, 2005). The results showed that

- 73 percent of students who reported being the most unhappy, tense, and nervous said they consistently did not get enough sleep;

- 55 percent of the students with the best mood reported getting adequate sleep most nights, while only 20 percent of those with the worst mood reported getting adequate sleep;

- 59 percent of students with the worst mood reported often feeling tired, compared to only 19 percent of those with the best mood; and

- 51 percent of students with the worst mood reported having trouble falling asleep, compared to only 18 percent of those with the best mood.

Though many people do not realize it, moods and emotions have a crucial physical component. Sometimes the best remedy for a short fuse and a bad attitude is simply to get more sleep. Any parent knows how greatly sleep affects a young child's temper, and no one grows out of the need for sleep.

## Cognitive Impairment

By the third day of Peter Tripp's wakeathon, his mental and cognitive abilities began to decline. Recall that instead of his famous fast-paced chatter, he began to speak in slow, cumbersome sentences and often seemed at a loss for words. He struggled to remember basic information and could no longer concentrate.

While this case study illustrates the consequences of extreme sleep deprivation, sleeplessness can significantly damage cognitive abilities in daily life. According to a Harvard experiment, people score significantly better on memory tests when they sleep soundly for at least 6 hours the night after they learn something. If people are deprived of sleep on the night after the information was learned, however, their memory of it will never improve, even if they sleep normally on subsequent nights (Moore-Ede, 1993).

Students do not have to choose between bed and books. Better grades come with more, not less, sleep. Researchers who compared academic records to sleep questionnaires for both high school and medical students found that those with the best grades consistently reported sleeping longer (Moore-Ede, 1993). One study even showed that people who did not sleep on the previous night scored substantially worse on cognitive performance tests than the subjects who were legally intoxicated but slept the night before (Kuo, 2001). No one would take an important exam while intoxicated, but these findings suggest that poor sleep can be even more detrimental! Quantitatively, one study has measured the difference in cognitive function following a night of sufficient sleep and then a night of insufficient sleep. The study found that after insufficient sleep, people score an average of 10 points worse on a test of cognitive function than they had previously (Miyata et al., 2010). It seems that sleep-deprived college students may not even realize the negative effect sleep loss has on mental ability. In a study of 44 college students, where half had 8 hours of sleep and half pulled an "all-nighter," those without sleep performed statistically worse than those with a full night of sleep. The most surprising finding, however, was that when asked to estimate their cognitive performance, the students with no sleep estimated a higher performance than the students with a full night of sleep (Pilcher & Walters, 1997). The moral of this story is that "the way to get more As is to get more Zs" (Moore-Ede, 1993).

## Physical Impairment

During his eight-day sleep deprivation, Peter Tripp's only sign of physical impairment was a core temperature drop. However, during these eight days, Tripp engaged in minimal physical activity, so other impairments may have been present but were not observed. Other research shows that sleep deprivation slows reaction time (see figure 10.6; Kribbs & Dinges, 1994). Sleep deprivation also diminishes muscular strength (Reilly & Piercy, 1994), and one study found that it could decrease cardiorespiratory endurance by as much as 11 percent (Martin, 1981). It has even been suggested that heart failure may be connected to a lack of sleep in some cases (Riegel & Weaver, 2009).

## Psychosis

After a few days with no sleep, Peter Tripp began to have mental delusions. He saw cobwebs in his shoes, ants running across his desk, and a rabbit in the broadcasting booth. He began to hear voices, and soon he could no longer remember where he was. He became paranoid and began to imagine that there was a conspiracy against him. During a checkup on the morning of the eighth and final day, he "realized" that the doctors were trying to bury him alive and ran screaming from the examination room, completely naked. His doctor had to tackle him to prevent him from running out of the building. Tripp's delusions and paranoia serve as illustrations of some likely consequences of extreme sleep deprivation (Bullman & Milne, 1998; Coren, 1996).

Political, military, and religious groups have long used sleep deprivation as a means of brainwashing and torture. Sleep deprivation causes people to become emotionally unstable and lose their grip on reality. Although the thought of seeing hallucinations of space aliens or singing frogs may seem funny, the consequences can be quite serious. For obvious reasons, few experiments have been performed in which human subjects are extensively sleep deprived, so many questions about these later stages of sleep deprivation in humans remain unanswered. Case studies such as Peter Tripp's therefore provide valuable information.

## Death

Any animal will eventually die if not permitted to sleep. Rats will die after 2 to 3 weeks of total sleep

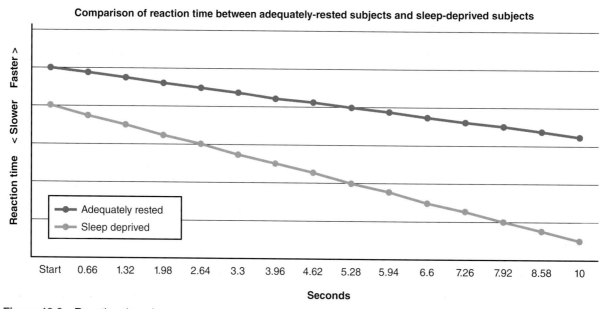

**Figure 10.6**    Reaction time decreases with sleeplessness.

deprivation or after 5 weeks of partial sleep deprivation (Rechtschaffen & Bergmann, 1995). For obvious reasons, this type of experimentation is not possible with humans. It is also very rare that a person would become sleep deprived to the point of death because severely sleep-deprived humans will begin to have 30-second intervals of "microsleep," brief periods in which the brain does not perceive environmental stimuli and brain waves briefly adopt sleep patterns (Science News, 2011).

The consequences of extreme sleep deprivation are tragically observable in humans who have **fatal familial insomnia**, a rare hereditary disease that completely eliminates the ability to sleep. The disease is incurable and leads to a coma and eventually death (American Academy of Sleep Medicine, 2001).

Mercifully, Peter Tripp never became deprived of sleep enough to endanger his life, but it is clear that his record-breaking time awake did have permanent consequences. His happy-go-lucky demeanor was replaced by a negative, argumentative one, and he lost his wife, his listeners, and eventually his job. His life was permanently changed.

Most people will never have the more severe and dangerous symptoms of sleeplessness, but many will go through their lives feeling tired and cranky. Without the energy to remember birthdays or write letters or return phone calls, or the spirit to make jokes or take risks or have adventures, they will find it hard to build meaningful relationships. Instead of being a "fountain of joy," these people become a drain. Worst of all, they may be so exhausted that they do not even care. Those who say, "I'll sleep when I'm dead" may miss out on a lot while they are alive.

## Sleep Regulation

Most people notice that they naturally have different levels of sleepiness and alertness throughout the day, but what causes these patterns? Sleep is regulated by two interacting body systems: sleep–wake homeostasis and the circadian biological clock.

When you have been awake for a long time, **sleep–wake homeostasis** tells you that a need for sleep is accumulating and that it is time to sleep. It also helps you maintain enough sleep throughout the night to make up for the hours of being awake. In this way, sleep–wake homeostasis creates a drive that balances sleep and wakefulness. Yet if this restorative process existed alone, without the circadian rhythm, it would mean that you would be most alert as your day was starting out, and the longer you were awake, the more you would feel like sleeping.

The circadian biological clock comes to the rescue by regulating the periods of sleepiness and wakefulness throughout the day. A **circadian biological clock**, also called a circadian rhythm, is an internal cycle lasting approximately 24 hours. The term *circadian* comes from the Latin *circa*, meaning *around*, and *diem*, meaning *day*. The circadian rhythm dips and rises at different times of the day, so an adult's strongest sleep drive generally occurs from 2:00 to 4:00 in the morning and from 1:00 to 3:00 in the afternoon, although there is some variation in this. The sleepiness experienced during these circadian dips will be less intense if you have had sufficient sleep and more intense when you're sleep deprived. The circadian rhythm also causes you to feel more alert at certain points of the day, even if you have been awake for several hours (Dement & Vaughan, 1999).

The internal clock hungers for consistency. This is seen most clearly when significant disruptions are made to this clock, as when one travels to a different time zone and experiences what is commonly called "jet lag." Jet lag is generally described as excessive sleepiness, loss of concentration, poor motor control, increased irritability, slowed reflexes, and nausea (Smolensky & Lamberg, 2000). But it is not necessary to travel to have these symptoms; stay awake several hours past your normal bedtime for a few nights in a row and you may have the same experiences.

The circadian rhythm is not constant throughout life but changes as people age. Significant changes to this circadian rhythm occur during adolescence, when most teenagers begin to have a **sleep phase delay**. This shift in the circadian rhythm of most teens causes them to naturally feel alert later at night, making it difficult for them to fall asleep before 11:00 p.m. Since most teenagers wake up early for school and other commitments, this sleep phase delay can make it difficult for teens to get the sleep they need (9 1/4 hours on average, 8 1/2 hours minimum). This sleep deprivation can influence the circadian rhythm; for a teen, the strongest circadian "dips" tend to occur from 3:00 to 7:00 a.m. and from 2:00 to 5:00 p.m., but the morning dip can be even longer if he or she has not had enough sleep and can even last until 9:00 or 10:00 a.m. This could be very detrimental to students and damage their ability to focus in class (National Sleep Foundation, 2010b).

The circadian biological clock is controlled by a part of the brain called the suprachiasmatic nucleus (SCN), a group of cells in the hypothalamus (an inner-brain region) that responds to light and dark signals. From the optic nerve of the eye, light travels to the SCN, signaling the internal clock that it is time to be awake. The SCN sends signals to other parts of the brain that control body temperature, the release of hormones, and regulation of other body systems that play a role in making one feel sleepy or awake (National Sleep Foundation, 2010b).

Melatonin is one hormone regulated by the suprachiasmatic nucleus. Released at night, when light levels decrease, melatonin promotes sleep. Research has shown that melatonin levels in the blood naturally rise later at night for teenagers than for most children and adults. Many teens may have difficulty going to bed early enough to get adequate sleep, a problem when they must get up early for classes. It may help to keep the lights dim at night as bedtime approaches, to reduce stimulation of the SCN and make it easier to fall asleep. It may also be helpful to get into bright light as soon as possible in the morning in order to feel fully alert (National Sleep Foundation, 2010b).

Circadian disruptions such as jet lag disturb natural sleep patterns, since the shift in time and light cues on the brain force the body to alter its normal pattern. But the negative symptoms of jet lag can also occur in everyday life when the circadian rhythm is disrupted by the long and irregular hours people keep. Because of this, it is important to maintain a regular sleep schedule and allow plenty of time for quality sleep, allowing these two vital biological components—the sleep–wake restorative process and the circadian rhythm—to help you perform at your best (National Sleep Foundation, 2010b).

# Architecture of Sleep

Although many mysteries pertain to sleep, advancing technology has allowed an examination of a host of physiological processes that occur while sleeping. A **polysomnography (PSG)**, also known as a **sleep study**, is a multilayered examination of what occurs during sleep. A typical PSG includes five physiological measures:

1. Electrooculography (EOG) for observing eye movements
2. **Electroencephalography (EEG)** for measuring brain activity
3. Electromyography (EMG) for evaluating and recording skeletal muscle activity
4. Electrocardiogram (ECG) as a measure of cardiac function
5. Various other devices for measuring respiration rate and airflow pressures

Research has enabled the classification of sleep into various categories. The two most general phases are **nonrapid eye movement** (NREM) and **rapid eye movement** (REM). NREM is a deeper sleep and the phase with the most physical restoration. NREM accounts for approximately 75 percent of sleep and includes all sleep except REM. Due to EEGs, NREM can be separated into three smaller **sleep stages**: Stage I, Stage II, and Stage III. These stages transition the body into deeper sleep: the deeper the sleep, the slower the frequency and amplitude of **brain waves** (see figure 10.7). To better understand NREM, a closer inspection of its three stages is necessary.

## Stages I and II of NREM

Stage I is a transitory phase, lasting approximately 10 minutes. Here, **beta brain waves** change into theta brain wave patterns, which have a slightly lower frequency and higher amplitude than beta waves. This very subtle transition from wakefulness to sleep can be disturbed by a gentle nudge or soft whisper. People awakened from Stage I sleep will often claim that they were not yet asleep (Coren, 1996).

Stage II is where some experts say sleep begins. The two distinguishing brain wave patterns in Stage II are sleep spindles and K-complexes. A **sleep spindle** is a short burst of brain activity, typically lasting no longer than half a second. These spindles occur when falling into a progressively deeper sleep and sometimes follow muscular twitches. Sleep spindle activity is thought to aid the integration of new information into existing knowledge (Tamminen et al., 2010). Since muscle twitches occur more frequently in children than in adults, this activity is also believed to be the body's early method of learning which nerves control certain muscles (Khazipov et al., 2004). A **K-complex** is the "largest event in a healthy human EEG." K-complexes are thought to have two functions: first, to "protect" sleep by suppressing cortical arousal in response to stimuli that the sleeping brain often evaluates as danger; second, to aid in sleep-based memory consolidation. K-complex electrical signals most often occur as part of regular Stage II sleep but can also occur as a result of external stimuli such as sounds or touch (Cash et al., 2009). Stage II sleep usually lasts from 5 to 20 minutes and is the transition between light sleep and deep sleep. People awakened at this point typically acknowledge that they were, indeed, asleep.

## Stage III of NREM

Stage III sleep begins as the body moves into a deeper slumber, characterized on an EEG by low-frequency, high-amplitude **delta brain waves**. This stage is also referred to as **slow-wave sleep**. As the deepest stage of sleep, blood supply to the brain decreases, and all

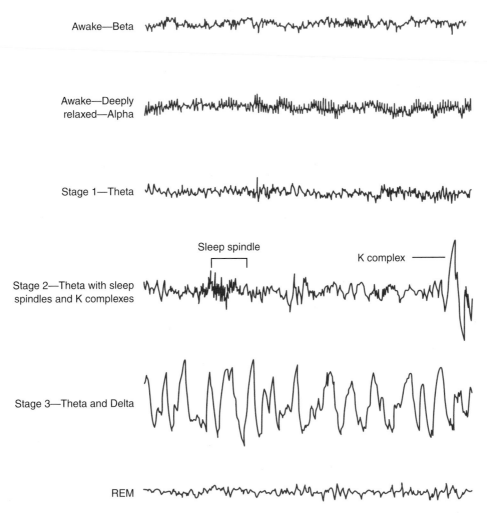

**Figure 10.7**   Electroencephalograph images of various stages of wakefulness and sleep.

but the essential bodily functions shut down. Lasting from 10 minutes to an hour, Stage III sleep is where the majority of physical restoration occurs. During this stage alone, 80 percent of the body's daily amount of growth hormone is released. Skin cells multiply at twice the normal rate, the body defends itself against pathogens, and the immune system regenerates. This stage is crucial for physical growth and development. Animal and human studies have both demonstrated that prolonged failure to get deep sleep can permanently stunt growth (Dement & Vaughan, 1999).

## REM Sleep

At the end of Stage III sleep, approximately one hour after initially falling asleep, REM sleep begins. One cycle of REM sleep lasts from 1 to 20 minutes. **REM sleep** is an active period marked by intense brain activity, similar to that of being awake. In this state, heart rate increases and blood pressure rises. Breathing becomes more rapid, irregular, and shal-

low; eyes move rapidly in various directions, and skeletal muscles become paralyzed. There is a good reason for this temporary paralysis—REM is when most dreams occur. Experts believe this paralysis prevents people from acting out their dreams. In rare cases, this protective mechanism becomes disabled, resulting in some rather bizarre behaviors such as shouting, swearing, grabbing, punching, kicking, jumping, and leaping during sleep (Moore-Ede & LeVert, 1998). In his book *The Complete Idiot's Guide to Getting a Good Night's Sleep*, Dr. Martin Moore-Ede describes an unfortunate young man whose mobile inhibitions during sleep often malfunctioned. One night he dreamed he was an NFL football player and leapt out of bed, trying to tackle the wall across the room (Moore-Ede & LeVert, 1998). Fortunately, most people do not act out their dreams.

Normal adults spend approximately 25 percent of sleep in REM, while newborns spend about half their sleep in REM (National Sleep Foundation, 2006). Although the purpose of REM sleep is not well understood, current experts believe it is critical for memory (Cai et al., 2009; Mitchison & Crick, 1983; Moorcroft & Belcher, 2003).

After REM sleep concludes, you have completed one **sleep cycle**. This entire sequence is repeated several times a night, depending on how much you sleep. In subsequent cycles, however, deep sleep is shorter and REM sleep is longer. Each cycle takes about 90 minutes.

# How Much Sleep Do You Need?

It depends. Here's how humans compare to other animals:

|  | Hours per 24-hour period |
| --- | --- |
| Giant sloth, koala: | 20 |
| Opossum: | 19 |
| Cat: | 16 |
| Dog: | 15 |
| Moose: | 13 |
| Jaguar: | 10 |
| Chimpanzee: | 9 |
| Human, rabbit, pig, rhinoceros: | 8 |
| Gray seal, dolphin: | 6 |
| Cow, goat, donkey, sheep: | 4 |
| Horse, elephant: | 3 |

Wells 2012; Becker 2005.

The first thing experts will tell you about sleep is that there is no magic number. Sleep needs for human beings are dynamic before age 20, as you can see in table 10.1 (Condor, 2001). For adults whose sleep schedules have stabilized, the general recommendation is to get about 8 hours of sleep a night. This figure comes from two sources: the statistical average for men and women who were allowed to sleep as much or as little as they wanted and a study published in the *Journal of Sleep Research* that examined sleep and mortality rates (Wingard & Berkman, 1983). Keep in mind, though, that this is an average, and individual sleep needs can vary significantly from it (Dement & Vaughan, 1999).

Not only do different age groups need different amounts of sleep, but sex and genetics may affect sleep needs as well. Other variations in sleep needs cannot be so easily explained, but just like different personality traits, the amount of sleep you need to function best may be different from that of someone else of the same age and sex. While you may

be at your absolute best after sleeping 7 hours a night, someone else may need at least nine hours of sleep to have a happy, productive life. A 2005 study confirmed that sleep needs vary across populations, and the study calls for further research to identify traits within genes that may explain how sleep needs differ among individuals (National Sleep Foundation, 2010a). During his presidency, Bill Clinton got by with only 5 or 6 hours of sleep a night. On the other hand, President Calvin Coolidge needed 11 (Coren, 1996). Sleep need is like shoe size: the average man wears a size 9 1/2 (8 1/2 UK; 42 1/2 Continental), but shoe stores still sell plenty of pairs of 8s (7s and 40 1/2s) and 13s (12s and 47s).

The relationship between sleep duration and life span is most frequently examined as part of large health screens given to thousands (or millions) of individuals. Respondents are typically asked, "How many hours do you usually sleep each night?" and the association between the responses and later mortality is evaluated. Two newer studies and a summary of 23 such studies from the past 30 years have shown that, compared to people getting 7 to 8 hours of sleep, there is an increased risk of dying in people who reported a short sleep duration (usually substantially less than 7 hours) and in those who reported a long sleep dura-

## Table 10.1   Changing Sleep Requirements of Children

| Age | Hours of sleep needed |
| --- | --- |
| Newborn | 16 to 18 broken up throughout the day |
| 1 year | 14, including one or two naps |
| 2 years | 11 to 12, including an afternoon nap |
| 3 years | 12 to 12.5; some children stop taking naps by this age |
| 4 years | 11.5 to 12; more children stop taking naps by this age |
| 5 years | 11; most children stop taking naps by this age |
| 6 years | 10.75 to 11 |
| 7 years | 10.5 to 11 |
| 8 years | 10.25 to 10.75 |
| 9 years | 10 to 10.33 |
| 10 years to puberty | 9.75 to 10 |
| Adolescent | 9.25 |

Adapted from Condor 2001.

tion (generally 9 hours or more; Ferrie et al., 2007; Gallicchio & Kalesan, 2009; Hublin et al., 2007).

Determining *your* personal sleep needs requires no special equipment or expert assistance, but it does take a little bit of discipline. First, set yourself a regular bedtime to stabilize your biological clock. Second, make sure you are not disturbed or awakened in the morning. A good time to do this experiment might be when you are on vacation and have no early morning demands. Finally, simply let nature take its course. Students who do this usually report sleeping 10 to 12 hours the first night, 9 to 10 hours the next few nights, and then progressively shorter periods until their sleep becomes regular. During the first few nights they are paying back accrued sleep debt. Within two weeks, most people find that their sleep time stabilizes between 7 and 9 hours. I must emphasize again, though, that sleep needs are individual. Do not force yourself into a sleep pattern; relax and see what happens. You will be amazed at how your body develops a natural sleep rhythm, how you no longer need an alarm clock, and how great you feel. People say they feel lighter and are charged with energy, able to focus like never before, and less troubled by people and circumstances. They are sleeping the way God designed it.

## How to Sleep Like a Log

The expression "sleep like a log" is somewhat inaccurate; first, because of how much goes on inside the brain while you sleep (as you have just learned) and second, because most people shift posture about 20 times during the night (Maas, 1998). "Sleep like a baby" is probably a worse comparison, however. Do you really want to sleep irregularly for 17 hours a day, frequently waking up and crying? Here are some suggestions for having good **sleep hygiene**—a term recently coined to describe quality sleeping habits.

**1. Establish a consistent sleep schedule.** To whatever extent possible, try to go to bed and wake up at the same time 365 days a year. Many experts believe that after getting enough sleep, this is the most important factor in waking up feeling refreshed (Dement & Vaughan, 1999). Eighty percent of shift workers, whose work schedules and therefore sleep schedules change weekly, report problems sleeping (Moore-Ede, 1993). Constantly changing your bedtime keeps your circadian rhythm, the 24-hour light-based cycle that regulates when the body feels alert or tired, from being established. Without an established circadian rhythm, your sleep cycle will constantly be unbalanced and difficult to regulate. Fortunately, you do not need to go to bed and get up at *exactly* the same time every day. Variations within 30 minutes will not adversely affect your biological clock (National Sleep Foundation, 2002). Sleeping consistently is the best thing you can do to be truly rested.

**2. Get regular exercise.** Some of the most troubled sleepers are elderly people. On average, they tend to sleep intermittently and get less deep sleep. Trying to discover how to improve this situation, researchers studied the effect of exercise on the sleeping behavior of older people. Sixty-seven adults aged 50 to 76 were divided into two groups. One group did 30 to 40 minutes of aerobic exercise at 60 to 70 percent of maximum heart rate, four times a week. The other group did not. After 16 weeks, the subjects in the exercise group took 50 percent less time to fall asleep and increased their quality sleep time by one hour (Dement & Vaughan, 1999). This is not an isolated study, and its results are not only true for the aged. A careful analysis of 44 studies shows that people who exercise consistently go to sleep faster, have longer bouts of deep sleep, and sleep longer than people who do not exercise (Kubitz et al., 1996). One caveat: For some people, exercising too late in the day acts as a stimulant. They find that exercising in the evening makes it harder to go to sleep (Stickgold et al., 2004). If you are one of those people, exercise at least four hours before you go to bed.

Many people wish they could sleep this soundly.

**3. Establish a bedtime ritual.** This is one of the most common recommendations made by sleep experts (Coren, 1996; Dement & Vaughan, 1999; Zammit, 1997). Many people say they nod off effortlessly after following a simple routine. Some popular rituals are drinking a glass of milk, reading a book, turning down the covers, taking a warm bath, or brushing and flossing teeth. The routine must be regular and consistent to be effective. Many proponents of these rituals also recommend using your bed only for sleep. They believe that doing work, talking on the phone, or watching TV while in bed sends conflicting messages about what should happen there.

**4. Create a quality sleeping environment.** The three crucial descriptors of a quality sleep environment are *quiet*, *dark*, and *cool*. Making a quiet sleep space can be difficult, especially if you live in a college dorm. Fortunately, earplugs can reduce noise, and there are other devices that produce "white noise," or soothing sounds like rain, waterfalls, or ocean waves, to mask disturbing noises. Many people find that they sleep better with a fan on.

You can make your room dark by getting opaque blinds for your windows, turning off your computer screen and other electronic devices, turning digital clocks away from you, and stuffing a towel under the door to eliminate light from the hallway. If those measures are not enough, you can purchase eye masks that block out light.

Though cool environments are generally preferred for sleeping, individual preference is a large factor in room temperature. Couples who sleep together often squabble about this. Preferences about covers and bed temperature vary, but the majority of people like the room they're sleeping in to be about 65 degrees Fahrenheit (18 degrees Celsius; Maas, 1999).

**5. Invest in a quality bed and sleeping accessories.** Most people will spend almost a third of their lives in bed—an average of 23.4 years! Making your bed comfortable is certainly worth the investment.

- Generally, bigger is better. Make sure your bed is at least 6 inches (15 cm) longer than you are (Maas, 1999). If you sleep with someone else, don't settle for anything smaller than a queen-size mattress.

- When it comes to sheets, a well-recognized independent consumer group reported cotton as the most preferred fabric (Consumer Reports, 2006a). In their investigation, the variables evaluated were comfort, ease of care, and durability. Cotton performed well in each of the three categories. Although choice of sheets is largely affected by personal preferences, cotton is a good place to begin looking. See the Consumer Watch sidebar for a more detailed discussion of the different types of mattresses and sheets.

- A pillow with proper support is key to a good night's sleep. Fold your pillow in half and squeeze out the air. A pillow with proper support will return to its original shape, but a broken one will stay folded. Down or feather pillows seem to be the most popular (Maas, 1999).

If after doing these things you still find yourself struggling to stay awake and alert throughout the day, it may be time to talk to your doctor. There are several types of sleep disorders that, at best, harm a person's ability to sleep deeply.

## Common Sleep Disorders

More than 70 sleep disorders have been identified; the following are four of the most common.

**1. Insomnia,** the most prevalent sleep disorder, is characterized by an inability to fall asleep or the tendency to wake up frequently during the night and then have difficulty going back to sleep. Insomnia is more common in women than men and tends to increase with age. Short-term or "transient" insomnia is a normal part of life and may be caused by emotional or physical discomfort, stress, environmental noise, extreme temperatures, jet lag, or as a side effect of medication. Problems arise when insomnia becomes regular, or "chronic." Treatment for chronic insomnia often includes adjusting behavioral patterns, such as following a specific nighttime routine, improving sleep environment, reducing caffeine and alcohol intake, or reducing afternoon napping. Phar-

### Only One Who Never Sleeps

I lift up my eyes to the hills—where does my help come from? My help comes from the Lord, the Maker of heaven and earth. He will not let your foot slip—he who watches over you will not slumber; indeed, he who watches over Israel will neither slumber nor sleep. (Psalm 121:1–4)

macological treatments may be helpful in eliminating symptoms in some cases (National Heart, Lung, and Blood Institute, 1995, 1998).

    **2. Obstructive sleep apnea (OSA)** is a potentially life-threatening disorder in which breathing is interrupted during sleep. An estimated 12 million Americans have OSA. This condition is commonly associated with excess fatty tissue, which can reduce or completely inhibit breathing. It is not uncommon for someone with severe sleep apnea to stop breathing 20 to 30 times per hour during sleep. These episodes cause frequent partial arousals from sleep and are typically associated with chronic loud snoring. The frequent arousals result in ineffective sleep and account for the chronic sleep deprivation and the resultant excessive daytime sleepiness that is a major hallmark of this condition. Treatment for adult OSA includes behavioral therapy (losing weight, changing

## Consumer Watch: Mattresses and Sheets

Egyptian cotton, jersey knit, flax linen, cellulose modal, pima cotton, synthetic polyester, or smooth satin—which type of sheets is best? Will your sleep quality improve on a mattress made of space-age memory foam or one with adjustable air pressure? These are some of the questions facing consumers making choices regarding what type of material they will spend one-third of their lives on. An estimated 70 million Americans complain about sleeplessness, so there is plenty of need for wise advice (National Sleep Foundation, 2005). One popular consumer magazine receives more inquiries about mattresses than about any other product except cars (Consumer Reports, 2006b). The following are some sound suggestions that will make you a savvy shopper.

1. A comfortable mattress is a matter of personal opinion. There are no clear winners when it comes to mattress preferences (Consumer Reports, 2006b). The optimal surface is purely subjective, says Dr. Clete Kushida, director of the Stanford University Center for Human Sleep Research (Kushida, 2006). Because preferences for firmness, materials, and size vary so widely, it is critical to try before you buy. Do not be embarrassed—try lots of different mattresses before making a purchase. A good sales person should encourage you to take your shoes off and spend some time on your back, stomach, and side to find the mattress that feels best to you.

2. Contrary to popular opinion, if you have lower-back pain, a firm mattress is not always better. One study published in *The Lancet* suggested that people who have lower-back pain can benefit from a medium-firm sleeping surface (Kovacs, 2003). If a mattress is too firm, it won't support all body parts evenly and may cause discomfort at the heaviest points (hips and shoulders). If it's too soft, the person could sink into the surface and have a hard time moving. Dr. Alan Hedge, professor of ergonomics at Cornell University, noted that the best mattress supports the spine at all points while allowing it to maintain its natural curve (Consumer Reports, 2006a).

3. Thread count of sheets matters up to a point. Thread count is determined by counting the number of vertical and horizontal threads in one square inch (2.5 square cm) of fabric. Many manufacturers suggest that higher thread counts are better. Yet a recent report examining the softness, durability, and comfort of sheets concluded that sheets from 200 to 400 threads per square inch rated highest overall. Thread counts exceeding 400 usually did not have increased benefits, only increased price.

4. When it comes to fabric, cotton is still king. In tests examining easy care, comfort, and durability, traditional cotton was the clear winner (Consumer Reports, 2006a). After 20 washings, many of the sheets made of luxury materials lost color, shrank so much they would no longer fit, or simply began to unravel.

5. Finally, you do not have to shop at specialty bedding stores to find high-quality cotton sheets with thread counts from 200 to 400. The highest-rated sheet in one consumer magazine was a cotton sheet with thread count of 300 from the retail store Target (Consumer Reports, 2006a).

sleeping positions, and avoiding alcohol and tobacco), using devices that force air through the nasal passages, using dental appliances that reposition the lower jaw and tongue, and undergoing surgery to increase the size of the nasal airway (National Heart, Lung, and Blood Institute, 1995/1999).

**3. Restless legs syndrome (RLS)** is a neurologic movement disorder often associated with sleep complaint. RLS sufferers report creeping, crawling, pulling, or tingling sensations in the legs (or occasionally the arms) that are relieved by moving or rubbing them. Periodic leg movements, which often coexist with restless legs syndrome, are characterized by repetitive, stereotyped limb movements during sleep. Some people with mild cases of RLS can be treated by exercise, leg massages, and eliminating alcohol and caffeine from the diet. Others require pharmacological treatment, and it may take some time to determine the right medication or combination of medications for the individual. Estimates suggest that RLS may affect from 10 to 15 percent of the U.S. population (Lin et al., 1999; National Heart, Lung, and Blood Institute, 2000).

**4. Narcolepsy** is a chronic sleep disorder that usually arises during adolescence or young adulthood. In the United States, it affects as many as 250,000 people, although fewer than half are diagnosed (Bassetti & Aldrich, 1996). The main characteristic of narcolepsy is excessive and overwhelming daytime sleepiness, even after adequate nighttime sleep. A person with narcolepsy is likely to become drowsy or to fall asleep at inappropriate times and places. Daytime sleep attacks may occur with or without warning and may be irresistible. REM sleep in people with narcolepsy frequently occurs at sleep onset instead of after a period of NREM sleep. Treatment is individualized depending on the severity of the symptoms, and it may take weeks or months for an optimal regimen to be determined. Treatment is primarily through medications, but lifestyle changes are also important (Lin et al., 1999).

## Next Steps

Robert Murray McCheyne (1813–1843) of Edinburgh, Scotland, was a young man ablaze with passion for Christ and his kingdom. Ordained a minister when he was only 23, McCheyne made such an impact that one listener said of him, "He preached with eternity stamped upon his brow. I trembled, and never felt God so near" (Rice, 2005). For the next six years McCheyne zealously and tirelessly presented the gospel of Jesus Christ to all who would listen. In 1839, he made a trip to the Holy Land to evangelize to Jews and upon his return contributed to a great revival that swept across Scotland and northern England. Soon afterward, however, his health began to fail. Ignoring the urging of his concerned friends, he refused to rest and continued to push himself to the limit. Finally, as the young preacher lay on his deathbed at only 29 years of age, he whispered to a friend at his side, "God gave me a message to deliver and a horse to carry it. Alas, I killed the horse, and now I cannot deliver the message" (Sanders, 1997, p. 136).

McCheyne's story dramatically and tragically shows that even a passion for the glory of God must be balanced with an understanding of physical limitations. Yet it is hard not to be completely engulfed by the vast ocean of the suffering of humanity, especially today when global needs are so evident. About one-sixth of the world's population goes to bed hungry every night, more than half the world's citizens earn less than a dollar a day, and the AIDS epidemic is expanding (World Health Organization, 2006). Resting amid crises like these can seem not only selfish but also ruthless, callous, and self-absorbed.

Respected pastor and teacher A.W. Tozer once said, "In an effort to get the work of the Lord done we often lose contact with the Lord of the work, and quite literally wear our people out" (Draper, 1992, p.155). God has infused rhythms everywhere in creation, from the rising and setting of the sun, to the ebb and flow of the ocean's tides, to the repeating stages of the sleep cycle. It is important to respect and live by these rhythms because the Lord has pronounced them "very good" (Genesis 1:31). Although the creator God does not sleep, he does not begrudge his children their slumber. "In vain you rise early and stay up late, toiling for food to eat—for he grants sleep to those he loves" (Psalm 127:2). Be reminded also of Jesus's words: "Come to me, all you who are weary and burdened, and I will give you rest. Take my yoke upon you and learn from me, for I am gentle and humble in heart, and you will find rest for your souls" (Matthew 11:28–29). Whether toiling for food or at a job or school, sleep is a cycle ordained by God as a blessing for his people.

# Keeping the Sabbath?

From ancient civilizations to modern society, people from every part of the globe have set aside one day of the week for physical and spiritual renewal. In fact, each of the seven days of the week has been designated as a Sabbath at one time.

### Sabbath Around the World

| | |
|---|---|
| Monday | Greek |
| Tuesday | Persian |
| Wednesday | Assyrian |
| Thursday | Egyptian |
| Friday | Turkish |
| Saturday | Jewish |
| Sunday | Christian |

Tan 1982.

Christians have argued the rules of the Sabbath for more than 2,000 years. The Talmud, which contains a vast array of ancient Jewish laws, has 24 chapters and 38 subcategories dedicated to Sabbath regulations.

In this point/counterpoint discussion, I am going to limit the focus to one simple question: Should twenty-first-century Christians set aside one day of the week for renewal? For sake of continuity, I will call this unique day a Sabbath. I will not discuss particulars, such as what day of the week Sabbath should be, spiritual practices that should be included, or behaviors that should be prohibited.

Proponents of setting aside one day of the week for rest are quick to point out God's example in the creation narrative in Genesis. After six days of work, the creator God rested.

> Thus the heavens and the earth were completed in all their vast array. By the seventh day God had finished the work he had been doing; so on the seventh day he rested from all his work. And God blessed the seventh day and made it holy, because on it he rested from all the work of creating that he had done. (Genesis 2:1–3)

When God gave Moses what is now known as the Ten Commandments, he referred back to his creation example and commanded the Israelites to do likewise.

> Remember the Sabbath day by keeping it holy. Six days you shall labor and do all your work, but the seventh day is a Sabbath to the Lord your God. On it you shall not do any work, neither you, nor your son or daughter, nor your manservant or maidservant, nor your animals, nor the alien within your gates. For in six days the Lord made the heavens and the earth, the sea, and all that is in them, but he rested on the seventh day. Therefore, the Lord blessed the Sabbath day and made it holy. (Exodus 20:8–11)

Many noteworthy Christians have chosen to abide by God's command to keep the Sabbath, in some cases to their personal detriment.

Perhaps one of the most notable examples in the twentieth century was Eric Liddell, a Scottish track star whose story became popular through the movie *Chariots of Fire* (Hudson, 1981), which won four Academy Awards. Liddell refused to run in a qualifying race of the 1924 Olympic Games because it was held on a Sunday, even though that meant he would not be able to compete in the race he had trained so long for.

Like Liddell, many Christians in the nineteenth and twentieth centuries were quite serious about not working on the Sabbath. The first man of flight, Wilbur Wright, refused an appeal of the king of Spain who requested an aerial display on a Sunday (Tan, 1982). Former president Ulysses S. Grant refused an invitation from the president of France to join his entourage for a day at the races saying,

> It is not in accord with the custom of my country, or with the spirit of my religion to spend Sunday in that way. I will go to the house of God. (Tan, 1982, p. 1,389)

History is filled with individuals who advised others of the merits of Sabbath renewal:

*(continued)*

*(continued)*

"Sunday is the golden clasp that binds together the volume of the week."
—Henry Wadsworth Longfellow (Draper, 1992, p. 956)

"If your soul has no Sunday, it becomes an orphan."
—Physician and missionary Albert Schweitzer (Gibbs, 2004, p. 90)

"Jesus spoke about the ox in the ditch on the Sabbath. But if your ox gets in the ditch every Sabbath, you should either get rid of the ox or fill up the ditch."
—Billy Graham (Draper, 1992, p. 109)

Some Christians, however, believe that the practice of keeping a Sabbath is not a model for Christians today.

Although God rested on the Sabbath, Jesus seemed to disobey many of the Jewish Sabbath laws right in front of religious officials. He

- picked grain for consumption on the Sabbath (Matthew 12:1–7);
- healed a man with a shriveled hand on the Sabbath (Matthew 12:9–14);
- healed a woman who had been crippled for 18 years on the Sabbath (Luke 13:10–17);
- healed a man suffering from dropsy on the Sabbath (Luke 14:1–6);
- healed an invalid by the pool of Bethesda and then ordered him to unlawfully pick up and carry his mat on the Sabbath (John 5:1–18); and
- healed a blind man with cakes of mud on the Sabbath (John 9:13–16).

Each time Jesus was questioned by the religious leaders about his disrespect for the Sabbath, he responded by showing he cared more about loving people than properly keeping the Sabbath: "The Sabbath was made for man, not man for the Sabbath" (Mark 2:27).

In addition to Christ's behavior, additional support for not keeping the Sabbath is the fact that the commandment to keep the Sabbath is the only one of the Ten Commandments not repeated in the New Testament (Richards, 1990).

Other passages add to the scriptural evidence for the argument that keeping the Sabbath was a command relevant to Old Testament believers but not required for New Testament disciples. Note what Paul said concerning the Sabbath in his letter to the Colossians:

When you were dead in your sins and in the uncircumcision of your sinful nature, God made you alive with Christ. He forgave us all our sins, having canceled the written code, with its regulations, that was against us and that stood opposed to us; he took it away, nailing it to the cross. And having disarmed the powers and authorities, he made a public spectacle of them, triumphing over them by the cross. Therefore do not let anyone judge you by what you eat or drink, or with regard to a religious festival, a New Moon celebration or a Sabbath day. These are a shadow of the things that were to come; the reality, however, is found in Christ. (Colossians 2:13–17)

In his letter to the Galatians, Paul urges followers of Christ not to be enslaved by the old system of keeping the law, which seems to include having particular days be "special."

Formerly, when you did not know God, you were slaves to those who by nature are not gods. But now that you know God—or rather are known by God—how is it that you are turning back to those weak and miserable principles? Do you wish to be enslaved by them all over again? You are observing special days and months and seasons and years! I fear for you, that somehow I have wasted my efforts on you. (Galatians 4:8–11)

Finally, some scholars argue that New Testament believers should strive for perpetual rest in Christ instead of resting only one day each week.

There remains, then, a Sabbath-rest for the people of God; for anyone who enters God's rest also rests from his own work, just as God did from his. Let us, therefore, make every effort to enter that rest, so that no one will fall by following their example of disobedience. (Hebrews 4:9–11)

As you can see from these opposing positions, scripture seems to support conflicting viewpoints. Which view do you believe God desires for you?

# Key Terms

| | | |
|---|---|---|
| beta brain waves | narcolepsy | sleep debt |
| brain waves | nonrapid eye movement (NREM) | sleep deprivation |
| circadian biological clock | obstructive sleep apnea | sleep hygiene |
| circadian rhythm | polysomnography (PSG) | sleep phase delay |
| chronic sleep deprivation | rapid eye movement (REM) | sleep spindle |
| delta brain waves | REM sleep | sleep stages |
| electroencephalography (EEG) | restless legs syndrome (RLS) | sleep study |
| insomnia | sleep apnea | sleep–wake homeostasis |
| K-complex | sleep cycle | slow-wave sleep |

# Review Questions

1. To what degree is sleep deprivation a problem?
2. What societal changes have encouraged people to sleep less?
3. Identify the effects of sleep deprivation in the order in which they occur.
4. Diagram the stages and cycles of sleep.
5. Identify the process for determining how much sleep you need.
6. List several reasons for improving the quality of sleep.

# Application Activities

1. Complete a more comprehensive sleep test to evaluate potential sleep problems at the Sleepnet website: www.sleepnet.com.
2. Keep a seven-day sleep/alertness log, like the following, to evaluate your individual sleep, nap, and alertness levels. This can be especially helpful to students who want to study during periods of maximum alertness.

# Sleep and Alertness Log

## Degree of Alertness

5: Feeling active, vital, alert, or wide awake

4: Functioning at a high level but not at my peak

3: Awake, relaxed; responsive but not fully alert

2: Lethargic, sluggish, slow

1: Foggy, losing interest in remaining awake

0: Fighting sleep

| Date | Bed-time | Time until sleep onset | Number of awakenings, total length | Rise time | Number of naps, total length (yesterday) | Sleep time | See degree of alertness scale |
|------|----------|------------------------|-------------------------------------|-----------|-------------------------------------------|------------|-------------------------------|
| | | | Fill out this section when you rise in the morning. | | | | Fill out during waking hours. |
| | | | _____ | | _____ | | 1A 2A 3A 4A 5A 6A<br>7A 8A 9A 10A 11A 12N<br>1P 2P 3P 4P 5P 6P 7P<br>8P 9P 10P 11P 12MN |
| | | | _____ | | _____ | | 1A 2A 3A 4A 5A 6A<br>7A 8A 9A 10A 11A 12N<br>1P 2P 3P 4P 5P 6P 7P<br>8P 9P 10P 11P 12MN |
| | | | _____ | | _____ | | 1A 2A 3A 4A 5A 6A<br>7A 8A 9A 10A 11A 12N<br>1P 2P 3P 4P 5P 6P 7P<br>8P 9P 10P 11P 12MN |
| | | | _____ | | _____ | | 1A 2A 3A 4A 5A 6A<br>7A 8A 9A 10A 11A 12N<br>1P 2P 3P 4P 5P 6P 7P<br>8P 9P 10P 11P 12MN |
| | | | _____ | | _____ | | 1A 2A 3A 4A 5A 6A<br>7A 8A 9A 10A 11A 12N<br>1P 2P 3P 4P 5P 6P 7P<br>8P 9P 10P 11P 12MN |
| | | | _____ | | _____ | | 1A 2A 3A 4A 5A 6A<br>7A 8A 9A 10A 11A 12N<br>1P 2P 3P 4P 5P 6P 7P<br>8P 9P 10P 11P 12MN |
| | | | _____ | | _____ | | 1A 2A 3A 4A 5A 6A<br>7A 8A 9A 10A 11A 12N<br>1P 2P 3P 4P 5P 6P 7P<br>8P 9P 10P 11P 12MN |
| | | | _____ | | _____ | | 1A 2A 3A 4A 5A 6A<br>7A 8A 9A 10A 11A 12N<br>1P 2P 3P 4P 5P 6P 7P<br>8P 9P 10P 11P 12MN |
| **7-day average (total of weekly averages)** | | | _____ | | _____ | | 1A 2A 3A 4A 5A 6A<br>7A 8A 9A 10A 11A 12N<br>1P 2P 3P 4P 5P 6P 7P<br>8P 9P 10P 11P 12MN |

From P. Walters and J. Byl, 2013, *Christian paths to health and wellness*, 2nd ed. (Champaign, IL: Human Kinetics).

# References

American Academy of Sleep Medicine. (2001). *International classification of sleep disorders, revised: Diagnostic and coding manual.* Chicago: American Academy of Sleep Medicine.

American College Health Association. (2011). *National College Health Assessment.* www.achancha.org/docs/ACHA-NCHA-II_ReferenceGroup_ExecutiveSummary_Fall2011.pdf.

Bassetti, C., & Aldrich, M.S. (1996). Narcolepsy. *Neurologic Clinics, 14,* 545–71.

Becker, M. (2005, August 10). How much do dogs sleep? *The Daily Item.*

Bullman, J., & Milne, C. (1998). *The sleep files* [3 videocassettes (ca. 156 min.)]. New York: Ambrose Video.

Cai, D.J., Mednick, S.A., Harrison, E.M., Kanady, J.C., & Mednick, S.C. (2009). REM, not incubation, improves creativity by priming associative networks. Proc Natl Acad Sci USA, 106, 10130–34.

Cash, S.S., Halgren, E., Dehghani, N., Rossetti, A.O., Thesen, T., Wang, C., et al. (2009). Human k-complex represents an isolated cortical down-state. Science, 324, 1084–87.

Condor, B. (2001, September 9). Early to bed. *Chicago Tribune*: 1, 6.

Consumer Reports. (2006a, June). Sheets: Wake-up call. *Consumer Reports.* 70(8).

Consumer Reports. (2006b, June). How to buy a mattress without losing sleep. *Consumer Reports*, 70(8).

Coren, S. (1996). *Sleep thieves: An eye-opening exploration into the science and mysteries of sleep.* New York: The Free Press.

Dement, W., & Vaughan, C. (1999). *The promise of sleep.* New York: Delacorte Press.

Draper, E. (1992). *Draper's book of quotations for the Christian world.* Wheaton, IL: Tyndale House.

Ferrie, J.E., Shipley, M.J., Cappuccio, F.P., Brunner, E., Miller, M.A., Kumari, M., et al. (2007, December 1). A prospective study of change in sleep duration: Associations with mortality in the Whitehall II cohort. *Sleep, 30*(12), 1659–66.

Gallicchio, L., & Kalesan, B. (2009). *Sleep duration and mortality: A systematic review and meta-analysis. Journal of Sleep Research, 18,* 148–58.

Gibbs, N. (2004). And on the seventh day we rested. *Time, 164*(5), 90–91.

Hublin, C., Partinen, M., Koskenvuo, M., Kaprio, J. (2007). Sleep and mortality: A population-based 22-year follow-up study. *Sleep Journal, 30*(10), 1245–53.

Hudson, H. (Director). (1981). *Chariots of fire* [Motion picture]. United Kingdom: Ladd Company & Warner Brothers.

Khazipov, R., Sirota, A., Leinekugel, X., Holmes, G.L., Ben-Ari, Y., & Buzsáki, G. (2004). Early motor activity drives spindle bursts in the developing somatosensory cortex. *Nature, 432*(7018), 758–61.

Kovacs, F.M. (2003, November 15). Effect of firmness of mattress on chronic non-specific low-back pain. *The Lancet, 362,* 1594–95.

Kribbs, N.D., & Dinges, D. (1994). Vigilance decrement and sleepiness. In J.O.R. Harsh (Ed.), *Sleep onset mechanisms* (pp. 113–25). Washington, DC: American Psychological Association.

Kubitz, K.A., Landers, D.M., Petruzzello, S.J., & Han, M. (1996). The effects of acute and chronic exercise on sleep: A meta-analytic review. *Sports Medicine, 21,* 277–91.

Kuo, A. (2001). Does sleep deprivation impair cognitive and motor performance as much as alcohol intoxication? *Western Journal of Medicine, 174*(3), 180.

Kushida, C. (2006). *Sleep deprivation: Basic science, physiology, and behavior.* Philadelphia: Taylor & Francis.

Leung, L., & Becker, C.E. (1992). Sleep deprivation and house staff performance. *Journal of Occupational Medicine, 34,* 1153–60.

Lin, L., Faraco, J., Li, R., Kadotani, H., Rogers, W., Lin, X., et al. (1999). The sleep disorder narcolepsy is caused by a mutation in the hypocretin (orexin) receptor 2 gene. *Cell, 98,* 409–12.

Maas, J.B. (1998). *Asleep in the fast lane: Our 24-hour society.* Ithaca, NY: Cornell University Psychology Film Unit.

Maas, J.B. (1999). *Power sleep.* New York: Harper Perennial.

Martin, B.J. (1981). Effects of sleep deprivation on tolerance of prolonged exercise. *European Journal of Applied Physiology and Occupational Physiology, 47,* 345–54.

Mitchison, G., & Crick, F. (1983). The function of dream sleep. *Nature, 304*(5922), 111–14.

Miyata, S., Noda, A., Ozaki, N., Hara, Y., Minoshima, M., Iwamoto, K., et al. (2010). Insufficient sleep impairs driving performance and cognitive function. *Neuroscience Letters, 469*(2), 229–33.

Moorcroft, W.H., & Belcher, P. (2003). *Understanding sleep and dreaming.* New York: Kluwer Academic/Plenum.

Moore-Ede, M. (1993). *The twenty-four-hour society: Understanding human limits in a world that never stops.* Boston: Addison-Wesley.

Moore-Ede, M., & LeVert, S. (1998). *The complete idiot's guide to getting a good night's sleep.* New York: Alpha.

Murphy, K., & Delanty, N. (2007). Review article: Sleep deprivation: A clinical perspecitve. *Sleep and Biological Rhythms, 5*(1), 2–14.

National Heart, Lung, and Blood Institute (1995). *Insomnia* (NIH Pub. No. 95-3801). Bethesda, MD: NHLBI.

National Heart, Lung, and Blood Institute. (1995, reprinted 1999.) *Sleep apnea: Is your patient at risk?* (NIH Pub. No. 99-3803). Bethesda, MD: NHLBI.

National Heart, Lung, and Blood Institute (1998). *Insomnia: Assessment and management in primary care* (NIH Pub. No. 98-4088). Bethesda, MD: NHLBI.

National Heart, Lung, and Blood Institute. (2000). *Restless legs syndrome: Detection and management in primary care* (NIH Pub. No. 00-3788). Bethesda, MD: NHLBI.

National Sleep Foundation. (1995). *Sleep in America*. Princeton, NJ: Gallop Organization.

National Sleep Foundation. (1999). *The sleep quiz*. Washington, DC: National Sleep Foundation.

National Sleep Foundation. (2001). *Sleep in America*. Washington, DC: National Sleep Foundation.

National Sleep Foundation. (2002). *Sleep in America*. Washington, DC: National Sleep Foundation.

National Sleep Foundation. (2005). *Sleep in America*. Washington, DC: National Sleep Foundation.

National Sleep Foundation. (2006). *Sleep-wake cycle: Its physiology and impact on health*. www.sleepfoundation.org/sites/default/files/SleepWakeCycle.pdf.

National Sleep Foundation. (2007). *NSF's Key Messages/Talking Points*. www.sleepfoundation.org/sites/default/files/Drowsy%20Driving-Key%20Messages%20and%20Talking%20Points.pdf.

National Sleep Foundation. (2010a). *How much sleep do we really need?* www.sleepfoundation.org/article/how-sleep-works/how-much-sleep-do-we-really-need.

National Sleep Foundation. (2010b). *Sleep drive and your body clock*. www.sleepfoundation.org/article/sleep-topics/sleep-drive-and-your-body-clock.

National Sleep Foundation. (2012). *Sleep in America: Planes, trains, automobiles and sleep*. Washington, DC: National Sleep Foundation.

Pasztor, A. (1996, July 1). An air-safety battle brews over the issue of pilots' rest time. *Wall Street Journal,* A1.

Pilcher, J. & Walters, A. (1997). How sleep deprivation affects psychological variables related to college students' cognitive performance. *Journal of American College Health, 46*(3), 121–26.

Rechtschaffen, A. & Bergmann, B. (1995). Sleep deprivation in the rat by the disk-over-water method. *Behavioural Brain Research, 69,* 55–63.

Reilly, T., & Piercy, M. (1994). The effect of partial sleep deprivation on weight-lifting performance. *Ergonomics, 37,* 107–15.

Rice, J.R. (2005). *Preacher bibliographies*. www.swordofthelord.com/biographies/MccheyneRobertMurray.htm.

Richards, L.O. (1990). *365 day devotional commentary*. Colorado Springs: Cook Communications Ministries.

Riegel, B., & Weaver, T. (2009). Poor sleep and impaired self-care: Towards a comprehensive model linking sleep, cognition, and heart failure outcomes. *European Journal of Cardiovascular Nursing, 8*(5), 337–44.

Sanders, O. (1997). Don't kill the horse. *Leadership, 7*(3), 136.

Schor, J. (1993). *The overworked American: The unexpected decline of leisure*. New York: Basic Books.

Science News. (2011). *Microsleep: Brain regions can take short naps during wakefulness, leading to errors*. www.sciencedaily.com/releases/2011/04/110427131814.htm.

Smolensky, M., & Lamberg, L. (2000). *The body clock guide to better health*. New York: Henry Holt & Co.

Stickgold, R., Winkelman, J., & Wehrwein, P. (2004, January 19). You will start to feel very sleepy. *Newsweek,* 58–60.

Tamminen, J., Payne, J.D., Stickgold, R., Wamsley, E.J., & Gaskell, M.G. (2010). Sleep spindle activity is associated with the integration of new memories and existing knowledge. *The Journal of Neuroscience, 30*(43), 14356–60.

Tan, P.L. (1982). *Encyclopedia of 7,700 illustrations*. Rockville, MD: Assurance.

Walters, P. (2000). *Sleep: The forgotten factor*. Paper presented at the annual National Wellness Conference, Stevens Point, WI.

Walters, P. (2005). *Sleep: The forgotten factor: Part II*. Paper presented at the annual National Wellness Conference, Stevens Point, WI.

Walters, P.H. (2009). Sleep thieves: College students identify what they do instead of sleep. (Oral presentation.) Wheaton College.

Wells, Virginia. (2012). *Sleep Behavior of Cats*. www.petplace.com/cats/sleep-behavior-of-cats/page1.aspx.

Wingard, D.L., & Berkman, L.F. (1983). Mortality risk associated with sleeping patterns among adults. *Journal of Sleep Research, 6*(2), 102–7.

World Health Organization. (2006). *Millennium development goals*. www.who.int/mdg/goals/goal1/en.

Zammit, G. (1997). *Good nights*. Kansas City, MO: Andrews & McMeel.

## Suggested Readings

Bass, D. (1997). Rediscovering the Sabbath. *Christianity Today, 41*(10), 38–43.

This journal article describes the process for learning "anew" the benefits of Sabbath rest.

Coren, S. (1997). *Sleep thieves: An eye-opening exploration into the science and mysteries of sleep*. New York: The Free Press.

This book explains the evident and the subtle effects of sleep deprivation on our mental and physical health, giving readers tips to improve the quality of their own sleep.

Dement, W., & Vaughan, C. (2000). *The promise of sleep: A pioneer in sleep medicine explores the vital connection between health, happiness, and a good night's sleep.* New York: Delacorte.

This may be the best book on sleep for the layperson.

Maas, J. B., Wherry, M.L., Axelrod, D.J., Hogan, B.R., & Bloomin, J. (1998). *Power sleep: The revolutionary program that prepares your mind for peak performance.* New York: Harper Perennial.

This is a good place to begin educating yourself about the importance of proper sleep hygiene.

Muller, W. (1999). *Sabbath: Restoring the sacred rhythm of rest.* New York: Bantam Books.

This book emphasizes the importance of sacred rhythms for emotional, physical, and spiritual renewal.

Peterson, E. (1994). The good-for-nothing Sabbath. *Christianity Today, 38*(4), 34.

Peterson describes the joy of following the Creator's example of Sabbath rest.

## Suggested Websites

**www.sleepfoundation.org**

The National Sleep Foundation is an organization dedicated to surveying sleep behavior and potential solutions for millions of Americans who have sleep-related problems.

**www.sleepnet.com**

"Everything you wanted to know about sleep but were too tired to ask."

**http://sleep.stanford.edu**

Stanford University Medical School is one of the leading sleep research institutions in the world. You will find a wealth of information related to sleep disorders.

# Personal Relationships and Wellness

Peter Walters

After reading this chapter, you should be able to do the following:

1. Identify your unique SHAPE.
2. Describe scientific evidence related to the interactions of relational and physical health.
3. Explain three spiritual principles for enhancing your relationships.

In the beginning, God created the heavens and the earth. (Genesis 1:1)

## So begins the book of Genesis, the first book

of the Bible. Yet the creation narrative is remarkably brief. This trend continues throughout the Bible—God, apparently, is a master of understatement. To jaded ears, scripture might sound minimalist and muted. Think about a few examples. After Jesus had fasted for 40 days in the harsh Judean wilderness, he was probably hallucinating with hunger, his reserves were depleted, and his organs and muscles were in a catabolic state. The Bible says only, "He was hungry" (Luke 4:2). Christ's excruciating death, graphically reenacted in the movie *The Passion of the Christ*, is sickening to watch. The gospel writer Luke described it with four simple words: "There they crucified him" (Luke 22:33).

God's modesty is even more remarkable in the Genesis creation account. He created the sun, a fiery ball of fusion reactions 1.3 million times larger than the earth; 400 billion stars in the Milky Way galaxy alone; microscopic single-celled organisms, each more complex than a jet engine factory; 2 million known animal species; and 260,000 known plant species. All that sprang solely from the mind and will of one mighty being, and the Creator described it with one word, "good" (Genesis 1:10, 12, 18, 21, 25).

Given the understatement of God, when he does choose to emphasize something, it is important to stop and listen. Only one event in the creation narrative is highlighted and pronounced "*very* good":

God created Adam from a fistful of earth.

the creation of people. Only humans hold the unique distinction of being created in the image of God and having the capacity of spiritual life and death.

In stark opposition to all of the goodness of God's creation, there was one issue he said was not good: It is *not good* for man to be alone (Genesis 2:18). Solitary confinement, as prisoners of war attest to, is one of the most damaging aspects of imprisonment (Drury, 2003). The isolation and loneliness can easily drive otherwise normal individuals mad.

This chapter runs parallel to the "very good" and the "not good" of Genesis. The first half examines five facets of humanity's God-given goodness.

This is like examining a diamond under a microscope. Take your time as you rotate from one facet to the next, seeing the wonderful and wounded parts (there are no perfect diamonds) of who you are.

It may seem strange or even too self-focused to begin a chapter on relationships with self. This approach is based on two ideas. First, if you fail to have compassion on yourself, it is nearly impossible to have compassion on others. The command of God is to love *others as you love yourself* (Mark 12:31). Loving the person that God created you to be is the first big step in loving those around you.

Second, as you develop a keener awareness of self you will be able to see others more clearly. Anne Morrow Lindbergh, in her book *Gift from the Sea* (1992, p. 38), said the following:

> When one is a stranger to one's self then one is estranged from others too. If one is not in touch with one's self then they can not touch others.
> . . . Only when one is connected to one's core can one be connected to others.

Realizing your own goodness (and shortcomings) places you in a much better position to celebrate and cultivate the goodness of others.

The second half of this chapter begins with a look at the biblical idea that it is "not good for man to be alone." While social scientists are not in agreement about why, there is almost universal agreement that a lack of loving, intimate relationships has a negative effect on many health-related issues, such as risk of heart disease and cancer, high blood pressure, high stress and anxiety, suicide, perceived happiness, and overall mortality. Several specific studies examining this link are presented. Given this correlation, it is disturbing that while the breadth (number of social contacts) of relationships has grown significantly during the past decades, the depth (level of social intimacy) of those relationships is at an all-time low. People have hundreds of Facebook friends but no one who deeply knows their heart or, for that matter, truly cares. Therefore, this chapter concludes with a discussion of three biblical principles for moving from social shallowness to relational depth.

## Identifying your SHAPE

Many jewelers believe that the shape of a diamond, or as they call it "the cut," is the most important aspect in determining value. *SHAPE* serves as an acronym for the five facets of your humanity:

**S**piritual gifts

**H**eart (i.e., values)

**A**bilities (i.e., natural gifts)

**P**ersonality

**E**xperience (Warren, 2002)

## Spiritual Gifts

There are different kinds of gifts, but the same Spirit. There are different kinds of service, but the same Lord. There are different kinds of working, but the same God works all of them in all men. Now to each one the manifestation of the Spirit is given for the common good. (1 Corinthians 12:4–8)

Eugene Peterson's (2003, p. 2083) New Testament paraphrase *The Message* translates the verse this way: "Each person is given something to do that shows who God is: Everyone gets in on it, everyone benefits. All kinds of things are handed out by the Spirit, and to all kinds of people."

The apostles and early church leaders frequently discussed and argued about spiritual giftedness, but today only about 25 percent of Christians say that they know their own spiritual gifts (Barna, 2001).

The New Testament mentions about 20 **spiritual gifts**. Each list of biblical gifts is a little different, but the lists overlap, and none is exhaustive. To avoid confusion and controversy, I have chosen to use the terms and descriptions from the book *Network: The Right People...In the Right Places...For the Right Reasons* by Bugbee et al. (1994).

To gain insight into which of the spiritual gifts you possess, complete the first application activity at the end of the chapter. Note that in this exercise you are asked not to rely solely on your own perspective. Most people have spiritual gifts that they themselves do not recognize, but others do. Seek feedback from at least two people who know you well, one a family member and the other not a blood relative.

Ask each to complete the application activity at the end of the chapter with you in mind. Where your results agree with theirs, treat it as confirmation of your own insights. You may find, however, that you have hidden gifts that others do not recognize or that others affirm gifts in you that you never knew you had. Either way, be open to what God wants to reveal to you about the special gifts he has divinely entrusted to you.

## Heart

What are your passions? What keeps you up at night and gets you going in the morning? A related question is "What are your **values**?" Most Christians know the "right" answer to this question, something like, "God first, others second, me last." Christians know they are supposed to love God and love others, glorify God in all they do, and seek first the kingdom of God. They cut their spiritual baby teeth on these things. So when you are asked, as a Christian, what is most important to you, the response is instinctive. The point of this exercise is not to try to identify what your highest values *should be* but what they *are*, and such automatic "spiritual answers" have a tendency to get in the way of real honesty. So what are your real values?

Here is a sampling of questions used in various value clarification exercises.

- If you were going on a trip you would not return from, what five things would you take with you?

- If you knew you would die tomorrow, or next week, or next month, how would you spend your last days?

- What would you want written on your tombstone?

Trying to answer questions like these can be useful, but it is hard to know what you would really do in those circumstances, and questions like these encourage the misperception that one's deepest values only emerge under extreme life-or-death situations. Better indications of your existing values are the innumerable small and seemingly insignificant actions and decisions you make day in and day out. Just as the Grand Canyon was created by slow erosion over millions of years, values are formed gradually, almost imperceptibly, a little bit at a time. What you wear, what gets your attention, and what you worry about says more about your true values than what you think you would do if someone put a gun to your head.

For some, this is not particularly good news. Rather, in this hyped-up, media-driven world many want the wealth of Mark Zuckerberg, the body of Paris Hilton, or the humor of Adam Sandler. If you are tempted to think this way, consider another perspective demonstrated by Susan Graham in an interview with Jamie Fields, writer for *Texas Monthly* (Fields, 1996). During the interview, Fields sought to compare Graham to one of opera's legendary mezzo-sopranos, Cecilia Bartoli. Fields asked Graham if she thought she could be the next Bartoli. Graham responded by saying, "I'm not sure I want to be the next anyone. I'd rather be the first Susan Graham" (Fields, 1996, p. 36). Graham's refusal to emulate other classical vocalists was perhaps one of the most important contributors to her unique voice. Graham's attitude is consistent with what the apostle Paul urged of the Galatian Christians:

> Make a careful exploration of who you are and the work you have been given, and then sink yourself into that. Don't be impressed with yourself. Don't compare yourself with others. Each of you must take responsibility for doing the creative best you can with your own life" (Galatians 6:4–5, *The Message*).

Those inspired words reflect the wisdom of how pride (being impressed with yourself) and comparison can kill one's inner spirit. You were created to be the person and do the work that God masterfully designed for you. At the end of your life, don't expect God to ask you why you were not more like Abraham, Moses, or the apostle Paul. Rather, expect to give an account of the person God created you to be and the work he gave you to do.

## The "No Goodness" of Being Alone

God said some 2,000 years ago, "It is not good for man to be alone" (Genesis 2:18). After a long history of consistent findings social and medical scientists are increasingly becoming convinced of the intimate connection between social and physical health. This section highlights some of those historical findings.

In 1979, Berkman and Syme published the results of their seminal work linking social relationships to mortality. In their study encompassing more than 20,000 subjects from California and Finland, they reported that independent of all other relevant factors such as cholesterol, blood pressure, family history, activity level, and body weight, the people who had the fewest social contacts were two to three times more at risk of death from heart disease than those who had the most social contacts (Berkman & Syme, 1979).

David Spiegel of Stanford University's School of Medicine, a self-proclaimed skeptic about the power of connection, divided 86 women with terminal cancer into two groups: one group received standard medical care, and the other received the same care but also met as a group once a week for social support. No medical information was given in the support sessions; subjects simply came together to talk about their feelings and experiences. Spiegel was shocked at what he found. The women not meeting in a support group survived an average of only 19 months, while the women in the support group survived an average of 37 months, nearly twice as long! After this work was published in the prestigious medical journal *Lancet*, Spiegel commented, "Believe me, if we'd seen these results with a new drug, it would be in use in every cancer hospital in the country today!" (Spiegel et al., 1989)

The Abkhazians of Georgia (in central Asia, not the United States) have caught the attention of health researchers. This group has the industrialized world's lowest mortality rate, and many of them live for more than 100 years. Scientists believe that one major reason for their longevity is their intricate web of social connections. The Abkhazians measure their worth and status by the quality and quantity of their family ties, and it is not uncommon for an Abkhazian to have more than 300 family members (Siegler et al., 1992).

The small town of Roseto, Pennsylvania, has the distinction of being one of the most studied communities in America. At one time the people of Roseto had about one-sixth the national average of heart disease (they also had much lower rates of ulcers, dementia, and other common disorders). Researchers went to Roseto to investigate their lifestyle, expecting to find a population with a low-fat, vegetarian diet and a focus on aerobic exercise. What they found, however, were people who were just as overweight, sedentary, and meat loving as the rest of America. Investigators did identify one difference between this community, made up largely of Italian immigrants, and the average American community. The town of Roseto functioned as one tight-knit family; people helped each other out, watched over each other's children, got together on the weekends, and had a very strong sense of belonging and community (Wolf, 1993).

One of the factors that impressed researchers the most was the attitude toward the elderly. In Roseto, the older residents weren't put on a shelf; they were promoted to "supreme court." No one was ever abandoned. Was this cardio protection simply a

## Social Snubbing Is Quite Painful

Social isolation comes at a high price, especially when manifested in rejection. According to a study published in the *Journal of Science*, social snubbing does affect more than just people's emotions. In fact, the feelings a person gets when ignored at a party or not chosen for a team generate exactly the same brain wave patterns that he or she gets when in physical pain. In the study, 13 volunteers were given a task and not told that it related to an experiment in social snubbing. During the experimental trials, each subject experienced social rejection. When that occurred, the EEG showed the same electrical patterns as when humans undergo visceral pain (Eisenberger et al., 2003).

function of good genetics? No. Years later, when the community atmosphere and family traditions began to dissolve and Rosetans became more industrialized and individualized (that is, more "Americanized") researchers went back to Roseto and found it had indeed achieved roughly the same incidence of heart disease and mortality as the general population (Egolf et al., 1992).

In a study of first-year college students, investigators found that those who reported less family support reported more negative physical symptoms than those who reported higher levels of family support (Zaleski et al., 1998). Similarly, in a study assessing college students' stress, support, and physical health, researchers reported that social support was highly correlated to fewer negative physical symptoms (Wohlgemuth & Betz, 1991).

Dr. Dean Ornish's book *Love and Survival* reviews much of the literature on this subject up until the turn of the twenty-first century (Ornish, 1999). Dr. Ornish, a cardiovascular physician, was in search of a more effective treatment plan for his patients when he discovered what he calls "the healing power of love." His book reviews more than 100 studies on the relationship between physical and relational health and concludes with the following statement, "When I reviewed the scientific literature, I was amazed to find what a powerful difference love and relationships made upon the incidents of disease and premature death from virtually all causes" (1999, p. 30).

More recent studies continue to support the connection between social isolation and illness and conversely social support and positive health outcomes.

Dr. Dorothy Espelage and colleagues from the University of Illinois conducted a study of 247 college students to determine the effect of social support and physical health. Their findings indicated that students who were more socially connected had significantly better health attitudes and suffered fewer negative health symptoms (Hale et al., 2005). In a study examining the social support of 1,378 college students, researchers reported a

sixfold increase in depressive symptoms for students who reported the lowest social support (Hefner & Eisenberg, 2009).

In a study conducted by Dr. Elaine Anderson and colleagues from Virginia Polytechnic Institute and Virginia State University, strong social support exerted a direct influence on the physical activity patterns of the 999 adults examined (Anderson et al., 2006). The subjects in this study came from 14 local church congregations.

In a large national epidemiological survey of 34,653 adults aged 20 to 99, investigators at Washington University School of Medicine discovered that low levels of interpersonal support were strongly correlated with increased prevalence of major depressive disorder, generalized anxiety, social phobia, and several physical health problems. Conversely, there was a strong association between excellent physical health and high social support (Moak & Agrawal, 2010).

Although the physiological mechanisms responsible are still being discovered, social scientists confidently assert that it is indeed "not good" physically, emotionally, or psychologically to be alone.

# Three Spiritual Practices for Enhancing Relationships

Despite the immense scientific evidence supporting the human need for intimate social relationships, according to social scientists, Americans are increasingly becoming socially isolated. Beginning in the mid-1960s, Harvard professor Robert Putnam began describing diminished memberships in parent–teacher associations, unions, and civic clubs and organizations. In his book *Bowling Alone*, Putnam (2000) reported that this trend continues with as much as a 60 percent decrease in attendance at dinner parties, civic meetings, family suppers, blood drives, and recreational leagues such as bowling.

A more recent study conducted by social scientists at Duke University and the University of Arizona

**New Homes Designed for the Dysfunctional Family**

The Ledbetter family likes to spend time at home together—just not in the same room. They built a 3,600-square-foot house with special rooms for studying and sewing, separate sitting areas for each child, and a master bedroom far from the other areas. The house also has what the family calls "the escape room" where, Mr. Ledbetter says, "any family member can go to get away from the rest of us."

The Mercer Island, Washington, industrial designer says his 7- and 11-year-old daughters fight less because their new house gives them so many ways to avoid each other. "It just doesn't make sense for us to do everything together all the time," he says.

After two decades of pushing the open floor plan—where domestic life revolved around a big central space and exposed kitchens gave everyone a view of half the house—major builders and top architects are walling people off. They are now touting one-person Internet alcoves, locked-door "away rooms," and his-and-her offices on opposite ends of the house. The new floor plans offer so much seclusion they are "good for the dysfunctional family," says Gopal Ahluwahlia, director of research for the National Association of Home Builders.

Fletcher 2004, p. W1.

---

revealed that almost one in four Americans does not have even one person to confide in (McPherson et al., 2006). These data were also compared to similar interviews conducted in 1985 and showed an unmistakable decline in the number of intimate relationships the average person has.

In the 2009 book *The Narcissism Epidemic*, Dr. Jean Twenge reported that today's college students are more narcissistic and relationally shallow than ever before (Twenge & Campbell, 2009). Her conclusions were derived largely from a longitudinal study begun in 1982 in which she served as the chief investigator. From 1982 to 2006, 16,475 college students completed an annual survey. In addition to displaying increased narcissistic tendencies, students revealed the following relational trends:

- More likely to have short-lived romantic relationships
- Increased relational infidelity
- Lacking emotional warmth
- Increased relational game playing
- Increased dishonesty
- Overcontrolling and violent tendencies

The irony is that today people have more social contacts than ever before, yet those contacts are shallow and superficial. See the New Homes Designed for the Dysfunctional Family sidebar for another example of social poverty despite financial abundance.

The adoption of three spiritual practices has time and again yielded a bounty of relational richness. Consider how they may enhance your relational connections.

## Practice 1: Realize Your Identity

Knowing who you are has a dramatic effect on what you do. Note the verse that precedes Jesus's washing his disciples' feet:

> Jesus knew that the Father had put him in complete charge of everything, that he came from God and was on his way back to God. So he got up from the supper table, set aside his robe, and put on an apron. Then he poured water into a basin and began to wash the feet of the disciples, drying them with his apron. (John 13:3–5, *The Message*)

Jesus, realizing that he had come from God and was returning to God, washed his disciples' feet and later that night was not terrorized by fear before Pilate. He then humbly laid down his life for the glory of God the Father. It was what he knew, his identity, that allowed him to act in such a selfless, fearless, and loving manner.

Identity answers the most basic questions of existence: where you came from, what group you belong to, and what you are capable of doing. Stealing another person's identity allows the use of someone else's rights and privileges as one's own. Elyse Fitzpatrick (2008), in her book *Because He Loves Me: How Christ Transforms Our Daily Life*, uses this metaphor to describe the identity Christians receive:

> Just in case you're unaware, identity theft occurs when someone steals your name and other personal information for fraudulent use. Most of us are dismayed by this new cyber-age crime, and we wouldn't assume that the

theft of another person's identity is acceptable behavior. The surprising reality, however, is that Christians are, by definition, people who have someone else's identity. They're called "Christians" because they've taken the identity of someone else: Jesus Christ. Not only have you been given an identity that you weren't born with or that you didn't earn the right to use, but you're invited to empty the checking account and use all the benefits this identity brings! This is so much better than identity theft—it's an identity gift! (p. 51)

The New Testament's authors consistently reaffirm this God-given identity Christians receive. Table 11.3 lists some of the promises and privileges that come with Christian identity.

Talk about a gift! What would Christians who really believe that they are this accepted, secure, and significant act like? They would undergo an amazing transformation in the way they saw themselves and others.

A wonderful example of how embracing an identity can transform a life is poignantly demonstrated in the animated movie *The Lion King* (Allers & Minkoff, 1994). The movie plays out as a struggle between good and evil through the adventures of a lion named Simba. Simba is born into an idyllic world in which his father, Mufasa, is the reigning king. Under Mufasa there is peace, goodness, and celebration in the kingdom. This tranquility is overturned when Scar, Mufasa's brother, kills Mufasa and usurps the throne. Scar's rule is one of tyranny, evil, and fear. Simba escapes Scar's plot to kill him as well and winds up frolicking with his new friends in the forest, completely oblivious to the larger realities of the kingdom. Simba's motto is "Hakuna Matata"—don't worry, be happy. But one

## Table 11.3 A Christian's Identity

| I am accepted . . . | I am secure . . . | I am significant . . . |
|---|---|---|
| I am God's child. (John 1:12) | I am free from condemnation. (Romans 8:1–2) | I am a branch of Jesus Christ, the true vine, and a channel of his life. (John 15:5) |
| As a disciple, I am a friend of Jesus Christ. (John 15:15) | I am assured that God works for my good in all circumstances. (Romans 8:28) | I have been chosen and appointed to bear fruit. (John 15:16) |
| I have been justified. (Romans 5:1) | I am free from any condemnation brought against me, and I cannot be separated from the love of God. (Romans 8:31–39) | I am God's temple. (1 Corinthians 3:16) |
| I am united with the Lord, and I am one with him in spirit. (1 Corinthians 6:17) | I have been established, anointed, and sealed by God. (2 Corinthians 1:21–22) | I am a minister of reconciliation for God. (2 Corinthians 5:17–21) |
| I have been bought with a price, and I belong to God. (1 Corinthians 6:19–20) | I am hidden with Christ in God. (Colossians 3:1–4) | I am seated with Jesus Christ in the heavenly realm. (Ephesians 2:6) |
| I am a member of Christ's body. (1 Corinthians 12:27) | I am confident that God will complete the good work he started in me. (Philippians 1:6) | I am God's workmanship. (Ephesians 2:10) |
| I have been chosen by God and adopted as his child. (Ephesians 1:3–8) | I am a citizen of heaven. (Philippians 3:20) | I may approach God with freedom and confidence. (Ephesians 3:12) |
| I have been redeemed and forgiven of all my sins. (Colossians 1:13–14) | I have not been given a spirit of fear but of power, love, and a sound mind. (2 Timothy 1:7) | I can do all things through Christ, who strengthens me. (Philippians 4:13) |
| I have direct access to the throne of grace through Jesus Christ. (Hebrews 4:14–16) | I am born of God, and the evil one cannot touch me. (1 John 5:18) | I am complete in Christ. (Colossians 2:9–10) |

From the International Bible Society 1984.

night everything changes. While looking into a pool of water, Simba encounters a vision of his father. His father says, "You have forgotten me and have forgotten who you are. Look inside yourself. You are more than what you have become—you are the son of a king!" This vision marks the turning point in Simba's life. No longer is he content to live for personal pleasure. His mission is to restore his father's righteous rule.

The same can be true for people when they realize who they are. Humans are completely forgiven, fully accepted, and have all the rights and privileges of a child of the creator of the universe. It is this realization, more than anything else, that transforms the way people interact with and relate to others. Perhaps the best place you can begin expressing this new transformed identity is at home with parents and siblings who you interact with day in and day out.

## Practice 2: Honor Your Parents

The first of the Ten Commandments that deals with how humans should treat others charges children to obey and honor their parents (Deuteronomy 5:16). That commandment is the only one with a promise attached: "So that you may live long and that it may go well with you." God's promise for increased well-being is linked to how children relate to their parents. Like it or not, one aspect of life that is undeniably in God's will is the parents you have.

For many, that statement is comforting and a strong reflection of God's goodness. To others who have been neglected, abandoned, or even abused by their parents physically, emotionally, or psychologically this statement is difficult to accept. How can a God of compassion place a defenseless child into a family to be neglected, harassed, and violated? Some thoughtful people have formulated responses to difficult questions like this (see Lewis, 1944; Yancey, 1997), but it's hard for a neglected or abused person to accept such a reality. Every family has their burdens, and each situation is unique, but you must ultimately remember scripture when considering your parents.

> Children, obey your parents in the Lord: for this is right. Honor your father and mother. (Ephesians 6:1–2)

Obeying and honoring parents (except when doing so violates God's authority) is no small matter to God. If severity of punishment indicates the gravity of the offense, consider the consequences of disobedient children spelled out in these passages. Be forewarned, the Old Testament passages that follow may seem extreme and need to be interpreted within the cultural context of that

time, but try not to miss the impoverished result the scriptures warn against.

> The eye that mocks a father, that scorns obedience to a mother, will be pecked out by the ravens of the valley, will be eaten by the vultures. (Proverbs 30:17)

> If a man curses his father or mother, his lamp will be snuffed out in pitch darkness. (Proverbs 20:20)

> Cursed is the man who dishonors his father or his mother. (Deuteronomy 27:16)

> Children obey your parents in everything, for this pleases the Lord. (Colossians 3:20)

> For people will be lovers of self, lovers of money, proud, arrogant, abusive, *disobedient to their parents*, ungrateful, unholy . . . lovers of pleasure rather than lovers of God, having the appearance of godliness, but denying its power. Avoid such people. (2 Timothy 3:1–5, italics added)

Because the commands of parental obedience and honor are so close to the heart of God and essential to people's well-being, Satan works overtime in creating a cultural disregard for parental authority. Gone are the days when children said "Yes, sir" and "No, ma'am" when speaking to parents and adults. Welcome to a culture in which songs and TV shows humor young audiences with their irreverent style and disregard for parental authority. In this era, even the most heinous language directed toward parents seems acceptable to many. In his song "Cleanin' Out My Closet," triple-platinum rapper Eminem raps about his mother who has been on welfare and addicted to drugs and sleeps around. His conclusion? He hopes "she burns in hell" (A-Z Lyrics Universe, 2006). As shocking as the lyrics are, his mother's response is even more startling: "That's just artistic expression," she said (ABC News, 2004). What does it say about the culture that such degrading language can be dismissed so casually?

Accepting your parents despite their imperfections is an initial step toward relational maturity. Honoring them is a lifelong process filled with many small steps of respect and love. It is all part of living out your identity as one who is created by God, placed on this earth but for a small season, and who will eventually return to the Creator.

## Practice 3: Choose to Forgive

American culture has made the path to forgiveness harder to follow through a spirit of entitlement that pervades society. People would rather the offender get justice than let the offense go. In life, everyone is wounded by others, from minor misunderstandings to serious strife. People inflict their fair share of wrongs, knowingly or unknowingly. These interpersonal offenses can cause chafing and blistering, like a rock in a shoe rubbing the same sore spot over and over again. But, if you choose to forgive and ask for forgiveness from others, the path of the offense mirrors the growth of a pearl in an oyster—what was once an irritant has become something beautiful and valuable. Offenses present you with opportunities to choose which way you will take—the way of the rock or the pearl.

You may have heard another metaphor for unforgiveness: unforgiveness is like drinking a poison and hoping someone else will die. Frederick Buechner (1993, p. 2) communicates this reality most eloquently:

To lick your wounds, to smack your lips over grievances long past . . . to savor to the last toothsome morsel both the pain you are given and the pain you are giving back—in many ways it is a feast fit for a king. The chief drawback is that what you are wolfing down is yourself. The skeleton at the feast is you.

A scene in the 1994 movie *Forrest Gump* exemplifies the futility of harboring unforgiveness. In this movie, Tom Hanks, who plays Forrest Gump, accomplishes the incredible despite being physically and mentally challenged. In this particular scene Forrest and his childhood friend Jenny are walking down an old gravel road shaded by hardwood trees. Jenny carries her sandals, and the walk seems pleasant until they happen upon an abandoned, weather-worn house. The sight is horrifying to Jenny. It's her childhood home, a place where Jenny had been abused by her alcoholic father.

Forrest sees the pain etched on Jenny's face as she walks ahead of him toward the abandoned house. Suddenly, Jenny throws her shoes at the house and then begins picking up rocks and furiously throwing them against the house. Years of pent-up anger are unleashed. When nothing is left to throw at the house, Jenny falls to the ground crying. Forrest sits down in the muddy driveway beside her and says, "Sometimes, I guess, there just aren't enough rocks" (Zemeckis, 1994).

Choosing not to forgive is like living in tornado alley. A tornado of anger and bitterness suddenly seems to come out of nowhere, creating a path of destruction. The real problem is that if this unforgiveness is not released the tornado returns again and again. Forgiveness is the only way of releasing the power of this destructive tornado. It's the key to setting yourself free from the prison of unforgiveness and bitterness.

On June 11, 1963, Vivian Malone, a young African American woman, was escorted by federal troops to ensure her admittance into the University of Alabama. She was hoping to become the first black student to attend the institution. Upon her arrival at school, her way was blocked by a staunch believer in segregation, Governor George Wallace. The governor's blockade failed, and Vivian eventually became the first African American student to graduate from the university.

Several years later, Governor Wallace regretted his actions. He was taken in his wheelchair to the Dexter Avenue Baptist Church in Montgomery, Alabama, where he formally apologized and asked the African American community to forgive him. After that service, he sought out a private meeting with Vivian to personally apologize. Vivian met with the governor and told him that she had forgiven him years earlier. In a 2003 interview, she was asked about this conversation.

"You said you'd forgiven him many years earlier?"

"Oh yes."

"And why did you do that?"

"This may sound weird. I'm a Christian, and I grew up in the church. I was taught that no other person was better than I—that we were all equal in the eyes of God. I was also taught that you forgive people, no matter what. And that was why I had to do it. I didn't feel as if I had a choice." (Nick, 2005, p. 10)

Her upbringing may have made Vivian feel like she had no choice, but she did. And her choice not only freed the governor, but it also liberated Vivian from years of anger and resentment. Hear these words of scripture, which are not crafted to create some type of human doormat but rather to show the pathway to freedom.

Be kind to one another, tenderhearted, forgiving one another, as God in Christ forgave you. (Ephesians 4:32)

Then Peter came up to him, "Lord, how often will my brother sin against me, and I forgive him? As many as seven times?" Jesus said to him, "I do not say to you seven times, but seventy times seven." (Matthew 18:21–22)

Forgiveness goes back to one's identity in Christ. Paul in a letter to the Colossians said, "As God's chosen ones, holy and beloved . . . forgive each other: as the Lord has forgiven you" (Colossians 3:12–13).

As you open yourself up to the forgiveness of God, as you accept his unconditional love, as you embrace your position of holiness, not as a result of your own behavior but from the grace of God, only then are you able to set others and yourself free through forgiveness.

Peacemaker Ministries is a nonprofit Christian organization committed to helping people find forgiveness and reconciliation. They have graciously given permission to reprint one of their significant tools in the process of reconciliation—The Peacemaker's Pledge (see sidebar). This pledge

## The Peacemaker's Pledge

As people reconciled to God by the death and resurrection of Jesus Christ, we believe that we are called to respond to conflict[1] in a way that is remarkably different from the way the world deals with conflict. We also believe that conflict provides opportunities to glorify God, serve other people, and grow to be like Christ.[2] Therefore, in response to God's love and in reliance on His grace, we commit ourselves to respond to conflict according to the following principles:

### Glorify God

Instead of focusing on our own desires or dwelling on what others may do, we will seek to please and honor God—by depending on His wisdom, power, and love, by faithfully obeying His commands, and by seeking to maintain a loving, merciful, and forgiving attitude.[3]

### Get the Log Out of Your Own Eye

Instead of attacking others or dwelling on their wrongs, we will take responsibility for our own contribution to conflicts—confessing our sins, asking God to help us change any attitudes and habits that lead to conflict, and seeking to repair any harm we have caused.[4]

### Go and Show Your Brother His Fault

Instead of pretending that conflict does not exist or talking about others behind their backs, we will choose to overlook minor offenses and will talk directly and graciously with those whose offenses seem too serious to overlook. When a conflict with another Christian cannot be resolved in private, we will ask others in the body of Christ to help us settle the matter in a biblical manner.[5]

### Go and Be Reconciled

Instead of accepting premature compromise or allowing relationships to wither, we will actively pursue genuine peace and reconciliation—forgiving others as God, for Christ's sake, has forgiven us, and seeking just and mutually beneficial solutions to our differences.[6]

By God's grace, we will apply these principles as a matter of stewardship, realizing that conflict is an assignment, not an accident. We will remember that success, in God's eyes, is not a matter of specific results but of faithful, dependent obedience. And we will pray that our service as peacemakers brings praise to our Lord and leads others to know His infinite love.[7]

[1]Matt. 5:9; Luke 6:27–36; Gal. 5:19–26.

[2]Rom. 8:28–29; 1 Cor. 10:31–11:1; James 1:2–4.

[3]Ps. 37:1–6; Mark 11:25; John 14:15; Rom. 12:17–21; 1 Cor. 10:31; Phil. 4:2–9; Col. 3:1–4; James 3:17–18, 4:1–3; 1 Peter 2:12.

[4]Prov. 28:13; Matt. 7:3–5; Luke 19:8; Col. 3:5–14; I John 1:8–9.

[5]Prov. 19:11; Matt. 18:15–20; 1 Cor. 6:1–8; Gal. 6:1–2; Eph. 4:29; 2 Tim. 2:24–26; James 5:9.

[6]Matt. 5:23–24; 6:12; 7:12; Eph. 4:1–3, 32; Phil. 2:3–4.

[7]Matt. 25:14–21; John 13:34–35; Rom. 12:18; 1 Peter 2:19, 4:19.

## What Americans Believe About Forgiveness

The Institute for Social Research (ISR), the world's largest academic survey and research organization, surveyed 1,423 American adults to determine their attitudes and behaviors related to forgiveness (Williams, 2001). Here are some of their findings:

- Three-quarters believe they have been forgiven by God for their mistakes.
- Sixty percent reported they have forgiven themselves for wrongdoings.
- Forty-three percent have gone to others to be forgiven.
- Women are more forgiving than men.
- Middle-agers and older adults are more likely to forgive others than younger adults are.

outlines four specific steps for interpersonal reconciliation.

The essence of Christianity has to do with relationships, and this section stresses some of the most fundamental aspects of developing healthy relationships. Beginning with an understanding of your new identity in Christ, you are then able to give honor to your parents and forgiveness to others (and also yourself).

## Next Steps

The self-analysis exercises at the end of this chapter focus on giving you a deeper understanding of the goodness that God has placed in you. Now it's time to hunt for the treasure in other people. Consider each person you meet as undiscovered territory, ripe with God-given potential. Take on the task of trying to discover at least one God-given attribute that you can encourage.

Next, take time to cultivate interpersonal relationships. Social, physical, and spiritual wholeness depend on it. A growing body of research suggests that the quality of social relationships affects your health and well-being.

Finally, although scripture is filled with relational guidelines, three of the most fundamental relational practices are knowing your identity, honoring your parents, and being quick to forgive.

## Key Terms

personality

personality type

spiritual gifts

values

## Review Questions

1. Identify the value God places on humans compared to the rest of creation.

2. Write one-sentence descriptions of each of the following spiritual gifts (see Application Activity #1):

   a. Administration
   b. Apostleship
   c. Craftsmanship
   d. Creative communication
   e. Discernment
   f. Encouragement
   g. Evangelism
   h. Faith
   i. Giving
   j. Helps
   k. Hospitality
   l. Intercession
   m. Knowledge
   n. Leadership
   o. Mercy
   p. Prophecy
   q. Shepherding
   r. Teaching
   s. Wisdom

3. List four characteristics the Myers-Briggs Personality Inventory measures (see Application Activity #4).

4. Identify at least two scientific studies that suggest a connection between relational and physical well-being.

5. Identify at least three cultural shifts that make intimacy more difficult.

6. Identify three spiritual principles from the text for enhancing your relationships.

## Application Activities

1. **Your spiritual gifts**

### Spiritual Gift Inventory

As you read through the following list, mark each paragraph according to how well you believe it describes you. When you finish, try to decide which three of the paragraphs you marked describe you most accurately.

Y: Yes, it very much describes me.

S: It somewhat or slightly describes me.

N: No, it doesn't describe me.

?: I'm not sure.

a. ____ Developing strategies or plans to reach identified goals; organizing people, tasks, and events; helping organizations or groups become more efficient; creating order out of organizational chaos.

b. ____ Pioneering new projects; serving in another country or community; adapting to different cultures and surroundings; being culturally aware and sensitive.

c. ____ Working creatively with wood, cloth, metal, paints, or glass; working with different kinds of tools; making things with practical uses; designing or building things; working with your hands.

d. ____ Communicating with variety and creativity; developing and using particular artistic skills (art, drama music, photography); finding new and fresh ways to communicate ideas to others.

e. ____ Distinguishing between truth and error, good and evil; accurately judging character; seeing through phoniness or deceit; helping others to see what's right and wrong in life.

f. ____ Strengthening and reassuring troubled people; encouraging or challenging people; motivating others to grow; supporting people who need to take action.

g. ____ Looking for opportunities to build relationships with nonbelievers; communicating openly and effectively about faith; talking about spiritual matters with nonbelievers.

h. ____ Trusting God to answer prayer and encouraging others to do so; having confidence in God's continuing presence and ability to help, even in difficult times; moving forward in spite of opposition.

i. ____ Giving liberally and joyfully to people in financial need or projects requiring support; managing money well in order to free more of it for giving.

j. ____ Working behind the scenes to support the work of others; finding small things that need to be done and doing them without being asked; helping wherever needed, even with routine or mundane tasks.

k. ____ Meeting new people and helping them to feel welcome; entertaining guests; opening your home to others who need a safe, supportive environment; setting people at ease in unfamiliar surroundings.

l. ____ Frequently offering to pray for others; expressing amazing trust in God's ability to provide; showing confidence in the Lord's protection; spending a lot of time praying.

m. ____ Carefully studying and researching subjects to understand them better; sharing knowledge and insights with others when asked; sometimes gaining information that is not attainable by natural means.

n. ___ Taking responsibility for directing groups; motivating and guiding others to reach important goals; managing people and resources well; influencing others to perform to the best of their abilities.

o. ___ Empathizing with hurting people; patiently and compassionately supporting people through painful experiences; helping those generally regarded as undeserving or beyond help.

p. ___ Speaking with conviction to bring change in the lives of others; exposing cultural trends, teachings, or events that are morally wrong or harmful; boldly speaking truth even in places where it may be unpopular.

q. ___ Faithfully providing long-term support and nurture for a group of people; providing guidance for the whole person; patiently but firmly nurturing others in their development as believers.

r. ___ Studying, understanding, and communicating biblical truth; developing appropriate teaching material and presenting it effectively; communicating in ways that motivate others to change.

s. ___ Seeing simple, practical solutions in the midst of conflict or confusion; giving helpful advice to others facing complicated life situations; helping people take practical action to solve real problems.

## Key to Spiritual Gifts

a. Administration

b. Apostleship

c. Craftsmanship

d. Creative communication

e. Discernment

f. Encouragement

g. Evangelism

h. Faith

i. Giving

j. Helps

k. Hospitality

l. Intercession

m. Knowledge

n. Leadership

o. Mercy

p. Prophecy

q. Shepherding

r. Teaching

s. Wisdom

From P. Walters and J. Byl, 2013, *Christian paths to health and wellness*, 2nd ed. (Champaign, IL: Human Kinetics). Adapted, by permission, from Bruce Bugbee and Don Cousins. Copyright © 1994, 2005. *The Network Curriculum Participant Guide*, by The Willow Creek Community Church and Bruce Bugbee and Don Cousins. © (2005) The Zondervan Corporation. For additional resources, go to www.brucebugbee.com.

2. **Your highest values**

## Values Clarification

The following is a list of 75 values (Kise et al., 2005). Feel free to add more of your own. Rate each value with an *A*, *B*, or *C*, according to how consistently it has affected your past choices.

Place an *A* next to values that have consistently affected your choices.

Place a *B* next to values that have occasionally affected your choices.

Place a *C* next to values that have rarely or never affected your choices.

| | | |
|---|---|---|
| Accuracy ____ | Fortune ____ | Perseverance ____ |
| Achievement ____ | Friendship ____ | Personal development ____ |
| Advancement ____ | Generosity ____ | Physical fitness ____ |
| Adventure ____ | Growth ____ | Possessions ____ |
| Aesthetics ____ | Happiness ____ | Power ____ |
| Artistic expression ____ | Health ____ | Prestige ____ |
| Authenticity ____ | Helping others ____ | Privacy ____ |
| Balance ____ | Honesty ____ | Productivity ____ |
| Challenge ____ | Humor ____ | Purpose in life ____ |
| Character ____ | Independence ____ | Recognition ____ |
| Cleanliness ____ | Influence ____ | Religious beliefs ____ |
| Competition ____ | Integrity ____ | Responsibility ____ |
| Conformity ____ | Justice ____ | Security ____ |
| Contribution ____ | Knowledge ____ | Self-respect ____ |
| Control ____ | Learning ____ | Service ____ |
| Cooperation ____ | Leisure ____ | Solitude ____ |
| Creativity ____ | Location ____ | Spirituality ____ |
| Efficiency ____ | Love ____ | Spontaneity ____ |
| Excitement ____ | Loyalty ____ | Stability ____ |
| Fairness ____ | Money ____ | Structure ____ |
| Faith ____ | Nature ____ | Success ____ |
| Family ____ | Orderliness ____ | Tolerance ____ |
| Financial security ____ | Organization ____ | Tradition ____ |
| Fitness ____ | Peace ____ | Variety ____ |
| Flexibility ____ | People ____ | Wisdom ____ |

Now, take all the *A* values and put them in clusters according to which ones seem similar to you. For instance, if you placed an *A* next to Authenticity, Honesty, and Integrity, and you see those as similar, put them together in a cluster. Some of these words may stand alone, in their own cluster. Don't limit the number of clusters you have. If you have fewer than five, repeat the process with the *B* values.

Counting a cluster as one value, write a brief phrase or sentence next to each cluster that succinctly describes what it means for you. Here are some examples:

*Accuracy:* Being correct, even in the tiniest details

*Competition:* Consistently outperforming my opponents

*Happiness:* Finding joy, pleasure, or satisfaction in the work I do and the relationships I have

*Prestige:* Being perceived as successful by my peers and associates

*Security:* Feeling safe and confident about my future

Finally, select the five values (clusters) that influence your choices the most. It may be difficult to narrow them down to five, so think carefully. You don't need to order them, since most likely they exert different levels of influence at different times. Identify your highest values in the following space.

_____

_____

_____

_____

_____

_____

_____

_____

_____

_____

From P. Walters and J. Byl, 2013, *Christian paths to health and wellness*, 2nd ed. (Champaign, IL: Human Kinetics). Based on Kise, Stark, and Hirsh 2005.

3. **Abilities**

   Identify your top three natural abilities.

   _____    _____    _____

   Now ask three people that know you well to identify what they believe are your most prominent abilities.

4. **Personality Profile**

   Reflect on the following information about the Myers-Briggs personality profile (see the Myers-Briggs Personality Profile sidebar on the following pages). What particular traits do you believe are truly reflective of your personality? Where do the strengths and weaknesses of that personality trait show up in your life?

5. **Life experiences**

   This particular exercise is not a joyride but rather an opportunity to walk barefoot down the gravel road of pain. The process, though difficult, is meant to yield fruitful and insightful outcomes.

   a. Identification. What is a painful memory that seems to come to my mind again and again? Where are the pain places in my past?

   b. What have been my coping mechanisms for dealing with the pain of my life? How satisfied am I with my coping strategies for pain?

   c. How has my pain affected my view of God? Self? And others?

# Myers-Briggs Personality Profile

Isabel Myers and Kathryn Briggs developed a personality type model based on Carl Jung's writings (Keirsey & Bates, 1984). Their model is more sophisticated than the medieval theory of the humors (which classified people as sanguine, melancholic, choleric, or phlegmatic personalities according to the bodily fluid they believed was dominant), or the popular but simplistic Type-A versus Type-B distinction. The Myers-Briggs model classifies personalities into 16 types, based on four variables:

1. How are you energized?
2. How do you prefer to receive information?
3. On what basis do you make decisions?
4. How do you structure your life?

Each variable can have one of two values, depending on preference in the four variables:

Source of energy: (E) Extroversion or (I) Introversion
Receiving information: (S) Sensing or (N) Intuition
Decision making: (T) Thinking or (F) Feeling
Orientation: (J) Judging or (P) Perceiving

You'll read about each of those terms in the next paragraphs. Then you will be asked to identify which characteristic best describes your preference. As you make your judgments, remember that rarely is anyone exclusively an introvert or exclusively an extrovert, exclusively a thinking type or exclusively a feeling type, and so on. Imagine each variable as a seesaw, or a balance scale. Different people have different "tilts" in one direction or the other. Also, most people can behave in both ways when necessary but prefer one of them. It's a lot like hand dominance: You can use both your hands, but you prefer to hold pens, eat soup, and throw baseballs with one hand rather than the other.

It is also important to keep in mind the following information about personality types:

1. **All classifications, even this one, are artificial.** They are useful and have a lot of explanatory power, but ultimately they are human creations. They are, at some level, arbitrary. It's not as if God made people out of 16 different molds, or that "ESFJ" (substitute your type here) is written into your DNA code.
2. **All classifications are fallible.** They are only as accurate as your answers to the questions.
3. **All classifications are personality *types*, not personalities.** Everyone's personality is different, including the personalities of people with the same test results. You may even find that none of the labels really fits.
4. **Your four-letter sequence does not define you.** Treat it as a description of, not a prescription for, how you think, feel, and behave. Don't let it put you in a box.
5. **The classifications are not value judgments.** There are no "bad" or "good" personality types. With those limitations in mind it's time to get started identifying your preferences. As you read the following descriptions, identify which letter best describes you (Kise, Stark, & Hirsh, 2005).

## How Are You Energized?

Extroverts (about 75 percent of the population) tend to be energized by being around people, working in groups or teams with tangible results. They process their thoughts by sharing them with others, getting their input, and modifying their views based on those interactions. Introverts, by contrast, are energized by the inner world of their ideas and imaginations. They prefer to work alone or to interact one on one. They would rather process their thoughts silently and share them only when they are finalized. For more information on these variables, see table 11.4.

## Table 11.4 Extrovert Type and Introvert Type

| Extrovert types (E) | Introvert types (I) |
|---|---|
| Find interruptions stimulating | Find interruptions distracting |
| Are outgoing | Are reserved |
| Invite others in | Wait to be invited |
| Say what they're thinking | Keep their thoughts to themselves |
| Are energized from without | Are energized from within |
| Want to live it first | Want to understand it first |
| Focus on the outside | Focus on the inside |
| Take over | Step aside |

## How Do You Prefer to Receive Information?

Sensing types (about 75 percent of the population) are focused on what they receive through their five senses: sight, hearing, touch, taste, and smell. They value hard facts; they pay attention to details; they are concerned with what is. Intuitive types listen to their hunches. They think in analogies, and they love to draw connections between different areas of knowledge. They rely less than sensing types do on their five senses and more on what you might call a "sixth sense." Other people may say that they live in their own worlds. They are concerned with what could be and with new developments and new possibilities. For more information on these variables, see table 11.5.

## Table 11.5 Sensing Type and Intuitive Type

| Extrovert Sensing types (S) prefer | Intuitive types (N) prefer |
|---|---|
| The useful | The innovative |
| Common sense | Insight |
| Accuracy | Creativity |
| Methodical approaches | Novel approaches |
| What is actual | What is possible |
| Practice | Theory |
| Identifying pieces | Identifying connections |
| The visible | The invisible |

### On What Basis Do You Make Decisions?

Thinking types (about 75 percent of men, 25 percent of women) try to make decisions according to the canons of logic, consistency, and fairness. When they have objectively analyzed the situation, they are ready to proceed. Right or wrong, they are often perceived as being more committed to ideas, goals, and tasks than to people. Feeling types, however, rely heavily on their gut instincts as they make decisions. They usually consider relationships more important than the work they are doing, so they seriously consider how their decisions will affect those relationships.

They feel most at home where they can focus on people's needs and live according to their own personal values. For more information on these variables, see table 11.6.

### Table 11.6  Thinking Type and Feeling Type

| Thinking types (T) | Feeling types (F) |
| --- | --- |
| Are logical and analytical | Are harmonious and personal |
| Are fair but firm, making few exceptions | Are empathetic, making many exceptions |
| Put business first | Put people first |
| Want recognition for exceeding requirements | Want recognition for personal effort |
| Decide with the head | Decide with the heart |
| Find flaws | Find strengths |
| Emphasize reasons | Emphasize values |

## How Do You Structure Your Life?

The terms *perceiving* and *judging* are not very helpful but, like the QWERTY keyboard, they have been so firmly established that they've stuck. Judging, in this context, has nothing to do with being judgmental, and perceiving has nothing to do with being perceptive. Judging types (about 50 percent of the population) like to plan their work, then work their plan. They like closure. Wherever they go, they leave organization and structure in their wake. They feel frustrated when things are out of place, and they must create some sense of order before they can work effectively. They believe that work should always come before play. On the other hand, perceiving types feel that planning gets in the way of living life to the fullest. They like things open-ended and spontaneous, and they tend to be adaptable and flexible. They want play to be part of work; they want work to be more fun. For more information on these variables, see table 11.7.

### Table 11.7 Judging Type and Perceiving Type

| Judging types (J) | Perceiving types (P) |
| --- | --- |
| Are organized and efficient | Are flexible, juggling multiple tasks |
| Prefer planned events | Prefer serendipitous events |
| Want things settled and decided | Are open to late-breaking developments |
| Put work before play | Allow work and play to coexist |
| Accomplish tasks through consistent effort | Accomplish tasks through last-minute effort |
| Are systematic | Are spontaneous |
| Like things scheduled | Like things spur-of-the-moment |
| Enjoy finishing things | Enjoy starting things |

What are your four personality preferences? List them here.

_____  _____  _____  _____

# References

ABC News. (2004). *Eminem, the boy who loved to bounce.* www.abcnews.go.com.

Allers, R., & Minkoff, R. (Directors). (1994). *The lion king* [motion picture]. United States: Walt Disney Co.

Amplified Bible. (1965). *The amplified Bible: Containing the amplified Old Testament and the amplified New Testament.* Grand Rapids: Zondervan.

Anderson, E.S., Wojcik, J.R., Winett, R.A., & Williams, D.M. (2006). Social-cognitive determinants of physical activity: The influence of social support, self-efficacy, outcome expectations, and self-regulation among participants in a church-based health promotion study. *Health Psychology, 25*(4), 510–20. doi: 10.1037/0278-6133.25.4.510

A-Z Lyrics Universe. (2006). *Cleanin out my closet.* www.azlyrics.com/lyrics/eminem/cleaninoutmycloset.html.

Barna, G. (2001). *The power of team leadership.* Colorado Springs: Waterbrook Press.

Berkman, L.F., & Syme, S.L. (1979). Social networks, host resistance and mortality: A nine-year follow-up study of Alameda County residents. *America Journal of Epidemiology, 128*(2), 370–80.

Buckingham, M., & Clifton, D.O. (2001). *Now, discover your strengths.* New York: Free Press.

Buechner, F. (1993). *Wishful thinking: A theological ABC* (Rev. ed.). San Francisco: HarperCollins.

Bugbee, B., Cousins, D., & Hybels, B. (1994). *Network: The right people. . .in the right places. . .for the right reasons.* Grand Rapids: Zondervan.

Buss, D.M. (1985). Human mate selection. *American Scientist, 73,* 47–51.

Drury, B. (2003). Lockdown in solitary. *Men's Health, 18*(8), 170.

Egolf, B., Lasker, J., Wolf, S., & Potvin, L. (1992). Featuring health risks and mortality: The Roseto effect: A 50-year comparison of mortality rates. *American Journal of Public Health, 82*(8), 1089–92.

ESPN. (2009). *Shaq vs. Phelps.* www.youtube.com/watch?v=b1q1y4HghBM&feature=player_detailpage.

Eisenberger, N.I., Lieberman, M.D., & Williams, K.D. (2003). Does rejection hurt? An MRI study of social exclusion—Rejection by other people in a social situation triggers brain activity resembling that produced by physical pain. *Science, 302*(5643), 290–93.

Fields, J.S. (1996, December). Face: Susan Graham. *Texas Monthly,* 10.

Fitzpatrick, E. (2008). *Because he loves me: How Christ transforms our daily life.* Wheaton, IL: Crossway Books.

Fletcher, J. (2004, March 26). The dysfunctional family house. *Wall Street Journal,* W1, W8.

Hale, C.J., Hannum, J.W., & Espelage, D.L. (2005). Social support and physical health: The importance of belonging. *Journal of American College Health, 53*(6), 276.

Hefner, J., & Eisenberg, D. (2009). Social support and mental health among college students. *American Journal of Orthopsychiatry, 79*(4), 491–99. doi: 10.1037/a0016918

Keirsey, D., & Bates, M. (1984). *Please understand me* (5th ed.). Del Mar, CA: Prometheus Nemesis.

Kise, J.A.G., Stark, D., & Hirsh, S.K. (2005). *LifeKeys: Discover who you are* (Rev. ed.). Minneapolis: Bethany House.

Lewis, C.S. (1944). *The problem of pain.* New York: Macmillan.

Lindbergh, A.M. (1992). *Gift from the sea* (50th anniversary ed.). New York: Pantheon.

McCarley, N. G. (1994). Validity of the Four Myers-Briggs Type Indicator Scales as a Function of Preference Score Strengths (Doctoral dissertation). Mississippi State University. (University Microfilms No. AAC94-00493)

McPherson, M., Smith-Lovin, L., & Brashears, M.E. (2006). Social isolation in America: Changes in core discussion networks over two decades. *American Sociological Review, 71*(3), 353–76.

Miller, D. (2003). *Blue like jazz: Nonreligious thoughts on Christian spirituality.* Nashville: Thomas Nelson.

Moak, Z.B., & Agrawal, A. (2010). The association between perceived interpersonal social support and physical and mental health: Results from the national epidemiological survey on alcohol and related conditions. *Journal of Public Health, 32*(2), 191–201.

Nick, S. (2005, October 24). Transition: Vivian Malone Jones. *Newsweek,* 10.

Ornish, D. (1999). *Love and survival.* New York: HarperCollins.

Peacemaker Ministries. (2004). *The peacemaker pledge.* www.peacemaker.net/site/c.aqKFLTOBIpH/b.1172255/apps/s/content.asp?ct=1245339.

Peterson, E. (2003). *The message: The Bible in contemporary language.* Omaha: Quickverse.

Putnam, R.D. (2000). *Bowling alone: The collapse and revival of American community.* New York: Simon & Schuster.

Rath, T. (2007). *Strengths finder 2.0.* New York: Gallup Press.

Siegler, I.C., Longino, C., & Johnson, C. (1992). The Georgia Centenarian Study: Comments from friends. *The International Journal of Aging & Human Development, 34*(1), 77–82.

Spiegel, D., Bloom, J.R., Kraemer H.C., & Gottheil E. (1989, October 14). Effect of psychosocial treatment on survival of patients with metastatic breast cancer. *Lancet, 2* 2(8668):888-91.

Tada, J.E. (2010). *A place of healing: Wrestling with the mysteries of suffering, pain, and God's sovereignty.* Colorado Springs: David C. Cook.

Twenge, J.M., & Campbell, W.K. (2009). *The narcissism epidemic: Living in the age of entitlement.* New York: Free Press.

USA Today. (2006, July 18). Snapshots, *USA Today*, p. 1.

Walters, P., Gustafson, J., Williams, B., & Carlson, K. (2006). *What your students are really thinking*. Paper presented at the Christian Society of Kinesiology, Sport, and Leisure, Boston.

Warren, R. (2002). *The purpose-driven life: What on earth am I here for?* Grand Rapids: Zondervan.

Watson, J.B. (1930). *Behaviorism*. Chicago: University of Chicago Press.

Williams, D. (2001). *How link between forgiveness and health changes with age.* www.umich.edu/news/index.html?Releases/2001/Dec01/r121101a.

Wohlgemuth, E., & Betz, N.E. (1991). Gender as a moderator of the relationships of stress and social support to physical health in college students. *Journal of Counseling Psychology, 38,* 367–74.

Wolf, S. (1993). Predictors of myocardial infarction over a span of 30 years in Roseto, Pennsylvania. *Integrative Physiological & Behavioral Science, 27*(3), 246–57.

Yancey, P. (1997). *Where is God when it hurts? A comforting healing guide for coping with hard times* (Rev. and expanded ed.). Grand Rapids: Zondervan.

Zaleski, E.H., Levey-Thors, C., & Schiaffino, K.M. (1998). Coping mechanisms, stress, social support, and health problems in college students. *Applied Developmental Science, 2,* 127–37.

Zemeckis, R. (Director). (1994). *Forrest Gump* [Motion picture]. United States: Paramount Pictures.

## Suggested Readings

Chapman, G.D. (2009). *The five love languages: The secret to love that lasts.* Chicago: Northfield.

In this guidebook you'll learn how to identify your love language (words of affirmation, quality time, gifts, acts of service, and physical touch) and how to speak the love language of others.

Goleman, D. (2006). *Emotional intelligence: Why it can matter more than IQ.* New York: Bantam Books.

Business leaders and outstanding performers are not defined by their IQs or even their job skills but by their "emotional intelligence." From this premise, Goleman describes how to quantify and develop your emotional skill.

Keirsey, D., & Bates, M. (1984). *Please understand me* (5th ed.). Del Mar, CA: Prometheus Nemesis.

Using the popular Myers-Briggs personality inventory, Keirsey helps people better understand themselves and others.

Kise, J.A.G., Stark, D., & Hirsh, S.K. (2005). *LifeKeys: Discover who you are* (Rev. ed.). Minneapolis: Bethany House.

This book is about discovering who you are, why you're here, and what you do best.

Matthews, G., Zeidner, M., & Roberts, R.D. (2004). *Emotional intelligence: Science and myth* (Rev. ed.). Cambridge, MA: MIT Press.

This book examines current thinking on the nature, components, determinants, and consequences of emotional intelligence.

Yancey, P. (2002). *Where is God when it hurts? A comforting, healing guide for coping with hard times* (Rev. and updated). Grand Rapids: Zondervan.

This book attempts to comfort those who feel abandoned, rejected, and isolated from a loving God.

## Suggested Websites

www.5lovelanguages.com

Five different ways people express love are examined.

www.haygroup.com/leadershipandtalentondemand/demos/ei_quiz.aspx

Test your emotional intelligence at this website.

www.queendom.com

If you like taking tests, you'll enjoy Queendom, offering the largest online battery of professionally developed and validated psychological assessments anywhere.

# Part V

# Conclusion

# Offering Your Life as a Living Sacrifice

John Byl

After reading this chapter, you should be able to do the following:

1. Understand how an eternal perspective shapes wellness.
2. Understand how prayer plays a positive role in wellness.
3. Review the seven steps to make wellness a reality.

**You've completed** a course focusing on physical, emotional, and relational wellness. But what does it all mean? Romans 11:36 points to what gives meaning: "For from him and through him and to him are all things. To him be the glory forever! Amen" (also restated in 1 Corinthians 8:6). To find meaning in the physical, emotional, and relational self, you need to own your past and recognize that all good things come from God, make decisions today and recognize that every breath depends on God's grace, and look to the next steps and your future and offer every part of your life as a living sacrifice to God. There is one purpose in the push for wellness: to glorify God (1 Corinthians 10:31).

Before concluding this book, I want to cover two more steps. The first step asks you to consider eternity and use prayer as help in a wellness walk. The second step asks you to review the main threads of each chapter to ensure success in improving and maintaining wellness.

## Tools for Achieving Wellness

At least two steps are particularly important in achieving wellness:

1. Understand the big picture. Your existence is eternal. Seeing the big picture ought to fundamentally change many attitudes.

2. The power of prayer, a time of communication with God, has many positive benefits.

## Eternity

To believe in God is to gain eternal life. **Eternal life** does not begin when you die but is a present reality. The well-known verse John 3:16 notes that everyone who believes in Jesus Christ "has eternal life." It does not say that believers *will get* it but rather that they *have* it. It has been said that "life is too short to worry about it." The Christian view is quite the opposite: Life is too long to worry about it.

Remembering that you live forever ought to change the way you think about rushing through your 70 or so years on earth. Whether a loan gets paid off in 10 years or 20, in the context of eternity, is rather inconsequential. A million years from now, as you sit drinking juice on a hillside overlooking the New Jerusalem, what do you think you will say about the big game you lost, the date that didn't work out, the exam you blew, or the business deal you just missed?

Viewing life as eternal does not contradict Paul's encouragement to "press on toward the goal" (Philippians 3:14), Jesus' declaration to use talents, not bury them (Matthew 25:14–30), or God's command to "fill the earth and subdue it" (Genesis 1:28). Ask yourself, What are you trying to build in this life? Houses or homes? Personal investments or kingdom investments? Remembering that life goes on forever ought to open people to the leading of the Holy Spirit and make them more dependent on God's providence. Resting in God will also improve wellness.

## Prayer

You've probably seen little sayings like "No prayer, no peace. Know prayer, know peace," or "Why pray when you can worry and fret?" Prayer is probably one of the most powerful ways of opening up to the Holy Spirit. Several scripture passages speak powerfully about the authority of prayer: "Is any one of you in trouble? He should pray" (James 5:13). "Cast all your anxiety on him because he cares for you" (1 Peter 5:7). "Do not be anxious about anything, but in everything, by prayer and petition, with thanksgiving, present your requests to God. And the peace of God, which transcends all understanding, will guard your hearts and your minds in Christ Jesus" (Philippians 4:6–7; see also 1 Timothy 2:1–2).

You wouldn't talk to a friend or lover only to get things. Rather, you talk to him or her because you want to share in that person's life. God wants you to do the same through **prayer**. Some academics would suggest that the effect of prayer is experienced more individually than empirically (Duckro & Magaletta, 1994), but others believe that "religiosity and prayer contribute without question to one's quality of life and perceptions of well-being" (Poloma & Pendleton, 1991, p. 81). Speak often with God.

## Seven Steps to Wellness

This text encourages you to not walk aimlessly through life but to walk with purpose and direction as you are led by God. Have a realistic and positive view of who you are; anticipate major obstacles and strategize how to move beyond them; and celebrate God, who you are, and what you are able to achieve. Life was meant to be abundant. Here's a review of seven steps toward successful wellness. The assignment in the Application Activities asks you to do one last review of your specific goals, obstacles to success, intervention strategies, and measures of success—so you know when and what to celebrate!

### Step 1: State the Goal

In Paul's letter to the Ephesians he said that a person oriented to God will not be tossed around in life like inner tubes in a water slide but will grow up to be a solid Christian (Ephesians 4:14–15).

Chapter 1 includes Paul's exhortation "to offer your bodies as living sacrifices, holy and pleasing to God—this is your spiritual act of worship" (Romans 12:1). Furthermore, in Christ's call to be perfect (Matthew 5:48), an overarching goal is to show God through the body.

Making life changes (as spiritual worship, as seeking godly perfection) is a difficult task and one that takes a lifetime. Writing down goals provides accountability in accomplishing them. The saying that Rome was not built in a day is a good reminder to always keep the big picture in mind and to paint positive strokes for today.

## Step 2: Assess Your Present Lifestyle

Know yourself, especially in relation to God. Remember the uniqueness of each fingerprint and personality—the past, present, and future. It is important to know yourself in relation to God and others and good to remember that God values you (Luke 12:23–25).

Consider Paul's reminder to value living in relation with others:

> Love must be sincere. Hate what is evil; cling to what is good. Be devoted to one another in brotherly love. Honor one another above yourselves. Never be lacking in zeal, but keep your spiritual fervor, serving the Lord. Be joyful in hope, patient in affliction, faithful in prayer. Share with God's people who are in need. Practice hospitality. Bless those who persecute you; bless and do not curse. Rejoice with those who rejoice; mourn with those who mourn. Live in harmony with one another. Do not be proud, but be willing to associate with people of low position. Do not be conceited. Do not repay anyone evil for evil. Be careful to do what is right in the eyes of everybody. If it is possible, as far as it depends on you, live at peace with everyone. (Romans 12:9–18)

## Step 3: Design a Specific Plan

Set goals that are realistic, specific, measurable, and concrete. Setting goals in this manner best helps achieve them. Do not count on good intentions alone to motivate you. Having concrete goals helps to direct your life and gives you specific accomplishments to celebrate.

## Step 4: Predict Obstacles

Predict obstacles that might keep you from achieving your goals for healthy living. The Lord's Prayer recognizes these with the request, "And lead us not into temptation, but deliver us from the evil one" (Matthew 6:13). Remember that temptations are not unique to you nor are they so powerful that they will inevitably overtake you. Paul said that the temptations each person has are not unique and that God "will not let you be tempted beyond what you can bear. But when you are tempted, he will also provide a way out so that you can stand up under it" (1 Corinthians 10:13).

Challenges in life bring growth. Paul writes that trials develop perseverance, and perseverance leads to maturity (James 1:2–4). Don't be beaten by obstacles, but rise to their challenges in God's strength and grow through them to become more than you are today.

## Step 5: Plan Intervention Strategies

Formulate intervention strategies to help you comply with the plan. Identify weaknesses and strengths and develop strategies to move forward. Remember that you don't need to go purely on your own strength. As Paul said, "I can do everything through him who gives me strength" (Philippians 4:13). You need to know ahead of time the likely obstacles to your goals for healthy living. How can you avoid these obstacles or successfully pass through these tough places without being derailed?

## Step 6: Assess Compliance With the Plan

Determine how well you are sticking to your plan. Looking back at yesterday's successes and challenges helps plan a more effective tomorrow. You've set concrete goals, but how do you know when you've crossed another bridge on the road to successful living? How long have you kept yourself from crossing back over again to unhealthy practices? Monitor your success.

## Step 7: Assess Progress of Your Overall Goal

Plan celebrations along the way to encourage progress in achieving your goals. Physical, emotional, and relational wellness is an opportunity to enjoy and glorify God. As you enjoy God you give him glory, and as you glorify God you give him enjoyment. Open

**Table B.2** *(continued)*

| | | | | |
|---|---|---|---|---|
| 12. I find myself cutting up my food into small pieces or hiding food so people will think I ate it, chewing it and spitting it out without swallowing it, or making certain foods off-limits. | 1: Often | 2: Sometimes | 3: Rarely | 4: Never |
| 13. People around me have become very interested in what I eat, and I get angry at them for pushing me to eat more. | 1: Often | 2: Sometimes | 3: Rarely | 4: Never |
| 14. I have felt more depressed and irritable recently than I used to or have been spending an increasing amount of time alone. | 1: True | 2: False | | |
| 15. I keep a lot of my fears about food and eating to myself because I am afraid no one would understand. | 1: Often | 2: Sometimes | 3: Rarely | 4: Never |
| 16. I enjoy making gourmet or high-calorie meals for others as long as I don't have to eat any myself. | 1: Often | 2: Sometimes | 3: Rarely | 4: Never |
| 17. The most powerful fear in my life is the fear of gaining weight or becoming fat. | 1: Often | 2: Sometimes | 3: Rarely | 4: Never |
| 18. I exercise a lot (more than four times per week and more than four hours per week) as a means of weight control. | 1: True | 2: False | | |
| 19. I find myself totally absorbed when reading books or magazines about dieting, exercise, and calorie counting to the point I spend hours studying them. | 1: Often | 2: Sometimes | 3: Rarely | 4: Never |
| 20. I tend to be a perfectionist and am not satisfied with myself unless I do things perfectly. | 1: Almost always | 2: Sometimes | 3: Rarely | 4: Never |
| 21. I go through long periods of time without eating or when eating very little as a means of weight control. | 1: Often | 2: Sometimes | 3: Rarely | 4: Never |
| 22. It is important to me to try to be thinner than all of my friends. | 1: Almost always | 2: Sometimes | 3: Rarely | 4: Never |

Add up the numbers on this questionnaire to get a total score.

From P. Walters and J. Byl, 2013, *Christian paths to health and wellness*, 2nd ed. (Champaign, IL: Human Kinetics). ©Copyright 1989. K. Kim Lampson, PhD, 206-232-8404, www.eatingdisordersupport.com.

# Table B.3 Scoring Key for Questionnaire 2

| Score | Response | Recommendations |
|-------|----------|-----------------|
| 38 or less | Strong tendencies toward anorexia nervosa | If you scored below 50 it is wise for you to seek more information about anorexia nervosa and bulimia nervosa. Contact a counselor, pastor, teacher, or physician to find out if you have an eating disorder. If you do, talk about what kind of assistance would be best for you. |
| 39 – 50 | Strong tendencies toward bulimia nervosa | See previous recommendations. |
| 50 – 60 | Weight conscious; may or may not have tendencies toward an eating disorder; not likely to have anorexia or bulimia; may have tendencies toward compulsive eating or obesity | If you scored 50 to 60, it is a good idea for you to talk to a counselor, pastor, teacher, or physician to determine if you have an eating disorder and if you do to learn how to get some help. |
| Over 60 | Unlikely to have anorexia or bulimia; however, scoring 60 does not rule out tendencies toward compulsive eating or obesity | If you scored over 60 but have questions and concerns about the way you eat or your weight, it is a good idea for you to talk to a counselor, pastor, teacher, or physician to determine if you have an eating disorder and if you do to learn how to get some help. |

From P. Walters and J. Byl, 2013, *Christian paths to health and wellness*, 2nd ed. (Champaign, IL: Human Kinetics). Reprinted, by permission, from D.W. Reiff and K.K.L. Reiff, 1999, *Eating Disorders: Nutrition Therapy in the Recovery Process, Life Enterprises* (Mercer Island, WA: Life Enterprises), 62. ©Copyright 1989. K. Kim Lampson, PhD, 206-232-8404, www.eatingdisordersupport.com.

## Phase I Strength Training Program

| 1 set/85–100% effort | | | | Week 1 | | Week 2 | |
|---|---|---|---|---|---|---|---|
| **8–10 reps/(2/0/2) repetition speed** | | | | Day 1 | Day 2 | Day 1 | Day 2 |
| **LEGS** Seated leg extension | | | | Wt. | Wt. | Wt. | Wt. |
| | | | | Reps | Reps | Reps | Reps |
| **BACK** Lat pulldown | | | | Wt. | Wt. | Wt. | Wt. |
| | | | | Reps | Reps | Reps | Reps |
| **BACK** Seated back extension | | | | Wt. | Wt. | Wt. | Wt. |
| | | | | Reps | Reps | Reps | Reps |
| **BACK** Abdominal crunch | | | | Wt. | Wt. | Wt. | Wt. |
| | | | | Reps | Reps | Reps | Reps |
| **CHEST** Chest press | | | | Wt. | Wt. | Wt. | Wt. |
| | | | | Reps | Reps | Reps | Reps |
| **SHOULDERS** Lateral raise | | | | Wt. | Wt. | Wt. | Wt. |
| | | | | Reps | Reps | Reps | Reps |
| **ARMS** Arm extension | | | | Wt. | Wt. | Wt. | Wt. |
| | | | | Reps | Reps | Reps | Reps |
| **ARMS** Arm curl | | | | Wt. | Wt. | Wt. | Wt. |
| | | | | Reps | Reps | Reps | Reps |

From P. Walters and J. Byl, 2013, *Christian paths to health and wellness*, 2nd ed. (Champaign, IL: Human Kinetics).

## Phase II Strength Training Program

| 1 set/85–100% effort | | | | Week 1 | | Week 2 | |
| --- | --- | --- | --- | --- | --- | --- | --- |
| 8–10 reps/(2/0/2) repetition speed | | | | Day 1 | Day 2 | Day 1 | Day 2 |
| **LEGS** Leg curl | | | | Wt. | Wt. | Wt. | Wt. |
| | | | | Reps | Reps | Reps | Reps |
| **BACK** Seated low row | | | | Wt. | Wt. | Wt. | Wt. |
| | | | | Reps | Reps | Reps | Reps |
| **BACK** Incline back extension | | | | Wt. | Wt. | Wt. | Wt. |
| | | | | Reps | Reps | Reps | Reps |
| **BACK** Seated torso rotation | | | | Wt. | Wt. | Wt. | Wt. |
| | | | | Reps | Reps | Reps | Reps |
| **CHEST** Chest fly | | | | Wt. | Wt. | Wt. | Wt. |
| | | | | Reps | Reps | Reps | Reps |
| **SHOULDERS** Seated overhead press | | | | Wt. | Wt. | Wt. | Wt. |
| | | | | Reps | Reps | Reps | Reps |
| **ARMS** Standing dumbbell curl | | | | Wt. | Wt. | Wt. | Wt. |
| | | | | Reps | Reps | Reps | Reps |
| **ARMS** Triceps cable pushdown | | | | Wt. | Wt. | Wt. | Wt. |
| | | | | Reps | Reps | Reps | Reps |

## Phase III Strength Training Program

| 1 set/85–100% effort | | | Week 1 | | Week 2 | |
|---|---|---|---|---|---|---|
| **8–10 reps/(2/0/2) repetition speed** | | | Day 1 | Day 2 | Day 1 | Day 2 |
| **LEGS** Incline leg press | | | Wt. | Wt. | Wt. | Wt. |
| | | | Reps | Reps | Reps | Reps |
| **BACK** One-arm dumbbell row | | | Wt. | Wt. | Wt. | Wt. |
| | | | Reps | Reps | Reps | Reps |
| **BACK** Deadlift | | | Wt. | Wt. | Wt. | Wt. |
| | | | Reps | Reps | Reps | Reps |
| **BACK** Hanging leg raise | | | Wt. | Wt. | Wt. | Wt. |
| | | | Reps | Reps | Reps | Reps |
| **CHEST** Bench press | | | Wt. | Wt. | Wt. | Wt. |
| | | | Reps | Reps | Reps | Reps |
| **SHOULDERS** Standing dumbbell lateral raise | | | Wt. | Wt. | Wt. | Wt. |
| | | | Reps | Reps | Reps | Reps |
| **ARMS** Seated alternating dumbbell curl | | | Wt. | Wt. | Wt. | Wt. |
| | | | Reps | Reps | Reps | Reps |
| **ARMS** Seated two-arm dumbbell triceps press | | | Wt. | Wt. | Wt. | Wt. |
| | | | Reps | Reps | Reps | Reps |

From P. Walters and J. Byl, 2013, *Christian paths to health and wellness*, 2nd ed. (Champaign, IL: Human Kinetics).

# Glossary

**actin**—A protein filament inside of the myofibril that combines with myosin to generate force.

**activating event, or stressor**—Any event or condition that triggers a stress response.

**active force**—The movement achieved in a joint through self-initiated muscle contraction.

**adenosine triphosphate (ATP)**—The body's most readily available source of energy. ATP is composed of one adenosine molecule and three phosphate groups.

**aerobic capacity**—The maximum ability to take in, transport, and use oxygen.

**aerobic endurance**—The body's ability to sustain prolonged physical activity that uses the cardiorespiratory system.

**aerobic exercise**—Activities that predominantly use the oxidative energy system.

**aesthetician**—One who studies aesthetics; one who studies the nature of beauty.

**alimentary canal**—The large, muscular tube in the digestive system through which food passes from the mouth to the anus.

**all-or-nothing thinking**—Looking at things in absolute, black-and-white categories.

**amenorrhea**—The absence of menstruation.

**amino acids**—The essential building blocks of proteins.

**anaerobic**—Activities that predominantly use the phosphagen and glycolytic systems and do not require oxygen for metabolic work.

**anorexia athletica**—Exercising compulsively in an effort to control weight and in a misguided attempt to gain a sense of power, control, and self-respect.

**anorexia nervosa**—An eating disorder characterized by an intense fear of becoming obese, a distorted body image, and extreme weight loss. A form of self-starvation.

**antioxidants**—Chemicals that reduces the rate of oxidation reactions in a specific context. These substances found in food help prevent cell damage.

**arousal**—A physiological and psychological state of increased activation, alertness, and readiness to respond.

**ascetic**—One who holds a view that through renunciation of worldly pleasures it is possible to achieve a higher spiritual or intellectual state.

**asceticism**—A view that through renunciation of worldly pleasures it is possible to achieve a high spiritual or intellectual state.

**Atkins diet**—A diet high in protein and saturated fat that avoids all forms of carbohydrate.

**ATP-PCr energy system**—Adenosine Triphosphate Phosphocreatine; the energy system that does not uses oxygen.

**atrophy**—A decrease in muscle mass.

**attribution**—Term used to represent the underlying meaning one places on the events or circumstances of life.

**a-$\bar{v}O_{2diff}$**—The difference in the blood oxygen content between the arterial and venous systems.

**balance**—Regularly eating neither too much nor too little food.

**ball-and-socket joint**—When the spherical end of a bone sits inside a cavity-like area. For example, the arm and shoulder and leg and hip meet in a ball-and-socket joint.

**ballistic stretching**—Moving through a range of motion with bobbing, bouncing maneuvers.

**barbell collar**—The protective clamps that secure plates on a weightlifting bar.

**behavior shaping**—The modification of situations or behavior consistent with your plan.

**behavior substitution**—When you substitute an undesirable behavior with a healthy behavior. For example, instead of having coffee and a cigarette after dinner, you go for a brisk walk.

**beta brain waves**—The brain waves that occur when we are actively thinking.

**binge eating disorder**—An eating disorder characterized by lack of control over eating; eating faster than normal; eating until feeling uncomfortably full; and feeling disgusted, depressed, or guilty after overeating.

**bingeing**—Characterized by eating, in a discrete period of time, an amount of food larger than what most people would eat in a similar period of time under similar circumstances.

**blood volume**—The volume of blood (both red blood cells and plasma) in a person's circulatory system. A typical adult male has approximately 5 liters of blood.

**body composition**—A measure of the distribution of fat and lean body mass in the human body most often expressed as a percentage of body fat. For example, *17 percent body fat* means that 17 percent of a person's body weight is made up of fat; the other 83 percent is lean body mass.

**body dysmorphic disorder (BDD)**—Reverse anorexia, when individuals, typically men, become obsessed with the perception that they are not muscular enough.

**body image**—Composed of the following: a perceptual component that relates how accurately a person estimates his or her body size; a subjective component that involves feelings, thoughts, and attitudes toward the body; and a behavioral component that refers to repetitive checking and the tendency to avoid situations where the person might feel uncomfortable about his or her body.

**bolus**—Term used for any fairly large quantity of matter. In the context of chapter 8, it refers to food making its way through the digestive tract.

**bone matrix**—The intercellular substance of bone tissue.

**brain waves**—The rhythmic waves of voltage arising from electrical activity within brain tissue.

**bulimia nervosa**—An eating disorder characterized by episodes of binge eating followed by fasting, self-induced vomiting, or the use of diuretics or laxatives.

**calorie**—A measurement of energy. One calorie is the amount of energy used to raise the temperature of 1 kilogram of water by 1 degree Celsius.

**capilarization**—The process of increasing the density of the smallest blood vessels in the body where oxygen and carbon dioxide are exchanged.

**carbohydrate**—Organic compounds (starches, sugars) that provide energy to the body.

**cardiac muscle**—A type of striated muscle found exclusively within the heart.

**cardiac output**—Amount of blood pumped by the heart in one minute. Cardiac output is the product of stroke volume and heart rate.

**cardiorespiratory assessment**—Evaluating the working capacity of the cardiorespiratory system.

**cardiorespiratory endurance/fitness**—The ability to sustain prolonged physical activity that uses the cardiorespiratory system.

**cholesterol (HDL-C, LDL-C)**—A sterol and a lipid found in the cell membranes of all body tissues.

An excessive level of cholesterol in the blood is a primary risk factor for heart disease. Most physicians consider blood cholesterol below 200 mg/dl as normal. HDL-C or high density lipoproteins, is what is often referred to as "good cholesterol" since higher levels of HDL seem to be correlated with increased cardiovascular health. On the other hand, LDL-C or low density lipoproteins have been correlated with diminished cardiovascular health, thus often referred to as "bad cholesterol".

**chronic sleep deprivation**—Occurs when one *consistently* does not get sufficient sleep.

**chyme**—Term used to describe the substance remaining after the bolus has been digested in the stomach.

**circadian biological clock**—*Circadian* comes from the Latin *circa*, "around," and *dias*, "day," meaning "around a day." This 24-hour cycle was first described by Franz Halberg.

**circadian rhythm**—Another name for the circadian biological clock; the 24-hour light-based cycle that regulates when the body feels alert or tired.

**clinical depression**—A condition identified by clusters of symptoms such as sadness, hopelessness, motivation, too much or too little sleep, restlessness or inability to sit still, feelings of worthlessness, and thoughts of death or suicide.

**cognitive–behavioral therapy**—A kind of psychotherapy that involves recognizing unhelpful or destructive patterns of thinking and reacting and then modifying or replacing them with more realistic or helpful ones.

**cognitive restructuring, or reframing**—The process of learning to refute cognitive distortions, or fundamental faulty thinking, with the goal of replacing irrational beliefs with more accurate and beneficial ones.

**collagen**—The main structural protein found in all human tissue.

**complete proteins**—Term used to describe foods that contain the nine essential amino acids (examples are meat, egg, dairy products).

**complex carbohydrate**—Multiple molecules of sugar that bond together to form starch and fiber (examples are bread, pasta, and cereal).

**creation**—The story of a personal God, and everything he made, who walked in the garden with Adam and Eve.

**creeping obesity**—A gradual increase of weight year after year, which eventually makes a person excessively overweight.

**deep breathing**—The act of breathing deep into the lungs by flexing the diaphragm, rather than breathing shallowly by extending the rib cage.

**delta brain waves**—Electromagnetic oscillations in the frequency range of 2 Hz or less, characteristic of the deepest stages of sleep.

**depression**—A state of sadness, loss of pleasure, or low mood.

**dieting**—A process of restrictive eating usually caused by body dissatisfaction, preoccupation with thinness, and the false belief that self-worth is dependent on body size. Dieting creates a physiologically driven preoccupation with food and can have devastating results such as eating disorders or even suicide.

**digestive enzyme**—Molecules that activate the breakdown of large molecules (usually food) into smaller molecules.

**digestive system**—A series of connected organs whose purpose is to break down, or digest, food.

**disaccharide**—A carbohydrate composed of two sugar molecules.

**discernment**—The ability to show godly and wise judgment.

**discretionary calories**—Additional calories allotted to people following the low-fat and -sugar MyPlate recommendations.

**disordered eating**—Eating behaviors resembling anorexia nervosa or bulimia nervosa but without the clinical diagnosis. Such people may continue to menstruate, regularly purge but not binge eat, or binge less than twice weekly.

**drive theory**—Within the context of stress management, this theory suggests a linear relationship between stress and performance. In other words, as stress increases, so does performance.

**duodenal ulcers**—A lesion in the lining of the duodenum.

**duodenum**—The first part of the small intestine; a hollow, jointed tube connecting the stomach to the jejunum.

**dynamic stretching**—Proceeding slowly and rhythmically through a full range of motion.

**easy cycle**—Cycling at an intensity at which your heart rate is 60 percent to 75 percent of your maximum.

**easy run**—Running at an intensity at which your heart rate is 60 percent to 75 percent of your maximum.

**easy swim**—Swimming at an intensity at which your heart rate is 60 percent to 75 percent of your maximum.

**easy walk**—Walking at an intensity at which your heart rate is 60 percent to 75 percent of your maximum.

**eating disorders not otherwise specified (EDNOS)**—Eating disorders characterized by unhealthy dieting practices, such as skipping meals, fasting, or using diet pills or laxatives.

**electrical impedance devices**—Devices that send small currents through the body to estimate body fat and measure the amount of water in the body. Blood and muscle have a lot of water, whereas fat and bone are highly resistive. The higher the resistance to the small currents, the more fat one has.

**electroencephalography (EEG)**—Test by a device developed in the 1920s that measures the electrical activity of the brain.

**Elhlers-Danlos Syndrome (EDS)**—A group of inherited connective tissue disorders.

**emotional reasoning**—Reasoning based on how you feel. "I feel lousy; therefore those people are lousy" is a statement based on emotional reasoning.

**empty calories**—See *discretionary calories*.

**endorphins**—Chemicals produced by the brain that increase feelings of well-being and decrease pain.

**esophageal sphincter**—A circular muscle that separates the esophagus and stomach. It relaxes during swallowing, forming an opening through which the food can pass.

**esophageal ulcer**—A lesion in the lining of the esophagus.

**esophagus**—The organ in the digestive tract that connects the mouth to the stomach.

**eternal life**—Life that does not begin when one dies but is a present reality.

**evolutionist**—One who believes that people were formed through an impersonal process of time and chance.

**exercise**—Activity directed at a goal.

**fall**—Refers to Adam and Eve's sin in the garden of Eden, precipitating people's universal and pervasive disposition to turn their backs on God.

**fascia**—Fibrous connective tissue surrounding and separating muscle bundles.

**fat**—Lipids in foods or the body, composed mostly of triglycerides..

**fatal familial insomnia**—A rare hereditary disease that completely eliminates the ability to sleep.

**female athlete triad syndrome**—The combination of three interrelated conditions associated with athletic training: disordered eating, amenorrhea, and osteoporosis.

**fiber**—The nonstarch polysaccharides not digested by human digestive enzymes.

**fight-or-flight response**—Theory first described by Walter Cannon in 1929 stating that humans react to threats with an urge to either fight or flee.

**FITT**—Acronym representing four exercise variables: frequency, intensity, time, and type.

**flexibility**—Generally defined as the range of motion (ROM) possible in a joint or group of joints.

**free radicals**—Molecules with one or more unpaired electrons that cause cellular damage in their effort to stabilize by regaining an electron.

**frequency**—The number of training sessions per week.

**fructose**—A type of monosaccharide.

**fulfillment**—God's honoring his promise that all things will be made new, and there will be an eternal "new heaven and a new earth" (Revelation 1:1).

**functional capacity**—The ability of the human body to perform physical activity, which is influenced by muscular strength.

**galactose**—A type of monosaccharide.

**gastric juices**—An acidic fluid secreted by the stomach glands to aid in digestion.

**gastric ulcer**—A lesion in the lining of the stomach.

**general adaptation syndrome (GAS)**—Describes the body's short-term and long-term reaction to stress. Alarm, resistance, and exhaustion are the three stages in this classic model first described by Dr. Hans Selye.

**glucose**—A type of monosaccharide, a simple sugar. It is one of the most important forms of carbohydrate.

**glycemic**—The presence of glucose (sugar) in the blood.

**glycemic index**—Rating of the food's potential to raise levels of blood glucose.

**glycemic load**—The amount of total carbohydrate in a particular food multiplied by the glycemic index (of that food) and divided by 100.

**glycogen**—Stored form of glucose in the liver, muscles, and kidneys.

**glycolytic energy system**—Term used to describe the physiological process of glycolysis.

**goal**—Specific target as you move toward fulfilling your mission statement.

**Golgi tendon organ**—Tendon organ stimulated by the high tension created when the related muscles contract with sufficient force. The reflex reaction is a contraction of the stretched muscle.

**goniometer**—An instrument to measure angles.

**happiness**—Feeling pleasure, contentment, satisfaction, or joy.

**heart rate**—Frequency of cardiac contractions, typically inferred from pulse.

**heart rate monitor**—A device used to accurately measure heart rate.

**hinge joint**—A joint which acts much like a door hinge. For example, the elbow or the finger joints.

**homeostasis**—The ability of the body to maintain healthy, steady conditions in spite of changes in the external environment.

**hydrochloric acid (HCL)**—A powerful acid secreted from thousands of gastric glands lining the stomach that serves to destroy harmful bacteria. As people age, the amount of HCL produced decreases.

**hydrostatic weighing**—Involves immersing a client in a tub of water and weighing the person. The more dense and muscular a person is, the more he or she is inclined to sink and be heavier on the scales. The more fat a person has, the more he or she is inclined to float and be lighter on the scales. This method is generally considered the best measure of body fat.

**hypermobility**—Excessive range of motion (ROM) in joints.

**hypertrophy**—Enlargement of muscle tissue. This can be done for a brief period of time via blood profusion during exercise or more permanently through overload adaptation to muscle fibers.

**hyponatremia**—A condition that occurs when the body's sodium level falls below normal as a result of salt loss from sweat.

**individualized zones of optimal functioning (IZOF)**—A performance model in which optimal zones of stress can vary from person to person and according to the task required.

**insoluble fiber**—Fiber that does not dissolve in water. It prevents constipation by making feces bulkier and softer so it passes more quickly and easily through the intestine.

**insomnia**—A sleep disorder in which a person has difficulty falling asleep or staying asleep.

**inverted-U theory**—This stress model purports a positive linear relationship between stress and performance up to a point, after which increased levels of stress result in decreased performance.

**isokinetic**—Resistance training in which the rate and speed of movement is controlled or held constant.

**isometric**—Resistance training in which contractions are made with no accompanying movement (an example is standing in a doorway and pushing against the frame).

**isotonic**—Resistance training in which the load (weight) is constant throughout the exercise.

**joint laxity**—Greater than normal range of motion (ROM) in joints.

**k-complex**—A waveform that occurs during stage 2 of NREM sleep.

**kilocalorie**—The amount of energy necessary to raise the temperature of 1 liter of water by 1 degree Celsius. Please note that this term is what is generally called a *calorie* when discussing nutrition and exercise.

**labeling**—Identifying with your shortcomings. Instead of saying, "I made a mistake," a person says, "I'm a jerk, a fool, a loser."

**lactate**—A fatiguing metabolite produced during glycolysis; also called lactic acid.

**lactose**—A disaccharide consisting of galactose and glucose connected together.

**lean body mass (LBM)**—The weight of the body minus fat. This includes muscle, all other organs, bones, and connective tissue.

**ligament**—A connective tissue that typically holds two bones together at a joint.

**love**—Commitment to care for others.

**macronutrients**—Nutrients required by the body in large amounts (water, carbohydrate, protein, and fat).

**maltose**—A disaccharide and an important component of sugar.

**maximal oxygen consumption ($\dot{V}O_2$max)**—Largest amount of oxygen the body can consume at work. Typically expressed in milliliters of oxygen per kilogram of body weight per minute. $\dot{V}O_2$max is the abbreviated notation.

**mental filtering**—Dwelling on the negatives and ignoring the positives.

**metabolism**—Series of chemical reactions that break down food particles to produce energy.

**micronutrients**—Nutrients that humans need only in very small amounts (vitamins and minerals).

**minerals**—Substances formed naturally that are needed in small amounts to help the body function normally.

**mission statement**—A big-picture, inspirational, and precise statement of where you want your life to go.

**mitochondria**—A structure found in all cells that increases the body's ability to use oxygen to produce work.

**moderate cycle**—Cycling at an intensity at which your heart rate is 70 percent to 85 percent of your maximum.

**moderate run**—Running at an intensity at which your heart rate is 70 percent to 85 percent of your maximum.

**moderate swim**—Swimming at an intensity at which your heart rate is 70 percent to 85 percent of your maximum.

**moderate walk**—Walking at an intensity at which your heart rate is 70 percent to 85 percent of your maximum.

**monosaccharides**—The simplest form of carbohydrate. They consist of one sugar molecule.

**monounsaturated fat**—Fatty acids with only one double-bonded carbon molecule held together by electrons, which results in lowered blood cholesterol levels compared to the consumption of polyunsaturated fats.

**motor unit**—A single motor neuron; groups of motor units coordinate the contraction of a single muscle.

**muscle dysmorphia**—A subcategory of body dysmorphic disorder. A disorder that straddles both anxiety and eating disorders, it is characterized by chronic preoccupation with body shape, which occurs in conjunction with changes in eating and exercise.

**muscle spindles**—Sensors scattered among muscle cells and fibers and stimulated by the extent and speed of muscle stretch. The reflex reaction is a contraction of the stretched muscle.

**muscular endurance**—The ability of a muscle or muscle group to sustain repeated contractions.

**muscular strength**—The maximal force that a muscle or muscle group can produce. This is generally expressed as any one-repetition maximum (1 RM).

**myofascia release**—A form of massage or stretching of the tough connective tissue (fascia) that surrounds the body.

**myofibril**—The parallel alignment of protein filaments within a muscle cell that interact and slide by one another during muscle contraction.

**myoglobin**—An oxygen-binding pigment in muscle, similar to hemoglobin in the blood, that acts as an oxygen store and aids in the diffusion of oxygen.

**myosin**—A protein filament inside of the myofibril that combines with actin to generate force.

**naloxone**—An intravenously injected drug administered in hospital settings to counter the effects of narcotics used during surgery or to treat pain. It is also used by athletes to block the euphoric feeling created by endorphins during exercise.

**narcolepsy**—A condition characterized by brief attacks of sleep that can happen at any time.

**net carbohydrate**—The total grams of carbohydrate per serving minus the grams of sugar alcohols and fermentable fiber.

**nonrapid eye movement (NREM)**—The majority of sleep is spent in this phase. There are four stages of NREM.

**nutrient density**—The amount of nutrients available in a single item of food.

**nutrition**—The science of how eating affects the body. A broader definition includes the social, economic, cultural, and psychological aspects of eating.

**obesity**—Having excessive fat (over 30 points on a BMI calculation).

**obstructive sleep apnea**—A common sleeping disorder which consists of repetitive cessation of breathing during sleep for 10 seconds or more due to complete closure of the throat, often characterized by snoring and feeling of tiredness.

**one-repetition maximum (1RM)**—The maximum amount of weight a person can lift for one successful repetition.

**Ornish diet**—A diet that relies largely on carbohydrate and includes only minimal amounts of animal protein.

**osteoblast**—The building of skeletal tissue.

**osteoclast**—Erosion of skeletal tissue.

**osteoporosis**—A skeletal disease in which bone mineral density is gradually diminished, making bones more vulnerable to compression and shear fractures.

**oxidative energy system**—Term used to describe oxidative, or aerobic, metabolism.

**pace cycle**—Cycling at an intensity at which heart rate is above 85 percent of maximum.

**pace run**—Running at an intensity at which heart rate is above 85 percent of maximum.

**pace swim**—Swimming at an intensity at which heart rate is above 85 percent of maximum.

**pandemic**—The outbreak of disease that affects people over a large geographic area.

**passive force**—Force applied in proprioceptive neuromuscular facilitation in which the patient or athlete lets the muscles relax while the therapist pushes a joint to stretch a muscle or set of muscles.

**peace**—To live in harmony with God and others and to experience personal wellness within.

**perceived exertion**—A subjective measure of intensity to determine how hard you are working.

**peristalsis**—Smooth muscular contractions that propel the food bolus through the esophagus to the stomach.

**personality**—A dynamic and organized set of characteristics that uniquely influences a person's cognitions, motivations, and behaviors in various situations.

**personality type**—The psychological classification of people according to particular traits, such as extroversion and introversion.

**physical activity**—Moving one's body.

**polysaccharides**—Carbohydrate that contain long chains of molecules bonded together.

**polysomnography (PSG)**—Simultaneous recording of brain waves and other measures of physiological functioning to assess sleep (such as eye movement, airflow, and muscle tension).

**polyunsaturated fat**—Fatty acids that have more than one double-bonded carbon molecule.

**posttraumatic stress disorder (PTSD)**—Certain psychological consequences of exposure to, or confrontation with, highly traumatic stressful experiences.

**prayer**—Talking to God as to friends and lovers for the purpose of sharing in their lives.

**proprioreceptive neuromuscular facilitation (PNF)**—A stretching technique, which uses a combination of passive stretching and isometric contractions (gentle resistance).

**protein**—A substance made up primarily of amino acids. An essential nutrient but not a major source of energy.

**providence**—God's loving care and protection.

**psychoneuroimmunology (PNI)**—A specialized field of research that studies the interactions among behavior, the brain, and the body's immune system.

**purging**—A method of ridding the body of food through self-induced vomiting or the use of diuretics, laxatives, or enemas.

**pyloric sphincter**—A hard ring of smooth muscle that separates the stomach and the small intestine. It lets food pass from the stomach to the duodenum (small intestine).

**range of motion (ROM)**—The flexibility around a joint.

**rapid eye movement (REM)**—This stage of sleep is characterized by rapid movements of the eyes. During this period, the body is paralyzed and dreams are more frequent than at any other stage of sleep. This accounts for about 25 percent of sleep.

**rational–emotive therapy**—A method of treatment, originally developed by Albert Ellis, that focuses on actively attempting to resolve cognitive, emotional, and behavioral problems.

**reciprocal inhibition**—The cooperation of the neuromuscular system to release the opposing contracted muscles.

**rectum**—The organ in the digestive process that temporarily stores fecal matter before it is excreted through the anus.

**redemption**—To make all things new in Christ.

**REM sleep**—An active period marked by intense brain activity, similar to that of being awake.

**repetition**—A quantity that represents the number of times a muscle or muscle group completes a predetermined movement pattern.

**repetition speed**—The length of time it takes to complete one repetition. The three specific phases of repetition speed are the concentric phase, eccentric phase, and the interval in between.

**resistance training**—Lifting weights of various sizes in order to develop increased muscular tone and strength.

**resorption**—A process by which cells called osteoclasts break down bone matrix and release minerals, such as calcium, into the blood.

**resting heart rate**—The heart rate of someone who has not eaten or exercised in the previous three hours and has remained in a prone position for at least 20 minutes before testing.

**resting metabolic rate (RMR)**—The rate at which energy is used by a body at complete rest.

**restless legs syndrome**—An uncontrollable need to move ones legs. Includes unexplainable feelings of crawling, creeping, pulling, tingling and twitching beneath the skin, usually between the thighs and ankles.

**runner's high**—A heightened condition or state of euphoria reported by people during or after aerobic exercise, generally associated with elevated level of endorphins.

**sarcomeres**—The basic building blocks of myofibrils. Sarcomeres are connected one to another in skeletal muscle, giving it a striated appearance.

**saturated fat**—Forms of fat that are normally solid at room temperature (e.g., butter).

**self-controlled**—To let God be in charge of your life.

**set**—A predetermined number of repetitions in strength training. For example, *two sets of 12 repetitions* means 12 repetitions, rest, and then 12 more repetitions.

**simple carbohydrate**—Single molecules of sugar that provide the body with glucose.

**skeletal muscle**—Muscle attached to the skeleton used to facilitate movement by applying force (via contraction) to bones and joints.

**skinfold measurements**—Fat measured beneath the skin with calipers at several key spots. There are more than 100 different equations and ways of doing this, showing that this type of measurement has potential but is also problematic.

**sleep apnea**—A disorder characterized by loud snoring and pauses in breathing during sleep. These episodes, called apneas ("without breath"), generally cause disruptive sleep.

**sleep cycle**—Term used to describe the process of going through all five stages of sleep. Generally, it takes approximately 90 minutes to transverse all five stages of sleep.

**sleep debt**—The cumulative effect of not getting enough sleep.

**sleep deprivation**—A general lack of necessary sleep.

**sleep hygiene**—A general term used to collectively describe one's behavioral habits surrounding sleep.

**sleep phase delay**—A sleeping disorder or syndrome s in which the circadian rhythm has the affected persons fall asleep and waking much later than most.

**sleep spindles**—Bursts of brain activity during Stage II sleep that consist of 12 to 16 Hz waves occurring for 0.5 to 1.5 seconds.

**sleep stages**—Term used to describe the various phases, or periods, of sleep. Most experts agree that there are four distinct stages of sleep. *Stage one:* light stage of sleep in which a transition from wakefulness is made. *Stage two:* lighter stage of sleep in which consciousness to external stimuli is decreased. *Stage three:* or deep sleep, is primarily associated with physical restoration. *REM sleep:* characterized by rapid eye movements (REM), mental restoration, and dreams.

**sleep study**—A test that measures the quality of your sleep and is specifically targeted to determining if an individual has diagnosable sleep problems.

**sleephomeostasis**—Denotes an equilibrium between the amount of sleep and individual needs and receives.

**slow-wave sleep**—Another term for Stage III of NREM.

**smooth muscle**—A type of nonstriated muscle found in the walls of organs, blood vessels, gastrointestinal tract, and elsewhere in the body. Most smooth muscle contracts involuntarily.

**soluble fiber**—Fiber that dissolves in water to form a gel. Some people think it lowers blood cholesterol and controls blood sugar.

**spiritual gifts**—Special abilities or capacities given by God for the edification of other people.

**sprain**—A joint injury, typically occurring from a sudden stretch (twisting and ankle…), in which some of the fibers of a supporting ligament are ruptured but the continuity of the ligament remains intact.

**static stretching**—The process of holding a stretched position.

**stomach**—A primary organ in the digestive system where food is broken down before passing into the small intestine.

**stress**—Any specific or nonspecific response of the body to any demand made on it.

**stress hardy**—Surviving and even thriving during unfavorable conditions.

**stroke volume**—The amount of blood being pumped in the heart by the cardiac muscle during exercise. As the heart becomes stronger, it becomes more efficient at pumping blood, and stroke volume increases.

**subluxation**—A partial dislocation at a joint.

**sucrose**—A disaccharide commonly known as table sugar.

**suicide**—The act of deliberately killing oneself.

**target heart rate zone**—Prescribed upper and lower limit of aerobic intensity.

**tendon**—The strong fibrous collagen tissue attaching a muscle to a bone.

**trace minerals**—Dietary minerals needed by the body in extremely small quantities.

**trigger points**—A sensitive area in the muscle or connective tissue (fascia) that becomes painful when compressed.

**values**—Accepted principles or standards embraced by a person or group.

**variable resistance**—Resistance training method in which the load (weight) changes during the exercise.

**vitamins**—Essential organic substances used by the body for metabolism, protection, and development.

**weight preoccupation**—An excessive concern with one's body weight.

**weight restoration**—Particularly for those who have anorexia, restoring weight through diet is one of the first steps in the process toward recovery.

# Index

# About the Editors

**Peter Walters, PhD,** is a professor in the department of applied health science at Wheaton College, a private, interdenominational Christian college in Illinois. Since 1996, he has directed the wellness program at the university level, during which he has evaluated the health and wellness behavior of more than 5,000 college students. He has taught health and wellness courses for almost two decades. Before his career in academics, Walters was actively involved in several parachurch organizations, including Campus Crusade for Christ, the Navigators, and the Fellowship of Christian Athletes. In addition to these ministry opportunities, he served as director of student ministries in three churches.

Walters has presented and published his wellness research at several national conferences and in peer-reviewed journals. He is certified as an educational trainer from the American Council on Exercise and the National Strength and Conditioning Association (NSCA). He is a certified USA Olympic weightlifting club coach and an NSCA-certified strength and conditioning specialist. He also competes in weightlifting and triathlons.

Walters is a member of the NSCA and ACSM and is past president of the Christian Society for Kinesiology and Leisure Studies (CSKLS). In 2009, he received the Literary Award from CSKLS. Walters holds a doctorate in kinesiology and a master of science degree in physical education from Texas A&M University.

In his spare time, Walters enjoys strength training, cardiorespiratory exercise, and adventure trips, which have brought him to the summits of Mount Rainier and Mount Kilimanjaro. He resides in Wheaton, Illinois.

**John Byl, PhD,** is a professor of physical education at Redeemer University College in Ancaster, Ontario, Canada, where he teaches wellness courses. Byl is a member of the Christian Society for Kinesiology and Leisure Studies (CSKLS) and is the host of their listserv. He is also a host of the listserv for Church Sports and Recreation Ministers (CSRM), an organization that connects church recreation and sport.

Byl has been a professor since 1986 and has edited, authored, or coauthored 20 books, including *Physical Education, Sports, and Wellness: Looking to God as We Look at Ourselves.* He is a recipient of the CSKLS Presidential Award, which recognizes those who have displayed actions compatible with the mission of the CSKLS.

Byl recently received the Queen Elizabeth II Diamond Jubilee Medal for his significant contribution to making physical activity a priority within his community and within Canada.

# About the Contributors

**Dianne M. Moroz** is an assistant professor and physical education department chair at Redeemer University College in Ancaster, Ontario, Canada, and teaches a course in wellness. Her mission statement is to respect, love, and honor all of God's creation. To act on this, she will work to grow emotionally, socially, and intellectually for the purpose of being a better steward and contributing to the well-being of all of God's children and creation.

**Heather Strong, PhD,** is associate professor and chair of health sciences at Redeemer University College in Ancaster, Ontario, Canada. Her dissertation research focused on how exercise can help improve body image concerns among women. She loves to go for long walks with her two Boston terriers, her husband, and her three children. She is passionate about helping those suffering from body image concerns and eating disorders.

**Bud Williams, PhD,** is an associate professor of applied health science at Wheaton College. He feels most fulfilled in his calling when introducing students to wellness and health science concepts so that they can be better stewards of their lives and more effective in serving God in their respective callings. He is refreshed by participating in a variety of outdoor activities with family and friends.

**Doug Needham, PhD,** is provost and vice president academic at Redeemer University College in Ancaster, Ontario, Canada. His teaching interests include introductory psychology, adolescent development, cognitive psychology, health psychology, and creativity. Dr. Needham's research interests include the following: the role of incubation (taking a break) in problem solving, analogical transfer in problem-solving tasks (i.e., using one problem to help solve another), and an examination of morality and values in adolescents. Dr. Needham hopes that his contributions to this book will provide useful information to students on how to prevent stress and depression, how to cope with them, and how to help others who are dealing with them. Above all, he hopes that readers understand that these conditions are treatable, that no one needs to experience them for long, and that a person's relationship with God can sustain and heal.

You'll find other outstanding
health and physical activity resources at
**www.HumanKinetics.com**